The Last Hockey Game

Also by Bruce McDougall

Non-fiction:

Ted Rogers (1995)
John Wilson Murray (1980)
Charles Mair (1978)

Fiction:

Every Minute Is a Suicide: Stories (2014)

The Last
HOCKEY GAME

Bruce McDougall

GOOSE LANE

Edited by Mark Anthony Jarman.
Cover and page design by Chris Tompkins.
Cover photo by Frank Prazak/Hockey Hall of Fame.
Printed in Canada.
10 9 8 7 6 5 4 3 2 1

Library and Archives Canada Cataloguing in Publication

The last hockey game / Bruce McDougall.

Includes bibliographical references and index.
Issued in print and electronic formats.
ISBN 978-0-86492-378-3 (bound).—ISBN 978-0-86492-724-8 (epub)

1. Stanley Cup (Hockey) (1967). 2. Montreal Canadiens (Hockey team)—History. 3. Toronto Maple Leafs (Hockey team) — History. I. Title.

GV847.7.M35 2014   796.962'648   C2014-902976-4·
                        C2014-902977-2

Goose Lane Editions acknowledges the generous support of the Canada Council for the Arts, the Government of Canada through the Canada Book Fund (CBF), and the Government of New Brunswick through the Department of Tourism, Heritage and Culture.

Goose Lane Editions
500 Beaverbrook Court, Suite 330
Fredericton, New Brunswick
CANADA E3B 5X4
www.gooselane.com

For Jan

THE LAST HOCKEY GAME:

Date: Tuesday, May 2, 1967
Place: Maple Leaf Gardens
Event: Sixth game, Stanley Cup finals
Teams: Montreal Canadiens, Toronto Maple Leafs
Toronto leads best-of-seven series three games to two

CHAPTER ONE
Pre-game Warm-up

Pete Stemkowski took one look at Terry Sawchuk coming through the dressing-room door and wondered if he'd make it across the room.

Sawchuk nursed his way to the coat rack at the end of the room and winced when he took off his rain-dampened overcoat. How could this guy perform so well as a goalie, Stemkowski wondered, when he could hardly walk? Careworn at the best of times, Sawchuk's face tonight looked drawn and haggard, his skin as grey as an abandoned wasps' nest. Stemkowski sometimes tried to amuse his teammates by following Sawchuk around the dressing room, imitating his old-man shuffle. But not tonight.

Sawchuk sidled along the rubber mats on the dressing-room floor to his stall, where Bobby Haggert, the team's trainer, had left his goalie pads, blocker, catcher's mitt, ratty-looking chest protector and blunt-bladed goalie skates, along with clean white underwear and three rolls of adhesive tape. Sawchuk used the tape to attach pieces of foam rubber to the parts of his body left most exposed by his decrepit equipment.

"He wore those battered old shoulder pads," said his teammate Ron Ellis, "the same ones he'd used since junior, and they were in tatters. And his chest protector was nothing more than a piece of felt." Stemkowski wouldn't wear Sawchuk's pads in a ball-hockey game.

Sawchuk's Leafs jersey hung on a hanger from a hook on the wall, along with his white Fiberglas facemask. The facemask looked like a bedpan with eyeholes. He'd worn it for the last couple of years to protect what was left of his mug that hadn't been cut by errant pucks and sticks. Sometimes, looking at Sawchuk, Stemkowski could hardly believe his eyes. This was the goalie that the Toronto Maple Leafs would depend on tonight to win the Stanley Cup. The biggest prize in professional hockey, and to win it, the Toronto Maple Leafs had to rely on a human train wreck.

Stemkowski himself was no prize. Tall and gangly, with a shock of wheat-coloured hair above a face like a hatchet and an Adam's apple that bobbed up and down like a pump handle, he relied on his youth, humour and personality more than his appearance to attract a woman's glance. One night, joking with a referee who'd just given him his third penalty of the game, he said, "You pickin' on me because of my good looks?" The ref said, "If I was, Stemkowski, I'd have given you six." But even if he lived to be a hundred, Stemkowski didn't think he'd ever look so wasted as his Ukrainian buddy did at thirty-seven.

If Sawchuk looked bad tonight, he felt even worse. His stomach ached. His chest was sore. His feet hurt. His back was still stiff from an operation last year, when he thought he might not walk again. The middle finger of his left hand had remained black and blue and throbbing ever since he caught a slapshot about six months ago, fired in a warm-up by Frank Mahovlich, his own teammate, for Christ's sake. The butterflies that always fluttered in his stomach before a game seemed tonight to have wings made of broken glass. But at least he didn't have a hangover.

Unlike some of the Pollyannas on this team, Sawchuk didn't claim to play hockey because he loved the game. He didn't yammer away to reporters about how fortunate he felt to play in the National Hockey League. He might have said something like that when he joined the Detroit Red Wings in 1949. But that was twenty years ago, and he'd been only seventeen. In those days, he did feel thrilled to play a game that he loved, in front of fans who adored him, put their faith in him and studied every move he made. Hockey had taken Sawchuk away from his Winnipeg home for good, at the age of sixteen, when most kids were still in high school. If those kids had any money, they'd earned it the way he did before he left: working in a foundry, manufacturing farm implements, or working for a sheet-metal company, installing canopies over giant ovens in bakeries. They'd earned it from shovelling manure or delivering newspapers, not from playing hockey in a town full of strangers a thousand miles away from home. As a kid playing junior hockey in Galt, not far from Toronto, Sawchuk had made in a week what most kids earned in four months. He sent most of the money to his mom, used most of the rest for room and board and kept twenty-five cents a week for himself, although he hardly needed it. The lumbermen, farmers, railroad employees and restaurant owners who watched him play gave him free donuts, free shirts and free advice and told him he'd make the NHL someday if he kept playing as well as he did.

Hockey had given Sawchuk a life that most kids could only dream about, although he knew now, after twenty years, that those dreams left out a lot of the details of the life of a professional athlete. No one dreamed about the long hours of road-trip boredom. No one mentioned the fans who thought that a ticket to a game entitled them to your friendship. No one told him about the newspaper reporters who wrote whatever they wanted, no matter what you said. And even though he probably would never have met his wife if he hadn't become a professional hockey player, no one had told him that marriage could be such a pain in the ass.

As long as Sawchuk stayed in Toronto, he didn't have to worry much about getting along with his wife. Pat had stayed in Detroit with their kids when he'd come to training camp at the beginning of the season. He visited occasionally, and now she was pregnant with their seventh child. In Toronto, he lived by himself in a dumpy efficiency apartment on Jarvis Street, around the corner from Maple Leaf Gardens. It had a couch, a chair, a coffee table, a TV in the living room and a bed in the bedroom, and you could rent the place by the week, so he wouldn't lose money when the season ended and he had to go home again.

If he wanted human contact, he had a girlfriend. He didn't spend a lot of time with her, but now she was pregnant, too. Sometimes he and the kid Stemkowski went out for dinner to one of the cheap restaurants on Church Street. They were both from Winnipeg, but Stemkowski was Polish, and he was the only unengaged bachelor left on the team, so he could stay out all night if he wanted to, although usually he took the streetcar back to the Beaches, where he boarded with a chiropractor and his wife in a house near the racetrack. At dinner, Sawchuk and Stemkowski might sit across the table from each other for an hour or more in complete silence. Sawchuk liked it that way. He spent most of his time alone.

Despite the difference in their ages, Stemkowski got along with Sawchuk as well as anybody else on the team did. Almost like a son with his father. In fact, Sawchuk could be as moody and remote as Stemkowski's own father had been before he'd died a few years earlier. Sawchuk was a strange cat, but Stemkowski knew how to deal with his ups and downs. He knew, for example, that if Sawchuk didn't say hello when they first saw each other, he wouldn't speak to him for the rest of the day. Stemkowski didn't mind. He was happy just to sit at the same table as Terry Sawchuk. He respected Sawchuk as a hockey player and appreciated what the man had accomplished in all his years as a goalie in the National Hockey League. In fact, respect wasn't the right word. Awe was more like it. The guy had won three Stanley Cups as a goalie for the best team in professional hockey, four Vezina Trophies as the best goalie in professional hockey and a Calder Trophy as the best rookie in professional hockey. Stemkowski felt privileged to sit in the same room with Sawchuk, let alone have dinner with him.

Sawchuk's achievements might have impressed the kid Stemkowski, but they didn't impress Sawchuk's wife in Detroit. He could have been a boilermaker for all she cared, as long as he kept paying the bills.

Sawchuk slumped onto the bench in front of his stall. The bench where he sat, along with the cinder-block walls and the concrete floor, was painted blue, the same colour as the Leafs sweaters. Everywhere he looked, he saw reminders of the team's priorities: order, discipline, hard work. As soon as you walked through the door, you saw words painted on the wall in white capital letters: "Defeat does not rest lightly on their shoulders." On another wall, closer to the door, more words, in smaller letters, said: "The price of success is hard work." A bench ran around the perimeter of the room. Vertical partitions defined the place where each of the twenty players sat to get dressed for tonight's game. In each stall, a Leafs sweater hung on a hanger, its white number facing out. The crest on the sweater had been modified a few weeks ago to an eleven-point maple leaf, similar to the one used on the new Canadian flag.

Other parts of the wall were festooned with rows of plaques, listing the players on each Leafs team since 1927, along with the number of games that each team had won, lost or tied and its playoff record, if it had one. Two more plaques identified all the Leafs players who had made all-star teams or won individual awards. Nine Leafs in the last thirty years had won the Calder Trophy, awarded since 1937 to the best first-year player in the NHL. Three Leafs in the room tonight had won it: Dave Keon, Frank Mahovlich and Sawchuk himself. Four more Calder winners were just across the hall, with the Montreal Canadiens in the visitors' dressing room: Gump Worsley, Ralph Backstrom, Bobby Rousseau and Jacques Laperriere. Winning the Calder was impressive. Mahovlich had done it when he was only nineteen. But Sawchuk took it with a grain of salt. On any team in the NHL, you were only as good as your next game, no matter what you'd accomplished in the past. Hell, within the last five years, two Leafs players, Kent Douglas and Britt Selby, had won the Calder, and they didn't even play in the league anymore.

Across the room, Sawchuk's teammate Eddie Shack was talking about the great-looking broad who had married Elvis Presley the day before in Las Vegas. When he wasn't yakking about cars, Shackie was always gassing about great-looking broads. The dressing room smelled of liniment, adhesive tape and sweat, with accents of Wrigley's Juicy Fruit gum, which a few players chewed during a game to keep their mouths from turning dry. Sawchuk didn't chew gum because it hurt the muscles in his face. He just guarded the goal from the beginning to the end of a game as the inside of his mouth turned as dry as a dusty gravel road. On NHL teams, neither the goalie nor the players drank water during a game. "We were never allowed water on the bench," said Shack. "If you drank water it meant that you were out of shape."

Sawchuk leaned over to untie his shoelaces. Almost forty years old, and he still bought himself only one pair of shoes a year. He glanced down the bench at Mike Walton sprawled against the wall. Walton was a hotshot. He was also the future of hockey. He dressed like a riverboat gambler. Yancy Derringer in hockey skates. Skintight brown trousers flared at the cuffs over a pair of brown leather cowboy boots. Gaping yellow shirt with long collar points, chains around his neck and a cocky look on his face, just daring the world to try to knock the chip off his shoulder.

Kids like Walton didn't have to pretend they respected the old guys on the team. Why should they? What difference did it make to Walton if you'd won a trophy or two, scored twenty goals a season, spent twenty years in the same uniform or the same league? What old guy on the team tonight hadn't done that? For Walton, things were different than they'd been when Sawchuk first started in the league. In those days, a kid kept his mouth shut when he joined an NHL team. But not Walton. Sawchuk would never forget the day that Walton sauntered into the dressing room in his suede jacket and shades, like Mohair fucking Sam, looked at George Armstrong, the captain of the team, for Christ's sake, and said, "How's it hangin', Chiefie Cat?"

If Sawchuk had been in Armstrong's shoes, he would have belted the kid. If Walton thought he was hot stuff, he was a nobody compared to George Armstrong. The Chief had arrived in the NHL on a wave of publicity that made Walton's press clippings look like a peewee's scrapbook. He'd played his first game for the Leafs in 1949, when Walton was still crawling on his hands and knees around the kitchen floor of his parents' house in Timmins or Kirkland Lake or wherever the fuck he came from, and he'd scored his first NHL goal against the Montreal Canadiens, the team they were playing tonight. When Armstrong joined the Leafs for good, Conn Smythe, the owner of the team in those days, gave him the number 10, the same number that another Leafs hotshot, Syl Apps, had worn, expecting from Armstrong the same miracles that Apps had performed in the 1940s. Smythe also gave him a $6,000 signing bonus. "My head went ding-a-ling, like a cash register," Armstrong said.

Armstrong was nineteen, and he wanted his money in cash, the way Sawchuk had taken his signing bonus when he'd signed to play for the Detroit Red Wings. Sawchuk got $2,000 in U.S. funds, exchanged the money at a bank for 2,100 Canadian dollar bills, then took the cash back to the room in Windsor, where he lived in a boarding house, and threw it all against the wall just to watch it flutter through the air. Instead of giving Armstrong the cash, Smythe said he'd invest the money. Smythe's company not only owned the Leafs, it also owned the arena in Toronto where they played their games, and Smythe, who owned most of the shares, said he'd buy some for Armstrong.

Armstrong was used to making money as a hockey player, just not in such quantities. Before turning professional with the Leafs, he'd made a few hundred bucks as a junior and twenty-five dollars a game playing with the Senior Marlboros when they won the Allan Cup as the best senior team in Canada. He used the money to buy two building lots in Sudbury, where he grew up, and he planned to build a house on the lots.

Smythe told Armstrong to hire someone else to build the house. He'd just invested $6,000 in the kid, more than he'd spent on some of his thoroughbred race horses, and he didn't want him to fall off a roof and break his leg. Smythe could shoot a crippled horse. What could he do with a crippled hockey player?

Armstrong took Smythe's advice about the house and the money. "He bought me 250 shares," Armstrong said, "and I had a little left over to buy my dad a brand new 1950 Studebaker." By tonight, Armstrong's shares had increased in value by about $100,000, but he never got the chance to roll around in the cash the way Sawchuk did.

Ordained by Conn Smythe as the second coming of the saviour, Armstrong hadn't behaved like Walton. Neither had Sawchuk or any other rookie. In those days, a rookie knew his place. If a veteran player told him to go to the store for a pack of cigarettes, he'd do it. If a veteran wanted a new pair of laces for his skates, he'd fetch them. In those days, a rookie was thrilled if an older player even spoke to him. And now here was Walton, young enough to be his son, calling the Leafs' captain Chiefie Cat.

If Walton weren't such a gifted hockey player, Punch Imlach, the Leafs' coach, would have sent him to Siberia and forgotten all about him, the way he did with other players who pissed him off. He'd already banished Walton for the last three years to the minor leagues in Rochester and Tulsa, but the kid kept scoring goals, and the Leafs needed more of those. So when Walton came back earlier this year to play in the big leagues, Imlach let him stay. It didn't make Imlach happy to have this punk-assed kid on the bench, though, so he left Walton out of the lineup as often as he could. He even forced the kid to get a haircut, just to show him who was the boss.

The older players turned Walton's presence to their advantage. If Imlach was preoccupied with Walton, they figured he'd have less time to bug them. When Imlach announced one afternoon at a team meeting that Walton wouldn't dress for a game that night, Armstrong and a few other players walked over to Yonge Street and bought Walton a Beatles wig. It cost $38.95, but they figured it was worth the price. They knew that long hair drove Imlach nuts. They also thought that the wig might knock the chip off Walton's shoulder. Maybe he'd get the message and smarten up. "I didn't think he'd have the nerve to wear it," said Armstrong.

Walton strutted into the Gardens that night with Candy Smythe, the owner's granddaughter, who was his fiancée, and sat in her grandfather's seats directly behind the Leafs' bench. Throughout the entire game, he sat five feet from the Leafs' coach with the Beatles wig on his head. "Punch had to walk back and forth in front of me all night," Walton said.

Even after eighteen years with the team, George Armstrong would never have pulled such a stunt himself. Sawchuk looked at Armstrong now, sitting in his place in the dressing room, closest to the door, the place he'd earned with almost two decades of service. Armstrong was one of those guys who insisted in public that he played hockey because he loved the game. Half the guys in the dressing room tonight said the same thing. But when the love ran out, the money kept them going.

Walton and the other young players in the league wouldn't have to worry about money as much as Sawchuk and Armstrong did. Sawchuk worried about spending ten bucks on a new shirt. Every week he scrambled to find the cash to send home to Pat to pay the kids' dentist bill or buy them new boots for the winter. Young players like Walton would make lots more money than he ever did, if they could stick with an NHL team. Even that wouldn't be so hard after this year. Next year, the NHL would add six new teams. Twice as many teams, twice as many jobs, twice as many chances to play in the big league.

Young players wouldn't even have to negotiate their own contracts anymore. Now a kid walked into his contract meeting with a sharp-eyed lawyer on his arm like Alan Eagleson, that profane, self-promoting legal hound dog with the big face, who knew every trick in the book and didn't take any shit from some bald-headed asshole like Punch Imlach. Imlach made you sweat for every penny, as if he was paying your salary out of his own pocket. But with Eagleson on your side, the tables were turned. The players came first. That's what Eagleson kept saying. Without the players, Eagleson said, an owner didn't have a team. Look at what he'd done for that kid Orr. Got him eighty-five grand just to show up this year at training camp. Imagine throwing a pile of cash like that at the wall.

How old was Orr again? He looked about eleven. Not so much younger than Sawchuk when he'd signed his first professional contract for $2,000.

The Omaha Knights, that was the name of Sawchuk's first team, in the United States Hockey League. He'd been rookie of the year. Now the league didn't exist anymore. Twenty years later, and along comes Bobby Orr. Thanks to Eagleson, he gets eighty-five grand to sign his first NHL contract. Sure, the kid was good, but not forty times as good. There were big changes coming, all right. Sawchuk could smell them, and they smelled like money.

Sawchuk took off his shirt. A yellow-and-green bruise covered his left shoulder like a topographical map. It marked the spot where Sawchuk had absorbed a slapshot fired by a young sniper on the Chicago Black Hawks named Bobby Hull. Hull's slapshots went more than a hundred miles an hour. Skating at full speed and putting all his weight behind it, he'd shot the puck at Sawchuk from the middle of the face-off circle, hardly twenty feet away. The shot had lifted Sawchuk right off his feet. His raggedy cotton-and-leather shoulder pads, made in the days when Micmac Indians carved one-piece hockey sticks from tree roots and wore skateblades made of caribou bones — those shoulder pads hadn't done any more to soften the blow than the padded shoulders of a sports coat.

The bruised shoulder was the least of Sawchuk's aches and pains. Over the last twenty years, he'd broken bones, ruptured organs, pulled muscles, torn ligaments. One of his arms was shorter than the other from a football accident in high school. A month after he started playing professional hockey in Omaha, he'd got hit in the eye with a stick. Doctors took the eyeball right out of his head, laid it on the table, told him he might go blind. But when they put it back in his head, he could see again. He played his next game two weeks later and got a shutout.

He'd feel better tonight when he got on the ice. Sawchuk felt best when he played hockey. Everything else became irrelevant. It was the other twenty-three hours in a day that gave him the heebie-jeebies. "When I'm actually on the ice I don't worry at all," Sawchuk said once to a reporter named Trent Frayne.

Sawchuk glanced again around the room. Ron Ellis, looking like a fresh-faced kid with a crewcut, sat next to Red Kelly, who'd started playing in the NHL when Ellis was six and was now half bald. Kelly was folding his trousers neatly over a hanger and whistling to himself a song by Henry Mancini called "Moon River." Sawchuk, Stemkowski and everyone else in the room knew that the Leafs could win the Stanley Cup tonight, but Kelly didn't look too concerned. "Gosh hang," Kelly said once, when a teammate asked him if he felt nervous, "not really." Christ, Kelly sometimes came into the dressing room between periods of a game, sat down at his stall, unlaced his skates, leaned back and fell sound asleep. "Thinking about the game," Kelly said, "with my eyes closed."

Stemkowski wondered how Kelly stayed so calm. Even before a nothing game in the middle of the season, Stemkowski felt like jumping out of his skin. What if I make a mistake? What if I give the puck away? Miss a check? Pass when I should shoot? What if I fall and break my leg? Take a slapshot in the face? What if we lose the game? We won't lose the game, he thought now. In the next instant, he thought this was the coolest thing in the world, to dress in the uniform of the Toronto Maple Leafs, about to step onto the ice under the bright lights in front of sixteen thousand screaming fans and play his favourite sport in the most famous hockey rink in the world, while the entire nation watched the game on TV, wishing they could all be him. Even the prime minister was here tonight. Stemkowski could hardly believe that he got paid to do this.

Stemkowski watched Sawchuk bending over his equipment and began to chuckle. Sawchuk could make him laugh without saying a word. When the Canadian Broadcasting Corporation had installed stronger lighting in Maple Leaf Gardens so it could start transmitting games in colour, Stemmer had stepped off the ice after a shift and found his pal hunched at the end of the bench, wearing sunglasses. That was Ukie: funny in one breath, surly in the next.

Next to Sawchuk in the dressing room, the toothless geezer who alternated with him in goal seemed just as strange. Johnny Bower took half an hour to change into his underwear. If he had to dress for a wedding, he'd take all week. Mike Walton had mentioned to Bower this year that his dad had a picture of the goalie at home. Bower said he was pleased to hear that the rookie's father was such a devoted fan. "He isn't a fan," Walton said. "He played with you in Cleveland, in 1946." That was the year when Walton was born. Stemkowski would have been three years old. Dressing with Bower, Stemkowski sometimes felt embarrassed, as if he was watching his school principal take off his pants.

All season, Stemkowski had wondered if he'd stick with the team. Most of the other players did, too, no matter how old they were. Jim Pappin had played his share of games in Rochester, and he was almost thirty. So had Larry Hillman. Christ, Hillman spent so much time going back and forth between Toronto and the farm team in Rochester that he'd rented a house for his wife, Marjorie, and their three kids in St. Catharines, halfway between the two cities. Hillman had joined the Leafs almost seven years ago, and Imlach still treated him like a disposable towel. He'd use Hillman on defence for a few games in Toronto, then send him back to play for a month or two in Rochester, then call him back to Toronto again if someone got hurt. One year, Imlach called when the family was decorating their tree on Christmas Eve and told Hillman to go to Montreal. Marjorie drove him to the airport with the kids in the back seat, and the next day they opened their presents without him.

The other players who filed into the dressing room tonight lived a little closer to the rink than Hillman. Hillman's defence partner, Marcel Pronovost, drove from Meadowvale, a new subdivision about forty minutes west of the city. Frank Mahovlich lived in Leaside, about ten minutes up the Bayview Extension. George Armstrong came from Leaside, too, but sometimes he walked over to Yonge Street and came downtown on the subway. So did Allan Stanley, another of the team's old codgers, who'd spent one winter living by himself in the suburbs and now rented an apartment within walking distance of the subway.

Ron Ellis and his wife, Jan, drove in together from Weston. If the Leafs had won their previous game in Toronto, the Ellises would have taken the same route tonight as they'd followed five days earlier, east along

Eglinton and then south down Mount Pleasant. But five days earlier the Canadiens had whipped the Leafs and tied the series at two games apiece before the two teams travelled to Montreal to play at the Forum. Now they were back in Toronto, but the Ellises took a different route tonight, one that might bring them better luck, and parked the car in the lot on Church Street across from the Gardens. They had no trouble finding a parking spot. Once the attendant recognized Ellis as a Maple Leaf, he let them park for nothing. In return, Ellis and the other players gave him a stick or a couple of pucks for his kids.

With the exception of Mike Walton, the players wore white shirts, well-pressed grey slacks and skinny ties under a tweed sport coat or blue blazer. Except for the aches, pains, scars and bruises, they might have been going to work in a bank.

A puck had cut Johnny Bower's little finger, and he could hardly move his hand. Unlike Sawchuk, he didn't wear a mask, and he had so many cuts on his face that he could hardly shave in the morning. That wouldn't have stopped him from playing tonight. Everybody played with injuries like that. But last week, in the fourth game of the series, Bower had pulled a muscle in his leg during the warm-up. That finished him for the season, but Imlach didn't want the Canadiens to find out. He told Bower today to get dressed anyway and sit on the bench as Terry Sawchuk's back-up. If Sawchuk got hurt, Bower would make his way to the net and pretend to re-injure the same muscle as he'd pulled last week. He'd hobble off the ice again, and Imlach would fetch the Leafs' third goalie, Al Smith. Until then, Smith would sit fully dressed in his goalie equipment, watching the game on TV in the dressing room. Imlach hoped he'd stay there all night. The Canadiens would have a much better chance of scoring on Smith than they did against Bower or Sawchuk. If they knew that Bower was hurt, they'd injure Sawchuk to get to Smith. Anything for an edge.

Worse than the injuries to the players' bodies were the bruises on their minds. Dave Keon had first played for the Leafs as a fresh-faced teenager, still in high school. He'd scored twenty goals or more every year since he joined the team, but this season, he'd scored only nineteen, and he attributed his performance — in private, at least — to his disillusionment with the organization and the men who made decisions about his life. Red Kelly had detected flaws in the organization, as well, and decided to quit.

Along the wall from Kelly, Brian Conacher, a rookie at twenty-six, was weighing his options in other lines of work. For Conacher, as it had been for his father and uncles, hockey was a means to an end. He'd agreed to play for two years and earn enough money from hockey to start a business or make some investments. If he still liked it after that, he'd decide then whether he'd keep playing. A few stalls from Conacher, Bob Baun, the defenceman, would spend tonight's game on the bench. Baun was only thirty, but he, too, intended to quit.

And then there was Frank Mahovlich, Big Gutch, the Big M, two stalls down from Kelly. Mahovlich didn't want to talk. Stemkowski could tell just by looking at him. Tall and shy, Mahovlich regarded the world with a wary expression on his face, and he hadn't wanted to talk for months. Stemkowski blamed the Big M's silence on Punch Imlach, and he wasn't the only one.

On a good day, Mahovlich could perform as well as any player in the game. He just needed confidence. In his first six full seasons in the NHL, Mahovlich had burned up the league, scoring 178 goals. Over the same period of his career, Gordie Howe, now the best player in the NHL since Rocket Richard retired, had scored only 150.

In the 1960–61 season, Mahovlich had scored 48 goals. Only four players in the history of the league had scored more often. But rather than reassuring Mahovlich that the Leafs valued his exceptional talents, Harold Ballard, one of the team's owners, got drunk with his cronies in a hotel room at the end of the season and offered to sell Mahovlich to Chicago for $1 million.

To the men who ran the teams in the NHL, Mahovlich was just another commodity, like a bag of cement or a load of lumber. No wonder Gutchie closed his mouth and hardly said a word in the dressing room.

"Frank was like a radio," said Conacher. "The moment he hit the dressing room door it was like he was turned off. All the life and fun were sucked out of him."

The press criticized Mahovlich because he didn't seem mean enough. But some of his teammates remembered the Big M's mean side, and so did some of the Canadiens who would play against him tonight. Mahovlich had fought Ted Harris, the Canadiens defenceman, to a draw. Then he'd shot the puck at Henri Richard and hit him in the mouth. Mahovlich had challenged the entire Montreal bench, and the ensuing brawl started on the ice and continued into the hallway. Punch Imlach called it Mahovlich's "finest hour." After the game, a reporter asked Mahovlich if he'd shot the puck intentionally at Richard's face. Mahovlich tossed the guy halfway across the dressing room.

The local news media were relentless in pursuing Mahovlich. Reporters followed him everywhere. At restaurants, they eavesdropped on his conversations. At his house, they picked through his garbage. They pestered his wife, his father, his mother and his brother. Once, when Mahovlich missed a workout, reporters went to his home, discovered that he had dysentery and printed the earth-shattering news in their papers. By tonight's game, Mahovlich had stopped clipping articles for his scrapbook. "Who cares about the garbage they write about me?" he said.

This season, Mahovlich had scored only eighteen goals, about half his usual output. The press hounded him. Instead of defending his player, Imlach kept pounding on him too, telling him to his face that he was useless, telling the press that Mahovlich wasn't playing up to his potential. "I don't know where you're from," Imlach hollered at Mahovlich one night in the crowded dressing room, after the Leafs had lost a game to New York, "Chicoutimi or some place. But you should've stayed there and then I wouldn't have to be bothered with you." When Mahovlich wound up in the hospital, suffering from stress — or, as the press called it, a nervous breakdown — everyone claimed to have seen it coming. The only person surprised was Imlach.

It might have been easier for Mahovlich if he'd just quit instead of trying so hard to meet the expectations of his coach, his fans, the media and, most of all, himself. But Mahovlich wasn't a quitter. Next season, he'd be back in the hospital. When he got out, he'd spend the month of November practising by himself at a rink north of the city called Tam O'Shanter, under the watchful eye of a nurse. Toronto was a tough place to play in the NHL, and it was even tougher to play under Punch Imlach.

Regardless of their ability, Imlach didn't extend favours to his players, probably because he himself had received no favours as he struggled his way to a career in hockey. Born in 1918, the only child of Scottish parents, he'd grown up around Coxwell and Gerrard in Toronto's east end, attended Riverdale Collegiate, and gone to work in a bank a few blocks away. His father preferred soccer to hockey and didn't think his son would amount to much no matter what he did. By tonight, Imlach had spent more than forty years in the game as a player, a coach, a general manager and an owner, first of the Quebec Aces and later of the Rochester Americans, the Leafs' farm team. He worked for more than thirty of those years to get a job in the NHL, and he wasn't about to coddle some young kid just because he was overly sensitive to criticism. As far as Imlach was concerned, every player on the team tonight, even the ones he'd chosen himself, thought the sun shone out his own asshole because he played for the Toronto Maple Leafs. It was Imlach's job to prove them wrong. No matter how gifted a player might be, the key to winning was hard work and obedience.

If younger players like Walton and Mahovlich had a hard time getting along with Imlach, the older, more conservative players respected his experience. He was like most coaches they'd met. They expected nothing from him but good decisions about the team. So far Imlach had made enough good decisions that the Leafs had won three Stanley Cups. "He was a great guy to play for," said Tim Horton. "He put a lot of money into our pockets."

Even the TV commentator and former minor-league player Don Cherry spoke highly of Imlach. Imlach coached Cherry with a minor-league team in Springfield then moved to the NHL to coach the Leafs. When the Leafs won a Stanley Cup, Imlach returned to the minor-league city for a visit. "He was wearing a white suit and he had a white hat tilted back on his head," said Cherry, who toiled in the minors for more than fifteen years. "He was the talk of hockey, and there I was, the tenth defenceman in a leper colony. He's swaggering along the street and he happened to see me. He walked right over and asked me how I was doing. He even remembered [my wife] Rose's name. He told me to hang in and kept on walking. He was the best motivator I ever saw and he was the best coach I ever played for."

But some players preferred a coach who did more than remember their names. For Mahovlich, Imlach didn't even do that. Mahulovich, Malellovick, Malollowitz: Imlach mispronounced his name at every opportunity, and it wasn't always by accident. "Punch was just insensitive to sensitive people," said a former Leaf named Billy Harris.

Insensitive he might have been, but Imlach never stopped worrying. He worried about his hockey team more than he worried about his own family. Imlach knew how much work it took to get these guys to play together as a team. It didn't matter to him if they liked him or not. A bunch of headstrong overgrown adolescents, most of them didn't even like each other. In the last few weeks, Stemkowski and Bower had barked at each other in practice after Stemkowski cut the goalie's finger with a slapshot. Pappin had argued with Bower, too, although Pappin argued with everyone at some point. Keon and Baun had pushed each other around a bit. Larry Jeffrey and Larry Hillman dropped the gloves and fought in practice. Baun disagreed with Bob Pulford, Pulford didn't like Stemkowski, Stemkowski didn't always get along with Conacher, Conacher didn't see eye to eye with Pappin, and Pappin didn't like anybody. Off the ice, these guys were as different as any group of twenty men picked at random off the sidewalk. All they had in common was their ability to play hockey. It was Imlach's job to make sure they did it well enough to win the Stanley Cup. And if anyone thought that was fucking easy, Imlach would set him fucking straight in a fucking minute.

Whether they liked him or not, Imlach had full confidence in the players he chose to work for him. He'd said so publicly since the beginning of the series. The Leafs would win the Cup, he'd said. The Leafs would win the Cup. If that wasn't going to bat for his players, he didn't know what was. Imlach had laid his credibility, his reputation and his job on the line. All he expected in return was a Stanley Cup.

After the first game of this series, in Montreal, Imlach had gone to a tailor on Rue Sainte-Catherine and ordered a new suit. On the way to the shop, pedestrians on the street made fun of him. The Leafs had lost the first game, six to two, and they told him he should quit before his team lost the next three. The Leafs didn't stand a chance against the Canadiens, they said. Imlach chose a green checkered suit, which he thought would look good on TV. He told the tailor to have it ready when he returned to Montreal after the fourth game. He wanted to wear it, he said, "when the Leafs win the Stanley Cup." The tailor told him he'd have to wait a long time to wear it. "Just get the goddam suit ready," Imlach said.

The Leafs won the second game, in Montreal, and they won the third game, in Toronto, after more than twenty minutes of overtime. Montreal tied the series, winning again by a score of six to two. Back in Montreal, the Leafs won the fifth game, and Imlach picked up his new suit. Now they were in Toronto again. The Leafs were ahead by three games to two. If they won the game tonight, they'd win the Cup. And there was Imlach, in the corridor outside the dressing room, wearing his green checkered suit.

Big, cold, grey and impersonal. That's Toronto, thought Henri Richard, as the taxicab made its way through the afternoon traffic on University Avenue. Even if it hadn't been raining, no one on the Canadiens walked around this city much unless he had someplace to go. The only place Henri Richard wanted to go was back to Montreal. Last night, he and Claude Provost had taken the elevator up to their room at the Royal York, and neither of them had gone outside again. They hadn't even opened the door, except when the bellhop delivered their luggage. The guy had spotted the crest on the breast pocket of their blazers, but he didn't say anything until after he hung up their suit bags, emblazoned with the same Canadiens logo, in the closet. Now he looked like a little boy, thrilled to stand in the same room with two Montreal Canadiens. "I shouldn't say this," he said, "but I hope you guys win tomorrow night." Provost gave the guy some loose change. It wasn't his cash. The Canadiens' coach, Toe Blake, had handed out tip money before the team's train pulled into Union Station, across the street from the hotel. Blake had also given each player a five-dollar bill for spending money. But where would they spend it in this dismal city unless they spoke English? The few people in this city who spoke French did it in the same way as they dressed, as if they had more important things to do.

Even with a morning skate, a team meal and a meeting in the afternoon, the day had dragged by. Now it was almost five o'clock, and Richard and his teammates were on their way for the last time, not just for today, but for the season, to Maple Leaf Gardens. Now they could focus their attention on the hockey game, instead of twiddling their thumbs and trying to distract themselves from the gnawing anxiety that they all felt when they thought about their jobs. The hockey game would start in less than three hours.

The taxi seemed to move at a snail's pace. Jammed into the back seat between Leon Rochefort and Jacques Laperriere, both six feet tall, Richard looked like an aging bank robber being escorted to jail. Hollow-cheeked, sunken-eyed, prematurely grey, he stared glumly at the law courts, hospitals and fortress-like bunkers of insurance companies that lined both sides of the wide boulevard. Provost sat in the front seat beside the driver, his anvil-shaped head emerging from the collar of his trenchcoat like an Easter Island statue. He and Richard had known each other since they were both fifteen years old, and Provost hated Toronto even more than Richard did.

The voice of the dispatcher called over the radio for "Cabs on the two-four? Anybody on the two-four? I need a car around Bay and Bloor."

A transistor radio hung from the rear-view mirror. From its tinny speaker came a blast of slashing guitar chords from a rock band called The Who.

"Tabernacle!" said Provost, holding his hands over his ears.

The driver changed the station. A news announcer said that a heavyweight boxer named Muhammad Ali had refused induction into the U.S. Armed Forces and had been stripped of his champion's boxing title. "I ain't got no quarrel with them Viet Cong," said Ali. "They never called me nigger."

"Just turn it off," said Jacques Laperriere.

The driver shrugged and turned off the radio.

Henri Richard didn't like travelling, didn't like leaving his family, didn't like leaving his house. He didn't like leaving his business or the familiar streets of Montreal. He didn't like having to make a long-distance phone call whenever he wanted to talk to his children. He especially didn't like travelling to Toronto, where he felt like a second-class citizen in his own country. Even buying a newspaper was a challenge in this city, although he seldom did that anywhere. He didn't read newspapers very often, except for the sports news, and he had as much chance of finding a copy of *Le Petit Journal* or *Montréal-Matin* in this city as he did of meeting the Pope at the Honey Dew Restaurant. He might watch the sports news on one of the five channels that the TV in his room picked up, but it was frustrating trying to figure out what the sportscaster was talking about, even if there was a picture on the wall behind him. Some of his friends in Montreal thought Quebec should become a separate country from the rest of Canada. Richard didn't pay much attention to politics, but after a visit to Toronto, he understood why. Why would anyone want to be a part of the same country as Toronto? Big, cold, impersonal and Anglo. And the rain this afternoon just made it worse. Richard watched a woman walking along the sidewalk, wearing a clear plastic rain scarf on her head like cellophane draped over a clump of wool. It was hard to tell if she was twenty-two or sixty. Women all looked the same in this city. Grim-faced, purse-lipped, tight-assed, with legs like a piano's: even the Queen of England was better looking, but not much.

At Dundas Street, the cab stopped for a red light. Another cab pulled up beside it. Richard glanced at the passengers and recognized four more of his teammates hunched inside like truants in a paddy wagon. Yvan Cournoyer, young, fresh-faced and apple-cheeked. Terry Harper, who had backed up Richard over the last five years in so many fights that Richard had lost count. Bobby Rousseau, probably thinking about playing golf. In the front seat, God, disguised as Jean Beliveau. With these guys as your teammates, you didn't waste time thinking about losing. Even in a godforsaken city like Toronto, Richard felt confident that the Canadiens would win the sixth game of the series tonight. Then they could go back to Montreal, play the seventh game on Thursday, two days from now, and win the Stanley Cup in front of the people who had supported them all year.

The Canadiens had already travelled once today to Maple Leaf Gardens. They'd come here for a midday skate, to make sure their blades felt sharp, their sticks felt comfortable in their hands and their nerves didn't short-circuit with anxiety. Except for their gloves, they didn't wear equipment. Dave Balon, the winger, had joked with the team's assistant trainer, Eddy Palchak, about putting some speed into Cournoyer's skates with the magic stone that Palchak carried in his pocket to take the burrs off the sharpened steel of the players' blades. Bosey joked a lot. That was his way of staying calm. So did Gump Worsley, one of the team's two goalies. When Gump wasn't puffing on a cigarette or taking a sip from a cup of tea, he kept up a steady banter that became part of the background noise like the buzzing of a fluorescent lightbulb. Jean Beliveau had talked for a few minutes to a reporter. He spoke English well, and most of the French-speaking players were happy to let him do the talking.

The goalies had skated, too, moving awkwardly in their big black goalie skates with blades as flat and dull as curtain rods. Skidding along beside the Canadiens' other goalie, a kid named Rogie Vachon, Gump looked like a paunchy little man out for some exercise with his grandson. Vachon wasn't much taller, but he had hands the size of pie plates. None of the players knew which of the two goalies would play tonight and which one would sit on the bench.

Just a few months ago, Worsley had been the team's starting goalie. But during a Canadiens game at Madison Square Garden, a fan had hit Worsley in the head with a hard-boiled egg. Worsley suffered a concussion, so the Canadiens recalled Vachon from their farm team in Houston. Vachon was twenty-one, but he'd impressed everyone, including the fans, the coach and the general manager, Sam Pollock. Everyone who saw him thought Vachon was an impressive goalie. Before he'd arrived in Houston, he'd impressed Gilles Laperriere, Jacques's brother, who had seen the kid playing in Abitibi. And before that, Vachon had impressed his friends, playing pond hockey in Palmarolle in grade eight. But he hadn't impressed his mother to the same degree. When a Junior Canadiens coach named Scotty Bowman went north to ask the kid to play for his team, Vachon's mother said her son would find a better future working for the local sawmill. Even now, his mother was still skeptical. Rogie would be almost thirty before he'd finally convince his mom that he'd made the right decision. By then, he'd be the highest-paid goalie in the NHL, earning $2 million for a five-year contract. Even his mom thought that was impressive. But tonight, he was earning one hundred dollars a game, and the sawmill still beckoned.

When the Canadiens brought Vachon from Houston this year to take Worsley's place, he played a game against Detroit. It wasn't the first time that Vachon had played with the Canadiens. He'd shown up for training camp in September, but so had thirteen other goalies. By tonight, Richard could hardly remember any of them. Over the first half of the season, the Canadiens had fallen into the doldrums, winning a few, losing a few, tying a few. When Worsley was hurt and Vachon joined the team to replace their first-string goalie, it looked as if the Canadiens would continue to flounder. The game against Detroit had just begun, when Gordie Howe, the best player in the NHL, got a breakaway. He skated toward the new kid in goal and took the first shot of Vachon's NHL career. The kid stopped the shot, and the Canadiens won the game. After that, the team began to pay attention. "It was like when you're sick, the doctor gives you the pill," said Yvan Cournoyer. "Well, Vachon was our little pill. When he came along we felt better all of a sudden."

With Vachon in goal, the Canadiens began to win again. The more the team won, the better they played. The better they played, the more they won. Of Vachon's nineteen games since his arrival, the Canadiens had lost only three. In the best-of-seven semi-finals against the Rangers, the Canadiens had won four straight, with Vachon in goal for each game.

In this final series against the Leafs, Vachon had started in all five games. One of those games had extended into two periods of overtime before a Leafs player, Bob Pulford, scored the winning goal. The Leafs had now scored fourteen goals against Vachon in this series. The Canadiens had scored fifteen against the Leafs' goalies, Terry Sawchuk and Johnny Bower, but they were behind in the series, three games to two. Last Saturday, Vachon's luck ran out. The Leafs scored four goals in the first two periods, and Blake yanked him, replacing him with Worsley.

After their morning skate, the Canadiens went back to the hotel for a lunch of steak, salad and Jell-O, followed by a meeting with Blake in the team owner's suite, which David Molson let them use so they wouldn't have to jam themselves into Blake's room. They talked about their last game: what had gone right and what needed improving.

Blake talked to his players individually, as well, speaking in English to some, French to others. That killed some more time. Then the players went to their rooms for a nap.

Lying in their underwear on top of their bedspreads, Beliveau and Cournoyer, roommates on the road, talked for a few minutes about the Leafs defence. Cournoyer would play tonight only if one of the Leafs got a penalty. Beliveau had played against these guys for years. He knew how they worked, and he gave Cournoyer some pointers on shifting past Marcel Pronovost and manoeuvring in the corners against Allan Stanley. Stanley,

Pronovost and the other Leafs defencemen tonight, Larry Hillman and Tim Horton, had almost 400 Stanley Cup playoff games between them, about 370 more than Cournoyer. "Stanley and Pronovost can both block shots," Beliveau said. "You can outskate Pronovost. But Stanley will get you on the angles every time."

The two Canadiens dozed for less than an hour. Any longer, Beliveau said, "and it slows me up in the game." When they got up again, Cournoyer opened the curtains. He got dressed slowly, tying the knot in his tie once, then doing it again until he got it just right. In the bathroom, Beliveau spent twenty minutes shaving. Downstairs, they milled around the lobby with their teammates dressed in identical blazers like members of a men's choir. "The Canadiens made sure we dressed properly," said Gilles Tremblay, "even when we were just kids."

For a French-speaking boy raised on hockey in Quebec, to play for the Montreal Canadiens was an honour, and they wore their uniforms proudly, on and off the ice. Of the twenty players on the team today, fourteen had been dressing as Canadiens since they were teenagers. Some had joined the organization before they'd left public school. Some had brothers, cousins and uncles who'd tried to play for the team.

The cabs turned onto Carlton Street and delivered the Canadiens to the front door of Maple Leaf Gardens. The players walked quickly through drizzling rain and into the lobby. A couple of rink attendants stood inside the door, assigned to the job of letting the players in and keeping everyone else outside. At four-thirty on a rainy afternoon in May, there were more pedestrians scurrying along the wet sidewalk than fans trying to catch a glimpse of their heroes. The rink attendants recognized each player. They'd already seen them at least ten times this year. They nodded at Dickie Duff, who'd played until three years ago as a Maple Leaf. A streetcar filled with rush-hour passengers rang its bell as it rumbled past the doors. The Gardens wouldn't start hopping for another couple of hours. The team had lots of time to dress in their equipment and uniforms. But at least they were in a hockey rink. "We could get dressed in ten minutes," Beliveau said. "But it's easier to have the time."

If they'd played tonight's game in Montreal, the Canadiens might have gone to the Forum even earlier. They'd have walked through the dressing-room door. They'd have glanced at the motto on the wall: "Nos bras meurtris vous tendent le flambeau / À vous toujours de le porter bien haut." They'd have lingered in their shirtsleeves for a couple of hours under rows of wood-grained plaques that displayed in gold type the names of all the Canadiens players who'd taken the team's motto to heart: "To you from failing hands we throw the torch. Be yours to hold it high." A bit overblown. But for the Montreal Canadiens, winning seemed like a life-or-death issue.

Cab drivers, grocery clerks, waitresses: everyone in Montreal had something to say to a Canadien who lost a game. "The pressure on Canadiens coaches and players to stay on top," said Bill Libby in the *Hockey News*, "is heavier than that on any other team in any sport in any city in Canada or the U.S."

"Your kids get it at school," said Gump Worsley. "Your wife gets it. What's wrong with your husband? What's wrong with your father's team?"

The pressure wasn't nearly so intense in other cities. Only Toronto came close. In New York, said Worsley, who played there for ten years, "you go a block and a half from the rink, and you're away from all that. Go into a restaurant, and nobody knows who you are. You can't do that in Montreal."

The team brought the pressure on themselves. They'd begun winning years ago and hadn't stopped. In twenty-five seasons of the six-team league, the Canadiens had won the league championship twelve times. They'd won the Stanley Cup ten times. They'd finished second eight times and missed the playoffs only once. When Henri Richard joined the team in 1955, he assumed the Canadiens would win the Cup every year, and they did, for five years in a row. They were so good over those years that none of their four-out-of-seven-game playoff series went to a seventh game. They went to a sixth game in the finals only once. Of thirty First Team All-Star positions over that period, Canadiens players took fifteen of them. Of the thirty Second Team positions, they took ten. Some teams awarded bonuses to their players if they won more than half their games. The Canadiens didn't receive a bonus unless they won them all.

The more games the Canadiens won, the more people paid attention. When the Canadiens travelled to London, England, for five days to play exhibition games there against the Black Hawks, the Chicago media sent one reporter. The Canadiens were covered by thirty-three.

"We were afraid to lose," said Yvan Cournoyer. "That's what made us a winner."

Even after the league expanded, salaries rose, and the game changed, the Canadiens kept living up to their own expectations. Five years after tonight's game, in 1972, Larry Robinson started playing as a defenceman with the team. For the next seventeen years, his team never missed the playoffs. When they lost in the playoffs instead of winning the Stanley Cup, fans demanded to know why. Except for Gump Worsley, who loved kibitzing over a beer with the team's fans, most of the players left town to get away from the incessant prodding. "The fans in Montreal love you," said another former Canadien named Steve Shutt, "win or tie."

Even their opponents acknowledged the Canadiens' winning tradition. "It was an honour to lose to Montreal," said a former goalie named Chico Resch.

To maintain their winning tradition, the Canadiens emphasized one particular skill over all the others: skating. There wasn't a player on the team tonight who hadn't improved his skating to become a Canadien and to remain with the team. "A coach can teach anything else," said the team's president, David Molson, "but a player who can't skate is a minor-leaguer with us."

It hadn't always been the case. In earlier days, when Molson's ancestors had first invested in the team, the Canadiens had a reputation as a bunch of nasty-minded bruisers who would rather knock their opponents out of the rink than score a goal. "Frightful collisions," considerable "hurt and blood" and young players "battling for victory with as much passion and eagerness as was ever expressed in war," said an observer of the team's first game, in 1910.

In the 1920s, the Canadiens' owners, who included an ex-goalie, a former hockey referee and a race-horse breeder, set out to build a team of "he-man hockey talent" that could "not only outplay the opposition but physically overwhelm them as well. Down in their hearts," said the ex-referee Leo Dandurand, "they should feel that they can beat the opposition in the alley as well as on the ice."

His players took him literally. With names like Newsy, Sprague and Odie, the Canadiens and their opponents clubbed and sliced each other with their sticks, only to become the best of friends off the ice. Playing for an opposing team one night, Newsy Lalonde bodychecked Sprague Cleghorn hard enough to draw attention from Cleghorn's brother, Odie, who chased Lalonde down the ice and bashed him over the head with his stick so hard that he left a twelve-stitch gash. Police arrested Odie for assault. In court the next day, Lalonde appeared as a witness, on Odie's behalf. "There was nothing personal about it," Lalonde would later say, when he was almost eighty. But the judge still fined Odie fifty dollars.

Looking for more mayhem, blood and violence, fans flocked to Canadiens games, and they got what they wanted. In a game against Ottawa, Sprague and Odie knocked three of their opponents out of action for two games each. The referee called the Cleghorns "a disgrace to hockey." Ottawa asked the president of the league to expel Sprague Cleghorn from the game. The league disagreed. It inducted Sprague into the Hockey Hall of Fame.

Brother Odie had a good head for hockey, and he used it as more than a punching bag. As a playing coach in Pittsburgh, Odie began to send players off the ice and replace them with players from the bench while the game was in progress. He was the first coach ever to try the tactic. He also alternated two forward lines, another first for the NHL. Until then, the same players from each team panted and sweated their way through an entire game. Odie Cleghorn also took a turn in goal for his team after Pittsburgh's regular goalie was injured. When another coach, Lester Patrick, pulled the same stunt with the New York Rangers during the 1928 playoffs, the man who replaced him as coach behind the bench was Odie Cleghorn.

The blood and violence might have attracted fans, but it didn't help the Canadiens win hockey games. By the 1930s, the Montreal Canadiens were known as the doormats of the NHL. Over six years, the team finished last or second-last four times. The fans grew tired of watching bloodied goons chase each other around an arena without winning the game, and they stayed away in droves.

Attendance dwindled in 1934 to two thousand a game. In desperation, the team's owners signed away revenue from all the popcorn, hot dogs, soda pop and five-cent programs sold during games, and the Canadiens were losing money. "The Canadiens' revenue stream was pathetic," said writer Michael McKinley.

The team teetered on the verge of bankruptcy, until a former player and co-founder of the league named Tommy Gorman took over as general manager in 1940. Gorman put a price tag on every player on the Canadiens and offered all of them to other teams, except for one player, a bilingual left-winger from Northern Ontario named Toe Blake. But the Canadiens were so bad that no other team would pay for any of them. In desperation, Gorman hired Toronto's coach, Dick Irvin, to come to Montreal and cultivate young players. More important, he asked Irvin to find ways to make money so the team wouldn't fold. Irvin invited the Quebec Senior League to play some of its games in the Forum. He added professional wrestling to the attractions staged in the arena. When the war started, he found jobs for Canadiens players in munitions factories around Montreal so they could keep playing hockey against rival teams whose best players had joined the armed forces. He also signed a player named Maurice Richard, Henri's elder brother, in 1942. Maurice Richard, Toe Blake and

Elmer Lach, known as the Punch Line, helped turn the Canadiens into winners and turn around the team's fortunes.

The Canadiens won their first Stanley Cup in thirteen years in 1944, but the team hardly behaved like champions. Off the ice, they sat by their stalls in the dressing room, smoking cigarettes and drinking beer. They seldom shaved, and they paid attention to their diet only when they couldn't pull their shorts over their stomachs. If they couldn't outplay their opponents, the Canadiens beat them up, sometimes with notorious results. After a brawl between the Leafs and the Canadiens in 1955, the referee, Frank Udvari, banished everyone to the dressing rooms except for eight players, who competed for the rest of the game by themselves, with no one on the bench.

The Canadiens finally began to behave as champions with the help of Frank Selke, another refugee from the Toronto Maple Leafs. As general manager, Selke succeeded in imposing some discipline on the players. At the same time, he built a network of amateur teams that could provide Montreal with a steady supply of talent. Most of the teams were in Quebec, but the Canadiens also operated an amateur hockey system in Regina, the home of a Canadiens defenceman named Terry Harper, who was in tonight's lineup; ten farm clubs in Winnipeg, where another defenceman playing tonight, Ted Harris, had grown up; and an amateur league in Edmonton, not far from an extensive French-speaking farming area, that cost the Canadiens $300,000 a year to maintain. After the mid-1950s, more than ten thousand amateur players on 750 teams owed their first allegiance to Montreal. Only one in a thousand ever skated with the Montreal Canadiens.

But this vast network of young players helped the Canadiens win five Stanley Cups in a row between 1956 and 1960. "I went six seasons," said Henri Richard, "before I found out that you didn't automatically get the Stanley Cup every year."

In 1960, Richard's big brother finally retired, and without him the Canadiens stopped winning the Cup, at least for a while. They won it again in 1965, and then in 1966, as well. Now it was 1967, the hundredth anniversary of Confederation and the fiftieth anniversary of the NHL. It just made sense that the Canadiens would win the Cup this year, too.

Every Canadien in the dressing room knew that his future depended on the way he played tonight. All-star, scoring champion, playmaker, shot blocker: he might have been the best in the league last year. But past achievements counted for nothing but a handshake and an invitation to the old boys' dinner in June. From the team that had won the Cup in 1960, the Canadiens had chopped, traded, demoted or bid farewell to thirteen players, and there was always another player to take each of their spots. "There always seems to be someone there to replace you," said Yvan Cournoyer. "You have to be number one. There is nothing else."

The team hadn't been number one this year. They'd reached the finals only after a mediocre season, finishing seventeen points behind the Chicago Black Hawks. They'd scored only 202 goals, their worst record in twelve years. Cournoyer in December had scored three power-play goals in one game, a feat achieved only once before, by his teammate Jean Beliveau. But of the team's other forwards, Henri Richard, Claude Provost, Gilles Tremblay and Dick Duff had all been injured at one time or another. Beliveau himself suffered a sprained thumb and a pulled muscle, and during a game in Chicago, his eye was struck by a stickblade, temporarily blinding him, sending him to hospital for three days and almost ending his career. He missed a total of seventeen games and played another twenty in a row without scoring a goal. Gump Worsley injured his knee, had surgery in December and re-injured his knee when he came back. On defence, J.C. Tremblay suffered a concussion; Terry Harper, a dislocated shoulder; Ted Harris, a broken finger. Jacques Laperriere missed nine games at the beginning of the season with a fractured ankle that hadn't healed from the previous April. The team's physiotherapist had administered more than five hundred treatments this season. Only Bobby Rousseau and John Ferguson had survived unscathed, although both of them had missed a few games with suspensions.

To add insult to injury, the season seemed to drag on forever. Who ever heard of playing a Stanley Cup final game in May? The major-league baseball season had started almost a month ago. "Since I entered the NHL as a player thirty-one years ago," said Toe Blake, "I've never known anything like it."

After hobbling through most of the season, the Canadiens finally regained their equanimity and started to win games. They ended the season with eight victories and three ties over eleven straight and then won four more against the Rangers in the opening round of the playoffs. Now they faced the Leafs. The two teams hadn't played for the Stanley Cup in eight years.

When this series began, a couple of weeks ago, Montreal players felt relieved to meet the Leafs instead of the Chicago Black Hawks. The Black Hawks had finished the season in first place. Five of them had finished in the top ten in the scoring race, including Bobby Hull, who'd scored more than fifty goals. The Leafs, on the other hand, had no top-ten scorers, three geriatric defencemen, two fossilized goalies who'd spent as much time this year on their backs in the infirmary as they had in the net, and an average age that seemed Biblical. Montreal had defeated the Leafs in the playoffs the year before, and the team hadn't changed anything since. "We couldn't believe our luck," said Terry Harper, the Montreal defenceman. "We thought it was going to be easy." Now, one game away from a humiliating defeat, they didn't think so anymore.

In their dressing room in Montreal, the players would have read the newspaper, opened their fan mail, signed some autographs. It was a place to get away, said Ken Dryden, who would later play goal for the Canadiens. "Our refuge." Everywhere else — restaurants, theatres, buses, grocery stores, charter flights — was cluttered with the media and "friends of the team," autograph hunters, friends of friends, petty crooks armed with out-of-town schedules. The Canadiens today could escape into Maple Leaf Gardens from the world outside, but it wasn't their home, and they entered like pilgrims visiting a foreign cathedral.

To reach their dressing room, the visiting team had to turn left instead of right. The air felt chilly and smelled sharp, the way it did in any hockey rink in any town in the world. In every hockey rink, ammonia was injected into the cold brine that ran through pipes under the ice to keep it frozen. In the corridor, the shiny painted floors felt sticky underfoot. In the Gardens, the corridor that led to the visitors' dressing room was particularly narrow, and the painted cinder-block walls were lined with alien photographs of Toronto Maple Leafs. And when the Canadiens got to their room, they had to pass a big maple leaf painted on the door across the hall.

Inside the cramped and airless room, they found their equipment set out and hanging from hooks over the spot where each of them had dressed throughout the season. The Canadiens' trainer, Larry Aubut, and his assistant, Eddy Palchak, had brought the players' skates back from Tommy Nayler's little shop under the stands before this morning's skate. If any blades needed a touch-up, Nayler would have done it this afternoon. Nayler was the assistant trainer for the Maple Leafs and could easily have run a file down the sharp edge of a visiting player's skateblade if he'd wanted to scuttle the visitors' chances of winning. But every NHL team that visited the Gardens relied on Nayler to sharpen their skates. So did figure skaters like Barbara Ann Scott and Don Jackson. "He was the best in the business," said Hall of Fame defenceman Harry Howell, who played seventeen seasons with the New York Rangers. "All the players in the league knew that he wasn't going to sabotage their skates. He wouldn't have lasted long if he did."

Around eight o'clock last night, Larry Aubut and Eddy Palchak had pulled up in a cab to the parking garage off Wood Street, following the five-ton truck that the Leafs had sent to Union Station to greet the Canadiens' train from Montreal. To help Aubut and Palchak transfer the Canadiens' equipment from the baggage car to the truck, the Leafs always sent the same two attendants. In the Leafs program, these guys had titles like "assistant equipment manager" or "transportation specialist." But Aubut and Palchak knew them only as Finkle and Jumbo. Like the trainers and rink attendants for all six of the NHL teams, these guys worked non-stop, it seemed, twenty-four hours a day, seven days a week, at least from October till April, when the season ended. No matter when you went to an NHL arena, you'd see a trainer or attendant dressed in his team jacket, lugging a bag of equipment or rolling a dolly loaded with hockey sticks through the empty hallways. The hours didn't bother them. They had no hobbies. Few of them had wives. They lived in bachelor apartments and basement boltholes, usually within a bus ticket from the rink. They loved their jobs, couldn't think of a better way to pass the time, couldn't wait for the next season to begin after this one ended. If they didn't work for an NHL team, what the hell else would they do? The Leafs had once held a birthday party for Jumbo at a restaurant called George's Spaghetti House. In addition to a cake, the team chipped in and said that Jumbo could call anyone he wanted, anywhere in the world. The team would pay the long-distance charges. Jumbo said thank you very much and called his mom in Scarborough to tell her he'd be late coming home that night.

Once inside the Gardens, Aubut and Palchak unloaded their team's shoulder pads, elbow pads, shin pads, gloves, sweaters, socks, pants, sticks, skates, tape, towels, soap, rubber mats, first-aid kits and the portable skate sharpener that Palchak used between periods to touch up the Canadiens' blades. The playoff schedule was a bit easier, and the finals were the easiest games of the whole year, spread apart by two or three days, with nothing in between but a practice. But no matter how easy it got, Aubut didn't like going on the road.

Neither did Palchak, although he'd been hired as assistant trainer only a year ago, and the novelty of travelling to a city like Toronto still compensated for the drudgery that he faced once he got there. Through a friend of his mother's from church, Palchak had started working for the Canadiens before he turned eighteen, doing odd jobs at the Montreal

Forum — dirty laundry, mostly — and running errands for Larry Aubut. Now in his mid-twenties, squat, pudgy and near-sighted, he made less in a year than the lowest-paid rookie, a bit more than $5,000, but the players expected him to appear on command. He had learned to sharpen their skates to their critical satisfaction and to sharpen them again, sometimes three times in a game, when they felt something was amiss. When a teammate played a trick on Cournoyer and cut the lace on his skate with a knife, Palchak unthreaded the pieces from the boot and laced it up with a new one. He fetched tape, towels, sticks, pop and underwear at a player's command. Long after they'd showered, shaved and left the building, he remained behind to dry out their equipment, do their laundry and put everything in order for the next day.

Palchak knew that most people would give their left arm to have his job. He knew that he worked for the greatest hockey team in the world. He had the Stanley Cup rings to prove it. The players called him Eddy and gave him a big tip at the end of the season. He could drink for free at taverns òwned by Toe Blake or Henri Richard. He had his summers off, and he spent the fall and winter rubbing shoulders with Jean Beliveau. Long after the players on tonight's team retired or were traded, Palchak would still have his job. A player might stick around till he was thirty-five, maybe a bit longer. Palchak would go to work every day with the Montreal Canadiens until he was sixty. Beat that with your nine-to-five, Palchak thought, brushing a button-sized wad of discarded hockey tape from his red team cardigan.

Palchak and Aubut had spent the entire day at the Gardens, and Palchak hadn't eaten anything except an omelette at the Diana Sweets around the corner on Yonge Street. In Montreal, he would have sent a kid out to buy a smoked meat sandwich at Bens. In Toronto, smoked meat was what you got when the butcher shop burned down.

Hunger made Palchak grumpy. It didn't help that the Leafs had beaten the Canadiens two days ago at the Forum in Montreal and scored four goals against the team's young goalie, Rogatien Vachon. That put the Leafs ahead in the series by three games to two. Now everybody was in a surly mood. Even Gump Worsley, a perennial wisecracker, had hardly spoken to Palchak last night on the train all the way from Montreal. Palchak could usually rely on the Gumper to say something funny. They were both friendly, conscientious men with round faces and smiles like sunshine. But not last night.

While Palchak bustled around the visitors' dressing room, Aubut stood outside in his Canadiens windbreaker, having a smoke. On the other side of the street, across the intersection, a few fans had already arrived for dinner at Le Baron Steak House. Pretty soon, the sidewalk would be teeming with Leafs fans. That concerned Aubut a bit.

Fans were unpredictable. In Boston, they threw marbles at the referees and tossed lit firecrackers at the players. In Chicago, they threw lightbulbs and harmonicas. In Detroit, a fan threw an octopus onto the ice. After a game in New York, a referee named Bryan Lewis found a note under his hotel-room door telling him that if he came back, he'd get shot. After another game, New York fans chased the referee down Fiftieth Street and threatened to kill him until he escaped in a cab. A fan in a tavern near Madison Square Garden punched a referee named John McCauley so hard, he toppled over and hit his head on the bar. It took him five months to recover.

Aubut had been attacked before a game in the Canadiens' semi-final series against New York by a fat woman who walked up behind him outside Madison Square Garden and stuck a hat pin into his ass. Palchak had laughed when Aubut told him about it. "She probably thought you were Yvan Cournoyer," he said. But to Aubut, it was no laughing matter. Someday, one of these lunatics would try to stab a player or shoot him with a gun.

A few kids had loitered all afternoon in the rain on the sidewalks outside the Gardens. Rink rats, probably, skipping school on a Tuesday to catch a glimpse of their heroes. Aubut felt sorry for some of them. They looked soaked and shabby, as if no one paid much attention to them and they didn't get enough to eat. The kids regarded the Leafs players as gods and thought Maple Leaf Gardens was the next-best thing to Heaven.

Aubut could understand that. Even Yvan Cournoyer said he'd almost fainted when he'd met his hero, Rocket Richard, and Cournoyer had been a junior at the time, one of the best junior-hockey players in the country, almost seventeen, with a good future ahead of him. These kids didn't even own a pair of skates.

Aubut also wondered about the adults around this place who took advantage of these skinny little kids. Conn Smythe had run the Gardens like a military base, and the staff all toed the line. But by the mid-1960s, the Gardens was a "world of tiny kingdoms, insider deals and scams," said Gord Stellick, a former Leafs executive. "An odd gang of rounders, drifters and ex-cons," with nicknames like "Yogi, Straw Hat, Freddie Cigar, Banana Joe, Popcorn Millie, George the Towel Guy."

Aubut didn't want to imagine what some of these characters might demand from a kid in return for a ticket to a game or a pair of gloves used by the kid's favourite player. He flicked his cigar into the gutter and went back inside. Through an open door that led into a cluttered workshop under the stands came a sound like a million caged cicadas on a summer night. Tommy Nayler stood over his skate-sharpening machine, running the blade of a Tackaberry skate across a grinding wheel.

Henri Richard pulled his shoulder pads over his head. They felt flimsy. A Canadian company called WinnWell made them: two leather-covered shoulder caps of Fiberglas held together by white cotton quilting, tied at the neck with a shoelace. When his head popped out above the pads, Richard's eyes focused on Yvan Cournoyer across the dressing room, draping his trousers over a hanger. Cournoyer got dressed before a game more slowly than Richard.

In the enemy territory of Maple Leaf Gardens, this dressing room wasn't home, but the Canadiens had been here often enough that it was at least familiar. It was like being a travelling salesman. Your job took you out of town. You recognized a few familiar sights. Sometimes you liked the change of scenery, sometimes you couldn't wait to get home again and sleep in your own bed.

A rubber mat covered the painted concrete floor. The benches were bolted to the painted cinder-block walls. There was a hook fastened securely to the wall above each player's spot and a dripping shower at one end of the room. It wasn't fancy, but compared to the Forum, it was a palace. The Forum hadn't been renovated for twenty years. The rubber mats were tattered, the pipes leaked, and an odour of sweat, liniment and unflushed urinals hung like mustard gas in the corridors. Old and crummy as it was, the French players on the team still called it "la maison."

"It wasn't my second home," said Yvan Cournoyer, "it was my first. I was more comfortable there than anywhere else on earth." Who cared if the taps leaked or the toilets flushed?

Only in his third year with the team, Cournoyer didn't say much in the dressing room. But then, who did, on this team?

For a team that caused so much hubbub and excitement, the Montreal Canadiens were pretty quiet guys. Trying to get a word out of Canadiens defenceman Ted Harris, said one reporter, was like trying to pry a sawbuck out of Jack Benny. John Ferguson, the left-winger, was usually wound up too tight to talk, especially before a do-or-die game like tonight's. Jean Beliveau, the captain, said everything he had to say just by existing. A visitor once asked Toe Blake if Henri Richard could speak English. "I don't think he even speaks French," Blake said. "He just doesn't speak."

Richard was the first to admit that he didn't like to talk. When he set up a hockey school one summer in Montreal to make some extra money, two hundred kids showed up, but Richard couldn't think of anything to say to them. "I hated the hockey school," he said. "I spend all my time skating, not talking."

The players weren't unfriendly with each other. But they had no illusions about why they came to the rink. They weren't coming to play, they were coming to win. It was their job. Idle chit-chat just distracted them, and none of them wanted distractions.

Dave Balon had heard from other players that the Canadiens had one of the quieter dressing rooms in the NHL. When he joined the team from the New York Rangers, almost four years ago, he noticed the difference right away. Sometimes you could hear the sound of a player trimming his fingernails with a nail clipper. At first he wondered if the French players didn't want to talk to the English players. But he quickly realized that language had nothing to do with it. Balon had played for the Lions in Trois-Rivières, Quebec, and for other teams that had their share of French-speaking players, and their dressing rooms had been as noisy as anyone else's. Balon just figured that the Canadiens had other things to do than talk.

Henri Richard kept quiet because he was shy and, in his first seasons with the team, because he felt awestruck by the other men in the dressing room. Even more than most French-Canadian kids in the 1950s, Richard regarded the Montreal Canadiens the way a novitiate regards the Catholic Church. Henri had watched his older brother Maurice play for the team from the time he was six. He'd tried not to bask in the reflection of his brother's glory, but it was hard not to feel proud of Rocket Richard. Henri never forgot the first time that he walked into the Canadiens' dressing room. Henri had walked past the door to the room many times when he'd played centre with the Junior Canadiens. They played and practised at the Forum, too. He'd looked at the crest emblazoned on the door and wondered how it must feel to go inside. He was nineteen when he arrived for his first game as a Montreal Canadien, and he never forgot the feeling. "It was like a chapel," he said. A red sweater on its hanger in each player's stall. Twenty sets of gloves, pants, shin pads, skates, all positioned by the trainers in the same way. His thirty-two-year-old brother was sitting just inside the door. So were Ken Mosdell, Doug Harvey, Bert Olmstead. Henri had watched them play for years. It took him five years, he said, before he could talk in such a hallowed place. "Ten before I shaved in it."

Tonight, twelve years later, every player in the visitors' dressing room understood how Richard had felt, even if they hadn't played their first professional game with the Canadiens. The youngest ones were pulling on their equipment to play on the same team as men they'd admired for years. The money mattered, too. Money allows you to think about hockey and nothing else. It changes your status from someone who plays the game when he's not working to someone who works at the game. Hockey is no longer just your hobby, it's your job. From hockey, you make a living, pay the bills, feed your family, keep a car on the road and a roof over your head.

Even if you play just a single game as a pro, the paycheque entitles you to membership in an exclusive club. Money provides another measure of your ability and qualifies you to compare yourself against everyone else who does the same job as you. No matter how much you make, though, no one plays for money alone. And in the eyes of a new player, the veterans were more than employees earning a paycheque. They were gods.

"I looked on the older players as something special," said John Ferguson, sitting two spots from Richard tonight. "It was two years before I even dared to go and have a beer with them."

Out of respect as well as his own inclinations, Ferguson dressed well, even when he came to practice. Tonight, he wore a light blue dress shirt with a red-and-blue military tie under his Canadiens blazer. To practices at the Forum, he wore sport coats with a pattern of houndstooth check, or casual suits tailor-made from a solid brown or rust-coloured gabardine. Twenty-eight years old and ruggedly handsome, Ferguson dressed so well that a clothing company asked him to model sweaters and sport coats for its fall catalogue. "He looks as if he's about to have his high-school graduation photo taken," said a writer named John Zichmanis.

Ferguson was no tailor's dummy, though. Within a few years, he would own the company. Tonight, his wife, Joan, was seven months pregnant with the first of their four children. Ferguson intended to support his family not just by playing hockey but by building a business, as well.

Ted Harris, sitting a couple of spots away from Ferguson, didn't pay as much attention to his wardrobe. You could tell by the scuff marks on his shoes and from the shoes themselves, round-toed, thick-soled brown lace-ups that you might find at a farm-implement store beside a bag of Vigoro fertilizer. Like Ferguson, Harris had played in Cleveland before he joined the Canadiens in Montreal. Harris would turn thirty-one this summer, the same age as Henri Richard, and Harris and his wife were expecting their first child, as well. Richard hadn't heard this news from Harris, though. Harris almost never spoke in the dressing room. Richard had heard the news one night from a complete stranger at the tavern that he owned in Montreal. He'd felt a bit embarrassed that a stranger knew more than he did about his own teammate. Until then, he hadn't even known how old Harris was.

It wasn't just Harris who didn't talk. All the Canadiens defencemen seemed to have taken a vow of silence. Jacques Laperriere sat two spots over from Harris. He seldom spoke, either, although at least people recognized the big guy on the Montreal streets where they walked together after practice. Laperriere lived in an apartment near the Forum. Richard had walked with him a few times on his way to Bens, where a few of the players went for lunch. All the way along De Maisonneuve Boulevard, people greeted them, stopped to talk or asked for their autograph.

But no one recognized Harris. Unless a better-known teammate went with him, Harris could walk down the middle of Rue Sainte-Catherine in his Canadiens uniform, and people would assume he was a weirdo who'd dressed up early for Hallowe'en. No one would suspect that he played for the Canadiens or that he'd helped the team win a Stanley Cup last year. Harris once stood with a reporter from the *Gazette* on the curb on Atwater, across from the front door of the Forum, and not a single pedestrian stopped to get his autograph or say hello or tell him he was a bum, the way Montreal pedestrians did with other players on the team. Harris didn't care. "There are people in this world who are just naturally meant to be in the limelight," he said. "I'm not one of those people."

Guys like Jacques Laperriere and Yvan Cournoyer had a harder time than Ted Harris staying anonymous, especially in Montreal. They couldn't go anywhere in the city without causing a commotion. "I went to an Expos [baseball] game," Cournoyer said in 1969, "and in two minutes they had me out in front of the crowd."

Like Henri Richard, Cournoyer and Laperriere had played hockey as teenagers in Montreal for the Junior Canadiens. By the time they joined the big team, they'd already appeared on TV every week for years. Cournoyer had flown up and down the ice like a rocket. Laperriere had been the captain of the team and set goal-scoring records as a defenceman. In those days, Laperriere stood out from his teammates like an eagle in a budgie cage. He was tall, skinny and gaunt, with a stony expression on his face, like a bust of Voltaire. Now he was twenty-five, and off the ice he wore his glasses on his aquiline nose, but people recognized him on the street, called his name, asked for his autograph, told him he played a good game. Laperriere certainly didn't ask for the attention. He just did his job. "It's a simple thing," he said.

Laperriere didn't have to talk in the dressing room to do his job. "He has no private agenda, no aspirations," said Steve Shutt, who would play with Laperriere a few years later. "All he wants to do, ever, is make that defence play well."

If the Canadiens wanted to talk to each other, they found opportunities off the ice, where they spent a lot of time together. A couple of months ago, the team had met in Saint-Hubert for its annual bowling tournament. It was snowing, the last night of February. The team celebrated Henri Richard's birthday at the bowling alley and presented him with a cake. Richard had been born in a leap year, on the twenty-ninth of February, so his teammates planted the icing with seven candles and three wooden matches.

Everyone showed up in a costume. Jean-Guy Talbot disguised himself as Charles de Gaulle, the president of France. John Ferguson came as Dracula. Richard wore a fake beard and army fatigues and stuck a big Cuban cigar in his mouth, trying to look like Fidel Castro. They had spaghetti and pizza for dinner that night. When they bowled, Terry

Harper had to roll the ball down the alley with his left hand because he'd broken his right one. Ferguson won the tournament by eight pins. That was just as well. Ferguson couldn't stand to lose. But while the other players hooted and hollered and watched Gump Worsley skidding around the lanes dressed as Little Bo Peep, Ted Harris sat quietly on a plastic chair by the wall and nursed his broken fingers. "That's the type of guy he is," said Worsley, after he and Harris had played together for almost ten years. "We haven't had a real conversation yet."

Tonight, even Worsley wasn't talking much. He sat at the far end of the room, next to Rogie Vachon, and distracted himself by sipping tea from a Thermos. He fiddled with a buckle on his left pad and wished he could light up a cigarette. Finally, he did. "Maybe he needs one, eh?" said his coach, when a reporter asked later why he allowed Worsley to smoke a cigarette in the dressing room.

Jean Beliveau had pulled his white wool stockings over his shin pads and put on his blue hockey pants, but he hadn't put on his skates yet. They sat on the floor at his feet. He usually put on the left one first. It was a half-size smaller than the right one. Now he leaned back and took a deep breath. The painted cinder-block wall felt cold against his shoulder blades. Beliveau wore a pair of light cotton socks. Bobby Rousseau, sitting beside him, wore no socks at all. Rousseau liked to feel the smooth kangaroo leather that lined his skate boots. He said it gave him more direct contact with the ice when he skated. Who could argue with him? Rousseau could skate as fast as anyone in the league.

All the players knew they had to win tonight. They didn't have to talk about it. They didn't even have to look at each other. They knew what they had to do and how they felt about it. All of them were tense. "All the good ones," said Beliveau. "If you're not, you don't get the jump."

Richard glanced again at Yvan Cournoyer as the youngster straightened his pants and hung the hanger behind his spot on the bench. Cournoyer ordered his pants from a tailor shop near the Forum, not because he paid attention to fashion, but because the muscles in his legs were so big that he couldn't wear pants off the rack without ripping the seams.

Cournoyer looked calm enough tonight, Richard thought. Certainly better than he'd looked the morning before his first Stanley Cup final, a couple of years ago. Cournoyer liked fast cars, and with the money he'd made in his first year in the NHL, he'd bought a Corvette. As the Canadiens proceeded to beat the Leafs in the semi-finals, he drove to and from the Forum in his flashy new car. But just before the first game of Cournoyer's first Stanley Cup finals, his mother called to tell him that someone had stolen his car. He looked a lot better tonight than he had then.

No one in the room dared to crack a joke or make a flippant comment, partly because they all took tonight's game seriously, but partly because they all knew that, if they didn't act seriously enough, John Ferguson might tell them to shut the fuck up or worse. Ferguson was wound up tighter than a G string on a violin. He'd glare at a teammate who showed even the slightest hint of flippancy before a game. He'd yell at his own teammates during a game if he thought they deserved it. Before he joined the Canadiens, Ferguson once fired a puck at the head of a teammate for kibitzing with an opponent during a warm-up. When J.C. Tremblay complained at dinner that he wasn't getting enough ice time, Ferguson threw a pitcher of beer in his face. "He intimidated as many of us in the dressing room as he did opponents on the ice," said Beliveau. "You wouldn't dare give less than your best if you wore the same shirt as John Ferguson."

Before he sat down in the Leafs' dressing room, Mike Walton had filled a glass with ice water. He'd wrapped the glass in a towel and placed it at his feet. Now he put his hockey stick on the floor between his feet, flanked by his gloves, palms up, and started dressing for the game in the same way as he'd dressed for hundreds of games before this one: He fastened his knee brace, then put his left shin pad against his leg and pulled the sock over it. He pulled the sock over his right shin pad. He pulled on his hockey pants. He laced up his left skate, then his right one.

Walton had followed the same routine as a junior in Toronto, as a minor-league player in Tulsa and Rochester and for the thirty-odd games he'd played this year with the Leafs. If he seemed superstitious, he had a good reason. A player's entire career can be decided by a single split-second decision to go left or right, to shoot high or low, to pass, to hesitate, to do nothing at all. If a player can duplicate the slightest detail associated with his good decisions in previous games, it becomes a source of reassurance. He might wear the same hat, take the same route to the rink, eat the same food, brush his teeth with the same number of strokes, place his stick on the floor the way Walton did.

Before he left the house today, Leafs defenceman Tim Horton had polished his shoes, just as he'd done before every game since the mid-1950s. He'd driven down Bayview Avenue to the Gardens, the same route as he took before every game, wearing the same overcoat. The overcoat had once belonged to Jean Beliveau. Beliveau stood six feet, four inches off the ground and weighed more than two hundred pounds. Some people had nicknamed him le Gros Bill. No one would call Tim Horton le Gros Tim, especially when he wore Beliveau's overcoat. The coat fit Horton like a set of living-room drapes. The sleeves dangled below his fingertips. The hem brushed the tops of his shoes, and he could have worn two more overcoats underneath. He looked like a kid dressed up in his dad's clothes. Horton had taken the coat by mistake one night from an all-star banquet. When it brought him good luck, he kept it. "It was a lucky coat," said Horton's wife, Lori. Fashion-conscious herself, she tried to get her husband to wear something more stylish, even buying him two new overcoats one winter. "He wore one of them one night," she said, "and the Leafs lost the game." So much for fashion.

Walton had just turned twenty-two, and he could hardly imagine what might happen if he neglected his rituals. With Punch Imlach in charge, he might never have had a chance to wear a Maple Leafs jersey at all. Imlach despised Mike Walton, his sideburns, his flared pants and everything he stood for, and so did Imlach's boss, Stafford Smythe, who would soon become Mike Walton's uncle by marriage.

Imlach tolerated Walton on the team only because he couldn't ignore him. "Blazing fast, tricky with the puck...the most exciting player in

Maple Leaf history," according to Trent Frayne, Walton had recorded almost two points a game, including forty-one goals, in his last year as a junior with the Toronto Marlboros. As the team rolled on to the Memorial Cup, Walton scored more points in the playoffs than any other junior-hockey player in Canada, more than his teammates Pete Stemkowski and Ron Ellis, more than Yvan Cournoyer, who played that year for the Junior Canadiens. In the summer after the Marlies won the Memorial Cup, Punch Imlach and the Leafs invited Stemkowski and Ellis to try out for the big team. But they didn't invite Walton.

For three years, Imlach had buried Walton in the minor leagues, initially in Tulsa, Oklahoma, with a team called the Oilers. Imlach figured a flashy player like Walton might draw a crowd. That would suit Imlach. He owned a piece of the team.

Walton attracted attention by racking up eighty-four points in sixty-eight games and winning a place on the league's first all-star team. In the playoff finals, Stafford Smythe came to a game in St. Paul, Minnesota, to watch his farm team perform. After the first period, the team's coach announced in the dressing room, in front of all the players, that Stafford Smythe said Mike Walton would never play for the Leafs. "He said I was a bum," Walton recalled. The league disagreed with Smythe's estimation and selected Walton as its rookie of the year.

That earned Walton a promotion to Rochester, New York, to play with a Leafs farm team in the American Hockey League. His teammates that year included Jim Pappin, Pete Stemkowski, Eddie Shack and Brian Conacher, all playing with him tonight for the Leafs. This time, he scored thirty-five goals and registered more than a point a game. His team won the league championship. Once again, Walton was named rookie of the year, the second time, in the second league, in two years that he'd earned that distinction.

Walton might have won his third rookie-of-the-year award in three years if he'd played more games in the NHL. Only Terry Sawchuk had ever done that. But the Leafs left Walton in Rochester for the first half of the season. There, he averaged more than a point a game and scored nineteen goals in thirty-six games, enough to earn him a chance, he thought, to play in the NHL. If the Leafs didn't let him play, he said, he'd quit. Finally, in January, around his twenty-second birthday, he got the call to come to Toronto. He didn't win his third rookie title, which went instead to a young defenceman on the Boston Bruins named Bobby Orr. But the next year, Walton scored thirty goals for the Leafs. The kid just didn't know when to quit. The fans loved him. But Imlach hated him more than ever, and so did Stafford Smythe.

The way he dressed, the way he wore his hair, the way he walked, the way he talked: Walton drove Imlach nuts, and some of the old farts on the team, as well. The harder they tried to make him conform, the more he resisted. He acted as if he owned the world. He also suffered from migraine headaches and intense bouts of anxiety. But to anyone who didn't bother to get to know him, he looked as if he didn't have a care in the world.

To play well, a player needed peace of mind, and a player's peace of mind depended on emotional stability. The fewer distractions, the better, although some distractions couldn't be ignored. Unfaithful wives, for example. There had been rumours in the dressing room lately that one of the players had started an affair with a teammate's wife. The anxiety over his wife's betrayal and his teammate's treachery had sent the player into a funk. Rated among the top scorers in the league, he'd had trouble this season even pushing the puck down the ice without letting it dribble away and slide between his skates. Only one man in the room knew if the rumour was true, and he wasn't talking. But everyone else had speculated one way or the other, based on conversations with the others and the gossip that all their wives brought home.

Perhaps that explained why Punch Imlach preferred old geezers like Allan Stanley and Marcel Pronovost to young whippersnappers like Walton. Sixteen years made a big difference to a man's equilibrium. At thirty-eight, you'd had time to figure out what mattered and what didn't.

...

Eddie Mepham had napped fitfully until four-thirty or five this afternoon, the way he'd done on a hundred game days before this one. Then he'd eaten a light dinner. He preferred eggs for dinner because he didn't have to chew them. A lanky, six-foot former junior-hockey player, Mepham had had his front teeth knocked out more than fifteen years ago by a stick that also cut him for seventeen stitches. Today, as usual on the day of a game, he ate two poached eggs. "A heavier meal affects his judging," said his wife, Myrt.

Mepham was a goal judge at Maple Leaf Gardens. Like the players, he felt the pressure of tonight's game, and he went through a familiar pre-game ritual to relax himself and clear his mind.

"You'd think a man would get used to it," Mepham said to Myrt. But Eddie never did.

After dinner, Mepham smoked a few cigarettes with his coffee, then dressed in a white shirt, maroon tie, grey flannels and a blue blazer with the NHL's crest on the chest pocket. Before he left the house, Myrt checked to make sure that he'd remembered everything. Eddie had once gone all the way to the Gardens before he discovered that he'd forgotten to wear his tie. Myrt thought most hockey men needed a mother as much as they needed a wife.

Fully dressed now, Eddie said goodbye to Myrt and headed off in his topcoat through the drizzle to the Eglinton subway station. It took about fifteen minutes to get to College Street. Mepham's stomach turned cartwheels all the way. "I always get the butterflies before a game," he said. "I think it's a good thing. It shows I haven't lost my desire."

At the Gardens, Mepham made his way under the stands to the little room where the goal judges, timekeepers, linesmen and referees gathered to swap tales and smoke cigarettes. The other goal judge, Grant Eason, was already there, a short, fat guy with white hair and a red face, smoking a cigar. Eason wore a blue blazer identical to Mepham's. Ace Bailey was there too, the penalty timekeeper and former Leaf. He'd worked every Leafs home game since 1937, hadn't missed one. Bailey knew a lot of good stories, and tonight he was telling a few of the best. Eddie Mepham had heard half of them before. He didn't care. Even if you'd heard a story three times, it beat thinking about tonight's game.

Terry Harper may not have been as fast as his teammates skating forward, but he could skate backwards as fast as anyone on the Montreal Canadiens. At twenty-seven, he'd been working on skating backwards for half his life. It was a useful talent for a defenceman.

As a kid in Regina, Harper had played forward from the time he could skate. He became known around town as a fast and shifty winger. His idols, like Billy Hicke, a local kid who'd already made it to the American Hockey League, and Eddie Litzenberger, another Regina kid who'd played for the Montreal Canadiens, were all forwards. Harper, too, intended to play in the NHL, as a forward. One summer afternoon, he was hanging around in his friend's garage, and they tossed a couple of lit matches onto a pile of gasoline-soaked garbage on the floor. As the trash burned, Harper leaned over the gas can just as the contents exploded into his face. For the next three months, in the Grey Nuns Hospital, doctors peeled flesh from his legs, buttocks and other parts of his body left untouched by the fire and grafted it onto his face, neck, hands and chest. Harper's mother wondered if her son would ever walk again without limping. Harper wondered how quickly he could get back on his skates and play hockey.

With his legs stiff from newly healed skin, Harper figured he'd switch positions. On defence, he thought, he wouldn't have to move so much. "But I was wrong," he said.

Over the next couple of years, Harper grew five inches and put on twenty pounds. Now he was six feet tall and almost two hundred pounds, built like a totem pole. He played well enough on defence in Regina to become an all-star with the Pats, a local junior team that the Montreal Canadiens owned. He was especially good at skating backwards. His teammate tonight, Dave Balon, played for the Pats, as well. They'd competed for the Memorial Cup together against Hull-Ottawa. The Montreal

Canadiens owned that team, too. Four other teammates tonight had played in that series: J.C. Tremblay, Ralph Backstrom, Gilles Tremblay and Bobby Rousseau. On the ice, where every player had a nickname that combined familiarity with convenience, Harper called Balon "Bosey." Balon called Harper "Harp." Off the ice, they hardly spoke.

At the end of the season, when Balon and Harper took the train together back to Saskatchewan, Harp didn't say more than three words in three days. He just sat in his seat, leafing through the sports section of the *Globe* or an old copy of *Reader's Digest*, looking out the window and napping, all the way to Regina. But watching Harper now as he shyly turned his back to the room to pull off his street clothes and dress in his equipment, Balon didn't care if he ever spoke at all. He knew how fast Terry Harper could skate backwards. He knew how often Harper had stood up for his teammates in a fight. He knew that no one wanted to win more than Terry Harper, and he was glad to play again on the same team.

With all the fighting, cross-checking, elbowing and slashing, not to mention a puck travelling at a hundred miles an hour, most hockey players had had their front teeth knocked out by the time they signed their first professional contract. Some players used their signing bonuses to have their remaining teeth removed, since they figured they'd lose them anyway. But Terry Harper and John Ferguson had never lost a tooth playing hockey.

Ferguson not only had all his teeth, he had few scars on his face for a man who made his living by stopping opponents' fists with his head. Ferguson's advantage was genetic. "He was very slow to bleed," said Joan Ferguson. When her husband tried to convince a referee that an opposing player had hit him on the head with a stick, the referee seldom believed him because he wasn't bleeding. You could pick up the skin on his head between your fingers, she said. "Like a shar-pei dog."

As for Harper, his teeth remained intact in his head despite the way he did his job. In just his first week with the Canadiens, he did his job so ferociously that the NHL eventually had to change its rules to accommodate him. In a game between the Leafs and the Canadiens, Leafs forward Bob Pulford, known for his doggedness, had bullied Bobby Rousseau, known for his speed. Harper conveyed his displeasure to Pulford by grabbing him around the throat and trying to lift him off the ice by his head. Pulford suggested to Harper that he should put him down by punching Harper in the eye.

The referee sent them both off for five minutes. At the time, an NHL rink contained only one penalty box for both teams. Inside the box, Pulford mouthed off to Harper again, over the shoulder of the attendant, Teedle Walker, who sat between them in his shirt and tie and navy blue blazer and tried to stay out of the way. Pulford yelled at Harper. Harper yelled back. Pulford reached across Teedle Walker and tried to pull off Harper's shoulder pads. Harper reached back and swung his fist at Pulford's head. Teedle Walker adjusted his tie. Then he jumped up on the bench and decided to take a walk. Harper and Pulford belted each other a couple of times, grabbed each other by the arms and toppled on their skateblades into the timekeeper. Then Harper tried to throw Pulford over the boards and back onto the ice. The linesmen separated them again, and the referee ordered each player to go to his dressing room. The fracas wouldn't have made such a lasting impression if half of Canada hadn't watched the fight on TV. In the dressing room, Harper calmly unlaced his skates and removed his equipment. A few years later, Harper would ask Pulford for a job with a team in Los Angeles, and Pulford would be glad to hire him.

Thanks to Harper and Pulford and the notoriety they'd attracted, Stafford Smythe and the other Maple Leafs owners ordered the maintenance crew at the Gardens to construct a barrier to divide the penalty box in half. This made it more difficult for a player on one side to reach out and hammer a player on the other side the way Harper and Pulford had done on national television.

At the time of his encounter with Pulford, Harper might have been feeling grumpy because he missed his defence partner, Jacques Laperriere. Lappy and Harp usually played together on defence. They hollered at each other constantly in a language that wasn't really English and wasn't really French, full of *yo*s and *yip*s, Lappy-Lappy-Lappy and Harp-Harp-Harp. They played as if they had eyes in the back of their heads. Off the ice, they didn't talk much. They were defencemen with the Montreal Canadiens, after all, about as gabby as Mount Rushmore.

The kinship between them had as much to do with their determination as it did with their skill. The two defencemen had persevered through injuries and pain and suffering, Harper in his burn-scarred body, Laperriere in his damaged pride. Laperriere grew up in Rouyn-Noranda, a mining town in northern Quebec just across the provincial border from Ontario. The area had a reputation for copper, gold and hockey players: half the players in the NHL seemed to come from that neck of the woods. Winter lasted about fifty-one weeks of the year, followed by bug season. To make a living, men went into the mines to beat the minerals out of the rock for money. When they came out, they went to the hockey rink to beat the crap out of each other for fun. Eventually the copper, gold and hockey players all left town. Laperriere's brother Gilles had gone to Quebec City to play for a junior team called the Citadelles. When his hockey skills would take him no further, Gilles returned to Rouyn. Jacques intended to go further than his brother and stay away longer.

In Rouyn, Jacques played organized hockey with St-Michel, the local school, then for a midget team sponsored by Restaurant Renaud, which the locals called Chez Butch. Most of the time he played shinny outdoors, all day long, starting in the morning and playing till the sun went down and no one could see the puck anymore. On some days, the temperature fell to thirty degrees below zero. When the snow and ice melted, the kids kept playing hockey in the mud with a tennis ball.

Like Harper, Laperriere caught the attention of the adults in town. When coaches suggested that they send Jacques to a bigger city, Laperriere's parents thought of his brother Gilles and said they didn't want to send another son on a wild goose chase for hockey glory. But a professional scout named Lou Passador finally convinced the Laperrieres to change their minds. Passador had discovered a kid in Fort William named Alex Delvecchio, who now played in the NHL for the Detroit Red Wings. He assured the Laperrieres that Jacques had as much talent as Delvecchio.

Laperriere lived for a year in Montreal, playing for a Junior B team called the St-Laurent Jets. Then, at fifteen, he spent the most miserable year of his life, in Brockville, about a hundred miles up the St. Lawrence River, in Ontario. The English-speaking boys of Brockville teased him — he was big, gawky and French and looked like Voltaire. The girls teased him because he had more interest in hockey than he did in them. None of them could pronounce his name right. Laperriere could have gone home to Rouyn and practised his water-skiing on Lac Témiscamingue. But he didn't intend to go home again until his hockey achievements had surpassed his brother's. At the end of the season, the Canadiens recognized their mistake and sent him back to Montreal to play with the Junior Canadiens. Not only did Laperriere play defence like a vine-covered wall, he also scored goals. For three years, he ranked among the highest-scoring defencemen in junior hockey.

Laperriere turned professional with Hull-Ottawa. When Terry Harper joined the team two years later, their young coach, Scotty Bowman, put the two of them together in the playoffs. They stayed together over the next year. When one was selected for the Eastern Pro League's all-star team, so was the other. Harp and Lappy came as a package.

The Canadiens intended to bring them to the NHL together, but Laperriere got hurt and didn't leave home until the hockey season had already started. The season before, in Hull, he'd broken his ankle so badly that it required surgery, and it didn't heal properly. Five games went by before he finally packed up his Doris Day records and joined his friend Harp in Montreal. But his injuries didn't stop. In December, he broke his nose, and he broke a finger in February. Laperriere would worry about those inconveniences in the summer, when the season ended. In the meantime, he was a Montreal Canadien.

When Lappy and Harp stepped onto the ice, the complexion of the team changed. Laperriere roamed his sector of the ice the way an eagle glides on geysers of air. Even the president of the NHL remarked on his talent. "Never in my years in professional hockey have I seen a young man take over and lead a team as Laperriere has done," said Clarence Campbell. Laperriere and Harper played together on the Canadiens defence for the next eight years. They remained close friends, as well.

One day, a reporter asked Jacques Laperriere a question: If Terry Harper was so good, why didn't the Canadiens use him on the power play the way they used Laperriere?

"Ah, those ding dongs," said Laperriere, unleashing an atypical blizzard of verbosity. "They don't know hockey like they think. Terry is the best of his kind."

In the Leafs' dressing room, defenceman Tim Horton lay face-down on a training table and winced as the team's trainer, Bob Haggert, rubbed liniment into the base of his spine. The guy had muscles under his muscles, Haggert thought. Like massaging a church pew.

It wasn't the first time in these playoffs that Horton had been injured. In the semi-finals against Chicago, he'd broken his nose. He'd injured himself this time in a much less dramatic way. At home last weekend in Willowdale, snoozing on the bed on his stomach, he'd been ambushed by his nine-year-old daughter, who jumped up and down on her father's back to wake him up.

Tim Horton had learned early in his career what it meant to get really injured in the NHL. About twelve years ago, when he was twenty-six, the Leafs were playing at Madison Square Garden. It was a shithole of an arena, whose glamorous reputation belied its dilapidated facilities. The owners of the Garden were so cheap, they wouldn't spend money to turn the lights on when the Rangers practised there. The team learned to keep their shots low to the ice to avoid hitting each other in the face. During a game against the Rangers, Horton rushed with the puck down the ice and caught his skateblade in a crevice at the same time as he looked down at the puck. Before he could look up again, a New York Ranger named

Bill Gadsby hit him with a bodycheck. With the crevice holding his skateblade like a vise, Horton's leg twisted more than a hundred degrees to the left, breaking his tibia and his fibula. For good measure, Gadsby's shoulder broke his jaw. When Horton fell unconscious to the ice, Gadsby saw blood trickling from the side of the player's mouth and out of his ear.

Until that game, Horton's pre-game ritual included polishing all the shoes that he owned. When his leg healed and he returned to play the next year, he modified his ritual. Now he polished only the shoes that he wore to the rink. The change must have worked. He hadn't broken his leg since.

When Haggert finished kneading, poking, rubbing and taping up his back, Horton minced his way to his cubicle to take his place beside Red Kelly. Kelly would turn forty in a couple of months. Horton was thirty-seven. Both players knew that their minutes as Toronto Maple Leafs were numbered.

In his twenty years in the NHL, Red Kelly had managed to avoid a serious injury. But he'd seen some doozies. Just to make sure he didn't tempt fate, he touched wood, tapping his knuckles against the blue-painted bench beneath him.

Kelly remembered a kid named Howie Harvey, who went to St. Michael's College, the Catholic high school in Toronto where Kelly and several teammates had played junior hockey. Harvey was a goalie, good enough to earn a tryout one fall with the Leafs. At the tryout, Harvey watched a deflected puck hit the Leafs' regular goalie, Baz Bastien, in the face. The puck dislodged Bastien's eyeball, rendering him blind in one eye.

Most other players, after seeing such an accident, would simply have adjusted their pre-game ritual, polished a different pair of shoes or worn a different hat, and kept right on playing. Unlike football and baseball players, said the Leafs' former owner, Conn Smythe, "Hockey guys play if they can breathe."

Howie Harvey was an exception. Harvey skated to the bench, took off his gloves, leaned his stick against the wall, unbuckled his goalie pads and quit pro hockey on the spot. Even Harvey's big brother Doug, an all-star defenceman with the Montreal Canadiens, couldn't entice him back to the game.

Red Kelly whistled a tune that he'd heard on the car radio called "Somethin' Stupid," by Nancy and Frank Sinatra. Kelly lived with the blessing of an uncluttered mind. Whistling helped keep it that way, as if he could blow his unwanted thoughts through his lips along with the music.

Even thinking about the possibility of an injury put a player at a disadvantage, so Kelly tried not to do it and usually succeeded. That was one of the reasons why he'd stopped wearing a helmet and why many goalies chose not to wear a mask. Sometimes they said the equipment made them sweat too much. But a mask or a helmet also revealed a player's fear of injury, and fear is a weakness. Professional hockey teams prey on each other's weaknesses, no matter how slight. It gives them a small advantage, and small advantages can make the difference between winning and losing a game. Better to intimidate your opponents with a mouth full of gaping holes and a face scarred like a Ukrainian Easter egg than hide behind a mask, a tooth guard or a helmet and reveal your fear.

Kelly had played in the NHL for fifteen years before he wore a helmet in a game. By then, he'd established himself firmly enough in the league that his opponents didn't try to intimidate him the way they might have done with younger players. Younger players might have known Kelly as a gentleman in hockey pants. Older players knew better. As a teenager, Cornflakes Kelly had won a light-heavyweight boxing championship and could probably have popped their lights out with a single punch if he'd felt mean enough to do it. Kelly seldom did.

"To win a fight in hockey," he said, "you have to hit the other guy on the head, and whenever you do that with a bare hand, you stand to lose just as much as he does."

Kelly was less interested now in fighting than he was in his future. After this series ended, he would never play again for the Toronto Maple Leafs or any other team in the NHL. Nor would he ever look forward again as a player to winning a Stanley Cup. He'd already won seven.

Maybe that was enough, although one more would make it an even number. Kelly preferred even numbers.

Kelly glanced at Terry Sawchuk and hoped the gods would smile on the goalie tonight. They'd played together in Detroit in the 1950s. Kelly moved to Toronto first, then Sawchuk came along two years later. Sawchuk wore a facemask now, but he never worried about his injuries. He only wore the mask because some players had started taking slapshots, which moved the puck at high speeds and in unpredictable directions.

Over twenty years, Sawchuk averaged two operations a year to remove bone chips from his right arm. He'd played with a herniated disc, severed wrist tendons, a broken right arm, a fractured instep, a punctured lung, infectious mononucleosis and a ruptured appendix. Not only was his right arm shorter than his left, but an operation on his back had cost him two inches in height, as well. No wonder he smoked cigarettes.

Like most other NHL players, Sawchuk accommodated the risk of injury by turning his scars and wounds into badges of honour, symbols of valour in the face of danger. He kept his lost teeth in a little jewellery box and pickled his own appendix in a jam jar. Of the sixty chips that doctors had removed from his elbow, Sawchuk kept twenty-two of them in another jar in his living room. Sawchuk's apartment looked like a high-school biology lab.

Considering the injuries they'd endured, it was a wonder that all the players in tonight's game didn't smoke like chimneys instead of whistling Dixie like Red Kelly. If one of them suffered an injury so incapacitating that he couldn't walk, a team would expect him to stay at home and recuperate. Otherwise, said Punch Imlach, "If he can fucking walk, he can fucking play."

To assess a player's ability to fucking walk, the Leafs depended on the team's doctor. The fact that the doctor tonight, Hugh Smythe, was also the brother of the team's co-owner didn't bother the players. They trusted Dr. Hugh. Even opposing teams consulted him when they came to Toronto. "Our assessment over-ruled the coach and the manager," Hugh said. But the owners had the last word, and they wanted their players to take a pill or a shot and return to the ice as soon as possible after an injury. A player didn't earn much for a team if he sat on his ass in a suit behind the bench instead of entertaining the paying fans.

"You weren't much good to a team if you couldn't play hurt," said Leafs goalie Johnny Bower. "They'd give you a needle and away you'd go."

For the players in tonight's game, the painkiller of choice was novocaine. Among the Leafs players, Red Kelly had taken a few shots earlier this season after he'd twisted the ligaments in his right knee and couldn't sleep. George Armstrong used it to numb a shoulder injury. A few years earlier, Bob Baun had scored the winning goal in overtime in a game against Detroit while playing on a broken ankle reinforced by surgical tape and a few shots of novocaine. His goal launched the Leafs toward their third consecutive Stanley Cup. The Canadiens used it, too. All teams did. "Some guys skip novocaine," said Terry Harper. "I ask for it."

To fill their prescriptions, Leafs players could walk down the corridor to the Happy Day Pharmacy, just outside the Gardens' front door. Or they could walk across the street to the R.L. Roach Pharmacy at Church and Carlton, which advertised itself in the team's program as "the drug supplier to the Maple Leafs."

Players didn't always know one drug from another. If they needed a boost, a stabilizer or a painkiller, they deferred to the greater wisdom of the team's physician. Unfortunately, team physicians often regarded the players in the same light as a team's owner regarded his stable of horses. They administered the same drugs to a crippled defenceman as they did to Northern Dancer. If it worked for one thoroughbred, it would work for another.

Gump Worsley injured himself during a playoff series against the Chicago Black Hawks badly enough that he thought his season had ended, so he went to a coffee shop before the seventh game to wait for the opening face-off. His coach, Toe Blake, decided that Worsley should play, injured or not, and he sent a messenger to the coffee shop to fetch him. Worsley hobbled back to the Forum. To make sure he played without faltering from the pain, a doctor injected him with a tranquilizer used on animals at the federal government's experimental farm. "They had to phone Ottawa to get permission," Worsley said.

Playing against Worsley that night, the captain of the Black Hawks, Pierre Pilote, had been medicated by his team's doctor with a red liniment to relieve the pain in his spine. Used primarily by veterinarians on dogs, the stuff made his skin burn for about twenty minutes. By the end of the game, his skin had absorbed the liniment into his respiratory system, tainting his breath so that he could taste it in his mouth. Later Pilote discovered that the red liquid, called dimethyl sulfoxide, could cause dermatitis, impair the functions of his liver and leave lesions on his blood cells.

Players defer to the expertise of others not only in medicine but in accounting, law, finance, fashion, real estate and fine dining, as well. As long as an expert has gained access to the magic circle of the professional hockey community, few players question his authority. When a puck hit Allan Stanley, the Leafs defenceman, in the face and left a cut that took thirty stitches to close, he said, "I was scared when it happened, but as long as the doctor says I'm all right, heck, there's nothing to stop me from getting back."

Players preferred to play rather than nurse a wound. They knew that the more games they missed, the more chance another player had of taking their place. The sooner they could numb the pain, the sooner they could play again.

Teams seldom admitted publicly that a player might lose his job if he used an injury as an excuse for missing a game, but everyone on both teams tonight knew that it happened. They'd known lots of players who'd been injured and never made it back to the NHL. That was one reason why Red Kelly had played most of a previous season for the Detroit Red Wings on a broken ankle. And when he admitted in public that his team had urged him to play, the Red Wings dumped him.

With his leg taped from his knee to his ankle, Kelly had one of his worst seasons since he'd started playing in the NHL. The team itself didn't do much better. But the fans knew nothing about Kelly's injury, and they began to boo whenever he stepped onto the ice. As the season passed and the Red Wings kept losing, they started to boo the whole team. Out of the playoffs at the end of the season, the Red Wings' coach, Sid Abel, blamed the team's poor performance implicitly on Kelly's mediocre play and fined every player $100 for lack of effort. "I was surprised when I got fined," Kelly said. After all, the team had encouraged him to play, despite his injury.

The Red Wings' manager, Jack Adams, didn't mind when Kelly admitted playing with an injury. He felt insulted, though, when Kelly implied that Adams had made him do it. When the writer Trent Frayne published the story, Adams and the rest of the Red Wings' management insisted that the team never forced players to play with an injury. Kelly had played for the Red Wings for thirteen years. He'd chosen Jack Adams to stand in for his father-in-law at his wedding. He'd helped the team win four Stanley Cups and had become the Red Wings' captain. But when he suggested in public that his team had made him play with an injury, Adams said he wasn't wanted any longer in Detroit. Kelly moved to Toronto and had now won three more Stanley Cups. Detroit wouldn't win the Cup again for thirty-five years.

In the officials' dressing room under the stands, the referee, John Ashley, hadn't started to dress yet for the game, hadn't even loosened his tie. Matt Pavelich, one of the two linesmen, had taken off his shirt and was looking in the mirror above the sink, rubbing some Brylcreem into his hair. The other linesman, Brent Casselman, pulled a small box out of his kit bag to show his colleagues the watch that he'd bought for his mom at Eaton's College Street, a block away from Maple Leaf Gardens. Casselman was only twenty-two. This was his first season as an official in the NHL.

Ashley had played junior hockey in Galt, west of Toronto, but hadn't made it to the big leagues. He'd moved back to his hometown of Kitchener, opened an auto repair shop, played amateur hockey for a senior team nearby in Stratford called the Indians, then tried his hand as a referee. "Just for something to do," he said. "It turned out longer than I expected."

Ashley figured he'd joined the NHL at the right time. At one time, the league relied on idle players to referee games in which their own teams weren't involved. The linesman in those days was just some spectator in the stands who wasn't blind or blind drunk and had brought a pair of skates. The ref wore a suit and a derby hat and rang a big brass bell like a schoolteacher. Ashley knew a few retired referees who wished they still carried a cowbell instead of a whistle. With three pounds of brass, they said, a ref could defend himself more effectively than he could with two ounces of fancy chrome-plated tin.

By the time Ashley signed up, the NHL paid referees about $18,000 a year. It beat fixing cars in Kitchener. And he liked his job: he travelled first class, stayed in fine hotels and didn't have to worry about autograph seekers. Ashley had become so good at his job, and the players respected him so much, that the NHL had chosen him, from the five referees employed by the league, to adjudicate the final game of each Stanley Cup series for the last three years, and the league would continue to select him for the job for another five years after tonight.

Pavelich examined his chin in the mirror. With his dark eyes and black hair, he looked like Burt Reynolds, the actor. Pavelich had worked as a carny in the circus before he became a hockey official. He was thirty-three, and he'd been an official for more than fifteen years, the last eleven of them in the NHL. Pavelich tossed his tube of Brylcreem to Casselman and sat down.

Pavelich, Casselman and the other two linesmen in the NHL earned about $150 a game and $10 a day for travelling expenses working seventy games in the NHL and about a dozen more games in the minor leagues. "It costs me more than that to plan my day," said a former player named King Clancy, Punch Imlach's assistant tonight with the Leafs.

Casselman adjusted the thin Fiberglas pads that he'd strapped to his shins. Each of the linesmen and the referee wore these pads, designed primarily for soccer players, under their black wool trousers to protect them from pucks and sticks. They also wore foam basketball pads over their kneecaps and a protective cup over their testicles. Otherwise, an official protected himself by keeping out of the way, unless he had to break up a fight.

Officials and most players regarded fighting as an integral part of the professional game. "No man can last in the NHL who backs away from a fight," said former Detroit Red Wings star Ted Lindsay. But not everyone agreed. Once in a while, a zealous politician or Crown attorney took the game out of the arena and into the public courts. John Ashley thought these politicians might just as well have handed out speeding tickets to drivers in the Indianapolis 500. "When they started bringing players into court," said Ashley, "I didn't think anything had to be done at all."

Almost since the first professional hockey game, intimidation, violence and fighting have given hockey the allure of a heavyweight boxing match on skates. In the 1920s, an owner named Tex Rickard had parked a fleet of ambulances outside the front door of Madison Square Garden and turned on their lights and sirens to lure pedestrians inside to watch a hockey game. For almost a century since then, owners of NHL teams have taken full advantage of the game's incipient violence to sell tickets. As Henri Richard once said, "Fighting helps fill arenas. It puts more money in the pockets of the owners."

Fighting was one reason why 15,977 fans in Maple Leaf Gardens tonight had paid as much as $7 and as little as $1.50 for their tickets. If the players didn't fight, the fans might. In New York, fans got into fistfights at almost every game.

Until a game began, Ashley worried more about the fans than he did about the players. Tonight, he'd left his young daughter Kristine upstairs in the stands with one of the Gardens' ushers, a guy named Pits, and asked him to keep an eye on her while he did his job on the ice. "Watch the game," Ashley told her, "cheer for everybody, and don't tell anybody who you are."

...

Clarence Campbell, the NHL's president, looked down from the stands and saw John Ashley at centre ice in his striped jersey and black trousers, holding his arms folded across his chest. Campbell remembered the way he'd felt as a referee before an NHL playoff game. More than thirty years earlier, Campbell had worked the semi-finals between Detroit and another team from Montreal called the Maroons, a five-game series that the Red Wings won. Campbell was too ambitious to work as a referee forever, but he remembered those days fondly. He liked the dynamic order that prevailed within the prescribed dimensions of the hockey rink. He liked to wield his authority on the ice like a judge in a courtroom. As a referee, he worked in full view of the fans, and the players usually did what he told them to do. They might yell at him and call him names if they disagreed with him, but they might also come to his rescue if the fans attacked him. As a spectator, he didn't feel so confident, especially after the Richard Riot.

Near the end of the 1954–55 season, nine years after he became president of the league, Campbell suspended the most famous hockey player in the world, Rocket Richard, for assaulting a linesman who had restrained Richard in a fight against a Boston Bruin named Hal Laycoe. Not only did Campbell jeopardize Richard's chances of winning the NHL scoring title (fellow Canadien Bernie Geoffrion would pass Richard on the last day of the season), he also threatened the Canadiens' chances of winning the Stanley Cup, by extending the suspension through the playoffs. After announcing his decision, Campbell and his secretary strolled a few blocks along Sherbrooke Street from the NHL's offices to the Montreal Forum to watch a game between the Canadiens and the Detroit Red Wings. They arrived ten minutes after the opening face-off. In full view of the fans, whose favourite player he'd just banished from the game, Campbell sat down with his hat on his head and his secretary by his side.

Campbell had hardly taken a breath when the fans around him attacked. They began by tossing peanuts, but Campbell just smiled. Then they started climbing over the seats to get at him. As the mob descended on

Campbell, the police arrived and dispelled them with tear gas. The fans took their hostility into the streets of Montreal, smashing windows, overturning cars, setting trash cans on fire. The riot lasted for three days. The rioters demolished taxicabs, streetcars and automobiles. Twelve policemen were injured, along with twenty-five civilians. Eight police cars were torched. For the first time, the game of hockey became front-page news in cities as far away as Los Angeles, London and Amsterdam. English Canadians could hardly believe the furor that followed Campbell's decision. But for many French Canadians, it was the flint that ignited their simmering resentment against Anglo indifference to their culture.

In the eyes of many historians, the Richard Riot marked the beginning of Quebec's Quiet Revolution. It led to federal bilingualism, the separatist movement and the repatriation of the Canadian constitution. Toronto's shocked newspapers called it "Savagery which attacks the fundamentals of civilized behaviour." In Montreal, French Canadians knew better. Anglos could talk all they wanted about civilized behaviour, as long as their civilization prevailed. In the Richard Riot, French Canadians had defied the prevailing force of English Canada with a power of their own. And it had all begun with Clarence Campbell's decision over a misdemeanour in a hockey game.

Most fans figured Clarence Campbell ran the league. They didn't realize that Campbell took his orders from the owners who paid him. They also figured Campbell knew more about hockey than anyone else in the world. Working late in his office in Montreal, the president of the NHL often received phone calls from drunks in bars asking him to settle an argument about the distance between the red line and the goal or the name of the player who scored the winning goal in the 1959 Stanley Cup finals. Campbell didn't mind. He liked to feel that he had one foot in the owners' camp, while he kept the other foot firmly planted on the ice. He still loved hockey. Campbell had grown up in Saskatchewan, after all, in a little farm town called Fleming, where the Trans-Canada Highway crosses the Manitoba border and little boys play hockey all day long. One of the boys on the Canadiens tonight, Bosey Balon, also came from Saskatchewan. When the league expanded next year, more boys from the province could look forward to someday playing in the NHL.

Campbell had spent the last two years putting the finishing touches on a plan to add six new teams to the league. He and his employers had resisted the idea for decades. NHL owners ran the league as a closed shop. They had no interest in sharing their revenues with outsiders. They didn't want to dilute their product or pay the additional costs of travelling to new cities. But over the last few years, U.S. television networks threatened to broadcast the games of another hockey league if the NHL didn't add some new teams in more distant markets.

Here in Toronto, while Campbell hunched in his seat and kept a wary eye out for hostile fans, a more menacing presence lurked over his shoulder a few rows back. Alan Eagleson wore horn-rimmed glasses and a fifty-watt smile that drew people toward him. "How are you, Clarence?" Eagleson hollered, when he caught Campbell's eye. "Big game tonight."

Campbell flinched as if he'd bitten down on a cherry pit. He regarded Eagleson as a buffoon. Eagleson regarded Campbell as the NHL's executive window-dressing, all show and no substance. As for Campbell's opinion about him, Eagleson couldn't have cared less. The more people recognized Eagleson, the better Eagleson liked it.

Like Campbell, Eagleson had trained as a lawyer, but he was half as old, twice as ruthless and ten times as ambitious. Already a member of Ontario's legislature and a force within the Progressive Conservative party, Eagleson had started his campaign to become the most powerful man in hockey, cultivating friendships among the players, including several Leafs. He'd been a high-school student in Mimico, near the lake west of Toronto, when he first encountered Bob Pulford. They met in a lacrosse game, a sport that Pulford played as well as anyone in Canada. More recently, Pulford had introduced Eagleson to Bob Baun, the Leafs defenceman.

Now Eagleson had become involved in the career of Mike Walton. Walton had finagled some tickets for Eagleson tonight from his future father-in-law, who managed the Gardens ticket office. Eagleson had also run for Parliament against another Leaf, Red Kelly, although Kelly had beaten him. Eagleson certainly didn't regard Kelly as a friend, especially now that Kelly was about to retire. To Eagleson, Kelly was just another old man.

Back when players in tonight's game were growing up, the best-paid labourers in Canada earned forty dollars a week. With an NHL team, a boy could earn five times as much for six months of work, and his job took fewer than four or five hours a day. No wonder players felt grateful to work in the NHL. But their sense of gratitude gave Eagleson a pain in the ass. How could you dig in your heels and insist on a higher salary from a team's manager when your client admitted in public that he'd gladly play the game for nothing?

About ten years ago, the NHL owners, hoping to placate their players and discourage the formation of a union, had set a minimum salary of $7,500 a season for players in the league. The strategy had worked for a while. But Eagleson knew that if the salaries couldn't go lower, they could certainly go higher, and as they did, he intended to get a cut.

Eagleson watched J.C. Tremblay and some of the other Montreal Canadiens skating around the ice. He'd met them as he was drumming up support for an NHL players' union. Eagleson's reputation had grown among NHL players ever since he'd landed a big contract last year for the rookie Bobby Orr. The Bruins had agreed to give Orr more money than most players in tonight's game had made in their first ten years in the league. With Eagleson's guidance, Orr used some of the money to buy a car wash in Toronto's east end. Orr visited the place every time the Bruins played in the Leafs' hometown. Bobby Orr, Mike Walton, Derek Sanderson, Phil Esposito — all young, all talented: these guys represented the future of hockey, Eagleson said, not the geriatrics like Kelly, playing out their last days on the Leafs, or the fossils who coached the teams here tonight.

The Leafs' coach, Punch Imlach, took Eagleson's threat to the NHL's future so seriously that he'd sold some of his stock in Maple Leaf Gardens

Ltd., the company that owned his team. He figured that players' rising salaries would reduce the company's profits.

Montreal's coach, Toe Blake, didn't even know that his players had agreed to join a union, let alone the reasons why they'd done it. Blake's time was up, Eagleson thought. Fuck Toe Blake, he thought, and anybody else who stands in my way.

From his seat in the reds, Eagleson glanced past his wife and over the heads of some men in suits at a spot in the stands above the red line at centre ice. The owners of the Maple Leafs had removed six seats from this spot, forfeiting about $1,200 in lost ticket sales over the course of a season. Owners didn't usually remove seats from their arenas. They added more, as many as they could legally cram into their buildings, and charged top dollar to fans who could squeeze themselves between the arm rests. But here the owners had sacrificed a buck to take the seats away. In their place, a television network had installed a camera. That proved Eagleson's point. As he knew, the owners might have sacrificed some ticket revenues to accommodate the technology, but they would earn ten times as much as they'd sacrificed, not just in broadcast fees, which were almost negligible at the moment, but also in razzle-dazzle and publicity in places where few people had ever seen an NHL game.

For every fan in the Gardens who'd paid a few dollars to watch the game tonight, another hundred sat in front of a TV somewhere in Canada watching the game and the commercials for nothing. For a long time, the owners didn't get the equation. Conn Smythe thought the Leafs would lose money if he allowed people to watch his team without buying a ticket. Even if a game were televised, he insisted that TV viewers receive only the last two periods. Recently, the owners had begun at last to realize the value of television exposure. You couldn't put a price on it, although some men had started trying. They were sitting now a few rows down from Eagleson, executives of MacLaren Advertising, right behind the Leafs' bench. Those men and their successors would eventually control the game of professional hockey. Some day Eagleson would sit in that row too.

Players' salaries were starting a steady ascent that would continue for decades. In the early 1950s, the Leafs' captain, George Armstrong, gave up $3,000 of his $7,000 NHL paycheque when the team sent him to Pittsburgh in the American Hockey League. Twenty-five years later, Armstrong's nephew, Dale McCourt, would earn more money in a single year of his career than his uncle had earned as a Maple Leaf over twenty seasons. Pension provisions for NHL players would reflect their rising salaries, as well, and Eagleson would get his hand in that cookie jar.

Even Clarence Campbell would board the gravy train as it chugged into the new age of television. Campbell's salary would hit the low six figures before he retired in 1977. His successor, John Ziegler, would live even higher on the hog. By the time the league owners moved his office to New York City in 1989 and then changed the title of their hired gun from "president" to "commissioner," the position would come with a salary of more than $3 million.

Alan Eagleson thanked his lucky stars that he hadn't lived a half-century earlier. In the last fifty years, poor boys had clawed and scratched their way from the shadows of a one-horse town into the bright lights of professional hockey. Now, like circus freaks and acrobats, they accepted money to provide a spectacle for the ticket-buying public. The faster the players skated, the harder they shot the puck, the more viciously they fought and the more blood they spilled, the more fans would pay to watch them. And so began the business of professional hockey that continues to this day. "We should never call the NHL sport," said Randy Gregg, who became an orthopaedic surgeon after winning five Stanley Cups with the Edmonton Oilers. "It's business."

Hockey players in the early 1900s said they'd play the game for nothing, but they could afford to do it. In Montreal, hockey players came from white Anglo-Saxon Protestant establishments like the Montreal Amateur Athletic Association. In Boston, which rivaled Montreal as the leading centre of hockey on the continent, they came from Harvard University, which operated two outdoor hockey rinks by 1903. A player at Princeton named Hobey Baker grew up in a well-to-do family of Philadelphia bankers and attracted as much attention in the first half-century of hockey as Bobby Orr in the second half. When he went to work on Wall Street, Baker played recreational hockey with teammates who brought their personal servants to the dressing room to lay out their uniforms.

Teams played their games, according to their amateur constitution, to "promote the cultivation of kindly feeling among the members of the hockey clubs." Between periods, both teams skated off the ice together to chit-chat with their fans over a buffet luncheon before resuming their game. Ink-stained sports reporters might write humdrum books about Frank Mahovlich and Bobby Orr; Hobey Baker captured the attention of one of the world's great novelists: F. Scott Fitzgerald wrote about him in *This Side of Paradise.*

Like Hobey Baker in the 1900s, the best-recognized men in hockey played the game for nothing, not because they were altruistic but because they already had all the money they'd ever need. The intrusion of money into sport offended writers such as Rudyard Kipling and Robert Baden-Powell, founder of the Boy Scouts. As the author Geoffrey Wheatcroft points out, when Kipling referred to "flanneled fools and muddied oafs" involved in sport, he was objecting to "professionalism, the jumped-up members of the lower classes who were now paid too much to hit or kick a ball, and, what was worse, the loafers who paid to watch them."

In Baden-Powell's opinion, "games were grand 'for developing a lad physically and morally', teaching him to play with unselfishness, 'to play in his place' and 'play the game', but 'games were vicious' when drawing crowds to be merely onlookers at a few paid performers... Thousands of boys and young men, pale, narrow-chested, hunched up, miserable specimens, smoking endless cigarettes, numbers of them betting, all of them learning to be hysterical as they groan and cheer and panic in unison."

Hobey Baker and his patrician teammates would have concurred wholeheartedly. They'd no sooner accept a paycheque for playing hockey than they'd take a dollar for helping an old lady cross the street. Only tradesmen, labourers and prostitutes worked for pay.

With money in the equation, a hockey game became much more than a mere social outing among amateurs promoting their kindly feelings. Players now made their living from the sport. Games became more cutthroat, the risks intensified, injuries became more severe, and rivalries extended across borders. Between periods, opposing teams no longer retired to the buffet tables to talk about the bond market. They went to separate dressing rooms to nurse their wounds and stew in their antagonism. In the midst of a maelstrom of passion and malevolence, one emotion informed the contestants in a hockey game: fear.

"Hockey's based on fear," said Frank Mahovlich. "When you take the fear away, it ruins the game."

As much as they feared their opponents, players also feared losing. Most of them could recover from an injury. Recovering from the humiliation of defeat was much more difficult. It was especially difficult when your team represented the hopes, delusions, prejudices and bigotry of an entire linguistic culture.

The rivalry between Montreal and Toronto, said the writers James Duplacey and Charles Wilkins, personified the competition between the two cities in finance and business, and the contrast between the "sometimes pinched Presbyterianism of southern Ontario and the mysterious etherealness of the Roman Catholic Church in Quebec." It went as deep as the defeat by the British of the French on the Plains of Abraham. As the writers observed, the Montreal Canadiens represented the common people of New France. The team and the people were both known as "les habitants." When the Canadiens won a game, their victory signified the emergence of les habitants from their subjugation at the hands of the English.

All this might sound a bit highfalutin for a hockey game, until you consider the men on the two teams tonight. They included a former member of Parliament, three aspiring politicians, a future senator, a perennial favourite for governor general, the founder of Canada's most successful restaurant chain, a couple of business executives and two men with their names on 45-r.p.m. singles that had sold more than a hundred thousand copies.

For the last twenty-five years before tonight's game, the same six teams from six North American cities had played in the NHL. Over that period, Montreal and Toronto between them had won nineteen Stanley Cups. But in all those years, Montreal and Toronto had met in the Cup finals only four times.

Tonight, the fans in Maple Leaf Gardens would groan and cheer and panic in unison, until one team on the ice won the hockey game. If the Leafs won, English Canadians would gloat about the superiority they'd felt over the downtrodden French for more than two hundred years. If the Canadiens won, they would keep alive the hope among French Canadians of restoring the pride they'd lost two centuries ago on the Plains of Abraham.

If you lived in Montreal, you expected to see the final game of the Stanley Cup playoffs in your city, especially this year, 1967, the centennial of the nation. The game began, after all, in Montreal, at least in the form that we watch today.

Everyone knew about the aboriginals who'd glided up and down ice-covered rivers on blades made from the sharpened shinbones of wild caribou. Everyone knew, too, about the soldiers on steel blades who'd whacked a ball around a frozen patch of ice with wooden sticks near Kingston or Halifax or someplace. But let's admit it: Organized hockey, the game that people like to watch as well as play, the game sponsored by beer companies, the game that made Don Cherry famous, the game that little kids play in their driveways wearing sweaters from their favourite teams — that game began in Montreal.

Two teams of one goalie and eight skaters each, roaring around the Victoria Skating Rink in March of 1875, trying to score a goal by firing a block of wood between two posts about six feet apart: that's hockey. One player elbows another player in the face, the other player retaliates with his stick and gets thrown out of the game: that's hockey, too. The details might have changed since then. Players use a rubber puck, not a block of wood, and they can pass it ahead of them now, up the ice, as well as behind them, like rugby players. But it's still hockey, men and women on skates chasing a puck and doing everything they can to beat their opponents.

From the first game they saw, Montrealers took to hockey like Spaniards to bullfighting. By the turn of the century, the city had built Westmount Arena exclusively for the game — not curling, not badminton, not horseshoes or horseback riding. Just hockey. Westmount was the largest rink in the world. Built at the intersection of Wood Avenue and Rue Sainte-Catherine, the arena soon smelled the way most hockey rinks would for the next fifty years: of sweat, urine, beer and tobacco smoke. The Canadiens played there. So did two other Montreal teams, the Wanderers and the Shamrocks. They played in front of seven thousand fans, all puffing on cigars and cigarettes and blowing smoke over the ice. By the second period, the players darted through the fog like characters through the streets of London in a Jack the Ripper movie.

Westmount was the first arena to offer reserved seating, so fans could gorge themselves before the game at the buffet tables in the dining rooms and chin-wag in the smoking lounges instead of sitting in the cold for an hour to make sure no one else took their seat. If fans got chilly, they could rent a blanket for a nickel to keep themselves warm.

Beginning a tradition that NHL owners would try to maintain for the next fifty years, one man owned almost all the professional hockey teams that played at Westmount Arena. His name was J. Ambrose O'Brien. He was the son of a lumber baron in Renfrew, on the Ottawa River, and he later became a Canadian senator, another tradition in the hockey world. More than one senator over the years has owned an NHL hockey team.

(Only the future senator on the Leafs tonight, Frank Mahovlich, has actually played for one.)

Prior to the formation of the NHL in 1917, O'Brien tried to gain admittance to another professional league for a team that he owned called the Renfrew Millionaires, whose name hinted at the size of the owner's bank account as well as the players' salaries. But the other league turned him down. It also turned its back on the Wanderers, from Montreal. Figuring if you can't join 'em, beat 'em, O'Brien formed his own league, the National Hockey Association, and invited the Wanderers to join, too. Then he created a team that would expand the league's reach and stir the hearts of French Canada. O'Brien was a smart businessman. French Canadians accounted for about three-quarters of the city's population, and most of them would pay a nickel to watch their fellow Frenchmen playing hockey.

French-speaking Montrealers didn't take immediately to the team, especially since its players wore jerseys emblazoned with a green maple leaf. They saw it as O'Brien's ploy to buy their support, while another team, le National, had already captured their hearts. But as the French-language press covered the team more extensively, support grew for the Canadiens among its French-speaking readers. Within three years, the Montreal Canadiens were wearing red, white and blue jerseys, the colours of the flag of France, with a logo on the chest: CAC, which stood for Club Athlétique Canadien.

The Montreal Canadiens won their first Stanley Cup in 1916. In fact, in the first eleven years after Lord Stanley donated his little silver basin to the world of hockey, teams from Montreal won it between ten and twelve times, depending on whom you asked, but certainly a lot of times.

When O'Brien and the Montreal Canadiens became founding members of the National Hockey League in 1917, they modified their jerseys again. As le Club de Hockey Canadien Inc., the team replaced the original logo on its uniform with a CH. Since then, for almost fifty years to the day before tonight's game, Montreal players had worn the logo on their jerseys as well as their gloves, pants, hockey bags, blazers, suitcases, keychains and underwear.

Over those years, the Montreal Forum, where the Canadiens played their home games, had become part of the city's urban fabric. Built in 1924 on the site of a roller-skating rink, the Forum could accommodate 9,300 fans when it opened for business. In the first game ever played there, the Canadiens scored seven goals against a team from Toronto called the St. Pats, who scored only one. The hockey-mad tavern dwellers in Montreal wished for a similarly lopsided result in tonight's game.

The Montreal Forum had been built in 159 days by men using picks, shovels, hammers and saws. Maple Leaf Gardens had taken four fewer days to build, but Conn Smythe had done it by performing a miracle, like Christ turning water into wine.

When the Gardens' doors opened in 1931, the legend of Conn Smythe had already started to circulate. It began with Smythe winning enough bets on football games and horse races to buy a stake in the St. Pats, the professional hockey team whose name he changed to the Maple Leafs because he didn't like Catholics. He disliked Irishmen, too, so he replaced the Leafs' green sweaters with blue, the colour traditionally worn by Toronto's top-ranked sports teams. In the midst of an economic depression, he offered to pay the tradesmen who built the Gardens with preferred shares in Maple Leaf Gardens Ltd. as an alternative to cash. As their shares kept doubling in value, he inadvertently helped several of them become millionaires.

No other facility in the NHL could match the Gardens for turning a buck. As of tonight, the Leafs organization had sold every available ticket for every home game for the previous twenty-one years. None of the Leafs tonight had ever played a game in Toronto when a ticket remained unsold. No wonder they thought the fans liked them.

No matter how many seats the owners added to the Gardens, Leafs fans kept paying to sit in them. The Canadiens might have called the Forum home; the Leafs called the Gardens a gold mine. It was "the original money machine," said the writer Peter Gzowski.

To keep the money pumping, Smythe hand-picked his employees according to their obedience and work ethic. Many staff members had served with him in the First World War. Billy Barker, the first president of the Maple Leafs, had been Smythe's flight instructor.

Smythe ordered his maintenance crew to wash the grey-painted floors at least twice a day, scrub the walls and keep the place as spic and span as St. James Cathedral, a few blocks south. He mounted framed photographs of hockey players in the hallways and plastered a jumbo-sized portrait of the King of England in full regalia on the northern wall inside the arena, where everyone could see it. With Maple Leaf Gardens, a new era began for long-suffering hockey patrons, said Frank Selke, who worked for Smythe in Toronto at the time. "Hockey crowds now had real class."

Smythe made his most astute and far-reaching decision when he installed a little dome-headed guy named Foster Hewitt in a box above the Gardens ice and told him to describe the hockey game below in words spoken into a microphone connected to a radio transmitter. Other NHL owners had had a similar idea. Throughout the 1930s, fans in Montreal could listen to their teams' home games, described in English and French, by announcers like Roland Beaudry, Michel Normandin, Doug Smith and Elmer Ferguson. But almost no one in the Gardens tonight had ever heard of those guys. Most of the English-speaking people in the building, including the players on the ice, had grown up listening on Saturday nights to the voice of Foster Hewitt. "I try to sell hockey," Hewitt said. And that's what he did, better than anyone, ever. Whether they lived in Joe Batt's Arm, Pickle Lake, Moose Jaw or Ladysmith, the brand name of Foster Hewitt became a synonym for the product itself, as well known in Canada as Kleenex, Coke and Zamboni.

With Hewitt's never-ending sales pitch, Leafs players became as familiar to millions of Canadians as movie heroes, said the writer Trent

Frayne. "People became as emotionally involved with them as if they were members of the family." Hewitt, who owned exclusive broadcast rights to Leafs home games, became rich.

At the urging of his father, Foster Hewitt had gone to work in the 1920s as a broadcaster of symphony concerts for the *Toronto Star*'s newly opened radio station. One Saturday afternoon on a snowy day in March, the station gave him an assignment that no one else would take. He trudged in his galoshes up to Arena Gardens on Mutual Street, one of only three indoor rinks in the city, and broadcast a hockey game between two amateur senior teams from Parkdale and Kitchener. Shivering in his overcoat on a stool inside a small glass-walled booth, Hewitt used a telephone as a microphone to describe the game to his listeners. The glass in his booth prevented him from leaning forward over the boards, so when the players skated into the corners, he could hardly see them. Even when he could see the players, he could hardly tell one from another because they didn't wear numbers on their sweaters. The more he talked inside his booth, the more the vapour from his breath kept steaming up the windows. And every few minutes, a telephone operator would come on the line and interrupt his broadcast to announce a call for Mr. Hewitt. "I couldn't wait for the game to end," Hewitt said.

Whether he liked it or not, though, listeners wanted more of Hewitt's play-by-play. A few years later, when Smythe moved his team a few blocks, from Mutual Street to their new home in Maple Leaf Gardens, he brought along Foster Hewitt.

Rather than sitting on a stool at ice level, Hewitt decided on the location of the broadcast booth inside the Gardens by walking over to a nearby department store and looking down through a window from each floor to the sidewalk below. When he could see all the pedestrians without losing sight of the pencils and pens in their pockets, he knew he'd gone high enough. By the time the Gardens opened, the NHL had copied an innovation of another hockey league out west and stuck numbers on the backs of players' sweaters. If Hewitt could see a pencil from five storeys above the ice, he figured he'd have no trouble seeing an eight-inch numeral. One day, a Gardens director saw Hewitt peering down at the ice and said the broadcast booth reminded him of the cabin of an airship. He called it a gondola, and the name stuck. For the next forty years, little kids from coast to coast imagined a radio announcer named Foster Hewitt sitting in his gondola, dressed like a Venetian cab driver.

Foster Hewitt parlayed his gig as the mouthpiece of Canadian hockey into a small fortune that included holdings in mining operations, oil wells, a radio station and a fourteen-room pile in Forest Hill. He earned enough money from his investments to send his son, Bill, to Upper Canada College, and then brought him on board the gondola. While Foster stuck to radio, Bill Hewitt became the voice of the Leafs on TV. By 1967, as the third generation of his family to make a living from sport, Bill Hewitt could look forward to even greater fame and fortune than his dad, if he wanted them. In the meantime, Foster Hewitt had joined a group of investors from Vancouver to bid for one of six new franchises in the NHL.

On the ice below the gondola, the players on each team warmed up by skating around one half of the rink, passing to each other and taking shots at their goalies. Then they went back to their dressing rooms before eight o'clock, leaving behind a few dozen black pucks clustered in the nets and scattered over the white ice.

At each end of the rink, a couple of Gardens attendants in blue cardigans shovelled the pucks into metal buckets. At the sound of an engine revving, the fans looked toward the north end of the rink, where the portrait of Queen Elizabeth hung on the wall, and watched a Gardens attendant named Doug Moore drive the Maple Leafs' Zamboni through a gate in the boards. Most of the fans tonight could remember when a phalanx of workers with snow shovels yo-hoed their way around the rink, followed by four attendants pushing steel oil drums filled with water and mounted on their sides on rubber wheels. Behind them came yet another kickline of attendants dispersing puddles of water with rubber squeegees. The big Zamboni, belching exhaust fumes into the stands, did a better job in half the time and required only one man to operate it. In the three years since the Leafs' owners had bought the Zamboni, it had paid for itself by cutting ice-maintenance costs in half. The owners of all six NHL arenas had now replaced their ice-making staff with a $3,500 Zamboni.

An attendant carrying a bucket of pucks skidded across the ice to the penalty box and handed it to the timekeeper. In the NHL, the home team had to provide pucks for each game. The pucks were frozen so that they wouldn't bounce. In previous years, the attendant would have taken the bucket to the Leafs' bench instead of the penalty box. If a player shot the puck over the boards in those days, the linesman would collect a replacement from the Leafs' trainer. But the attendant stopped leaving the pucks behind the Leafs' bench because Bob Haggert, the Leafs' current trainer, would sometimes get so upset with the officials on the ice that he'd wind up and hurl the puck into the far corner of the rink and make the linesman fetch it himself, in front of fifteen thousand jeering spectators.

Bob Haggert had grown up a few blocks from the Gardens. His mom, Elsie, worked there, serving sandwiches to newspaper reporters in the press room. As a boy, Haggert rode his bike past the Gardens after school at Duke of York to sell the *Toronto Telegram* on the sidewalk at Yonge and Carlton. In high school at Jarvis Collegiate, he caught the attention of the manager of the Toronto Marlboros, Harold Ballard, who hired the skinny kid as a stickboy and dressing-room attendant. Because of her confidence in Harold Ballard, Haggert's mom allowed her teenaged son to go on road trips with the junior team. "Mr. Ballard was like a surrogate father to me," Haggert said.

Haggert became the junior team's trainer and was on the job in 1955 when the Marlboros won the Memorial Cup as national junior champions. Eventually, he joined the Leafs, becoming in 1959 the youngest head trainer in the NHL. Since then, he'd been selected four times as the trainer for the First All-Star Team.

For the rest of his life, Haggert remained loyal not only to the Leafs but also to the man who hired him as a teenager: Harold Ballard.

For a young boy like Haggert, who had been raised by his mother to mind his manners and respect his elders, Harold Ballard seemed larger than life. Swaggering through the world with no fear and little regard for convention, the big, beefy Ballard brawled and boozed his way through Olympic Games, speed-boat competitions and hockey championships and had as much energy now, in his sixties, as the players on the ice who were a third of his age. Like Conn Smythe, Foster Hewitt and Smythe's son Stafford, who was Ballard's partner, Ballard had attended Upper Canada College. But he'd dropped out to cruise through the streets of Toronto in his Pierce-Arrow, cruise across Lake Ontario in his Sea Flea, draw attention to the Ballard skates manufactured by his father's company, and raise as much hell as he could without getting caught. Ballard had set Canadian records as a speed skater, but he'd distinguished himself even more by leading the men's hockey team in a brawl after they lost the world championships to the United States in 1933, for which he'd spent time in a Paris jail cell, and by stealing the Olympic flag from St. Moritz in 1928. Until someone stole it in turn from him, Ballard used the Olympic flag as a bedspread.

In the 1930s, Ballard ran a business that supplied machinery to the garment industry in Toronto, while he became more deeply involved in managing sports teams. At sixty-three, Ballard now owned a piece of the most successful hockey franchise in the world, drove a white Cadillac, had a keen eye for plump women and remained irrepressibly exuberant in his larceny.

At the moment, Ballard and Stafford Smythe, two of the three current owners of the Leafs, were mingling in their suits with the throngs of sponsors, advertising executives, reporters and hangers-on who congregated in the corridor outside the teams' dressing rooms. Soon they would make their way to their seats behind the Canadiens' goal.

Almost twenty years younger than his partner, Staff Smythe had known Ballard all his life. Ballard used to take the kid for rides in his convertible when he visited Conn Smythe, Stafford's dad, near the Old Mill, in the west end of Toronto. The Smythes and the Ballards were neighbours. Not only did they share a passionate interest in hockey, they also shared an equally passionate interest in money.

Conn Smythe called Ballard a buccaneer. He went where he wanted and took what he could get, Smythe said, without conscience. Ballard returned the compliment. Conn Smythe, he said, "is a miserable old bastard."

When Conn Smythe relinquished control of the organization in 1961, he demanded more than $2 million from his son. To pay the old man, Ballard and Smythe persuaded a third partner, John Bassett, to join them. In addition to the Leafs, Bassett owned the *Toronto Telegram* and the local Canadian football team, the Argonauts. With the Leafs firmly in their control, the new owners intensified their focus on squeezing money from the operation.

Over the next few years, Ballard, Smythe and Bassett enlarged the rink's capacity by four thousand seats. They steadily increased the price of tickets and cluttered the Gardens with advertisements for beer, cigarettes, cars and chocolate bars. They opened a bar and restaurant called the Hot Stove Lounge, charging a $100 initiation fee plus $50 dollars a year or $1,000 for a lifetime membership. In 1965, they sold broadcast rights to all Leafs home games for six years to a Toronto advertising agency for $9 million. Then they tore apart the Leafs' farm system, selling teams in Victoria and Rochester for $900,000.

As the hockey team showed signs of strain, the company that owned it became more prosperous than ever. In November 1965, stock in Maple Leaf Gardens Ltd. hit ninety-three dollars. Gardens management split the company's shares five for one. Shares purchased for a thousand dollars by bricklayers, electricians, masons and carpenters, along with anyone else who'd bought Gardens stock in 1935, were now worth $30,000. (The same amount invested in a savings bond would have grown in value to less than one-tenth of that amount.) Since Ballard and Smythe owned most of the Gardens' shares, they were very happy campers tonight, although, true to their nature as owners of an NHL hockey team, they wanted more. An NHL owner could never have enough money.

Anyone in Canada who owned a television set could watch tonight's game on the CBC. Another six million people listened to Foster Hewitt's radio broadcast. Some people did both. To reach these fans and try to sell them Edsels, Esso Extra and Molson Ex, advertising agencies had started competing for multi-year TV contracts. Yet NHL owners still regarded all the publicity merely as a way to sell more tickets. The greater the demand for tickets, the more games they scheduled, and the harder their players worked. Now the players wanted to get paid for their efforts, and Alan Eagleson had persuaded most of them that he could get them what they wanted.

Why not give him a chance? the players argued. Players had tried for more than forty years to get a fair deal from their teams' owners, and they hadn't succeeded yet.

In a more equitable world, the superstars of hockey would have worked together with their less talented brethren to get what they wanted. People bought tickets to see a superstar. In the years that Howie Morenz played for the Montreal Canadiens, the NHL doubled the number of games in its schedule so that more people could pay more money to watch him play. With Gordie Howe, Bobby Hull and Bobby Orr in the league, NHL teams now played seventy games. Players toiled over a season that was now three times as long as it had been in the 1920s, generating at least three times the gate receipts for their teams' owners, but in more than forty years, their average salary hadn't even doubled.

Owners became even happier when their teams made the playoffs. Then they could increase the price of a ticket, knowing that they'd sell every seat. With another six teams in the NHL next year, the playoffs would require even more games, allowing the owners to sell even more tickets at inflated prices.

Rather than exercise the influence that came with their box-office status, most superstars in the league took their pay and kept their mouths shut. Lesser players who thought they deserved a bigger piece of the action kept their mouths shut, as well. A man who complained about the demands of an NHL career might find himself playing in another city, possibly in another league at a lower salary. He might even find himself out of a job: no matter how much he contributed to his team, his team would get rid of him.

A player named Ted Lindsay had discovered this the hard way. Lindsay played in Detroit for thirteen years. He'd won the NHL scoring championship, was named to the NHL all-star team eight times and had become captain of the Red Wings. Lindsay defended his teammates on the ice with such ferocity that the league had created two new categories of penalty just for him, for elbowing and kneeing. "My kind of hockey player," said the Red Wings' manager, Jack Adams. But in 1957, when Lindsay led the formation of the NHL Players' Association and publicly accused the league's president, Clarence Campbell, of prejudice, Adams banished him to Chicago with the rest of the cast-offs and shit disturbers after a season in which he'd averaged more than a point a game.

To discredit Lindsay further and smear his reputation, Detroit executives planted false rumours with local newspapers that Lindsay had belittled his teammates. To substantiate the rumours, they fabricated statements from Lindsay about his teammates' shortcomings and planted them with local reporters. Then the managers showed reporters a doctored version of Lindsay's contract to prove that he'd made more money than he'd admitted to his teammates. The smear tactics worked. When other players in the league saw the newspaper reports, they accused Lindsay of double-dealing, stopped talking to him and gave up trying to form a union. In the world of hockey, Lindsay's name was mud, not because he'd tried to injure another player, but because he'd apparently betrayed his brothers within the fraternity of professional hockey. At the same time as Detroit was blackballing Lindsay, the Leafs did the same thing to Tod Sloan in retaliation for his support of Lindsay. By harassing, belittling, ostracizing and trading Lindsay and his supporters, the owners shut down the players' association in less than twelve months.

If they had to, NHL owners would shut down entire teams rather than capitulate to players' wishes for a fair shake. In 1925, players on the Hamilton Tigers asked for an additional $200 to play in the playoffs, after they'd already played an additional six games in the regular season. Instead of giving them what they wanted, the president of the league suspended the team, fined each player $200 and dismantled the franchise. That was the last time a team from Hamilton ever played in the NHL.

By banishing uppity players, owners not only got rid of troublemakers, they often made a profit, as well, by sending the player to another team in which they had a financial stake and generating some additional publicity. NHL owners like the Norris brothers were masters of self-dealing. Between them, the brothers owned at least a portion of the Red Wings in Detroit and the Black Hawks in Chicago, as well as Chicago Stadium and Madison Square Garden in New York. In 1967, when the NHL announced the names of the six new cities in the league selected from more than a dozen applicants, one of them was St. Louis, Missouri. No one from St. Louis had asked for a franchise, but James Norris owned the city's arena.

NHL owners got away for years with behaviour that a more conventional company's customers, employees, shareholders, suppliers and regulators wouldn't tolerate for five minutes. Even the league's president, Clarence Campbell, capitulated to the moral flu that prevailed among the top ranks of the league. At the age of 74, Campbell, the man responsible for maintaining the NHL's ethical standards, was charged with conspiracy to bribe a Canadian senator in return for his influence in leasing a duty-free shop at a federally run airport in Montreal. Although the NHL paid his legal costs, the ailing Campbell was found guilty and served a brief jail sentence.

NHL owners are not just headstrong and temperamental rich guys, said Eric Nesterenko, who played for twenty years in the 1950s and '60s for the Leafs and the Black Hawks. They're "nasty, vicious, greedy, self-serving people." Players in the 1960s could do nothing about it except play for the team that owned them or quit, and no one reaches the pinnacle of professional hockey by quitting.

Most players felt grateful to their teams' owners for giving them a chance to play in the NHL and treated them with respect proportionate to the owners' wealth and status. If the wealth had come with the help of embezzlement, theft, slander, bribery or conspiracy, players didn't let these quibbles temper their gratitude.

Owners didn't have to try hard to win the loyalty of a professional hockey player. He lived in constant fear of losing his job, and the owner of his team had total control over his professional destiny. "If an owner or manager decided he didn't want you — or, worse still, didn't like you — you were dead," said Nesterenko. "They buried some guys so deep, they never surfaced."

NHL players resembled kidnap victims, stricken by a variation of Stockholm Syndrome and falling in love with their captors. An owner merely had to make an unexpected gesture of generosity, and a player would become his defender for life.

Harold Ballard was especially adept at tossing crumbs to his minions. Ballard earned the gratitude of Leafs player Eddie Shack by paying to have Shack's dune buggy painted Maple Leaf blue. He won commendations from Red Kelly, a former member of Parliament, because he drove with the Stanley Cup to Kelly's house after Kelly had damaged his knee so badly helping the Leafs win the thing that he couldn't walk. "I don't know of anybody else who would ever have thought about doing that," Kelly said.

In Chicago, the president of the Black Hawks, Bill Wirtz, made similar gestures. According to Bobby Hull, Wirtz was "tighter than a buzzard's ass in a power dive." Wirtz once resisted a city order to install drinking fountains in Chicago Stadium because he wouldn't make any money from fans who drank water instead of an overpriced drink from a Stadium snack bar. When he finally installed a drinking fountain, he ran hot water through the pipes. But he earned the admiration of Bob Pulford because Wirtz sometimes treated people with kindness and "paid for quite a few funerals. No one knew that," Pulford said.

Conn Smythe merely had to talk to George Armstrong to win the player's respect. When the Leafs' owner named a horse after him, called Big Chief Army, Armstrong was over the moon. "The horse couldn't run much faster than I could skate," said Armstrong, interviewed at his bungalow in Leaside. Smythe paid more to maintain his horse than Armstrong had paid for his house, and he didn't need a second and third mortgage to cover the cost. Armstrong felt even more grateful to Mr. Smythe when the Leafs' owner appointed him as the team's captain.

NHL owners named horses after Jean Beliveau and Brian Conacher's Uncle Charlie, and they regarded their two-legged animals on the ice in the same way as they regarded their four-legged animals on the track. Conn Smythe demanded as much effort and obedience from his players as he did from his horses. He expected "one hundred per cent loyalty," he said, and he expected them to play "when, how and where our organization tells them." Even John Ferguson, playing tonight for the Canadiens, would compare raising thoroughbreds to "building a stable of hockey players. I don't see that there's any difference."

To his credit, Smythe didn't play favourites. He took the same hard-nosed attitude toward his own family as he did toward his stable of two- and four-legged chattels. When a puppy belonging to his nine-year-old grandson, Tommy, spooked one of Smythe's horses, the horse stumbled and broke a leg. Angered that he had to put the horse down, Smythe shot the kid's dog, as well.

John Ferguson knew that the Canadiens would play tonight at a disadvantage. During the pre-game warm-up, the ice at Maple Leaf Gardens felt heavy, like walking in mud. The young players on the Canadiens preferred fast ice that allowed them to streak toward the other team's goal with the puck on their stick like a yo-yo on a string. At the Montreal Forum, the players usually got what they wanted. But this was enemy territory.

The Canadiens forwards could skate faster than anyone on the Leafs, even Dave Keon. Most of them were in their twenties. Ferguson was twenty-eight. Yvan Cournoyer was twenty-three. Claude Larose was twenty-five. Gilles Tremblay was twenty-eight. So was Bosey Balon, one of the faster players in the league, although hardly anyone ever noticed him. Bobby Rousseau was twenty-six. Jim Roberts was twenty-seven. Ralph Backstrom was twenty-nine. At thirty-one, Henri Richard was regarded as one of the team's elder statesmen. He and Jean Beliveau had both played on the Canadiens team that won five Stanley Cups in a row, beginning when Yvan Cournoyer was only twelve. They all had young legs, but those legs wouldn't make much difference if they had to mush their way through slushpiles, with the puck rolling on its edge like a quarter through a rain gutter.

Because of the Canadiens' emphasis on speed and passing, the Forum maintained the best ice in the NHL. Even the referees said so. Unlike other arenas, the Forum also had hard boards. They didn't give when one player slammed into them after an opponent's bodycheck. A few years after tonight's game, a Montreal defenceman, Larry Robinson, would hit a Philadelphia Flyers forward named Gary Dornhoefer so hard that he dented the boards. The referee had to stop the game so that workmen could repair the damage. Most Montreal players could skate fast enough to elude the full impact of a bodycheck. Their slower opponents suffered more than they did.

Detroit had good ice, as well, in the Old Red Barn where the Red Wings played. "Like vanilla ice cream," Red Kelly said. "Smooth as a pool table."

The other rinks weren't so good. Earlier this season, in Chicago, a Leafs player named Larry Jeffrey had hurt his leg so badly after catching his skateblade in a rut that he'd spend the game tonight on crutches beside his team's bench. Madison Square Garden in New York had bad ice, too, and even worse dressing rooms. When the Canadiens played the Rangers there, Montreal's assistant trainer, Eddy Palchak, made sure that the team packed their equipment immediately after a game rather than leaving it overnight on the floor. Palchak had once returned to the visitors' dressing room in New York after a night on the town in Manhattan to discover the Canadiens' salt-stained gloves and skates all chewed beyond recognition by rats.

Like Ferguson, Jean Beliveau had noticed the ice, as well. The puck wouldn't sit flat, and it didn't snap crisply off the players' stickblades the way it did when they warmed up at home in the Forum. Beliveau thought the Canadiens seemed stiff and dull. "You can tell in the warm-up how you're going to be skating," he said, and tonight he felt as if he was skating through melted cheese.

The Leafs would gain more tonight from their grizzled experience than they'd lose from the soft ice, and Beliveau knew it. Older on average than the Canadiens, veterans of at least a hundred more Stanley Cup games, the Leafs stuck to their knitting and waited for their chances. Beliveau had seen it happen before: age in its wisdom outsmarting youth with all its energy. Soft ice would favour old slow guys who play defensive hockey over the fleet-footed youngsters on the Canadiens.

A buzzer sounded through a speaker in the wall. The players had one more minute to wait before they could file down the corridor and onto the ice. In Montreal, a bell rang three times in the Canadiens' dressing room, ding, ding, ding, like a little clock, to indicate that the game would start in three minutes. In New York, the voice of the timekeeper announced over a loudspeaker, "On the ice in three minutes, please." But in Toronto, the sudden blast of a rasping buzzer scared the shit out of you. That was okay: it also made John Ferguson angry. A few players raised their heads.

Ralph Backstrom and Jacques Laperriere had unlaced their skates. Now they leaned over to tie them up again.

The dressing-room door opened and Toe Blake walked in. He looked around the room but didn't say anything to the players. He handed a puck to the trainer, Larry Aubut. Aubut walked over to Gump Worsley and put the puck in the goalie's catching mitt. Everyone on the team recognized the gesture. Blake had chosen Worsley to start tonight's game. Rogatien Vachon would watch the game from the end of the bench.

"Give your best," Blake told the team.

The two goalies leaned forward and let the weight of their goalie pads pull them to their feet. The rest of the players shoved their hands into their gloves, picked up their sticks and filed past the coach out of the room and into the hallway.

Bald-headed, grey-faced, Punch Imlach stood just inside the door, where everyone could see him in his ugly green suit and a fedora that looked as if he'd found it under a seat cushion. Pinned to the ribbon of his hat, Imlach wore an emblem of the U.S. 101st Airborne Division, given to him for luck by a Canadian soldier who had served in Vietnam.

No one in the room was more focused than Imlach on winning the game tonight. If he could have helped his team by lacing on a pair of skates himself, he would have done it. "His single purpose in life is to win hockey games," said the writer Peter Gzowski.

At forty-six, Imlach couldn't do much good now as a player. He never could, actually. Imlach had never played in the NHL. But he'd already won three goddamn Stanley Cups as coach of the Leafs, and he intended tonight to win another one, goddammit. "You're going to win it tonight," Imlach said, "or you won't win it at all."

Imlach tossed a box into the centre of the room. When it landed, he said, "This is what you're playing for." A thousand one-dollar bills spilled across the concrete.

What a fucking asshole, thought Mike Walton. Imlach's gesture made him angry, more angry than he'd ever felt in his life.

The other eighteen players stared at the scattered cash. Then Terry Sawchuk shoved his mask into the space between his left goalie pad and his knee, stood up and led the team out of the dressing room. No one said anything to Imlach until George Armstrong, the captain, walked past. "Don't worry, Punch," he said. "We'll get this one."

The assistant trainer, Tommy Nayler, remained behind with Imlach, to lock the door. Imlach walked over to the rack of sticks that Nayler would carry to the players' bench and knocked his knuckles on them. He went to the blackboard on the wall of the dressing room and drew an arrow on it with a piece of chalk. He kicked the metal pails that the trainer had filled with ice chips. Then Nayler handed Imlach a stick of spearmint gum. Imlach removed the wrapper, dropped it on the floor, put the gum in his mouth and walked out of the room. Nayler bent over to pick up the gum wrapper, put it in his pocket, then pushed the rack of sticks into the hall and closed the door behind him.

On the ice, the two teams skated in a circle around their end of the rink. At the Leafs' end of the rink, Tim Horton watched the TV camera in the stands until the red light on top indicated that it was operating. Horton skated past the camera, leaned forward and slapped the blade of his wooden stick on the ice. He did that before every period of a televised game. It was his way of saying hello to his six-year-old daughter, Traci, who was watching her dad at home on TV.

A fan hollered, "Let's go, Timmy!" His voice was so loud, even Horton's daughter could hear it over the TV set in the rec room.

Foster Hewitt looked pale. He never ate on the day of a game. He got too nervous. He'd also lost about twenty pounds again this season, just as he'd done almost every year since he started doing this job in the 1930s. Thirty-five years, twenty pounds a year: Bill Hewitt figured his dad had lost the equivalent in weight of five small men.

Father and son had walked together up a staircase along the west wall of the building and carried their light raincoats to the public-address control room in the northwest corner of the Gardens. The Gardens announcer, Paul Morris, was there, looking down at the ice.

Passing Morris, the Hewitts made their way across a catwalk to the row of booths suspended from the ceiling above the seats. Bill Hewitt went into the TV booth and sat down. His dad walked a little farther and sat down in front of a microphone to describe the game to his audience over the radio. Below him the teams skated in counter-clockwise circles at each end of the rink. On some nights, Foster's grandson, Bruce, sat on a folding chair beside him. Bruce was Bill's son, and he was good with numbers — Foster referred to him as his statistician. Sometimes Foster let Bruce say a few sentences into the microphone. But not tonight. There was too much riding on this game to give a kid any airtime. Tonight, in the seat next to Hewitt sat a rep from MacLaren Advertising, the agency that represented Imperial Oil. The ad rep kept track of shots on goal, goals, penalties, times and other details on behalf of his client. That was fine with Foster Hewitt. Imperial Oil paid Hewitt's fee.

Like his son, Bill Hewitt liked to play with numbers. Sitting above the ice in the designated TV booth with a commentator named Brian McFarlane, Hewitt would multiply players' numbers during commercial breaks. Then he'd see how the product of his calculation compared to the time of the last goal. But now, prompted by a flashing green light, Bill Hewitt drew a breath and said, "Hello, Canada and hockey fans in the United States."

CHAPTER TWO
First Period

John Ashley, the referee, stood motionless at the centre of the rink. He moved his right hand forward as if he was brushing lint off his pantleg, spread his fingers, and let the puck drop to the ice.

With stickblades flicking like lizards' tongues at a bug, Ralph Backstrom and Pete Stemkowski stabbed at the falling puck. Leafs winger Jim Pappin darted toward the puck, chased by grim-faced John Ferguson. Ashley backed away from the commotion. The game was on.

Pappin pulled the puck out of the thicket of legs and skates and flicked it blindly toward the Canadiens' end of the rink. When he turned to follow it, he ran smack into Terry Harper, the defenceman, who had skated toward centre, turned sideways and bent forward to block his way. Pappin vaulted across Harper's back, landed face-down on the ice, regained his footing and started skating again.

Young linesman Brent Casselman straddled the blue line beside the boards. When the puck crossed the line in advance of any of the Leafs players, Casselman held out his arms like Christ on a crucifix to indicate that the play was onside.

Gump Worsley, the Canadiens' goalie, guided the rolling puck away from the goal as Stemkowski chased Jacques Laperriere to the puck.

"Man on you, Lappy," Worsley shouted.

Fired by adrenaline, charged by the noise of sixteen thousand screaming Leafs fans, hearing the skateblades of his two-hundred-pound pursuer
chopping into the ice behind him, Laperriere remained as calm as a gar-
dener tending to a tomato plant. With the puck on his stick, he shifted his
head, his arms and his gloves to the right, just enough to signal to Stemkowski
that he would turn behind the net. Stemkowski shifted his weight to follow
him. Then Laperriere dug his skateblades into the ice and turned the other
way. When he reached centre ice, he lifted the puck over the Leafs defencemen into their end, timing his shot so that the three Canadiens forwards
could burst over the blue line together without breaking stride.

Claude Larose swept toward the goal, grazed the puck with his stick
and sped past Terry Sawchuk so fast that the crouching goalie felt a cool
breeze through the eyeholes of his facemask. Sawchuk couldn't see John
Ferguson barrelling from his blind side toward the goal, but he could hear
Ferguson coming, because the Canadiens forward skated as if he was
chopping onions with his feet. Ferguson stormed past the goalie and
followed Ralph Backstrom and Bob Pulford, the Leafs winger, into the
corner.

The puck skittered toward the face-off circle, and Sawchuk watched
his defencemen, Larry Hillman and Marcel Pronovost, skating to retrieve
it. Sawchuk, Hillman and Pronovost had all played their first games in
the NHL as teenagers with the Red Wings in Detroit. Hillman had joined
the Red Wings at seventeen and was still the youngest player ever to have
his name engraved on the Stanley Cup. Pronovost was the most popular
French Canadian in the NHL who didn't play for the Canadiens. Before
a game between the Canadiens and the Red Wings at the Montreal Forum,
the fans had helped him celebrate his thirtieth birthday by presenting him
with a new car. Pronovost had also broken his nose fourteen times and
now looked as if he was squishing his face against a pane of glass.

Pete Stemkowski took the puck and turned in front of Sawchuk. The
puck was rolling on its edge. He looked down at the puck as Larose lowered
his shoulder to ram it like a piledriver into his head. In the split second

before this happened, Stemkowski leaned to his left, angled his weight onto his inside foot, glanced up the ice and made a pass that landed right on the stick of Jim Pappin, who was skating away from him at twenty miles an hour. While Stemkowski avoided Larose's shoulder, Pappin felt the puck on his stick without looking down at the ice and kept skating.

Stemkowski had made similar passes so many times throughout his career that no one paid much attention anymore. Certainly he no longer impressed his coach. Punch Imlach had said more than once in the last couple of years that Stemkowski was "a stupid hockey player."

Pappin slapped the puck into the Canadiens' end. Terry Harper skated in to retrieve it. "You got time," Worsley yelled at him. "You got time."

A moment later, three players kicked at the puck against the boards. When it disappeared within a maze of skateblades, John Ashley blew his whistle to stop the play. Thirty seconds had passed since the game had begun.

Ferguson, Backstrom and Larose left the ice. Despite his French-Canadian surname, Rosey had grown up in Ontario, in a whistle stop north of Lake Superior called Hearst, the Moose Capital of Canada. Since joining the Canadiens, he'd worked hard to prove to them that he deserved his place on the team. But they still had reservations about Larose. So did his mother in Hearst. She worried that her son would get hurt, and she wished he'd never played hockey at all.

Jean Beliveau, Gilles Tremblay and Bobby Rousseau skated from the Canadiens' bench to replace them. Laperriere and Harper stayed on the ice.

From the Leafs' bench, Punch Imlach sent Dave Keon, George Armstrong and Frank Mahovlich onto the ice, along with two fresh defencemen, Tim Horton and Allan Stanley. Of the five Maple Leafs on the ice at the moment, Imlach had the least confidence in Mahovlich. He hoped the son of a bitch wouldn't let him down.

...

"Take a fucking look," Jim Pappin snapped to Bob Pulford as he slid along the Leafs' bench. "I was open."

Pulford rested his gloved right hand on top of the boards as he caught his breath. "Y're open, lemme know, fucksake," he said.

Gibberish came out of Pulford's mouth like porridge bubbling in a pot. "Pulford was always mumbling," said former NHL referee Bruce Hood. Pulford was always miserable, as well. His teammates had seldom seen him smile, even when he scored a goal. Over beers in a bar, they joked that Happy Hour couldn't start until Pulford went home. But they'd seen him argue. Pulford argued with the other team. He argued with his own team. He argued with the officials. He challenged every penalty, every offside. Some officials expected him to argue even when he scored a goal. "A most miserable player," said Hood.

Pappin and Pulford both lived in Weston, northwest of the city. They often drove together to practice at Maple Leaf Gardens, and they shopped together at the same grocery store, where Pappin picked up baby food for his new kid. But during a game, they bickered like romantically challenged parents. "On the ice," said Stemkowski, their linemate, "they didn't get along so well."

Pappin was as miserable as Pulford. Lean and moody, with a chip on each shoulder, he had an abrasive personality that could scour a frying pan, and he didn't play favourites with his criticism. He said stuff about his coaches and teammates that they didn't like to hear, and he said it right to their faces. "Pappin had the most cutting tongue of any person I've ever met," said Don Cherry, "cruel and to the point."

Pappin called the coterie of Leafs players who followed Punch Imlach the Punch Platoon, Punch Drunks or Imlach Lackeys. But as often as he criticized others, he turned his caustic eye inward. "He gets down on himself a lot," Stemkowski said.

For eight years as a professional hockey player, Pappin had spent countless hours on a bus, travelling with his minor-league teammates between small-time cities like Cleveland, Providence and Rochester.

Occasionally, Punch Imlach would call him up to play a game or two with the Leafs, then send him back to Rochester. He did this two or three times a year. At the beginning of this season, with his wife, Karen, pregnant with their second child, Pappin figured he'd had enough. "Either I make it this time or I quit," he'd said.

Pappin's life had improved since he'd started playing this year with Pulford and Stemkowski. He'd scored fifteen goals in the last twenty-two games of the season and another six in the playoffs. He now led the Leafs in scoring. Less than a week ago, his wife had given birth to a baby girl. Maybe life wasn't so bad after all.

Like Pappin, Stemkowski had commuted back and forth to Rochester from Toronto like a travelling salesman for Kodak cameras. This year, his third as a professional, he'd finally stayed with the Leafs for a full season, but that didn't give him much reassurance. Until about three months ago, Stemkowski had spent most games sitting on the bench. Now he'd earned a regular shift on a line that scored goals, and he tried hard to make the most of his opportunity. Lately, even Punch Imlach had admitted that Stemkowski made some good plays, although he was too slow.

Gilles Tremblay had watched Jean Beliveau take about ten thousand face-offs. He'd played on the same line as Beliveau for six years, and he'd watched him for three times that long, from the time he was twelve and his older brother, Ludger, had played in Quebec with Beliveau. Beliveau had written a small book about taking face-offs. Yet Tremblay still couldn't explain exactly how Beliveau did it or how he made it look so easy.

Leafs centre Dave Keon had taken a lot of face-offs, too. Playing against kids who were almost twenty, he'd been good enough to earn a tryout with the Detroit Red Wings when he was fourteen. Keon had grown up in Rouyn-Noranda, Quebec, near the Ontario border, and spoke French and English with equal fluency.

Facing off against Beliveau, he intended to intercept the falling puck and drive it past Gump Worsley into the Canadiens' net before the goalie had a chance to move. He'd done it before. But when John Ashley dropped the puck, it skidded past their sticks and into the corner. A few seconds later, when the puck came close to the Canadiens' goal again, Worsley darted from his crease and cleared it down the ice.

Tim Horton skated after it. Horton looked as if he lifted ten-pound weights with his jaw, but he also had such bad eyesight that he wore horn-rimmed glasses as thick as Coke bottles when he wasn't playing hockey. Dave Keon called him Magoo. "Corner, Timmy," yelled Allan Stanley, his partner, as if he was giving him directions. "Corner."

Horton reached the puck just as two fleet-footed Canadiens caught up to him. To elude them, he circled behind his goal, ducked, circled again and went the other way. Bobby Rousseau apprehended him in the corner and pulled the puck away from him with his stick, then skated into Dave Keon. Together, they weighed about as much as one big defenceman, and each of them was known for his speed.

Rousseau, too, had earned a tryout with the Red Wings but caught the flu and had to stay in bed. Around the same time as he'd become a professional hockey player, he'd become a professional golfer, as well, playing in three Canadian Opens and finishing third in the Quebec Open. But the pressure of competing for money against the best players in two different games had left him exhausted, and now he had an ulcer. In case it acted up during a game, he kept a bottle of milk beside him on the bench.

At the moment, neither Keon nor Rousseau would give up the puck without a fight. They pushed, shoved, pushed some more, until the puck disappeared underneath them.

In the next sixty seconds, the players skated four times from one end of the two-hundred-foot rink to the other. Twice, the Canadiens stormed into the Leafs' end of the rink, buzzing around Terry Sawchuk like speeding cars past a stranded pedestrian. Twice, the Leafs stormed back into Montreal's end, knocking Canadiens forwards off their skates and leaving defencemen sprawled on the ice.

One rush began in the Leafs' end of the rink, when Gilles Tremblay pinned George Armstrong face-first against the boards. Armstrong slid the puck between his skates to Dave Keon, who took three strides to cross the blue line and then passed the puck forward to Frank Mahovlich. As Mahovlich drew his stick back, the crowd greeted its home team's highest-scoring player with a chorus of boos. Mahovlich took a slapshot. The puck caromed off Gump Worsley's pads into the corner. "You stink, Mahovlich!" yelled a fan.

Before they perfected their slapshots in the 1950s, NHL players sometimes slapped the puck, but they didn't do it often, because they frequently broke their stick or broke the puck. In those days, sticks were made of two pieces of wood held together with glue. Pucks were once made from wood, as well, until they were succeeded by disks made from two circular pieces of natural rubber, glued together. Occasionally, the blow from a player's stick would break the puck in half. If one half ended up in the net, a referee would disallow the goal. If you wanted to score a goal in the NHL, you had to do it with the whole puck.

In the 1940s, a former player, coach and manager of the Boston Bruins named Art Ross patented a one-piece puck made of synthetic rubber and adorned with an orange circle bearing his name. Three inches in diameter, one inch thick, weighing about five-and-a-half ounces, "the roll-preventing hockey puck," as Ross called it in his patent application, slid more smoothly and was easier to manufacture than the two-piece version. It also remained intact when players smacked the bejeebers out of it. The new puck allowed players to take a harder shot that travelled at a higher speed, in a less predictable direction. For Art Ross, the new puck put a few pennies in his pocket. NHL teams went through about five thousand pucks a season. Until the patent expired in the mid-1990s, each one had Ross's name on it.

At the leisurely pace of a wrist shot, a hockey puck remains intact but can still inflict pain. A slapshot can kill. After stopping Bobby Hull's slapshot with his padded glove, a goalie named Bruce Gamble compared it to "handling a red-hot rivet."

But as more players took slapshots, more players had to block them or declare themselves cowards by dodging the rubber bullets. Defencemen in particular learned to hurl their bodies in front of pucks travelling faster than a major-league pitcher throws a fastball. So did some forwards.

Defencemen on the Canadiens had an additional incentive to block shots. Every time a Montreal goalie recorded a shutout, his defencemen received a bonus of $100. If he won the Vezina Trophy, awarded until 1981 to the goalie who allowed the fewest goals in a season, they earned another $1,000. Winning the Vezina required a team effort, especially from the defencemen.

To make life on the blue line even more precarious, players in the 1960s started to bend the blades of their sticks. Launched from a curved blade, the puck not only accelerates like a bullet, it also dips and skips and bounces.

The bigger the curve, the more unpredictable the puck's acrobatics. Until 1970, when the league imposed restrictions, some players put such a wow in their stickblades that they called them bananas. Pucks flew in all directions. Even if a defenceman didn't fall down to block a shot, he still risked getting hit in the head.

To protect themselves, defencemen lined their pants with foam rubber. Allan Stanley wrapped leather-covered ankle guards around his skates. Johnny Bower, the goalie, stuffed hockey socks into the unprotected space between the tops of his pads and the bottom of his padded shorts. Many goalies began to wear a mask, as well, although Gump Worsley wouldn't wear one until the last few games of his career, seven years after tonight's game.

At the other end of the rink, Terry Sawchuk wore a mask, and he was glad he did. Only a few games before tonight, in the semi-final series against the Black Hawks, Bobby Hull had taken a slapshot that hit Sawchuk in the face. Bob Haggert, the Leafs' trainer, skidded across the ice from the Leafs' bench, knelt down beside the fallen goalie and asked if he was okay. Sawchuk glared at him through the eyeholes of his mask. "I stopped the fucking shot, didn't I?" he said.

After he stood up, the Leafs won the game, four goals to two, and Sawchuk stopped another thirty-six shots.

Just seconds after Mahovlich tried and failed to score on a slapshot, the Canadiens got their chance, when Jean Beliveau burst out of his own end with Bobby Rousseau. Tim Horton was trapped in the Canadiens' zone, leaving Allan Stanley alone between the two Canadiens forwards and the Leafs' goal.

Stanley skated backwards, positioned between the two Canadiens so that he could block a pass with his stick while keeping Beliveau to the outside of the rink. From there, Beliveau could see only a portion of the goal. If he wanted a better view, he had to position himself directly in front of the goal. Trying to do just that, Beliveau feinted, ducked, moved his eyes, shifted, nodded, faked, moved his hands, turned slightly to his left, moved his hips as he skated toward Stanley, "six or eight different things in under two seconds," said the writer Hugh Hood, who'd once skated with Beliveau.

Sometimes Beliveau's tactics worked, sometimes they didn't. Tonight, they didn't. Stanley backed over his blue line, unflustered and unperturbed, still angling Beliveau to the outside of the rink, still positioned to intercept Beliveau's pass to Rousseau. So Beliveau chose a third option. When he crossed the blue line, he drew his stick back and fired the puck like a bullet at the two feet of open net that he could see between Terry Sawchuk and the far goalpost. But Sawchuk kicked out his left pad and directed the puck away from the net.

The play stopped when Frank Mahovlich shot the puck up the ice and hit the linesman Matt Pavelich in the back of the head. John Ashley blew his whistle, and Pavelich clambered to his feet. The players lined up for the face-off.

John Ashley had known some of these guys for years. The best hockey players in the world, he thought. Certainly the best in Canada. And half of them had grown up within a hundred miles of each other.

Ashley knew Tim Horton and George Armstrong from his own brief experience as a professional hockey player in Pittsburgh. He and the two Leafs were almost the same age, all born within six months of each other. Ashley knew from the moment he'd set foot on the ice with them in Pittsburgh that these two players would make it to the NHL. He wasn't surprised to see them here tonight.

Horton and Armstrong had first met long before they got to Pittsburgh. They'd played together as fifteen-year-old kids for a team called the Redmen, in Copper Cliff, a couple of hundred miles north of Toronto. Inco, the mining company, had built the town outside of Sudbury, upwind from the company's smelter, so its managers could eat dinner without breathing the stench of melting rock and molten nickel. The town imported its hockey players from surrounding areas like Cochrane, where Horton grew up; from Falconbridge, where Armstrong remembered being "the only Indian kid in town"; and from Skead, a predominantly native village that clung to the rocks like a jumbled pile of oiled lumber on the south shore of Lake Wanapitei.

Armstrong had been born in Skead, the son of an Irish father and Ojibwa mom. At the age of six, he'd contracted spinal meningitis, diagnosed only after a doctor inserted a needle into his spine. He thought he would die, if not from the disease, then from the pain of the needle. Compared to that, the aches and pains of playing hockey didn't seem very daunting.

When Armstrong joined the Leafs organization at fourteen, they gave him $100, his room and board and $2.50 a week. But the team had no place for an unproven native kid in Toronto, so they sent him to Stratford, a furniture-making town in the hardwood forests a hundred miles west of the city. Already wearing his jet-black hair in a jagged crewcut that he'd keep for the rest of his career, Armstrong played in Stratford for a junior team called the Koehlers, sponsored by a local furniture company. Alone in a strange town full of white men, he led the league in scoring and won the Red Tilson Trophy as the outstanding junior player in the province. He also earned a nickname: Chief. At first, he said, the name just reinforced his feeling of inferiority. He didn't tell anybody, though. Armstrong never talked about his feelings. He wasn't that kind of guy.

Unable to ignore such a gifted player, the Leafs moved Armstrong the next year to Toronto to play junior hockey for the Marlboros. He played so well with the Marlies that he won the Red Tilson Trophy again. No one else has ever done that. Other winners of the Tilson Trophy have included such luminaries as goalie Andrew Raycroft, unfulfilled superstar Eric Lindros and Doug Gilmour, another former captain of the Leafs. But only George Armstrong has ever won the trophy twice. In three years of junior hockey, competing against some of the best players in the game, Armstrong recorded 250 points in 120 games. The year Armstrong won the trophy for the second time, a reporter involved in selecting the winner submitted his three top choices on a ballot: His first choice was George Armstrong. His second choice was George Armstrong. His third choice was George Armstrong. There was no one in junior hockey as good as George Armstrong.

By tonight, Armstrong had been the captain of the Maple Leafs for the last ten years and had turned his derogatory nickname to his own advantage. Twenty years after he'd left his home in Northern Ontario, Armstrong had grown into his nickname. He truly had become the Chief. "The best captain I ever played with," said Marcel Pronovost. "The best captain any club ever had," said Bob Pulford.

. . .

Defence partners Tim Horton and Allan Stanley knew without looking what the other would do tonight — especially, it seemed, against Henri Richard. The first time Richard carried the puck toward the Leafs' blue line, Stanley stepped out, forcing Richard to go between him and the boards. Behind Stanley, Horton squeezed Richard into the boards and knocked him down. A few minutes later, Richard tried again to carry the puck over the Leafs' blue line. This time, Horton left no room for Richard in the middle of the rink. When Richard skated to the outside, Stanley knocked him over. They pulled the same manoeuvres on Yvan Cournoyer, Ralph Backstrom and Jean Beliveau, never allowing a Canadiens player to travel unmolested across the line.

Horton had grown up in Cochrane, a railway town about seventy miles from Ontario's border with northern Quebec. Stanley had grown up a few miles away, in Timmins, where his dad was the fire chief. As a young teenager, Stanley played for a local team called the Holman Pluggers, sponsored by a British company, Holman Brothers Ltd., that made hand drills for underground miners. Stanley left town at seventeen and went to Boston, then to Providence, where he played so much better than anyone else that the New York Rangers acquired his services for the equivalent of ten players' salaries. Stanley might have worked in New York, but his heart was in Northern Ontario, and he still came home in the off-season.

One summer, a former teammate from the Pluggers invited him to come on a fishing trip. The teammate, Bill Barilko, was the son of a chef who worked with mining crews in the nearby bush camps. Like Stanley, Barilko had also become a defenceman in the NHL. Earlier that year, he'd scored the overtime goal that earned the Leafs their fourth Stanley Cup in five seasons. Barilko and Stanley might have played hockey on different NHL teams, but when the season ended, no one could stop them going fishing together.

It was a Friday, and Stanley was working. When he didn't show up, Barilko and another fishing buddy took off without him. They flew in a small floatplane into the woods across the Quebec border. On the return trip, they hit bad weather, and the plane crashed. Lost in the thick woods of Northern Ontario, the wreckage stayed hidden for eleven years. The Leafs brought Tim Horton to Toronto from Cochrane to fill the spot left vacant by Barilko's death. Stanley mourned the loss of his friend and returned to New York to play for the Rangers.

After another seven years, the Leafs acquired Stanley in a trade, and Stanley and Horton became partners. Horton told Stanley that he had bad eyes and couldn't always see a pass in time to reach for it with his stick. Stanley said that didn't matter. As long as Horton placed his stick on the ice, Stanley would make sure that Horton felt his passes when they landed on the tape. "You don't have to see it," Stanley said.

Horton and Stanley had now played together in more than five hundred games. They ate and roomed together when the team travelled to other cities. "Tim and I got to understand each other," Stanley said. "We fit perfectly."

When Henri Richard won the face-off outside the Leafs' blue line, he slid the puck to his right to Leon Rochefort. Rochefort backhanded the puck into the Leafs' end, while Dave Balon chased after it.

The fans recognized Richard as the most menacing of these Montreal forwards, but all three of them could skate, shoot and score goals. Balon and Rochefort had moved together to Montreal, along with the goalie Gump Worsley, in a trade a few years earlier from New York. That year, Balon scored twenty-four goals. Everyone in Montreal assumed he was French, and they pronounced his name as if he should have worn a beret and smoked Gauloises. But Balon was Ukrainian, from Saskatchewan, and his last name rhymed with Malone.

Rochefort had grown up in Cap-de-la-Madeleine, now a suburb of Trois-Rivières, on the St. Lawrence River, about halfway between Montreal and Quebec City, and he'd spoken French all his life. As a teenager, he'd played hockey for a team called the Mad Hatters, sponsored by the Biltmore Hat Company, in Guelph, Ontario, where almost no one spoke French or understood why Rochefort couldn't speak English like everyone else. In Guelph he boarded with Rod Gilbert, the only other French-speaking player on the team. The owners of the house spoke no French, either, so Rochefort and Gilbert taught themselves to speak English using a dictionary and listening to records by the Norman Luboff Choir.

If a player scored three or more goals in a game in Guelph, the company awarded him a new hat. This gave added significance to the term *hat trick*. The phrase was first used in the mid-nineteenth century to describe the dismissal by a bowler in cricket of three consecutive batsmen. Unlike fans in his hometown, the fans in Guelph took the term literally, and it took Rochefort a while to figure out why a player's third goal prompted people in the stands to toss away their hats.

Like Rochefort, Bosey Balon had as much skill as almost every player in the league, but he couldn't hold a steady job in the NHL. He could skate fast, probably because he'd skated against the wind for hours every day, playing with his two brothers on the prairies near his home in Wakaw, Saskatchewan. At sixteen, Balon left the pond to play organized hockey, hitchhiking forty miles to Prince Albert to try out for the junior-league Mintos. In Prince Albert he met a nursing student named Gwen Gillies, who agreed to go out with him for a Coke and then agreed to marry him. "I knew right off the bat that we'd get married," she said. "He's such a kind man."

Balon played well enough to win a spot with the Regina Pats in 1957–58, when the team lost in the Memorial Cup finals to the Hull-Ottawa Canadiens. Both teams belonged to the Montreal Canadiens.

One of his teammates tonight, Terry Harper, had played with Balon for the Memorial Cup. Three of his teammates tonight had played against him: Ralph Backstrom, Bobby Rousseau and Gilles Tremblay. All five players had worked hard to get to the NHL, but the others had earned a more permanent position than Bosey Balon, and no one could quite figure out why, least of all Balon himself.

Unable to find a permanent place on an NHL team, Balon packed his bags, and he and his wife drifted around the minor leagues for three years, first to Vancouver, then to Saskatoon, three games with the Rangers in New York, then back to Vancouver, east to Trois-Rivières, then to Kitchener-Waterloo, back to New York for thirteen more games, to Kitchener-Waterloo again, back to New York, and then, in 1963, to Montreal, a team that seemed to appreciate his speed and aggression. "He fits right into our pattern," Toe Blake said, when Balon arrived.

Balon scored as many goals in his first twenty-one games with the Canadiens as he'd scored in seventy games the year before with the Rangers. He also established himself as a fighter. In a game against Chicago, he decked a brawler named Howie Young with a single punch. The Canadiens relied on Bosey Balon to stand behind the team's lighter, fleet-footed players the way John Ferguson did, especially if Ferguson got a penalty or couldn't play. Two years ago, playing with a cracked ankle, Balon had scored eighteen goals for the Canadiens. But last year it all turned sour, and the magic touch eluded him again. Blake criticized Balon openly. "Balon skates like the wind, is always hustling," he said. "He can get the puck up the ice and lay down a neat pass, but he just can't score."

Unable to rely on Balon to score goals, Blake used him in fewer games, then sent him a thousand miles away to Houston, in the Central Pro League, for nine games. At the end of the season last year, in 1966, Blake brought him back to Montreal and teamed him with Rochefort and Henri Richard for the playoffs. When Balon assisted on the goal that Richard scored to win the Stanley Cup, he figured he'd redeemed himself. But redemption didn't last.

Balon played now as well as any Canadien on the ice. He out-skated, out-passed and out-hustled his opponents. He made two passes to Leon Rochefort that looked as if they'd been guided by a laser beam, one of them from his backhand, the other between his legs, right onto Rochefort's stick.

No matter how well he played, Balon would remain a newcomer in the eyes of Henri Richard. Until last year, Richard had played for more than a decade on a line with his friend Claude Provost. He and Provost had known each other as youngsters growing up in Montreal, and they spent as much time together off the ice as they did at the rink. Now Richard's friend had been replaced by this Ukrainian guy with a French name who didn't speak French, who had come to Montreal from New York and would probably go somewhere else in a year or two.

Unlike Balon, Richard had lived his whole life in Montreal, started playing with the Canadiens twelve years ago, and didn't intend to go anywhere else. He and his wife had never even taken a trip beyond Quebec. Richard had four brothers and three sisters, a mother and a father in the city. All the Richards could play sports well, and they all played in Quebec. One of Richard's brothers had played senior amateur hockey in Quebec City; another had played for the Junior Canadiens in Montreal. Henri's eldest brother, Maurice, was one of the greatest hockey players who ever lived. As a brother, though, Maurice didn't make a big impression on Henri. Growing up, Henri spent more time with Claude Provost than he did with his famous brother. "He was more like an uncle," Henri said.

Henri was only six years old when Maurice Richard first joined the Montreal Canadiens. By the time Henri and his pal Claude Provost joined the team, thirteen years later, Maurice had become a superstar. Henri was a pretty good player himself. But he was so short, he could hardly reach the top shelf of a clothes closet, and he weighed less than a wheelbarrow full of wood chips. No one expected him to survive long in the NHL.

Henri Richard knew better. When he was thirteen, he played Junior B hockey against twenty-year-olds, and he weighed just ninety-five pounds. At fifteen, he moved up to the Montreal Nationales and began playing at the Forum, just like his older brother. Later, playing with the Junior Canadiens, Henri led the league in scoring for two years in a row. One afternoon, more than twelve thousand fans came to Maple Leaf Gardens just to watch him play. By then he'd bulked up to 120 pounds.

Before Henri's first year in the NHL, his older brother thought he would protect him. Then, in training camp, the two brothers collided while playing against each other in a scrimmage. Henri received a six-stitch cut in his head. The Rocket received twelve stitches, and both players had to be carried unconscious on stretchers from the rink. When he woke up, Maurice realized that his little brother could take care of himself. "Nobody has to look out for him," he said.

Henri not only survived in the NHL, he played in the league for twenty years, the last three as captain of the team. With Henri Richard on the team, the Canadiens won the Stanley Cup eleven times.

By tonight's game, Richard had scored more goals against the Leafs than he'd scored against any other team in the league. Earlier this season, against Terry Sawchuk, he'd scored the 250th goal of his career.

Now, as Richard buzzed toward the Leafs' goal, Brian Conacher kicked the skates out from under him. The referee, John Ashley, raised his arm, blew his whistle and ordered Conacher to spend two minutes in the penalty box for interference. Two minutes was more time than Conacher had spent in the game.

The teams had played so far for 150 seconds, and the Canadiens had taken only one good shot at Sawchuk. Over the next 120 seconds, they'd take six more.

Yvan Cournoyer looked forward to a penalty, as long as the other team got it. If the referee called one, Cournoyer would play tonight. Otherwise, he'd just sit at one end of the Canadiens' bench, studying his teammates on the ice and wiggling his toes inside his skate boots to keep his feet warm. Thanks to Brian Conacher, Cournoyer got what he wanted: another chance to play, another chance to score a goal against the Maple Leafs.

"A penalty disrupts the game," said Ken Dryden, "changes its rhythm, and in twenty per cent of the cases, changes its score."

Cournoyer jumped over the boards. So did Jean Beliveau and Dick Duff. Unlike Balon and most other players, Yvan Cournoyer could score goals almost at will. The average player scores one goal in every ten shots that he takes. Cournoyer had begun his second season in the NHL by scoring one goal in every three: twenty-nine shots, nine goals. For some reason, he was especially sharp against the Leafs. This year, he'd scored ten power-play goals against them. Two weeks ago, he'd scored the first goal of this series. Later in the same game, playing with two different linemates, he'd scored the third.

If a power play ever looked as if it would live up to its designation, the Canadiens power play did. It included four forwards and one all-star defenceman, J.C. Tremblay, a left-winger before he'd joined the Canadiens a few years ago. One of the forwards, Bobby Rousseau, stood on the blue line now with Tremblay. Some players said Rousseau had the most accurate slapshot in the NHL. He'd once scored a goal on a penalty shot with a slapshot from the blue line. He could also set up his teammates to score goals. This year, Rousseau had recorded more assists than all but two players in the NHL.

The Canadiens power play included Dick Duff, who'd scored no goals in this series, but who had the capacity to score as fast as anyone on the ice and held an NHL record to prove it. The power play also included the only two players in the history of the NHL, Beliveau and Cournoyer, who'd ever scored three power-play goals in a single game.

Five years before tonight, Duff was playing for the Toronto Maple Leafs and had scored a goal in Chicago that won the team its first Stanley Cup since the days of Bill Barilko, and its first under Punch Imlach. The team had played by then for eleven years without winning a Cup, the longest dry spell in its history. "One of the greatest playoff hockey players I ever coached," said Imlach.

The next year, when the Leafs won it again, Duff played on the starting line in the finals against Detroit. From the opening face-off, he scored not once, but twice, in sixty-eight seconds, faster than anyone had ever scored two goals from the opening face-off of an NHL playoff game.

One of thirteen children, Duff had come to Toronto with his older brother Les from Kirkland Lake to attend St. Mike's and play hockey.

When he finished high school, he could have played junior for one more year, but he won a spot on the Maple Leafs at the age of nineteen and moved directly into the National Hockey League. By tonight, like Henri Richard, Red Kelly, Bob Pulford, Dave Keon, Ron Ellis and Frank Mahovlich, Duff had never played a single game as a professional hockey player in any other league than the NHL.

Imlach's daughter, Marlene, liked Dick Duff better than any other player on her dad's team. For one thing, he was exceptionally handsome. Blue-eyed and blonde-haired, Duff combined the looks of a California surfer with the unassuming raffishness of James Bond. He was also a good guy. A reporter once asked Imlach to name an NHL player whom he would advise his son, Brent, to model himself after. Imlach said, "Jean Beliveau or Dick Duff."

In recognition of his loyalty and his contribution to the Leafs' two Stanley Cups, Punch Imlach traded Dick Duff to New York. When Duff heard the news one gloomy day in February, he sat down in his North Toronto rooming house and wrote an open letter to the *Globe and Mail*. "I came to the Maple Leafs as a boy of 14," he said, "and I leave as a man of 28. May I always carry the highest traditions of St. Michael's College and the Maple Leaf organization with honour." When Imlach's daughter heard the news, she didn't speak to her father for a week.

Less than a year later, Duff was traded again, from New York to the Montreal Canadiens. The Canadiens were going through hard times. They hadn't won a Stanley Cup in several years, hadn't made it to the finals in four. This presented Duff with an opportunity. He'd spent nine years with the Leafs and contributed to two Stanley Cups, and then the team had traded him away. Duff would spend about half as much time with the Canadiens, but he'd help them win twice as many Stanley Cups. By tonight, they'd won two in a row, and Duff hoped to make it three in a row. This one would come at the expense of the team that had sold him to the highest bidder like a few pounds of pork bellies.

So far in this series, though, Toe Blake had left Duff on the bench with Cournoyer, using him only on special occasions. As a result, Duff hadn't scored any goals, and he had only two assists. Duff didn't mind. He'd do anything to win another Stanley Cup for his team, and he'd certainly score if he got the chance. Maybe he'd score now, if Beliveau won the face-off.

Beliveau won the face-off and passed the puck back to J.C. Tremblay. Tremblay and his teammates kept the puck in the Leafs' end until George Armstrong sent it sailing down the ice toward Gump Worsley. Beliveau and Cournoyer skated back together to fetch it, Cournoyer checking his speed so that he didn't get too far ahead of his captain. Dave Keon followed them.

Beliveau and Cournoyer turned in unison and skated the other way, back toward the Leafs' net. Cournoyer accelerated up the ice on legs like pile drivers. Beliveau, who'd started playing for the Canadiens when Cournoyer was ten years old, kept the puck long enough to draw Keon toward him. When Keon poked with his stick toward Beliveau, the Montreal captain slid the puck past him. By the time Keon turned away from Beliveau, Cournoyer had rocketed with the puck into the Leafs' end of the rink.

Two Leafs defencemen, Tim Horton and Allan Stanley, stood in Cournoyer's way. But Cournoyer's linemates couldn't keep up with him and hadn't even crossed the blue line. If he'd passed the puck to one of them, he would have put himself offside. Instead, he fired a low slapshot. Sawchuk stopped the puck with his glove. The crowd breathed a sigh of relief.

A moment later, Horton passed the puck up to George Armstrong. Armstrong took a few gangly strides and prepared to shoot it into the Canadiens' end, but Dick Duff glided up behind him and lifted his stick. Cournoyer swept past, corralled the puck onto his stickblade, drove across the Leafs' blue line and took another slapshot. This time, Sawchuk didn't make the save look so easy. He did the splits, reached out with his catching glove, blocked the shot and let the puck drop to the ice. Then he fell forward and curled himself around it like a boy with his teddy bear. John Ashley blew his whistle.

As the period progressed and Montreal tried and failed to score a goal, the frustration was building in Jean Beliveau. Unable to break free of the close checking of the Maple Leafs and with the Stanley Cup on the line, Beliveau began to lose his self-discipline.

First he raked his padded elbow across Allan Stanley's head, after Stanley pinned him in the corner beside Sawchuk. Two inches lower, and his elbow would have collided with Stanley's nose. John Ashley let him get away with that one. A few minutes later, Beliveau did it again when he and Stanley tangled along the boards outside the Leafs' blue line. This time, as the two players kicked at the puck, Beliveau raised his stick and bounced it off the back of Stanley's head. It didn't look accidental, and the fans yelled their disapproval. Again Ashley let Beliveau get away with it.

Beliveau erupted for a third time, targeting Dave Keon at the end of the rink in front of Eddie Mepham, the goal judge. Shivering on a blue stool behind the net, chewing Chiclets to keep his mouth from going dry and to compensate for the cigarettes that he couldn't smoke on the job, Mepham sat with his knees pressed against the crack in the big gate that swung inward to allow the Zamboni onto the ice. Every time a player collided with the boards behind the net, the gate banged against Mepham's knees. When a two-hundred-pound player like Beliveau started throwing his weight at one-hundred-sixty-pound players like Dave Keon, Eddie Mepham's knees told the tale. When Beliveau scoured the Leafs centre along the boards like an eraser over a pencil mark, Mepham almost jumped off his seat.

The other goal judge, Grant Eason, told Mepham later that Beliveau had looked angry at his end of the rink, too. In the Leafs' end, Eason said,

Beliveau tried to nail Tim Horton's head to the glass with his stick. "If Horton hadn't ducked," Eason said, "he'd still be lying on the ice."

This time, Ashley had seen enough. Even the captain of the Montreal Canadiens couldn't break the rules without eventually paying a price. Ashley gave Beliveau a penalty for cross-checking. It was Beliveau's thirteenth penalty of the playoffs. Considering the way the Leafs took advantage of these occasions, though, the Canadiens could have played with no men on the ice at all. After ten minutes of play, the Leafs had hardly taken any shots, let alone scored any goals. They just couldn't get rolling.

When Toe Blake first became the coach of the Canadiens, a player in the NHL who received a minor penalty had to stay off the ice for two full minutes, no matter how many goals the other team scored. Blake himself had scored more than a few times while an opponent sat in the penalty box. When he became a coach after breaking his ankle so badly he could no longer skate, he passed Montreal's power-play torch to Jean Beliveau. As with every other aspect of the game, Beliveau excelled at power plays.

Other teams in the league wanted to change the rule. Instead of sitting in the penalty box for two minutes, a penalized player should return to the ice after the opposing team scored just one goal. The Canadiens disagreed. Why wouldn't they? With Beliveau on the power play along with Rocket Richard and Dickie Moore, who broke Gordie Howe's record for total points in a season, the Canadiens scored almost every time the other team received a penalty, sometimes more than once. During a power play in a game against the Boston Bruins, Jean Beliveau scored three times in forty-four seconds.

The NHL finally changed the rule after Toe Blake's second season as coach of the Canadiens. That year, in the finals against Montreal, a Detroit Red Wing received a penalty and watched helplessly from the box for two minutes as Jean Beliveau and Rocket Richard scored two goals against his team. The Canadiens won the game, two to one, and won the Stanley Cup for the second consecutive year. The rest of the league decided once and for all to change the rule, whether the Canadiens agreed or not. The penalized player in that game, Marcel Pronovost, was playing tonight for the Leafs. He watched now as Beliveau skated toward the penalty box, wishing perhaps that the league hadn't changed the rule after all. With Beliveau imprisoned for two full minutes, the Leafs might have scored twice, enough to win a close game like this one. As it happened, the Leafs didn't score at all.

Each coach in the game tonight tried to match the other team's players on the ice, strength for strength. If the wrong players faced each other, a good coach could take advantage of the other team's momentary weakness. "Line changes were critical," said Jean Beliveau. "Matching the right players with the opposing team's fast skaters or bruising bodycheckers could make all the difference."

Bobby Hull, who won a Stanley Cup with the Chicago Black Hawks in 1961, said that part of the reason his team never won it again was that "the wrong guys would get out on the ice at the wrong time. That's all it took to lose it in those years."

With 210 seconds left to play in the first period, Ralph Backstrom, the Canadiens centre, glanced toward the bench, expecting Toe Blake to replace him and his linemates. But Blake had just called his power play off the ice, and the Canadiens' next line wasn't ready to go. Blake left Backstrom on the ice with John Ferguson and Claude Larose, both bruising bodycheckers.

Seeing Blake's predicament, Imlach pulled a fast one. Even though they'd been on the ice for only a few seconds, he called the Leafs' bruising bodycheckers to the bench and replaced them with George Armstrong; Frank Mahovlich, the Leafs' highest goal scorer; and Dave Keon, the Leafs' fastest skater.

Within ten seconds, Keon had eluded the Canadiens forwards, carried the puck into their end of the rink and taken a backhand shot at Gump Worsley. Worsley blocked the shot, but he looked shaky.

Laperriere tried to shoot the puck down the ice. The Leafs fired it back into the Canadiens' end. Ferguson chased it around the boards and ended up on the wrong side of the rink.

Within thirty seconds, the Canadiens' forward line was in such disarray that it looked like the aftermath of a traffic accident: all the Montreal players seemed to be drastically out of place. When Backstrom skated past the Canadiens' bench, Blake ordered him off the ice. Jean Beliveau jumped over the boards to take his place.

A moment later, Brent Casselman blew his whistle as the Leafs went offside. With the play stopped, Blake sent Bobby Rousseau and Gilles Tremblay onto the ice to join their linemate, Beliveau. This was the line that Blake wanted to face Keon, Armstrong and Mahovlich.

Once again, though, Imlach pulled a fast one. Keon, Armstrong and Mahovlich had spent only thirty seconds on the ice. Blake expected them to stay there for at least a minute longer. But no sooner did the Canadiens players step onto the ice than Imlach called his forwards to the bench and sent Red Kelly whistling toward the face-off circle to stand in front of Beliveau. And here came Brian Conacher, as well, and Ron Ellis. Blake sensed another traffic accident in the making. The home team in a hockey game gets the last chance before a face-off to change its players on the ice. Toe Blake had no more chances. The Canadiens on the ice were mismatched. There was nothing that he could do about it, but that didn't stop him from trying.

"Richard!" Blake growled.

Henri Richard leapt off the Canadiens' bench, along with his linemates, Dave Balon and Leon Rochefort. Blake wanted these three guys to face Kelly's line. In particular, he wanted Balon on the ice against Conacher. Conacher liked to throw his weight around, and Balon could throw it right back at him.

Blake certainly didn't want Bobby Rousseau to face Conacher. Conacher outweighed Rousseau by twenty-five pounds and towered over him by five inches. Even wearing a helmet, as he did tonight, Rousseau was no match for Conacher. Nor did he want Beliveau to play against Red Kelly.

Kelly played with a deceptively effortless style. Even in high school, he'd played with such grace that people missed half of what he really accomplished. As a junior, no NHL team bothered to offer Kelly a contract until his flashier teammates had already signed one. The Leafs' local scout, Squib Walker, thought Kelly was a no-hoper. Finally, the scout for Detroit asked Kelly to sign with the Red Wings because he thought he might lose his job if he didn't return with the signature of at least one player from Kelly's junior team. Squib Walker bet the Leafs' team doctor a hat that Kelly wouldn't last ten games in the NHL.

By the time Kelly moved from Detroit to Toronto, Walker had lost his hat, and Kelly had lasted in the NHL for more than eight hundred games. The kid with technicolour hair, as a Detroit newspaper described him, played defence so well in Detroit that the children of the team's recently deceased owner convinced the league to create an award named after their dad, the James Norris Memorial Trophy. They wanted the award to honour the NHL's best defenceman so that Red Kelly would receive some recognition for his abilities. By tonight, Kelly had made the NHL's all-star team eight times and would have made it nine times if he hadn't played half a year as a left-winger. As a defenceman, Kelly seldom allowed a team to score against the Red Wings. As a forward during that half-season, he led the league in goals and assists. When it came time to select an all-star team, the league didn't know where to put him.

Since he'd joined the Leafs a few years ago, Kelly hadn't played defence very much, but he was still the highest-scoring defenceman in the NHL, and he was the only NHL player to make the league's all-star team as both a defenceman and a centre. When he first skated onto the ice in Toronto after the Red Wings traded him away, the fans at Maple Leaf Gardens stood up and applauded his arrival for four minutes. "I felt so tight, I nearly burst," Kelly said.

After twenty years in the NHL, Kelly's reputation as a nice guy who lacked a mean streak remained intact. He'd won four Lady Byng Trophies for his gentlemanly play. In the previous forty years, only one Canadien, Toe Blake, had ever won the Lady Byng. Kelly had also won three Stanley

Cups, which required far more than good manners and a cheery disposition. Kelly might have played like a gentleman, but he also played to win — not just at hockey, but at everything he did. "Would you feel disappointed," his wife, Andra, once asked him, when he ran for a seat in Canada's House of Commons, "if you lost the election?" "I don't know how I'd feel," Kelly said. "I've never thought of losing."

As Kelly took up his position at the face-off circle, Jean Beliveau and his linemates skated toward the Canadiens' bench to let Richard's line take their places. But the referee saw what they intended to do. He skated with Beliveau toward the bench, tooted quickly on his whistle, raised his arms and shook his head at Toe Blake. Then he ordered Henri Richard off the ice. "Henri," he said, pointing at the Canadiens' bench, "let's go."

Beliveau returned reluctantly to the ice to face Red Kelly. When the puck dropped, Kelly chased it past Beliveau into the Canadiens' end of the rink and, inadvertently, it seemed, left the captain of the Montreal Canadiens lying on his back.

Beliveau sprang like a gymnast to his feet and followed the play down the ice. When the puck came to him just inside the Leafs' blue line, he took a slapshot that Terry Sawchuk caught with his glove and tossed behind the net. As Marcel Pronovost retrieved it, Beliveau wheeled toward his bench. Henri Richard leapt over the boards onto the ice.

After almost twenty minutes, the soft ice of Maple Leaf Gardens had turned into a swamp. Instead of sliding smoothly, the puck bounced over mounds of snow, tipped onto its edge and rolled erratically. Red Kelly fumbled the puck and left it behind him for Conacher. Unaware of Henri Richard accelerating from his bench toward his right side, Conacher skated toward his blue line. Twice in the period Conacher had knocked Richard off his feet. A few minutes earlier, he'd driven Richard backwards into the boards like a train engine colliding with a rag doll. Now Richard saw his chance to even the score. When the puck skipped on a chunk of loose ice, Conacher looked down at his stickblade. He looked up again just in time to see Richard's shoulder driving like a piston straight into his chest. The collision sent Conacher flying and almost jolted the stick out of his hands. It was the most dramatic bodycheck of the period, executed against a six-foot-three-inch, two-hundred-pound bully by a player who was thirty pounds lighter and eight inches shorter, nicknamed the Pocket Rocket.

Humiliated, Conacher lost his temper. He chased Richard up and down the ice until Larry Hillman froze the puck against the boards behind the Leafs' net. By then, Richard's linemates had joined him on the ice. As Conacher yapped at Richard and threatened to punch his lights out, Bosey Balon stepped in front of Richard. Mess with my teammate, Balon suggested, you mess with me first. With only two minutes left in a scoreless period, Conacher chose discretion over valour. Head down, he glided away from the fracas straight back to the Leafs' bench.

To the extent that their talent distinguished them from other boys their age, hockey players like Dave Balon, Brian Conacher and their teammates received privileges as they grew up that other boys could only dream of. Hardly old enough to drive a car, still too young to legally drink a beer, hockey players who made it to the NHL drew the attention and admiration of adults by the thousands. Anonymous fans deferred to them and asked for their autographs. Even Canada's post office dispensed services to hockey players that it would extend to no one else but Santa Claus. When John Ferguson beat up one of their favourite players, irate fans in New York sent him angry letters addressed to "The Penalty Box, Montreal Forum." Canada's letter carriers delivered every one of them.

They also received special treatment from politicians, judges and police. As a direct result of this sanctioned indulgence, some of the players tonight would remain emotionally immature and suffer without reason; some would find themselves in their mid-thirties still behaving like adolescents at a frat party; at least one of them would die. "Hockey players live in a world of their own," said journalist Peter Gzowski. That world sometimes resembles a fool's paradise, where a man can remain hypnotically unaware of his shortcomings until he steps back through the looking glass and meets them head-on.

For all their accomplishments in sport, at least four players on the ice tonight already suffered from acute anxiety. Frank Mahovlich had sought treatment in hospital for his battered nerves. Ron Ellis would quit hockey temporarily when the game lost its meaning. Gump Worsley suffered from depression. Terry Sawchuk, "a moody man of exuberant peaks and mute hollows," according to the writer Trent Frayne, was haunted by ghosts.

A professional goalie since he was seventeen, Sawchuk found peace only during the sixty minutes of a hockey game, when he stood in front of fifteen thousand screaming fans and used his body to stop pucks travelling toward him at a hundred miles an hour. In the rest of his life, he could never escape from the demons of his own insecurities.

The third son in a Ukrainian household, Sawchuk shared a bed with his older brother Mitch as they grew up amidst the smells of kasha, cabbage rolls, chicken soup and kutya. When Mitch died of heart failure at seventeen, Sawchuk was ten years old. He never forgot his brother's death, no matter how much he drank, how much he ate or how many women he used to distract himself. Hockey became his only refuge. For many years, he wore his late brother's goalie pads, and he played as well as any goalie in the game.

By the time he turned twenty-one, Sawchuk had been voted rookie of the year in three different leagues over three consecutive seasons. Over those years, he perfected his own crouching style of play that enabled him to see the puck more clearly through the maze of players in front of him without leaving his feet. Bent at the waist, with his chin almost touching the tops of his goalie pads, Sawchuk influenced the style of every goalie who came after him, including Patrick Roy, the most successful NHL goalie of all time.

At the beginning of his career, Sawchuk gorged himself on food and beer until he weighed 228 pounds. A few years later, he starved himself with singular intensity until the flesh on his face hung like a chamois on a clothesline. He lost almost one-third of his weight. His five-foot-ten-inch body shrunk to 162 pounds. Throughout the ups and downs, he wondered why he couldn't feel the same undistracted serenity off the ice as he felt when he played in a hockey game. "He constantly needed assurance that he was great," said a coach named Lynn Patrick.

Doctors repaired the collapsed lungs, herniated discs, broken bones, flesh wounds and bruised eyeballs that Sawchuk suffered, but no one ever repaired his broken soul. In the 1950s, he sat out for three games one season because he felt so depressed that he couldn't face an opposing team. A few years later, he took more time off when he thought he was on the brink of a nervous breakdown. A morose, nervous, short-tempered man, as one writer described him, Sawchuk had said at the beginning of this season that he intended to quit the game. Now he was playing against the Montreal Canadiens for the Stanley Cup. Perhaps if he'd stuck to his intention, he'd have lived longer. But how could a man quit a game that brought him the only moments of sustained satisfaction in his life?

A few days earlier, on the day before the fourth game of this series, Sawchuk had left practice just after noon and strolled down Church Street to a bar called the Sapphire. The Leafs were ahead of the Canadiens in the series by two games to one. Punch Imlach had selected Johnny Bower to play in goal in the next game, the following evening. Sawchuk didn't like sitting on the bench, didn't like sharing goaltending duties with anyone else, even Bower. "It's difficult to stay sharp," he explained. It was also hard on the nerves and hard on the ego to sit on the bench and watch another man on the ice getting all the glory.

Sawchuk stayed at the Sapphire for about twelve hours. The next day, the day of the fourth game, he showed up at the Gardens for the morning skate around eleven, hungover and blurry eyed. "He'd had lots of sleep," said Marcel Pronovost with his tongue in his cheek. Assuming he'd just have to strap on his pads that night, sit on the bench and watch Bower play, Sawchuk retreated to his rented motel room around the corner and came back to Maple Leaf Gardens a few hours later to dress for the game. But in the pre-game warm-up, Bower pulled his groin and couldn't stand up in the goal. Dragooned into a game that he didn't expect to play, Sawchuk allowed the Canadiens to score six goals. The Leafs scored two. An irate fan sent Sawchuk a telegram from Nova Scotia asking how much money he'd taken to throw the game. Sawchuk went on the wagon. "I didn't have a good night," he admitted.

He was having a good night tonight, though. Sawchuk had already stopped fifteen shots, including two hard slapshots from Jean Beliveau, a point-blank shot from Leon Rochefort and a couple of deflections from Cournoyer and Larose. Against any other goalie, the Canadiens would have scored at least one goal by now.

With the Leafs controlling the puck and with hardly more than a minute to go in the period, John Ferguson launched himself at Pete Stemkowski as the two players skated near centre ice. Ferguson hit the Leaf with his stick, his gloves, his shoulder, his elbows, his knees and his skates, which were a foot off the ice. Stemkowski weathered the check, but the referee raised his arm to indicate a penalty.

A few years ago, the Boston Bruins' coach, Milt Schmidt, had started calling his team's goalie to the bench when the referee held his arm up to signal his intention of calling a penalty against the Bruins' opponents. As long as the Bruins controlled the puck, the play would continue. But as soon as a player on the opposing team touched the puck, the referee would blow his whistle. The other team couldn't score, even on an empty net, because the referee's whistle would invalidate the goal. So Schmidt removed his team's goalie and replaced him with an additional forward to give the Bruins a brief scoring advantage.

With Ashley waving his arm in the air now, Punch Imlach could have tried that stunt tonight, signalled to Terry Sawchuk to skate to the bench so he could replace him with Mike Walton. But Imlach had never tried the manoeuvre, and he wasn't about to try it now. Within a second or two, the puck drifted into the Canadiens' end of the rink. Ted Harris hovered over it until Ashley blew his whistle and gestured at a scowling Ferguson to leave the ice.

With seventy seconds left in the period, Gump Worsley crouched in the Canadiens' goal and watched Ashley drop the puck. Keon slid the puck cleanly back to the blue line, where Jim Pappin took a slapshot. Worsley blocked the shot with his chest but let the puck ricochet away from him. Laperriere took Keon out of the play, which allowed Mike Walton to collect the rebound unmolested. Mahovlich was standing alone near the post at the far side of the open net. Walton passed, but the puck hit J.C. Tremblay's skate, changed direction, slid between Worsley's legs and hit the goalpost. As Worsley fell on top of the puck, Jim Roberts slammed into Mahovlich. The impact seemed to jar Mahovlich awake. As if he realized that he'd come close to scoring a goal to win the Stanley Cup, Mahovlich shoved back.

Now the Canadiens seemed desperate to prevent the Leafs from scoring. Larry Hillman took a slapshot from the blue line that caromed off Roberts into the corner. Frank Mahovlich shot from six feet in front of Worsley, but Laperriere dropped to the ice and blocked it like a tree limb. Gilles Tremblay finally cleared the puck down the ice. When Keon tried to pass it back to the Canadiens' blue line, Laperriere dove in front of the puck, and Jimmy Roberts held it against the boards until Ashley blew his whistle.

The period ended before the Leafs could take another shot at Worsley, but along with all his teammates, Worsley knew that the damage had been done. The Canadiens had taken seventeen shots at Terry Sawchuk. Sawchuk had stopped them all. The Leafs had taken only eleven shots on Worsley, but they'd also hit the post and come as close as either team in the period to scoring a goal. To make matters worse, Frank Mahovlich was awake now and mad enough to fight. And when the second period began, John Ferguson would have to sit in the penalty box for another fifty seconds.

CHAPTER THREE
First Intermission

The period ended with the sound of a bell. From the stands, the fans erupted like bees from a hive hit by a stick. While the theme from a movie called *Zorba the Greek* thundered through the rafters from Jimmy Holmstrom's Kawai organ, ten thousand men sprang toward the exits, leaving their hats, their topcoats and a few of their wives behind them. They shunted down the painted concrete stairs and into the spartan washrooms, where they wedged themselves between strangers at the trough that ran along three of the cinder-block walls. If they timed it right, they'd still have a few minutes before the intermission ended to stand in another queue, at the concession stand, for two syrupy Cokes and a Shopsy's hot dog that tasted like a mustard-covered novelty worm in an oven mitt.

In the maintenance corridor, a short man in a beige trenchcoat and a black fedora strutted briskly past a couple of hockey nets, stepped over a rubber hose coiled on the floor and slipped out the side door of the Gardens onto Church Street. Stafford Smythe, co-owner of the Leafs, was almost as short as a jockey. At forty-six, he was losing his hair. He had bad teeth and a receding chin, an ulcer and a plague of aches and pains that would have alarmed a man twice his age. His left arm sometimes went numb for no apparent reason.

Under the stands, Doug Moore hopped onto the driver's seat at the back of the Zamboni, turned the ignition switch to start the engine and waited for Al and Diz, dressed like him in dark blue flannel pants and white cardigans, to swing the gates open so he could drive the machine onto the ice in a glory of exhaust fumes. Moore was twenty-eight, had a degree in electrical engineering and studied ice-making the way some men study nuclear physics. His two older buddies had worked at the Gardens since they'd returned to Canada from the war more than twenty years ago with their commanding officer, Conn Smythe, who was Stafford's father.

Under the streetlights outside the Gardens, Stafford Smythe pulled up his collar and walked north through the rain. A few cars passed, their tires spattering over the wet pavement. Even under ordinary circumstances, Smythe worried when he watched his team play, and he often took a walk between periods to calm his nerves. Tonight, Smythe's circumstances were far from ordinary.

If the Leafs lost the game tonight, they'd play the final game of the series in Montreal, where the Canadiens would enjoy the advantage of a home crowd. If the Leafs won tonight, they'd win the Stanley Cup. People would congratulate Smythe because he owned the team. But Punch Imlach would take all the credit for making it work.

In the six seasons since Smythe and his partners had taken over the team, the Leafs had made the finals four times and won the Cup three times, yet Imlach marched around as if the team owed its success entirely to him. He never gave Smythe credit or acknowledged the support he received from the owners, seldom even mentioned their names. Yet Imlach was using players tonight who'd won the Memorial Cup two years in a row with the Toronto Marlboros, and Smythe had managed those teams. Now he and his partners oversaw Imlach, too. Imlach didn't change his socks without Smythe's approval, and he knew it. Without the owners' approval, Red Kelly wouldn't be on the ice tonight. Neither would Marcel Pronovost or Terry Sawchuk. Christ, Sawchuk was keeping them in the game tonight. Imlach would find a way to take credit for that, too. Smythe sometimes wished that he could run the team as general manager. Then he might get some of the accolades that rained down on Imlach. But if the Leafs won tonight, Imlach would keep the manager's job for himself, at least for another year. Even Smythe couldn't take the job away from a guy who'd just won the Stanley Cup.

At Wellesley Street, Smythe turned west and walked past the Orthopaedic and Arthritic Hospital, a five-storey brick building where the team sometimes sent its players to repair their broken bones, twisted knees and bad backs. The doctors there kept Leafs paraphernalia in their offices: hats, jerseys, sticks, calendars, pucks emblazoned with the team's insignia. The souvenirs distinguished them, apparently, from run-of-the-mill doctors. If a sawbones was good enough to minister to Tim Horton's aches and pains, he was good enough for the no-names who cluttered up the rest of his schedule.

The hospital had been built as a sanitarium for tuberculosis patients more than fifty years earlier, before Smythe's father had built the Gardens and assembled the team that played there. In those days, a one-hour hockey game had consisted of two thirty-minute halves. Now, a period lasted for only twenty minutes, and it took three of them to complete a game. The first period tonight had taken much longer than twenty minutes because the referee and linesmen kept blowing their whistles and stopping the clock. Twenty-three times they'd tooted on their little black plastic Acme Thunderers: seven times when a player held the puck against the boards with his skate; five times to call a penalty; four offsides; three saves by Terry Sawchuk when he fell on the puck; two smothering saves by Gump Worsley; one time when the puck went over the boards; and once again when Frank Mahovlich hit linesman Matt Pavelich in the back of the head with the puck and knocked him down. Thirty-five minutes the period had lasted. Smythe had felt so anxious, he'd already left his seat and started through the corridor to the side door before it ended.

Worrying was bad for his health. Smythe knew that. But he couldn't help worrying. That worried him too. He lived with anxiety the way some men live with a backache, which he also had. Most of the time, Smythe worried about money. At the moment, he was swimming in a sea of debt, and he felt uneasy about discrepancies in the finances of Maple Leaf Gardens Ltd. Under the stewardship of Smythe and two partners, the public company owned the building, the team, the jerseys, the sticks, the spare hockey nets and the Zamboni. Every fan who bought a ticket to watch a game at Maple Leaf Gardens put money into the company and its shareholders. And Smythe, along with his partner, was stealing some of that money back as if he owned the company himself.

As his partner Harold Ballard explained it, they weren't really stealing. They controlled the bloody company, didn't they? Why shouldn't Smythe go along with the scam? Ballard was almost twenty years older than Smythe and had the irresistible enthusiasm of ten men. He'd blazed a trail through his life as wide as a four-lane highway and had swept up young Smythe in his wake. As a teenager, Smythe felt flattered by the attention paid to him by such a rambunctious swashbuckler. No one in Smythe's family had ever driven through downtown Toronto the way Ballard did, dressed in his raccoon coat at the wheel of a Stutz Bearcat with three blonde cheerleaders in the back seat. More important, Harold Ballard treated Smythe as if he mattered, gave him the validation that he'd never received from his own father. In the presence of Harold Ballard, Stafford Smythe could be one of the boys, instead of Conn Smythe's boy. Stafford Smythe loved Ballard like a father, but sometimes he wished that his partner would be more discreet.

Smythe's concern about their larceny had less to do with the ethics of the crime than the piss-poor job they'd done to conceal it. Someone might notice the missing money. What would happen if the two of them got caught as they siphoned cash by the bucketful into their own accounts?

Ballard didn't care what people thought of him. Already in his early sixties, he still acted like an irresponsible teenager. But Smythe cared about his reputation.

Harold Ballard loved attention, revelled in his notoriety and didn't give a rat's ass about his reputation. He was a one-man parade, and he welcomed everyone from princesses to prison guards to march along with him. For Ballard, Maple Leaf Gardens was like a comfortable pair of pants. He and Smythe were just moving money from one pocket to the other. That didn't reassure Smythe. He was more calculating than Ballard. Maple Leaf Gardens was a public company. It was one thing to fleece your partners in a private business. What could they do except sue you? With a good lawyer, that could take years. But the government regulated a public company on behalf of its shareholders. The penalties for stealing from a public company were stiff indeed, not to mention the scrutiny that resulted as soon as the newspapers got wind of a potential scandal.

Ballard told Smythe not to get his shorts in a knot. For more than fifteen years, everything that the two men had done together had made money. Their money-spinning talents had even impressed Smythe's father, an accomplishment that Stafford knew he could never have achieved on his own. Now, as the Tweedledum to Ballard's Tweedledee, Smythe had access to power and money. The problem was, he kept spending more than he had. How much longer could they keep their act alive?

Smythe turned south and plodded in his rubber-soled shoes down Yonge Street under the neon signs of the grubby shops until he reached the Westbury Hotel. Except for a couple of pedestrians trying to keep dry under the eaves of the storefronts, the night was quiet. It was a weeknight, after all. People in Toronto stayed home on weeknights, unless they went to a Leafs game.

The two partners had started small, skimming a few bucks here and there from the wads of cash that accumulated in the Gardens box office inside the front doors on Carlton Street. Enough for dinner at Le Baron or Winston's or to pay for a tune-up on the Cadillac. Nothing big. But once they saw how easily they could lift a few bills from the till of a cash-only business, Smythe and Ballard turned as greedy as two kids in an ice-cream factory. When his daughter got married a couple of months ago, Ballard used Gardens money to pay for the limo. The partners took more money to pay contractors to renovate their houses. They even rented an apartment in a new high-rise around the corner on Alexander Street, where Ballard and his cronies took floozies after hockey games, leasing the pad under the name of S.H. Marlie: *S* for Stafford, *H* for Harold. That was Ballard's idea. Over the next few years, Ballard and Smythe would siphon off folding money from the box office and the concession stands, a little bit here, a little bit there, until it all added up to almost $1 million.

Returning to the Gardens along Wood Street, Smythe passed the CBC truck parked on the asphalt pad beside the building. Under the truck, a gas-powered generator droned like a choir of monks. Cables dribbled from a panel on the side of the truck, across the pavement and under the sliding door that led to the building's loading dock. Smythe barely nodded at the attendant who perched on a stool inside the door to stop strangers from sneaking into the building.

Inside, Smythe passed a white Cadillac parked on the loading ramp. The car belonged to Harold Ballard. Who else would drive such a pimp-mobile? Their third partner, John Bassett, an exemplar of patrician discretion, drove a dark grey Buick. Smythe wondered what Bassett would say if he found out that his two partners were plundering the treasury of the very company that he'd helped them buy. Now Smythe made his way under the stands to the ramp where the rink attendants parked the Zamboni and stored their squeegees, shovels, buckets and scrapers. Thirty-five thousand dollars, Smythe thought. That's how much the Zamboni had cost.

Smythe worried about his investment in the Maple Leafs. To buy their controlling share from Smythe's father, the partners had gone into hock to the Bank of Nova Scotia for $2.3 million. Two-and-a-half times cash flow: that was the price they'd paid. The box office at the Gardens collected about $1 million a year in receipts. But Smythe and his partners didn't give a damn about box-office receipts. Fans would always pay to watch the Toronto Maple Leafs, so that money was practically guaranteed. The real money lay elsewhere, in television broadcasts.

Smythe's father had seen the possibilities of selling the game through TV. Clarence Campbell hadn't, and he was still the NHL's president. Campbell regarded TV as a threat. He figured people would stop buying tickets to the games if they could watch them for nothing at home. But Campbell took his marching orders from the owners, and most of them couldn't wait to get their hands on the money that TV would bring. In Toronto, the three owners of the Maple Leafs figured they could make as much money in a year selling advertising rights to hockey broadcasts as they made from ten years of box-office receipts. With expansion next year, that bonanza would get even richer.

Smythe looked through the open gates to the ice surface. Musical notes bobbed like bubbles on the hubbub from the crowd, as if the organ was underwater. He recognized the tune of "Lara's Theme" from that movie that his wife liked, *Doctor Zhivago*. On the ice, Doug Moore had already completed two trips on the Zamboni around the perimeter of the rink and was just crossing the blue line where Frank Mahovlich had hit the linesman in the back of the head with the puck in the first period. Smythe regretted that he and Ballard had caved in to public sentiment instead of unloading Mahovlich while he still had some value. The partners could have used a million dollars to pay down their $2-million debt to Conn Smythe. Though Stafford would never admit it, he agreed with Imlach, at least when the discussion turned to Frank Mahovlich: the Big M had seen better days.

What difference would it make if they'd sold him? Would people have stopped coming to the games? Not bloody likely. The way to make money in this business was to pay as little as possible in overhead and salaries, sell as many tickets as you could, pump up your concession prices and drive a hard bargain with advertisers. Companies would pay millions to get their messages onto televised broadcasts of hockey games, especially Leafs games. In that context, how much was a single player worth?

Smythe did the math as he walked under the stands toward the Leafs' dressing room. No player in tonight's game had skated for more than sixty seconds without hearing the sound of a whistle. In the entire twenty minutes of play, the forwards had skated for an average of only six minutes apiece. Four players hadn't skated at all, but spent the period on the bench. One Montreal Canadien, Jean-Guy Talbot, had skated for less than thirty seconds. Only the two goalies had stayed on the ice throughout the period. For this, the players in the game tonight got paid an average of $14,000 a season. The Leafs had a payroll of almost $300,000, earned by twenty men who spent no more than half an hour a night, three nights a week, performing physical labour, and they worked for only seven months of the year. The rest of the time, they sat on their duffs and watched the game along with the rest of the paying public. Who were the real thieves, Smythe wondered: the owners of the team or the players who took their money?

Smythe and his partners had already pared their overheads by about a third, mainly by dismissing the slackers and dimwits who'd worked for years on the Gardens payroll as rink attendants, ushers, pop-stand clerks and ticket takers. Dozens of them, mostly military veterans of Vimy, Passchendaele, Ypres and the Somme, all pulling in a paycheque that came directly out of the shareholders' pockets. Everyone who worked at the Gardens seemed to be related, like one big family. The announcer was the son of the sound man. The TV announcer, Bill Hewitt, was the son of the radio announcer, Foster Hewitt, whose own father, William, had been the first events manager at the Gardens when it opened, in 1931. Two of the rink attendants were brothers of a former Leafs goalie, Turk Broda. The penalty timekeeper was a former player. All of them relied on the Gardens to supply them with a white shirt, blue tie, dark blue pants and white cardigan with a Leafs insignia on the chest. In return they took orders from the owner and kept the facilities spic and span. In the days of Conn

Smythe, people said you could eat off the floor in Maple Leaf Gardens. "Who eats off the floor?" said Ballard. "It's a fucking hockey rink."

So the partners began to lower their standards. They dropped employees or didn't replace the ones who left voluntarily. They put less syrup and more water in the soft drinks and salted the popcorn so much that fans needed to drink pop by the gallon to quench their thirst. On the ice-maintenance crew, they'd replaced about six guys with one: Doug Moore. Harold Ballard had hired the kid. Moore had been a goalie like Broda, drafted by the Chicago Black Hawks. But Moore had an education, which gave him other options besides hockey, and he'd never played pro. Now he drove the Zamboni and advised the owners on getting the most from the pipes, compressors, gizmos and doodads involved in making ice.

Thank God for the Zamboni, Smythe thought as he watched the machine lay a strip of water down the centre of the rink. As a kid, Smythe had helped out on the ice crew at the Gardens, clearing snow with a wide shovel, then flooding the ice from a reclining steel drum on a four-wheeled chassis that he pushed around the rink like a baby carriage.

Smythe was in his mid-thirties when the Montreal Canadiens started using an automated ice-flooding machine. It was one of the first in Canada. It appeared for the first time in a game when the Leafs were playing the Canadiens at the Montreal Forum. Everyone thought the Canadiens' management had gone nuts, driving a truck around the ice. Why take a chance on new technology, especially when it cost money and came from a foreign country? Hockey was a Canadian game, after all. What did an Italian ice manufacturer from California know about it? Frank Zamboni had spent most of his working life making ice to keep milk cold for dairy farmers in the Hollywood Hills. He'd sold his first machine to a figure skater named Sonja Henie, who lugged it from town to town as she toured the United States with her ice show. Even after they'd seen the beast in action, NHL owners remained skeptical. A bunch of movie starlets dressed up as snowflakes didn't put the same demands on a skating rink as a team of professional hockey players from Canada.

But Smythe's father saw what the Zamboni could do: once the Canadiens started using a Zamboni, the team won the Stanley Cup for five consecutive years. Whether or not the machine had anything to do with the team's success, almost every skating rink in Canada now had one.

He also saw how much money he could save, and he didn't hesitate to buy one for himself. The tractor-like machine did the job of ten men. And unlike Diz, Bernie, Lou and the crew of semi-literate army veterans who'd once scraped and flooded the ice, the Zamboni moved at nine miles an hour, didn't get sick, didn't stop for a smoke break and finished the entire job in ten minutes. With one man at the wheel, it cleaned and scraped the surface, removed the snow and slush and laid down a thin sheet of water in ten-foot strips that froze as hard and smooth as a windswept pond on a cold December morning.

Unlike a pond, which answered only to Mother Nature, the ice in Maple Leaf Gardens or any other NHL arena could be monitored for texture, hardness and durability. By adjusting the temperature and the flow of the brine that ran through ten miles of piping below the concrete pad of the arena floor, an engineer could make the ice harder, softer, stickier or smoother, all with the flick of a switch and the twiddle of a dial. The ice itself was less than an inch thick.

With his engineer's approach to machinery, Doug Moore paid special attention to the technology that kept the ice at Maple Leaf Gardens in good condition from September to May, and he'd welcomed the chance to drive the Zamboni. He'd also helped the owners of the Gardens cram as many events into their building as they could. He showed them how they could remove the boards on a Monday, cover the ice with wooden flooring and accommodate six thousand visitors to an auto show or a Shriners convention, then put the rink back together again on Tuesday and flood the ice in time for a hockey game that night.

Moore felt that he had a tradition to uphold. In the early days of the NHL, Toronto had been the only city in the league with artificial ice. Moore had marveled at the old ice-making technology. It wasn't much more advanced than the equipment used in the world's first artificial-ice rink, built in London, England, in 1876. In North America, Canadian hockey players went to Pittsburgh to extend their seasons and make more money playing on artificial ice at Duquesne Gardens. In Canada, the first hockey arenas with artificial ice were built in Vancouver and Victoria, by a family of lumber barons named the Patricks, who started the Pacific Coast Hockey Association in 1911.

That was long before Stafford Smythe's time, but even he could remember when teams played on the same ice from the beginning of a game to the end. In those days, attendants might have shoveled the snow off the ice between periods, but if they'd tried to flood the ice during a game, the players would have needed rubber boots, not skates.

By the time NHL owners decided to flood the ice between periods, Smythe was eighteen years old. Jack Adams, the general manager of the Detroit Red Wings, had come back from a trip to Europe with a bag full of miniature Eiffel Towers and a recipe on a piece of paper for making water freeze quickly on top of artificial ice. In a restaurant in Paris, Adams had seen a curling demonstration, during which attendants swept the ice with sheepskin brushes, then flooded it for the next show. When Adams returned to Detroit, he convinced all the teams in the NHL that they could improve the game if they followed the restaurant's example.

The improvements, of course, helped NHL owners make more money. The more efficiently they could make artificial ice, the more games they could schedule in a season. More games meant more ticket sales. At the turn of the nineteenth century, a season lasted from January to March. Now, with artificial ice, it extended over eight months, if you counted exhibition games.

Smythe felt lucky to have a kid like Doug Moore on his staff to keep the ice in good shape. Some owners weren't so lucky. Chicago, for example, had bad ice. So did New York. Bad ice not only irritated the players, it could also cause injuries, jeopardizing an owner's investment. Tim Horton had broken his leg after catching his blade in a rut in Madison Square

Garden. Henri Richard broke his ankle when he caught his skateblade in a crevice beside the boards. Dave Keon injured his knee when he caught his skate in a crack in the ice.

As far as Smythe was concerned, the Zamboni was the best $35,000 that his father had ever spent. An investment in ice-making technology put at least as much money into an owner's pocket as the escalators that carried fans into the cheap seats of the Gardens or the new clock above centre ice that the owners had installed this year to replace the four-sided Sportimer. You had to spend money to make money, Smythe thought, as he passed the corridor that led to the Leafs' dressing room. This was show business, and an owner had to keep pace with the times. So did the manager, he thought, when he spotted Punch Imlach pacing the hallway.

Imlach was only three years older than Smythe, but he sometimes seemed as hide-bound, self-centred and conservative as Smythe's father. If he could only get Imlach out of the way, Smythe and his partner Ballard would show this city what an NHL hockey team could really do.

If Smythe ran the team, his company would save about $20,000 a year by eliminating Imlach's salary, and the Leafs might join the swinging sixties before the decade ended. And when the Leafs won another Stanley Cup, maybe Smythe would finally get some credit, as well.

Punch Imlach paced in his brown suede Hush Puppies up and down the painted concrete corridor, sipping coffee from a paper cup and muttering to himself. He wore thick wool socks to keep his feet warm. He passed the blue door of the Leafs' dressing room, to his right. To his left, the Canadiens had disappeared into the visitors' dressing room. In an unused equipment room farther along the corridor, two commentators named Frank Selke Jr. and Bob Goldham discussed the previous period in front of a bank of bright lights and a tripod-mounted television camera as big as a V8 engine. "I've never seen Terry Sawchuk's left hand going any better," said Goldham.

Imlach had first set foot in this arena as a 120-pound teenager, more than thirty years ago. Known then as just plain George, he'd humped his hockey bag on the streetcar before dawn from his parents' house in the east end of Toronto to try out for a local junior team called the Young Rangers. When he made the team, his father, a disgruntled two-hundred-pound Presbyterian Scot, said it was too bad his son had chosen to play hockey. Imlach's father had coached a local soccer team, Ulster United, to the Connaught Cup, Canada's national amateur championship. He wanted his son to play soccer, too, although he doubted that a scrawny kid like George would amount to much in any sport. Imlach's father had crippled himself in an accident as a yardman at the Toronto Transit Commission's stables on Eastern Avenue. After that, he became even more taciturn and more demanding of his diminutive son. Comparing him to the brawny lads who played for his soccer team, Imlach senior pushed George to play beyond his weight and push himself beyond his limits. But no matter how hard he worked, Imlach always seemed to fall short of his father's expectations. He could do better, his father said. Life wouldn't hand him a living on a silver platter. So far, his father had been right. No one had done George any favours to get him where he was today. He'd worked for everything he had, and he still did. No one else had given him any help, and he didn't go out of his way to help anyone else, including his team's players. "A real queer kind of guy," Frank Mahovlich said.

Born in Toronto around the same time as the first indoor artificial-ice rinks arrived in the city, in 1918, George had taken violin lessons as a child and could still play a passable version of "Twinkle, Twinkle Little Star" on the instrument that he kept in the hall closet at home in Scarborough. After high school, he took a job in a neighbourhood bank and started playing senior hockey in his spare time with the Toronto Goodyears, sponsored by the tire company. In his later years, he claimed that he'd acquired the nickname Punch during a game in Windsor, when he collided with another player, fell unconscious to the ice and woke up "wanting to fight everybody on the ice," he said, including his own teammates and the team's trainer, who tried to help him to his feet. After that, he said, his teammates called him Punchy—Punch for short.

With its elements of violence, anger, stoicism and endurance, the story gave Imlach all the attributes that his father would have admired in a man and that Imlach still looked for in a hockey player. But there was a more prosaic explanation for the nickname. With his sabre-shaped nose, prominent chin, protuberant eyes, glabrous cheeks and bald head under a battered fedora, Imlach resembled the hunchbacked male puppet from the Punch and Judy shows, which were still popular in Toronto in the 1930s.

Imlach paced back down the corridor. He'd give his players time to themselves in the dressing room. They were adults, most of them. They knew what they had to do to win the game tonight. An all-star NHL defenceman named Harry Howell once said, "You've got to be a psychiatrist to be a coach." Between periods, Imlach allowed his inmates to run the asylum.

A producer from MacLaren Advertising stood beside the camera, muttering into a headset that connected him, via a black cable snaking along the wall, to the CBC truck. The producer wore bell-bottomed corduroy pants and a gold turtleneck, and his moustache and sideburns ran in a continuous furry strip from one ear to the other like an ill-fitting chinstrap. The ad agency that employed him had owned the broadcasting rights to Maple Leaf hockey games for forty-five years, ever since Jack MacLaren and Conn Smythe had shaken hands to clinch the deal during a golf game at Big Bay Point Golf and Country Club, near Smythe's cottage on Lake Simcoe.

A gaggle of executives watched the commentators from the shadows around the perimeter of the room. Dressed in blue suits, white shirts and striped rep ties, the executives worked for the ad agency and for Molson and Imperial Oil, the companies that had paid MacLaren to insert their advertisements into tonight's broadcast. Through MacLaren, the companies also paid the interviewers, their guests and the CBC to broadcast the intermission show. During the game, all of them sat behind the Leafs' bench in the two rows of seats that MacLaren had owned for years. The way they strutted and puffed out their chests when they swaggered down to watch the intermission, you'd think the real show was not on the ice but here, under the stands, in front of those bright lights.

The producer looked at his watch, then held up his hand and signalled to announcer Ward Cornell to wrap up his interview with a sports reporter from Los Angeles. A former schoolteacher and radio actor, Cornell had worked full-time until this year as the manager of a radio station in London, Ontario, commuting to Toronto for his part-time Saturday-night gig as an intermission host on the Leafs games.

Cornell got the message. A commercial for Molson Export, "The Big Ale in the Big Land," was scheduled to air in ten seconds.

Imlach tried to ignore the camera, the beatnik in the sideburns and the money men in the sleek suits. They all had their jobs to do. He had his. In fact, he had two, for he was the general manager of the Leafs as well as their coach. Like a corporate president whose shareholders pressured him to plan for the next decade while generating a profit every week, Imlach knew he had to win games to make money. Hardly a day passed when the owners didn't remind him of their expectations and his obligation to meet them. Imlach could handle the bombast of Harold Ballard, and he could reason with John Bassett. But Stafford Smythe was a different story, and Imlach had just seen him step across the cables on the concrete floor at the end of the corridor.

Smythe not only wanted a profitable and winning team, he also wanted Imlach's job and the reputation that came with it, and sometimes Imlach felt tempted to let him have it. See how Smythe liked managing a team of bull-headed hockey players while answering to a bunch of owners who thought they knew more than he did about the game, all for $20,000 a year, a company car and a spot to park it behind the Gardens. But Imlach also knew that if he ever gave up the manager's job and stuck to coaching, he'd lose his advantage. Coaches in this league were like players: a dime a dozen. As soon as the Leafs hit a losing streak, Imlach would have no job at all.

When the Second World War began, Imlach had left his job in the bank and enlisted in the Canadian army. He was in his mid-twenties, married to Dodo, short for Dorothy, whom he'd met at the curling club up the street from the bank. In the army, he served his time in Canada, as a player and coach with the country's military hockey teams. When the war ended, the Detroit Red Wings invited him to their training camp, but by then Imlach was almost thirty, overweight and married, with a child on the way. He accepted a job instead with Anglo-Canadian Pulp & Paper and moved with Dodo to Quebec City. For $135 a week, Imlach followed a similar routine to the one he'd left behind in Toronto before the war, working by day as an accounting clerk in the company's office and playing in his spare time for the company's hockey team, the Aces, an abbreviation of "Anglo-Canadian Employees." After a few years as a player, Imlach became the team's coach, general manager and vice-president. By then, the Imlachs had spent eleven years within an English-speaking enclave in a French-speaking province. With two children now, George could have stayed with the company for the next twenty years until he collected a pension.

Imlach didn't go far as a company accounting clerk. But as coach and general manager of the Aces, he did his job so well that he was voted minor-league executive of the year. It didn't hurt that the team's lineup included a tough forward named Jean-Guy Talbot, now finishing his twelfth year with the Montreal Canadiens, or a gangly kid named Jean Beliveau, the best young player in the country. "Play well for Punch," said Beliveau, "and he'll never forget you."

Not that anyone ever forgot Beliveau. In Quebec City, fans packed the rink to see him play. Imlach tried to discourage him from leaving the team. "You'll never reach your potential," he said. "The National Hockey League isn't good enough to bring it out."

Imlach had a good reason to keep Beliveau in Quebec City. He wanted to buy a piece of the team, and Beliveau was good for the box office. With the departure of the Aces' star player, Imlach and a few friends bought the team at a discount. It was still a good investment, "but the big profit years had been the ones when Beliveau was playing," he said. More recently, Imlach had also bought a share of the Leafs' farm team in Rochester, the Americans. One of Imlach's friends from Quebec, Joe Crozier, now coached that team. Three days ago, the Americans had lost to the Pittsburgh Hornets in the finals for the league championship. The team had played its final games in front of sell-out crowds. That put a few extra dollars in Imlach's pocket. The Americans might have done even better if Imlach had left Mike Walton and Jim Pappin in Rochester, where they'd started the year. But they'd both threatened to quit if he did that, so he'd reluctantly brought them to Toronto.

Imlach did well with the Aces, but he knew that he had to move to the NHL to prove himself in the world of hockey. He did it the same way he'd done everything else, through hard work and a little skulduggery. At the age of forty, when many men began thinking about paying off the mortgage, Imlach moved his family to Springfield, in western Massachusetts, where the Boston Bruins hired him to coach their farm team, the Indians. The Indians played in the American Hockey League, a step up from the Quebec league in which the Aces played. To make sure he could operate the team in his own way, Imlach took the general manager's job, as well. It didn't make much difference, though. The Indians under Imlach finished out of the playoffs, in last place, more than thirty points behind the Rochester Americans. While the Indians packed their bags and went home to their off-season jobs, the Americans went all the way to the league finals. Based on the Americans' performance, the Leafs promoted the coach of the team, Billy Reay, to work in Toronto.

The Leafs needed all the help they could get in 1957. They'd finished out of the playoffs the year before and looked doomed to a dismal season again. When they finished last under Reay's coaching, the Leafs hired two assistant general managers. Punch Imlach was one of them. The other was King Clancy. As the team faltered over the opening few weeks under Billy Reay, Imlach seized the opportunity to promote himself to the honchos who ran the team. They elevated him to general manager. In his new position, Imlach took about thirty seconds to make his first big decision. He fired Billy Reay and took over the coach's job himself. Just as he'd done in Quebec and Springfield, Imlach had manoeuvred himself into the two most important jobs on the team. The Leafs finished the season in fourth place and lost in the Stanley Cup finals to the Montreal Canadiens, four games to one. If Stafford Smythe wanted to dislodge him now, he thought, he'd have to do it with a fucking crowbar.

In the Leafs' dressing room, Pete Stemkowski took a quick nibble from the hunk of kolbassa that he'd hidden on the shelf under his scarf. Punch Imlach took a dim view of players who ate solid food during a game. But Stemkowski's mom had sent the Polish sausage from her favourite deli in Winnipeg. Maybe it would bring good luck.

Allan Stanley glanced at Terry Sawchuk and said, "Nice going, Terry," but the goalie just stared at the tops of his pads and didn't look up.

With his jersey off, George Armstrong stood up and headed to the washroom. Johnny Bower followed him, tromping across the rubber mat in his goalie pads.

Side by side against the far wall, Red Kelly and Tim Horton leaned back and closed their eyes. Dave Keon tried to relax, but he didn't want to relax too much in case he lost his edge, so he fidgeted instead, leaned forward, unlaced his skates, sat back, stood up, checked the blade of his stick, grabbed an orange slice, sat down again, sucked on the orange, threw the peel across the room toward the trash bin outside the washroom door.

Now Marcel Pronovost followed Bower and Armstrong into the washroom. The three players stood together under the ceiling vent, passing a cigarette between them and waiting for Bob Pulford to come through the door and bum a smoke. When he did, Bower said, "Here, take mine," and handed him the half-finished Export Plain.

...

When the period ended and George Armstrong headed down the corridor to the dressing room, a guy in the stands yelled at him, "Nice going, Chief!" Armstrong let the words roll over him. He wondered if the guy used the nickname because of Armstrong's aboriginal heritage or because he really was a chief, an honour conferred on him by a native band back in 1950.

That was the trouble with being an aboriginal in this league, or in Canada, for that matter. No one knew any better. Over the years, people had suggested to Armstrong that he should take a more prominent stand on behalf of native people. As captain of the Toronto Maple Leafs, he should use his fame to draw attention to the poverty, despair and neglect that had settled for decades like a shroud over Canada's native cultures.

Like most players in the NHL, though, Armstrong had no interest in fighting political battles, not in public, anyway. He wasn't like his teammate Red Kelly, who'd run for Parliament a couple of years earlier and sat in the House of Commons as an MP. Kelly hadn't been elected on the ethnic ticket to stand up for the Irish Catholics of the nation. He'd been elected because he played hockey for the Toronto Maple Leafs. That's all Armstrong wanted to do: play his best to make a living and stay in the NHL.

In the NHL, men who stuck their necks out usually lost their jobs. It was one thing to run for Parliament. You didn't have to rock the boat to become a politician in Canada. Even Conn Smythe had supported Kelly's decision to become an MP, although they disagreed politically about pressing issues of the day, like the design of the Canadian flag. But if you stepped outside the officially sanctioned political circle, stood up for your rights, formed a union, spoke out against bigotry and racism, then you paid the price. Smythe and every other owner in the NHL made sure of it.

Look at Jimmy Thomson, Armstrong's teammate back in the 1950s. Captain of the Leafs at one time, played about seven hundred games for the team over twelve years. Then Thomson decided that players should get more than forty bucks a game for risking their lives to line the owners' pockets. He organized the Leafs players into a union or an association or whatever he called it, and that was the end of Jimmy Thomson as a Maple

Leaf. "A traitor and a quisling," Conn Smythe called him after he sold him to Chicago.

The same thing happened to another of Armstrong's former teammates, a guy named Tod Sloan: played in Toronto for eight years, scored thirty-seven goals one year, thirty-one another, ranked by sports writers the second-best centre in the NHL behind Jean Beliveau. But as soon as Smythe heard that Sloan supported a union, he was gone, too, to Chicago.

Armstrong didn't want to play in Chicago. He had kids in school, a family to support, a house in Leaside. What good would it do for anyone if he spoke his mind in public? As far as he was concerned, Thomson, Sloan and the rest of those guys hadn't accomplished anything. Give me one example of anything that's changed in the last fifteen years, he'd say. Even Davey Keon agreed with him, and he was Sloan's cousin, for crying out loud. Let's just play hockey, Armstrong thought. Someone else can solve the world's problems.

Still, it rankled when some jerk called him Chief or when he read newspaper stories that said the NHL represented Canadian culture at its best. "In hockey, no one worries about religion or race," said one reporter in 1961. "Hockey is a melting pot of nationalities." "Hockey cuts across language, race, age and distance," burbled another writer, Bruce Hutchison, "our only truly national expression."

When Armstrong read that, he wondered if he and the reporters lived on the same planet. If hockey represented the best of our nation, he thought, then Canada has a long way to go. Like the men who ran the country, the men who ran the game didn't tolerate anyone who bucked the party line or deviated from the status quo. Armstrong could count on one hand the number of aboriginals who'd even come close to playing in the NHL, and it sure wasn't for lack of effort. Freddie Sasakamoose, from the Whitefish Reserve in Saskatchewan, learned to skate on a pond, played with broken sticks held together with nails and tape, and used rocks and frozen apples for pucks. Another Saskatchewan native, named Ron Ratte, played for his residential school's team, he said, because hockey players got better food.

Yet miracles did happen. Against the odds, Freddie Sasakamoose made it as far as the Chicago Black Hawks one year and played his first NHL game against Armstrong's team at Maple Leaf Gardens, but he walked away when his wife said she didn't want to move to the big city. Who could blame her? Even a player like Armstrong had a tough time in the NHL, with boneheads calling him Tonto, Hawkeye and Chingachgook, and he wasn't even a Treaty Indian.

As a Maple Leaf, Armstrong had spent a few summers visiting reserves around the country for the federal Department of Lands and Forests. Part Algonquin on his mother's side, he'd been an honorary chief of the Stoneys in Alberta since 1950, when the Senior Toronto Marlboros won the Canadian championship. "I'm proud to be an Indian," he said before his induction into the Indian Hall of Fame in Brantford, "and if the youngsters can identify with me in this regard, that's great."

Armstrong bristled, though, when he thought about black players like the Carnegies or Manny McIntyre. Herb Carnegie had been as good as any player in the league when he played for a Quebec senior team in Sherbrooke. He'd played later with Jean Beliveau for the Aces, under Punch Imlach, but he was ten years older than Beliveau. Beliveau was on his way up by then. Carnegie was on his way out.

Every team in the NHL had had a chance over those years to take Herb Carnegie. His brother Ossie was pretty good, too. The New York Rangers invited Herb to their training camp but made it obvious from the first day that he didn't fit their plans. He ate by himself, dressed by himself, separated for most of the time from the other seventy-five players trying to make the team, all of them white except Carnegie. "Comical," Carnegie said.

He'd played senior hockey in the backyard of the Montreal Canadiens, but they'd ignored him. The Maple Leafs could have had him, too, and they knew how good he was. "I'd pay $10,000," said Conn Smythe, "to the man who can turn Herb Carnegie white."

Smythe thought he was being witty, and most of the hockey reporters in the league went along with him. "Why are there no Negro skaters in the

National Hockey League?" asked Stan Fischler in the *Sporting News*. "The answer is amazingly simple. There are very few Negroes in Canada." No one wrote back that Fischler was full of crap. No one said anything at all.

"With Herbie being black, we wouldn't have been able to put him in the same hotels with the rest of the team and have him eat at the same restaurants," said Red Storey, who played against the Carnegies before he became an NHL referee. In the States, Storey said, people might have stayed away from games if a black man had participated, and the NHL couldn't afford to lose fans.

So that was that: ignore a talented black man so you don't lose ticket sales to racist bigots in the United States. Even to Armstrong, it didn't seem right. Where was the NHL's answer to Jackie Robinson? Armstrong wondered. A baseball executive named Branch Rickey took the risk of employing a black man in baseball with the Brooklyn Dodgers. Armstrong would have felt prouder of his own team if Conn Smythe had taken a similar stand with the Toronto Maple Leafs. Before he became the first black player in major-league baseball, Robinson had spent a season in Montreal with the Royals, partly owned by the father of Pierre Trudeau, Lester Pearson's justice minister. Even in Montreal, Robinson had met with bigotry. French people should have known better, Armstrong thought. At the very least they should have understood how it felt to ride at the back of the bus. The Montreal Canadiens, les Habitants, employed more English-speaking players than French. Did anyone believe that was because there weren't enough good hockey players in Quebec?

"If he weren't a negro, he'd be playing for the Leafs," Conn Smythe said of Herb Carnegie. When it came to giving everyone a fair shake, that was about as much risk as Smythe would take.

Smythe didn't even like to let black men into Maple Leaf Gardens, let alone hire them to play for his team. A year before tonight's game, he'd quit as a director of Maple Leaf Gardens Ltd. and sold his remaining shares when his son and the other new owners staged a heavyweight championship fight between George Chuvalo and a black man named Muhammad Ali. Local luminaries in the sports media like Milt Dunnell,

Annis Stukus and Dick Beddoes joined the chorus against the black anti-war boxing champion of the world. "Anyone who buys a ticket will be making a contribution to the Black Muslims," said Dunnell.

The USA was different, these people said. It had a problem with the coloureds. But there was no racism in Canada, they said. And the funny thing was, the victims of racism went along with the myth. Instead of offending public sentiment and defying the bigots, blacks in Canada formed their own hockey organization, creating the Coloured Hockey League in the Maritimes long before the Americans formed the Negro American and Negro National baseball leagues, and long before the NHL came along. But unlike the Americans, no one went any further. They just put up with the status quo, as if it had been ordained by God or the Queen. What's good for Canada is good for the NHL, as well. You just don't buck the system. If a black player wants to play hockey in the NHL, he can go to an American city, not a Canadian one, like Willie O'Ree, who'd played for Boston in the 1950s.

Now it was 1967, and times apparently were changing. Even Syl Apps said so. Another former Leafs player who'd become an officially sanctioned politician in Ottawa, Apps chaired a parliamentary committee on youth. Apps had said recently in an interview that a neighbourhood in Toronto called Yorkville, which attracted crowds of long-haired, marijuana-smoking hippies, was "a festering sore on the face of the city."

Regardless of Apps's opinion, teenagers were challenging their teachers, women were demanding equal access to jobs on the police force, soldiers were questioning the authority of their governments to send them to war and minorities were defying their status as second-class citizens. But most hockey players didn't pay much attention to the world beyond the rink, and neither did their wives. When someone told her about a riot at a university in Montreal called Sir George Williams, Karen Pappin was surprised. "I guess these problems are universal," she said.

But hockey players couldn't ignore the changes that affected them directly. How could you ignore Mike Walton? He showed up for training camp with sideburns and challenged Punch Imlach to send him home.

Tim Horton had let his daughters convince him to grow his hair. "I looked about eighty," said Horton, who'd worn a crewcut for most of his life.

Haircuts were one thing. No one in the NHL had gone so far as a baseball player named Curt Flood. Flood had challenged a clause in a player's contract that allowed a team's owner to decide where the player could go to make a living from his sport, even after the contract expired.

The same conditions prevailed in the NHL. The Maple Leafs had owned the rights to Armstrong as a hockey player from the time he signed a contract called a C Form in Falconbridge when he was fourteen. The team still owned those rights tonight. Armstrong couldn't make a move without the team's permission. Either Armstrong did what the team told him to do, or he lost his job as a professional hockey player.

Armstrong didn't care. He'd felt flattered when the Leafs had first signed him as a boy. From then on, he didn't have to make many decisions. He just had to play hockey. The team would take care of everything else. In fact, he wished his teammates would see things his way. If they wanted to make changes, let them do it in private. He'd act as the mediator. That was his job as captain of the team.

Armstrong felt his allegiances torn, though, when he had to act as a go-between, with players agitating for an association, and Stafford Smythe and the other owners telling them to go fuck themselves. After all, Armstrong was a player, too, but he was also a shareholder in Maple Leaf Gardens. The shares that Conn Smythe had given him almost twenty years ago were worth a lot of money, and a players' association might compromise their value.

Other players stood firmly against the owners and all their privileges. "The owners sit in their offices and play chess with players' lives," said a former Leafs defenceman named Carl Brewer. Brewer, of course, was no longer playing for the team. If he was, Armstrong thought, he wouldn't have lasted long, not with that kind of mouth.

Hockey players had opinions just like everybody else, but it was best to keep them to yourself. A player named Andy Bathgate, whose deliberate slapshot to the side of Jacques Plante's head prompted the Montreal goalie to start wearing a mask, ratted on Gordie Howe in a U.S. men's magazine called *True*, accusing the NHL's most famous player of deliberately injuring his opponents and calling him "a recognized master of high sticking [who'd] carved his signature on [many players'] faces." For his candour, the league fined Bathgate $500, about twenty per cent of his annual income, and fined his team's manager $100 for letting his player put his name on the story. The next year, the Rangers made Bathgate captain of the team. Maybe they gave back his $500, too, although Armstrong doubted that.

Even reporters paid a price for sticking their necks out. Scott Young had done it in 1962, suggesting in his *Globe and Mail* column that the Leafs weren't serious when they'd announced the sale of Frank Mahovlich for $1 million. They'd done it just to deflect attention from baseball's World Series, he said. When the owners of the Maple Leafs read that, they felt "extreme concern," they said, at Young's insinuations. Young not only wrote for the *Globe*, he also appeared as a between-period commentator on televised Leafs games. Who needed a rabble-rouser like that on a hockey broadcast? A Leafs game reached more people than any other show on TV. The owners didn't want to jeopardize that advertising opportunity.

"We took our case to [MacLaren Advertising], the people responsible for the program," said John Bassett, one of the owners. Bassett owned a TV station in Toronto whose news reporters were as objective as he was. "We told them, A, what Young had written was detrimental to hockey, and B, he was an inefficient television personality," Bassett said. "At the end of the season, I guess they saw our case." Young was fired.

But then, the NHL had always seemed more conscious of its image than its substance. This was show business. Even in 2006, Don Cherry, who could have talked about more important things if he'd wanted to, spent five minutes on national TV admonishing rookies like Dion Phaneuf to wear a jacket and tie in public. There's nothing wrong with that, as long as no one mistakes the tie for a reflection of the character who wears it and as long as people remember that sometimes the bigger the swindler, the nicer the tie. Just ask Alan Eagleson.

As a players' agent, the well-dressed lawyer negotiated contracts with the team's owners on behalf of Mike Walton and a few other players in the Leafs' dressing room tonight. As a wheeler-dealer, Eagleson also spent a lot of time hobnobbing with the owners, flying around with Stafford Smythe on Smythe's private Lear jet, for example. Taking care of league business, he said.

But maybe Eagleson could succeed where the players had failed. Maybe he could persuade the owners to give players more control over their careers. He'd have to fight for it, though. Like any business, the NHL operated its franchises to make money, not to create a more just society or an equitable system for the players. If the fans didn't like the product, they didn't have to buy it; it was just like a hamburger or a bucket of chicken. Whether or not the NHL was run by a bunch of bigoted white men, NHL teams prospered, especially Armstrong's. The Toronto Maple Leafs might have missed the playoffs a few times over the years that he'd played for the team. But the owners had never had a losing season financially. For that reason alone, the Chief thought twice about rocking the boat and felt glad that he'd hung on to his shares in Maple Leaf Gardens.

Earlier tonight, a fan had leaned over the back of the players' bench and offered the trainer, Bob Haggert, fifty bucks for one of Frank Mahovlich's sticks. Haggert had ignored the guy, but it reminded him of all the wasted value on this team.

Haggert received offers like that all the time. Fifty dollars for a stick, two hundred for a pair of gloves, a thousand for Johnny Bower's goalie pads. What did people expect him to do: lift the equipment off a player's back when he wasn't looking?

The guy who'd offered to buy Mahovlich's stick for fifty dollars could have bought a new one for less than ten at Doug Laurie's sporting goods store in the lobby. It wasn't the stick that the guy wanted, any more than an art collector lusted after a framed picture of a smiling woman when he ogled the *Mona Lisa*. Collectors didn't want the thing itself as much as they wanted the aura that went with it. No one could put a price on that.

Few Leafs players in tonight's game had figured out how to capitalize on their fame. Most of them used it as a calling card. Mike Walton sold real estate. Frank Mahovlich ran a travel agency, on Bay Street near Bloor. Red Kelly ran a bowling alley in Simcoe, where he also owned a thirty-six acre tobacco farm. When he played in Detroit, Kelly had also sold electric motors and power drills for a company called Re-Nu Tool Co. The rest of them made ends meet in the best way they could find. Eddie Shack bought old cars, fixed them up and sold them for a profit. Jim Pappin went to work at six in the morning at Woodbine Racetrack to train thoroughbreds before he went to the Leafs practice at eleven. In the summers, Pappin taught little kids how to skate at the Holiday Hockey Ranch in Pickering, east of Toronto, and took their parents on horseback rides in the afternoons for sixty-nine dollars a person. Other players invested in the stock market. "We were always hustling," said Bob Baun. "We'd finish practice and have a phone in each ear and one in our ass."

As for endorsements, a few players, like Pulford and the Big M, made a couple of hundred dollars a year for appearing in advertisements for hats or ice cream or hamburgers. The Leafs program ran ads in which Tim Horton endorsed Studebaker automobiles, "as stingy on gas as Johnny Bower is on goals." He also owned the dealership. Haggert appeared in the program, as well, representing Ticknor Volkswagen in Weston, where he worked as a salesman in the off-season. But an ad in the Maple Leafs program didn't influence anyone beyond the hockey fans who bought one. The fame of athletes in other sports had started to spread further.

You didn't have to be a football fan to recognize Joe Namath or a baseball fan to recognize Roger Maris. These guys were making millions from their image. Namath, a big-cheese jock from New York, made ten times as much money hustling Ovaltine, easy chairs, aftershave and pantyhose as he did as a quarterback for the New York Jets. Maris, who had broken a home-run record set by Babe Ruth, now commanded a hefty six-figure fee to peddle Camel cigarettes, Post Alpha-Bits and Spalding baseball gloves. By comparison, Frank Mahovlich, who'd come close to breaking the NHL scoring record set by Rocket Richard, was lucky to make a hundred dollars for appearing at a Shriners' convention. Even within the small world of professional athletes, the Big M was still a no-name. When he sat down one night beside Roger Maris at the head table of a celebrity dinner in New York, Mahovlich had to introduce himself. Maris had never heard of him, didn't even know what sport he played.

"The greatest names in hockey aren't known throughout the States," said the owner of the New York Jets, Sonny Werblin. "They either lack awareness of merchandising or just don't know how to do it."

Haggert could count on one hand tonight the hockey players whose reputations extended beyond their sport the way Maris's and Namath's and Muhammad Ali's transcended theirs. Mr. Hockey, Gordie Howe, the equivalent of Babe Ruth in baseball, had capitalized on his reputation by trundling with Red Kelly around the state of Michigan in a station wagon, showing films in school gymnasiums of the Stanley Cup playoffs on behalf of Stroh's Brewery and by appearing in magazine ads for Camp Wee-Gee-Wa for Boys, in Parry Sound. When Howe finally signed a contract with Eaton's department store to pitch TruLine hockey equipment, he became the first NHL player ever to negotiate such an endorsement deal. The deal earned him less than $2,000.

Haggert had talked a few times after team practices with Alan Eagleson about the untapped earning power of NHL players. Eagleson and Haggert had both grown up in Toronto. They were both about the same age, and they'd both worked hard to get where they were tonight. Eagleson suggested that Haggert should start an endorsement company, and in another couple of years, Haggert would do just that. Eagleson would refer players to Haggert's company. Haggert would receive ten or fifteen per cent of their endorsement fees and reimburse Eagleson by paying legal fees to the agent's law firm. It was a lucrative set-up, especially as the league expanded into the United States. For the rest of his life, Haggert would remain grateful for Eagleson's help.

Haggert had seen first-hand how doors opened when an NHL player came knocking. A few years before tonight, he'd gone into business with a former Leaf named Bert Olmstead, distributing a hockey helmet designed in Sweden. At first, buyers for department stores dismissed the product as just another long-shot from a foreign country. But as soon as they learned that Haggert would show up with an NHL player to yak about his product, they welcomed the visitors with open arms, just for the chance to talk to Bert Olmstead.

When the money came at last, most of it would come from TV. Ten years before tonight's game, CBS had paid just $100,000 to carry ten NHL games in the U.S. Two years later, the network doubled the schedule to twenty games at fifteen thousand apiece. Now the NHL had added six more teams, all based in U.S. cities. Television would introduce these teams and their players to a vast new audience, and U.S. broadcasters would pay millions to reach it. Hockey had "all the potential of pro football," said the president of ABC Sports, Roone Arledge. In the U.S., nothing could be bigger than that.

Fame comes at the cost of relentless probing into a player's life, and after tonight's game, it would only become more invasive. Hockey was becoming a big business, and the game was only a small part of it. Like all other aspects of the entertainment industry, enormous profits rested on the integrity of the game's public image. The more valuable the image, the greater the scrutiny of the players' private lives.

As the NHL prepared to expand into the U.S., the league's owners, players, agents, executives and even trainers like Bob Haggert anticipated big money ahead. What better sport to appeal to Americans than a violent game in the most violent nation in the world?

And yet, for all its success in the U.S., hockey would fall short of the league's expectations. Nothing seemed to drum up interest, not the naked blonde streaking down the ice at the LA Forum or the electronic pucks that left a red trail like a comet across the TV screen so a viewer in Peoria could follow the action. To this day, the NHL still has not captured a U.S. audience as loyal as football's, as knowledgeable as baseball's or as hip as basketball's. All the razzle-dazzle in the world hasn't persuaded Americans to become fans of the NHL. And by far the most serious obstacle standing between professional hockey and the embrace of American sports fans is fighting.

Less than a decade after the league expanded, a U.S. magazine called *Hockey* said violence in the game contradicted every principle of fair play. The magazine challenged the assertion by Leo Dandurand and, later, by Conn Smythe that "if you can't beat 'em in the alley, you can't beat 'em on the ice." "Until the rationale behind this statement is discarded," the magazine said, "there will continue to be problems with violence in hockey."

Not only did the magazine encourage fans to complain in writing to the NHL about violence in the game, it also advised defencemen to extend a helping hand to their opponents after they'd bodychecked them to the ice.

In Canada, knowledgeable hockey fans who'd grown up watching Sprague and Odie Cleghorn, Newsy Lalonde and John Ferguson slamming their fists into other men's faces scoffed at the naivety of the American media. Yet gormless U.S. journalists weren't the only ones to suggest that excessive violence was hurting the game. Some of the players themselves were concerned.

"Allowing violence to become a characteristic of the game will not engender long-range interest," said Brian Conacher, shortly after he left the Maple Leafs.

Even Jean Beliveau spoke out, in his inimitable way, against violence in hockey. "Hockey is a game that demands physical strength and endurance," he said, "and you can get hurt playing it. It's like life in that way. But you don't have to be violent."

In America and most other places in the world, many people question the values of a culture like the NHL that measures the capacity of a man's soul and the depth of his courage by the way he bashes someone in the head for making him angry while he plays a game that has nothing to do with fighting. As every mother tries to teach her children, no one settles disputes with any satisfaction through violence. It's a stupid way to resolve differences, and the millions of people who don't watch NHL games know it, even if the NHL doesn't.

As Ken Dryden, a graduate of Cornell University, a lawyer, a former member of Parliament, a writer and a former goalie for the Montreal Canadiens, observes, "Fighting degrades the sport, turning it into a dubious spectacle and confining it to the fringes of sports respectability."

CHAPTER FOUR
Second Period

John Ferguson skated across the ice and sat down in the penalty box. He had fifty seconds left to serve in the sentence he'd received for mugging Pete Stemkowski at the end of the first period. During those fifty seconds, the Canadiens would play with four skaters on the ice, the Maple Leafs with five.

The Leafs had many strengths tonight, but the power play wasn't one of them. Other than sending Mike Walton over the boards to play right wing and putting Jim Pappin on defence with Larry Hillman, Punch Imlach did nothing especially innovative. "We didn't work on the power play," said Ron Ellis. "Punch's approach was to send out whichever line was up next."

When the Canadiens took control of the puck, J.C. Tremblay skated out of his end and cut toward the centre of the rink, hoping to find more room to manoeuvre. Anticipating Tremblay's move, Pappin veered along the centre line toward Tremblay and stuck out his knee, slamming his hard plastic pad into Tremblay's leg. The collision could have ripped Tremblay's tendons from his patella and crippled the player for life. This had happened more than once to an NHL player. Knee injuries are as common in hockey as black eyes in boxing. But in hockey, kneeing is an offence. Not only does a player receive a two-minute penalty for kneeing, he also risks losing his front teeth when an injured player's teammates avenge the crime.

They have good reason to retaliate. A knee injury threatens their livelihood. Jean Beliveau missed twenty-five games one season after a rookie slammed into his knee during a scrimmage in training camp. A knee injury had prevented Pappin's teammate Larry Jeffrey from playing tonight and would ultimately prevent him from completing all but one of his eight seasons in the NHL. Surgeons had first started chopping away at Jeffrey's knee when he was a twenty-year-old junior in Hamilton, around the same age at which many young men were entering their second year of university. Between then and his retirement from the NHL two years from now, at twenty-nine, Jeffrey underwent eleven operations on his knee. When he skated hard, he felt as if someone had stuck a sheet of hot sandpaper under his kneecap. For his previous five seasons in the NHL, he'd gone to a hospital after every game to have fluid drained from his knee and painkillers injected so that he could go to sleep. This season, he'd started to wear an aluminum brace on his knee, fastened with four wing nuts. If he managed to finish a game, he had to sit afterwards in the dressing room with a hose aimed full blast at his knee to loosen the joint before he could put his pants on. Tonight would have been one of the biggest games of his career, but Jeffrey spent the entire game in a jacket and tie, leaning on a pair of crutches behind the Leafs' bench. In the code of the game, players who inflicted that kind of injury on another player deserved what they got.

The force of the collision lifted Tremblay's feet off the ice. He landed on the right one, kicked back his left one and bent forward to keep his balance, gliding like a swan on one foot while looking down at the ice. The puck fluttered beneath him, but he couldn't kick it quickly enough when his left foot came down, and it drifted harmlessly into the centre-ice face-off circle. John Ashley didn't call a penalty on Pappin.

...

The players on both teams tonight made their living in much the same way as their fathers, with the strength of their back and the sweat of their brow, and they risked serious injury every time they went to work. More than half the players on the ice tonight came from places where men went to the hospital as often as they went to the local tavern.

Dave Keon had worked in a copper mine in Noranda, 2,300 feet below the ground. Frank Mahovlich had spent a summer or two peeling and loading logs in the forests near Timmins. "It was hard work," he said. When he became a professional hockey player, Mahovlich persuaded his father to quit mining, after seventeen years, and move to Toronto. "I would have been dead by now," his dad said later, "if Frank hadn't ordered me out of the mines."

In the logging camps around northern Quebec, where Jacques Laperriere and Leon Rochefort grew up, accidents were so common that men hardly noticed if one of their crew arrived on the job without a finger or an ear. Men lost their lives almost by routine, their bodies laid out beside the tree trunks near the worksite until another worker could notify the police, possibly a day or two later. "Even now, loggers must sometimes carry their dead partners out of the woods like sacks of flour," said the writer John Vaillant in 2005.

In the gold mines around Kirkland Lake, home of Dick Duff, Larry Hillman, Ralph Backstrom and Mike Walton, a man would spend forty years underground, scaling slabs of rock off the ceiling of a mine shaft, holding over his head an iron bar that weighed as much as a seven-year-old boy.

Not only were their fathers' jobs hard, but their fathers' bosses also made even the toughest NHL hockey coach look like Howdy Doody. "[Lumber] camp foremen saw their workers as expendable, interchangeable units to be hired and fired at will," said Vaillant. "There were camps that were known for having three crews: one on the job, one that had just been fired, and another coming in on the next boat." Compared to that, a whimsical demotion by Punch Imlach to Rochester was a busman's holiday.

When he'd first joined the Leafs, Tim Horton had driven a dump truck in the off-season, hauling sand and gravel for the team's owner, Conn Smythe. So had Bob Baun. Around the same time, Eddie Shack had a job driving a coal truck in Guelph, where he'd gone from Sudbury at fifteen to play junior hockey for the Biltmores. "Even with his overalls on he was exciting," said the Biltmores' coach, Eddie Bush.

If players didn't drive trucks, they found other ways to earn a living. Jean Beliveau, who'd ranked among the top players in Canada since he was nineteen, had become a certified electrician. Yvan Cournoyer had recently earned his ticket as a machinist, like his dad, "and I have the papers to prove it," he said.

A few players took university courses, although it was hard to focus on a textbook after a tough game, and the NHL didn't encourage them to venture too far into the alien realm of the intellect. Gilles Tremblay had received scholarships from the University of Ottawa after he was named the best athlete in Northern Ontario and Quebec. Tremblay's teammate Terry Harper took classes at the University of Saskatchewan. Dick Duff had taken courses at McMaster University in Hamilton and Assumption College in Windsor.

On the Leafs, Brian Conacher and Pete Stemkowski had studied economics at university. So had Bob Pulford, whose academic credentials made him far more attractive to advertisers than he'd been when he first joined the team. As a cantankerous, bone-headed high-school graduate who played left wing for a professional hockey team, Pulford had landed nothing but a fifty-dollar gig pitching Schick razor blades. After he earned his degree as a part-time student in history and economics from McMaster, he attracted his first big endorsement deal: $500 to tell the world to buy an *Encyclopaedia Britannica*.

Despite Pulford's achievement, most NHL owners thought that educating a hockey player was like pouring honey into a Swiss watch. Conn Smythe, the Leafs' founder, objected to players attending school, because they would then have to serve two masters, only one of whom was him.

Punch Imlach felt the same way. When Ron Ellis received an offer to continue his education, at no cost, while playing hockey for a small college called Michigan Tech, near the south shore of Lake Superior, Imlach said he'd be wasting his time. Why should a player like Ellis fritter away four years of his life in the isolated boonies of Michigan, he said, when he could be making money as a Toronto Maple Leaf? Once those four years were gone, he said, Ellis wouldn't get them back.

Intelligence on the ice had nothing to do with Jean Beliveau's understanding of hydroelectric power or Bob Pulford's understanding of the GDP. It had nothing to do with thinking. "The more you think, the more things there are to think about," said Yvan Cournoyer. "So you make a mistake. One mistake," he added, "and the puck is in your net."

Intelligence on the ice had everything to do with a player's instinct, reflexes and intuition, acquired through years of practice and experience. And for the next fifty-four seconds on the ice, the Leafs had more intelligence than the Canadiens.

At the face-off, Dave Keon, twenty-seven years old, the Leafs' fastest skater and the team's top scorer this year, competed for the puck against Jean Beliveau, thirty-five, the Canadiens' captain. Beliveau had already won seven Stanley Cups. Since he'd first started to play hockey, he'd skated more than thirty thousand miles, enough to cross Canada seven times. Skating had overdeveloped the muscles in his dominant foot to such an extent that he wore mismatched skates, a larger one on his right foot, a smaller one on his left. Beliveau had won a lot of face-offs, but he didn't win this one.

Keon slid the puck back to Allan Stanley at the blue line. Stanley was forty-one and had been playing professionally since Keon was nine. In the course of his career, Stanley had been purchased from another team for the equivalent of ten players' salaries, booed out of New York and traded to Chicago in return for Brian Conacher's cousin. In the same trade, New York acquired a defenceman named Bill Gadsby, who with one check had broken the leg and the jaw of Stanley's partner on defence tonight, Tim Horton. The same loopy patterns of fate and coincidence link the random events of any man's life, but they look more meaningful under the klieg lights of an NHL player's career.

Looking down at the puck, Stanley saw from the corner of his eye the Canadiens right-winger Bobby Rousseau speeding toward him from the face-off circle. Rousseau had led the Canadiens this year in scoring. He was twenty-six years old, fifteen years younger than Stanley, and was one of two players on the ice wearing a helmet. He'd left school after the ninth grade to make a living from playing golf and hockey. He kept himself mentally sharp by reading *The Power of Positive Thinking*, by Norman Vincent Peale. Now, as he sped toward the defenceman, he extended his stick, hoping to block a pass or knock the puck into the centre zone, then chase it at a speed that Snowshoes Stanley could only dream of matching.

Positioned on the blue line toward the middle of the rink, Stanley's partner, Tim Horton, saw Rousseau approaching and turned to skate toward the Leafs' end of the rink, intending to place himself between Rousseau and the Leafs' goal if the Montreal player captured the puck. Horton was thirty-seven. He'd made the NHL all-star team for the first time when Rousseau was a twelve-year-old playing bantam hockey in Montreal. Like Rousseau, Horton also took inspiration from *The Power of Positive Thinking*. He copied passages from the book on pieces of paper and taped them to the wall of his cubbyhole in the Leafs' dressing room. On road trips to New York, he attended services at the Marble Collegiate Church to hear Norman Vincent Peale deliver his inspirational sermons in person, and he encouraged his teammates to come with him.

The other Canadiens forward, Gilles Tremblay, also sped from the face-off circle up the middle of the rink toward the blue line. Tremblay had joined the Canadiens organization on a Friday night almost twelve years ago, when he was fifteen. He'd driven with his home team from Montmorency, Quebec, about three hours down the St. Lawrence, to play a game at the Montreal Forum. He scored three goals that night and was invited right after the game by Sam Pollock, an executive with the Montreal Canadiens, to play for one of Montreal's junior teams. When he'd left Montmorency that morning, Tremblay hadn't expected even to stay overnight in Montreal, so Pollock gave him some money to buy a suit and a toothbrush. He also said he'd phone Tremblay's parents to let them know that their son might be a bit late returning home. Tremblay didn't go home again for six months. Over the next week, he played four games in four different leagues with the Canadiens' junior affiliate. In the meantime, Pollock found a family to provide room and board for Tremblay and enrolled him in a local high school. "I have been with the Montreal Canadiens ever since," Tremblay said.

According to Jean Beliveau, who was drifting behind him toward the blue line, Tremblay "was the fastest left-winger I've ever played with." In bolting for the blue line, though, Tremblay skated away from the Leafs' captain, George Armstrong.

Almost thirty-seven, Armstrong had played more than twice as many games in the NHL as Tremblay. Unlike many of his teammates, Armstrong inspired himself with his own motivational wisdom, which he jotted on scrap paper from the hotel rooms where he and his roommate, Johnny Bower, stayed during road trips, and taped to the walls of his dressing-room stall. "I've got to skate harder now that I'm older," Armstrong wrote on a page from the Commodore Hotel in New York. "Always keep myself between my check and our goal," he scribbled on a scratch pad from the Sheraton Cadillac in Detroit. On an envelope from the Parker House in Boston, he wrote, "Don't stay out on a shift too long." He was thirty-two when he wrote that and had played in the NHL for ten years.

Seeing his teammate under siege at the blue line, Armstrong skated toward the only spot inside the Canadiens' zone to which Stanley could safely pass the puck. Stanley spotted him, pulled the puck to his forehand and flipped it high over Tremblay's outstretched stick. Armstrong caught up to it as it bounced off the boards. Before it reached the net, the puck hit the Montreal defenceman Ted Harris and bounced toward the far corner.

Harris was thirty years old but had played in the NHL only for the last three years. Before that he'd spent eight years in the minor leagues with the Philadelphia Ramblers, Victoria Cougars, Cleveland Barons and Springfield Indians, earning admiration for his winning spirit from his coaches and teammates, who'd included Eddie Shack, Gump Worsley, Larry Hillman and Don Cherry. He'd also spent an average of a hundred minutes a season in the penalty box for beating up his opponents. His opponents had included three of his teammates on the ice at the moment, Gilles Tremblay, Bobby Rousseau and J.C. Tremblay, none of whom he'd fought, as well as two of their brothers, both of whom he'd beaten twice in fist fights on the ice.

J.C. Tremblay was now Harris's defence partner. He was covering Keon in front of the Canadiens' goal. Even though Tremblay was two years younger than Harris, he'd played twice as many games over twice as many seasons in the NHL. This year, he'd been the Canadiens' highest-scoring defenceman. In more than four hundred games in the league, J.C. Tremblay had received fewer minutes in penalties than Harris received in a single season. He also was the only player in the game tonight other than his teammate Bobby Rousseau to protect his head with a helmet.

J.C. Tremblay chased the puck into the corner. So did the fifth skater for the Leafs, Frank Mahovlich. Mahovlich had played for the Leafs for ten years and had scored twenty goals or more in each season except two. On any other team, Mahovlich would have been a superstar. Not only had he scored almost fifty goals in a season, but he could lift an entire rink full of fans to their feet as he thundered down his wing like a Kentucky Derby thoroughbred down the home stretch. The only other player in the league who could do that was Bobby Hull. Knowing that Hull could score goals, his coach sent him onto the ice at every opportunity. He played an average of thirty minutes a game. In Toronto, Punch Imlach refused to give Mahovlich more ice time than any other player on the Leafs, and he restricted Mahovlich's ice time to twenty minutes a game.

With two-thirds as much time to score, Mahovlich scored two-thirds as many goals as Hull. After tonight, Mahovlich would move to Detroit to play for the Red Wings and then to Montreal to play for the Canadiens, and he would never again score fewer than thirty goals a season. Though Mahovlich never said it in public, he could easily have blamed Punch Imlach for squandering some of the best years of his career as a professional hockey player.

Counting Mahovlich, a comparative youngster at twenty-nine, the cumulative age of the five Leafs skaters on the ice at the moment was 171 years. The ages of the Canadiens players added up to 148. The Leafs players might have been a bit slower and a lot older, but they were twenty-three years more experienced. Allan Stanley alone had played in almost as many NHL games as all the Canadiens on the ice combined except Jean Beliveau.

Between them, the Leafs skaters at the moment had played 2,073 more NHL games than their opponents. Of that number, 459 were NHL playoff games. The Canadiens skaters had participated in only 297 playoff games. The difference of 162 games amounted to more than eleven years' playoff experience in the Leafs' favour.

Defencemen in particular improve with experience. With hundreds of additional games in their favour, the Leafs defencemen enjoyed an enormous advantage, and it showed. Stanley and Horton together had played in 212 NHL playoff games. Their counterparts on the Montreal defence, J.C. Tremblay and Ted Harris, had played in only 89.

As for the team's goalies, Terry Sawchuk and Gump Worsley were the same age, thirty-eight, but Sawchuk had played in more than twice as many playoff games as Worsley and 234 more games in the regular season. Of course, they were goalies, and goalies seldom conform to statistical norms.

With twenty-three years more experience, the Leafs practically had an extra player on their side. The phantom helped the Leafs at the moment in preventing the Canadiens from clearing the puck out of their own end of the rink. But the Habs finally succeeded when Jean Beliveau eluded Marcel Pronovost's outstretched stick and carried the puck across the

Leafs' blue line. Beliveau's linemate, Gilles Tremblay, had already flashed across the blue line, putting himself offside. Toe Blake sent five Canadiens over the boards to replace their teammates on the ice and told Henri Richard to take the face-off.

Henri Richard had had brown hair when he signed his first contract to play for the Montreal Canadiens. He was nineteen then, and he felt as if his dream had come true. Now he was thirty-one. After twelve years, anxiety had turned his hair as grey as ashes. "I worry every year about making the team," he said.

Richard had started dreaming about the Montreal Canadiens when he was six years old. If he couldn't play hockey, he intended to become a bricklayer or perhaps work for the railway like his dad, Onésime, who'd supported his family of twelve by working for the CPR since 1922. At thirteen, Henri concentrated more on his dream than he did on his schoolwork. But with Rocket Richard as an older brother, Henri had a lot to live up to.

Growing up in a French family in Montreal, Henri learned to speak English from players in his childhood hockey games. But he could hardly conduct a conversation, so the Canadiens organization sent him one summer to a camp in Algonquin Park, north of Toronto, to improve his language skills. "The only word I learned was 'same,'" he said. "Every time they asked me what I wanted, I'd point to the guy next to me and say, 'Same.'"

Even now, Richard never read a book in either language, and he still had difficulty speaking English. But he didn't care much. He just wanted to play hockey, and he could do that whether he spoke English, French or Urdu. "Within the range of intelligence required on the ice, there's no politics, no rhetoric, so the guy with words has no advantage," said former player Eric Nesterenko. "The smartest guys, period, survive."

When Henri earned his spot on the Montreal Canadiens, his older brother was still playing for the team, wearing the number 9 on his jersey.

The Rocket's former linemate, Elmer Lach, had retired. He'd worn the number 16, and he said Henri should wear that number, too.

For Henri Richard, the heritage of the number on the back of his jersey and the honour of wearing it meant more than the numbers on his paycheque. When he first joined the Canadiens, hockey hadn't yet become a job, and money was just the icing on the cake.

For the men who ran the NHL teams that employed them, however, money wasn't the icing, it was the cake. NHL managers took pride in paying their players as little as possible, and a youngster's wide-eyed enthusiasm for the game just made their job easier. The less money a team gave to its players, the more its owners could keep for themselves. In the game tonight, ten of forty players might have won the Memorial Cup, awarded to the best junior team in Canada, but none had succeeded in winning a few extra bucks from their manager at the beginning of the season.

In Toronto, players bickered over their contracts with the same man they relied upon for their inspiration and support. As their coach, Punch Imlach drove his players to accomplish more than they thought they could for the sake of the team. As general manager, Imlach then diminished a player's accomplishments to justify a lower salary and save the team some money.

"It's tough discussing contracts with a manager who's also your coach," said Frank Mahovlich.

Imlach negotiated thirty-five contracts a year. His players, who paid as much attention to a legal contract as they did to a dry-cleaning bill, didn't stand a chance. When the Leafs won the Stanley Cup in 1962, Johnny Bower asked Imlach for a raise. Most of his teammates by then were making about $19,000 a year. Bower, who'd also won the Vezina Trophy in the previous year as the NHL's best goaltender, was making $11,000, less than two-thirds as much.

Imlach pointed out that Bower was nearing forty but still hadn't played in the NHL for ten years. Until he did, Bower would not be eligible to collect his full pension. If Bower insisted on a raise, Imlach said, "I'll bury you so deep in the minors that the *Hockey News* won't be able to find you."

If Imlach sent him back to the minors, Bower would forfeit his pension and all the money he'd contributed to the NHL plan, $900 a year from an annual salary that was sometimes as low as $7,000. "Then I told him to go fuck himself," Imlach chuckled later. When a reporter asked him if he felt bad about shortchanging such a decent man, who'd contributed so much to the Leafs' success, Imlach said, "I didn't lose any fucking sleep over it."

The Canadiens operated with a different style. But every NHL owner regarded his players as expendable, and they used uncertainty, worry and anxiety to keep them off balance.

None of this had occurred to Henri Richard when he walked up the stairs at the north end of the Montreal Forum to discuss his first contract with Frank Selke. Maurice went with his brother that day, but Henri didn't expect the Rocket to negotiate the contract. He just wanted him to explain in French what Mr. Selke said in English.

The two brothers joined Selke in his wood-panelled manager's office. Selke, wearing a navy blue suit, sat in a leather chair behind a big wooden desk. From a marble plinth on the desk, two Parker pens pointed like javelins at the ceiling. Selke peered across the shiny walnut desktop and asked the kid how much money he wanted to play for the team.

Henri shrugged. "Pas d'importance," he said. "Pay me what you think I'm worth."

"He just wants to play for the big team," said the Rocket.

The Rocket suggested that the Canadiens pay Henri $2,000, the standard bonus paid to a player when he signed his first contract. The contract committed a player to the team for the rest of his life. Without the permission of the Montreal Canadiens, Henri could play for no other team in the NHL or any of its affiliates. The same contract allowed the team to demote or drop a player at a moment's notice. The Rocket also suggested that the team pay Henri $100 a game.

Selke frowned like an owl through his horn-rimmed glasses. He agreed to pay Henri $100 a game, the same amount as every other Canadien had received in his first year with the team. But he refused to pay Henri a bonus of $2,000. "That's not enough," he said. Selke said Henri should receive a bonus of $5,000 for signing his contract.

From his desk drawer, Selke took a sheet of his own personal stationery with "F.J. Selke" engraved at the top. He pulled one of the pens from the marble stand. With a scratching sound, he scribbled Henri's name and the date, "September/55," on the page. He wrote down the basic salary and the additional amounts that Henri would receive if he played a full season with the Canadiens, if the team finished in first or second place and if the team won the first round of the playoffs. Over the years, Richard would become more adept at building bonus clauses into his contract. Claude Larose, his teammate tonight, earned an additional $100 for every point he recorded in a season beyond thirty. Larose had also negotiated a bonus of $100 for every goal he scored in a game beyond the total of the winger playing opposite him. That bonus clause had earned him an extra $800, after he'd scored fifteen goals while allowing opposing teams' wingers to score only seven. But as Henri Richard began his first season with the team, he had yet to devise such ingenious schemes for earning more money. Selke wrote his signature at the bottom of the contract, then slid the sheet across the desk so Henri could sign the page, as well.

"I would have signed anything to play with Maurice and the Canadiens," he said later.

Apart from the signing bonus, the Canadiens paid the same amount in their rookie years to Henri Richard, Bobby Rousseau and J.C. Tremblay: $7,000.

By the end of his career, Henri Richard would win eleven Stanley Cups, more than any player in NHL history. For each Cup victory, he and his teammates would receive a payment of $500. They'd also receive about $2,000 for winning the semi-finals and appearing in the finals. The owners of his team would make enough money from the sale of popcorn and soda pop to cover these payments in six games. They'd cover the team's entire payroll with the sale of TV rights and box-office receipts from about ten games. The rest of the cash generated by the twenty players on the Montreal Canadiens went into the owners' pockets. If a player didn't like it, the owners could easily find someone to take his place. Lots of players had come and gone since Henri Richard had joined the Canadiens. That worried Henri Richard, even on a good day. And tonight was shaping up to be not so good.

Richard won the face-off, but Brian Conacher sent the puck down the ice toward the Canadiens' goal. Jacques Laperriere retrieved it and passed it back up the ice to Leon Rochefort, who redirected it ahead to Dave Balon, who flipped it to his left, to Henri Richard. With three passes, the Canadiens had moved the puck more than 120 feet up the ice in two seconds, a rate of more than forty miles an hour. Even the fastest player couldn't skate that fast.

Richard took the puck at full speed across the Leafs' blue line, cut behind the net and, at the last instant, snuck a pass through the crease to Dave Balon. Balon could score goals. He'd received $250 one year when he'd scored five game-winning goals and tied with Frank Mahovlich as the left-wing candidate for the NHL's Second All-Star Team. Now he rushed to the net, shoulder-to-shoulder with Leafs defenceman Marcel Pronovost. While the puck skittered toward Brian Conacher, Pronovost tried to drive Balon away from the net, but Balon warded off the check and slid his foot under Pronovost's left skate. Pronovost lost his balance, spun around and toppled backwards like a six-foot pine tree. He managed to lift his head just before the back of his skull struck the ice, but his momentum carried him on his back head-first toward the goalpost, anchored in concrete beneath the ice as firmly as a parking meter in a sidewalk. If Pronovost's head were to collide with a goalpost, the post wouldn't budge. It took the NHL another seventeen years after tonight to modify the design using magnets that released on contact. After another ten years, the NHL modified the system again with a length of flexible plastic called the Marsh Peg. The new design was a mixed blessing, especially for goalies. Knowing that the net would slide away in a collision, players raced toward the goal without slowing down.

Tonight, as the unstoppable force of Pronovost's head approached the immovable object of the goalpost, Terry Sawchuk turned away from the play, reached out with his stick and nudged the big defenceman out of harm's way.

Meanwhile, three Canadiens forwards and one defenceman had all skated deep into the Leafs' end. When the puck landed on Brian Conacher's stick, he launched himself the other way toward the Montreal goal, with only Terry Harper in a position to stop him.

Conacher and Harper both stood more than six feet tall and weighed close to two hundred pounds. Even at the best of times, they skated as if they had anvils in their pants. With a full head of steam, Conacher stormed across the Canadiens' blue line and bulled his way past Harper. Rather than allow Conacher an open shot on Gump Worsley, Harper grabbed the Leafs player around the waist, pinned his arms so he couldn't shoot and steered him away from the net as if he was hoisting a telephone pole across a parking lot.

John Ashley raised his arm. Harper's manoeuvre might have saved a goal, but it cost the Canadiens another penalty.

"What did I get the penalty for?" Harper yelled at the referee over the din of the crowd. But Ashley glided past Harper, as if he hadn't heard a word.

Henri Richard skated to the bench. For the second time in three minutes, he and the rest of Montreal's top goal scorers would have to watch the game from the sidelines while their team killed a penalty. Terry Harper stepped through the open door of the penalty box and sat down.

"You're a bum, Beliveau!"

From twenty rows above the ice, the voice pierced the cloud of sound that drifted through Maple Leaf Gardens.

Betty Armstrong flinched, then adjusted her navy blue skirt. A few rows away, the human foghorn yelled again.

"You suck, Frogman!"

The man wore a blue suit, a white shirt and a green tie, and he was sitting in a red seat, one of the most expensive seats in the Gardens. Eyes as big as headlights, the man gestured at Jean Beliveau on the bench, as if the Canadiens' captain had insulted his mother.

"Frappez la rue!" he screamed.

The man beside him laughed. He, too, wore a suit and tie.

Betty Armstrong looked around to find Elise Beliveau, but she couldn't pick her out of the crowd. Perhaps because of her husband's stature, Elise had found it more difficult than many wives to adjust to the fans. It didn't help that she'd never seen a hockey game until she met her husband in Quebec City.

Fans did more than just yell at Jean Beliveau. A few years ago, they'd spread a rumour about an affair between Elise and a professional wrestler named Jean Rougeau. No matter how hard they tried to deny it, the Beliveaus couldn't put the rumour to rest. From what Betty had heard, Jean Rougeau's wife wasn't too happy about the rumour, either.

Perhaps Elise wasn't here tonight, Betty thought. Few of the Canadiens' wives had made the trip to Toronto. Six of them were pregnant. Perhaps the others were superstitious. Maybe they thought their husbands stood a better chance of returning to Montreal for a seventh game if they stayed home.

The NHL didn't care what the wives thought. The league seemed to have a higher regard for hookers than it did for them. On a player's journey through the NHL, the league would turn a blind eye if a stripper sat on his lap or snuck into his hotel room, but it frowned upon wives and children who didn't sit quietly on the sidelines and keep their mouths shut. Betty remembered when the local newspapers had carried some photos of Lori Horton, Tim's wife, modelling some of the outrageously short skirts that kids had started to wear a few years earlier. Lori had the looks to wear one, but Betty knew there'd be trouble. Sure enough, George, as captain of the team, had to pass along a message to Tim the next day from the Leafs' owners. George hated doing that. Tim had been the only witness at the Armstrongs' wedding. That's how close they were. Now here was George telling his friend to keep his wife under control. Lori flipped her lid, said it was none of their goddam business. But that was Lori for you. The other wives, the older ones who knew the ropes, tried not to rock the boat. They dressed conservatively in knee-length skirts and sensible shoes. They even went to the same hairdresser. None of the women wanted to put their husbands' careers in jeopardy by drawing attention to themselves.

Sometimes it felt as if the league didn't want the wives around at all. Players couldn't even get married till the hockey season ended. A woman who agreed to marry an NHL player either organized a quick summer wedding or endured a long engagement. When Pat Sawchuk married Terry, she almost had to sprint down the aisle to make sure the Red Wings' season didn't start before she got to the altar. Susan Davis and Candy Smythe, sitting near Betty tonight, had waited all year for this season to end so they could marry their fiancés. Susan's wedding was scheduled for next Thursday to Brian Conacher. They'd met six years ago on board a ship crossing the Atlantic. Candy would marry Mike Walton two days later.

Marriage didn't mean much to the men who ran an NHL team. Women and hockey just didn't mix, they said. Even in the 1970s, NHL coaches instructed players' wives by mail to leave their husbands alone during the playoffs. Don't ask them to cut the grass or take out the garbage, said a coach in Philadelphia named Fred Shero, and above all don't have sex with them. Punch Imlach wouldn't let his players skip a practice to visit their wives in hospital after their children were born. The wife would get mad, of course, but what could she do? In a contest for her husband's attention, hockey came first, far ahead of old what's-her-name. If she didn't like it, she could take him to court, the way Mrs. Cleghorn did when her husband, Sprague, a member of the old Ottawa Senators, belted her with his crutch when he was recovering from a broken leg. That was in 1918, and things hadn't changed much since then. The court dismissed the charge, in any case. Sprague played in the NHL, after all. Now he's in the Hall of Fame. Who remembers his wife's name?

No one perpetuated this antediluvian tradition more enthusiastically than Punch Imlach. On an ideal team, his players would never marry, never age and never read a book. "Usually when I get a guy in young," Imlach said, "he's single to start with and hungry as well. He makes the team. That takes away some of the hunger. He gets married, and maybe that takes away some of his fight. I mean, it's no longer only him. I know one player who got into one hell of a fight one night in the penalty box and got told off by his wife for acting like a barroom brawler. He lost an awful lot of his aggression right from that one incident."

At home, Betty and George could laugh about Punch's attitude toward women. They felt pretty secure in their marriage, and George felt pretty confident in his job with the Leafs, especially now that he was captain.

Betty and George had met as teenagers at a dance in Capreol, Betty's hometown, near Sudbury. As George had advanced in his hockey career, Betty had moved right along with him. When George played in Pittsburgh for a couple of years in his early twenties, Betty had travelled with him, and then to Toronto when he joined the Leafs. For the first nine years, they moved home every summer to Falconbridge, where George made extra money working in a nickel mine. Three years after he became captain of the team, he finally bought a house, for $22,000, in Leaside, a leafy middle-class enclave in Toronto, a couple of miles north of the Gardens.

Some wives had known their husbands even longer. On the Canadiens, Nicole Tremblay had met Jean-Claude on a skating rink in Bagotville when they were both six years old. Henri Richard first skated with his wife, Lise, when they were six and her name was Villiard. John Ferguson had known his wife, Joan, longer than he'd known how to skate, ever since they'd met in public school in Vancouver when they were eleven.

Like Betty, most wives learned over the years to accommodate the strange rituals and secret codes that remained inaccessible to anyone who didn't play in the NHL. The longer a couple spent together, the better a wife could learn the drill, although some of them learned the hard way, especially if their husbands played for Punch Imlach.

Punch treated his players as if they were little kids and disregarded their wives altogether. He told his players how to dress, what to read, how to cut their hair. If they showed up late for a practice, he fined them twenty-five dollars. One day, Lori Horton wrote a note for her daughter's teacher explaining why Jeri-Lyn was late for school and then wrote another one for her husband asking Punch to excuse Timmy for being late for his skating drills. When Imlach caught Johnny Bower smoking a cigarette on the bench during a practice, he sent him home. His wife, Nancy, couldn't believe it, she said. Her husband was almost forty years old.

Since they were treated as kids, a lot of players behaved that way, too, especially when they travelled. Betty knew all about the road trips: the drinking, the horsing around, the hockey hags, the parties. Nothing knits a team more closely together, said Norma Shack one evening as the wives were having coffee before a game, than cheering for your third-line left-winger at a party on a road trip as he stands with his pants down, having sex with a drunken woman on the kitchen table. Betty couldn't tell if Norma was being sarcastic, although it didn't really matter. These things happened, and Betty knew it. All the wives did.

George didn't talk much about that side of a hockey player's life, perhaps because he didn't get involved himself. Besides, under the code of the professional athlete, what happened in the dressing room stayed in the dressing room, and the same code applied to hotel rooms and strangers' kitchens, as well. Sometimes it seemed that there was a code for everything that their husbands did, on or off the ice: a code for fighting, a code for defending a teammate, a code for initiating a rookie, a code for modesty, a code for keeping secrets from a wife. It was like being married to a spy. There might be differences between one team and another, but the code was universal.

The Canadiens' coach, Toe Blake, treated his players differently than Imlach. He imposed no curfew, applied no rules about clothing or haircuts and allowed players to behave as they wanted, as long as they wanted to perform like Montreal Canadiens on and off the ice. Still, the code prevailed on the Canadiens, just as it did on other teams. The younger players on the Canadiens followed the example set by the older ones. The older ones had learned to wear a blazer, shirt and tie. They'd been punished for showing up without a hat. They knew the standards that the Canadiens expected, and they didn't need their coach to enforce them. "Toe demanded first-class play, but he treated us first-class, as well," said Terry Harper. "We had a mutual trust."

No matter what team employed him, though, hockey took priority in the life of an NHL player. If his mind was a labyrinth, hockey was the Minotaur that guarded his soul from intruders, including his wife. Love and affection might have their places, but not in the game itself. Even teammates criticized each other if they allowed their attention to wander from the game. Not long ago, a few of the Leafs had accused Frank Mahovlich of malingering because he was worried about his pregnant wife, Marie. On the Canadiens, Ralph Backstrom took a box of cigars to the Montreal Forum to celebrate the birth of his daughter, Diana, and offered one to Toe Blake. Blake took a cigar and then said, "Now maybe you'll get off your ass and play hockey." And he meant it. The code of the NHL allowed no room for emotional distraction.

When all was said and done, though, Betty Armstrong couldn't complain. None of the wives could, really. George and the rest of them earned as much money as a doctor and far more than a schoolteacher to dress up three times a week and play a game that lasted sixty minutes, while fifteen thousand people paid to watch them do it. Most women felt privileged to be married to an NHL player and proud of their husband's accomplishments. "I boast about him whenever I get the chance," Betty said.

Grown men sent George gifts and photographs, bought him drinks and dinners, told him how much they admired him, offered him a job in the off-season. Children came to the front door and asked George to come outside and play. Women introduced themselves in drug stores and dairy bars and left their phone numbers on the windshield of his car. If the fans thought he deserved it, they'd yell at him, too, right in the middle of Bayview Avenue. It placed peculiar demands on a wife to handle the celebrity of her husband. As Andra Kelly said, "People cheer for Red because he's good on the ice. I cheer for him because he's good all the time."

Some wives appreciated the pressures and privileges that came with celebrity because they'd skated professionally with the Ice Capades, as Lori Horton had, or the Ice Follies, as had Joan Ferguson and Gladys Harper, Terry's wife. They'd learned how to deal with the public, how to present a facade to strangers who greeted their husbands as if they were best friends. They understood the specious relationship that fans created with a performer and the hazards a performer faced if he misinterpreted a fan's affection for something deeper. Especially if they'd never received much affection from their own parents, some players drove themselves to the limit to earn the adoration of their fans. Meanwhile, the fans fantasized that their hero cared about them. Like patrons and performers at a strip bar, all of them could maintain the illusion as long as no one turned on the lights. Trouble started, though, when people began living in the fantasy.

Sometimes it was hard to resist. Even Betty had to admit that it felt exciting, being married to a man who never had to introduce himself at a party, who could always find a table in a crowded restaurant or get immediate service from an auto mechanic. Brain surgeons didn't receive that kind of deference. Lola Keon said that one day she'd been standing in line with her husband at the bank, when a teller pulled them aside and told Dave that, from now on, he should go directly to the assistant manager's desk for help. A few days later, when Lola went back to the bank by herself, the assistant manager didn't recognize her until she told the man her name: Keon, as in Dave, the Maple Leaf.

The spoils of celebrity seemed harmless enough at first. Celebrity was, after all, just a charade. It didn't help anyone change a diaper or stay up all night with a colicky baby. Celebrity didn't keep a wife company when her husband went away for five days in a row, and it didn't scramble the eggs when her husband returned home with a teammate at two in the morning to discuss the previous night's game at the kitchen table. Celebrity didn't last forever, and even in the midst of the glory days, someone still had to shop for the groceries, feed the kids, wipe their chins, wash their hands, talk to their teachers, do the laundry, make the beds, keep in touch with the in-laws and phone the plumber when the pipes froze. Unlike celebrity, that rebop never ended.

For nine months of the year, the player himself demanded as much attention as the kids, and second-hand celebrity hardly compensated a wife for providing it. It began on the night before a game, when the house had to be kept quiet so the player could go to sleep by nine or nine-thirty at the latest. In the morning, the player's wife fed the children and sent them off to school or outside to play, preferably far away from the house, while her husband rested. Before noon, he might head downtown to the rink for a team meeting, then drive home for a nap. In the middle of the afternoon, his wife prepared his pre-game meal, usually a steak, unless you were Jim Pappin, who preferred liver, or Johnny Bower, who'd lost so many teeth that he could only chew a hamburger. After dinner, the wife kept the house quiet again while the player rested or listened to Mantovani on the hi-fi. Before he left for the game, the wife might bring the kids to him the way a nursery maid herded the little princes and princesses into the royal drawing room at Buckingham Palace.

At five, some wives drove their husbands to the rink, making sure to take the same route every time in case a deviation caused the team to lose the game. Some players would make their wives wear the same dress and drive around the block if a black cat crossed their path. By the time they reached the arena, the players were so wound up that they couldn't speak, not that they had much to say. A player usually had nothing on his mind all day but the game, and his wife wouldn't dare to distract him from that.

At first, it came as a relief when her husband went on a road trip, leaving the wife at home by herself. But after a day or two, living in a rented house with second-hand furniture, in a neighbourhood full of strangers who lived according to a nine-to-five schedule that seldom corresponded to hers, a woman began to feel bored and lonely. When Karen Pappin remarked on the boredom she felt in their empty house in Weston, Jim would buy her a round-trip ticket to Sudbury so she could stay there for a few days with her parents. No wonder some wives started to drink, especially if the marriage turned sour. If Lori Horton got mad at Tim before he left on a road trip, she'd lock him out of the house. When he came back, he'd have to knock down the front door. Now he never returned from a trip to the States without two or three bottles of Mogen David wine for his wife. "She was basically stoned for fifteen years," said their daughter Jeri-Lyn.

There wasn't much to do anyway in a suburban house on a weekday afternoon in the middle of winter. A player might sleep for eight or ten hours and then, after he woke up, while away the time reading magazines or, like Frank Mahovlich, listening to the soundtrack from *Oklahoma!* Mahov and his wife, Marie, had at least learned to play bridge, so they'd occasionally get together with Bob Pulford and his wife, Ros, for a few rubbers. Mahovlich had also learned to weave on a loom. But few other players had cultivated such a wide range of pastimes.

"If you're a kid with lots of interests," said a former Canadien named Bobby Smith, "you're probably going to be a well-rounded adult, but forget about being a professional athlete."

For a couple of months in the summer, a player might enjoy a more conventional life with his wife and family. At the end of this week, Betty and George planned to take the kids to Capreol to visit her mom. Tonight, Betty's mom was probably in the kitchen, baking pies. She didn't like to watch George play, in case he got hurt. George's own mother wasn't so timid. Or perhaps she was used to the danger and the violence by now. She was married to a nickel miner, after all. Easier to watch your son on

TV get his teeth knocked out by a hockey stick than worry about your husband getting crushed by a ton of rock in a mine shaft half a mile below the ground. ·

After a couple of summer months, the peace and tranquility would come to a grinding halt. In September, when their kids went back to school, the players went to training camp, and they stayed away for five or six weeks. The Canadiens held their training camp in Victoria, on the other side of the country. They practised five hours a day, from eight-thirty to eleven in the morning and again from two to four-thirty in the afternoon.

Unless they occurred during the summer, a player usually missed the major events of his family's life: the birth of his children, a child's first steps, first words, first teeth, first day at school. A player seldom attended a school play or a graduation ceremony. He never took a winter vacation unless he suffered an injury serious enough to keep him out of the game. He didn't have time to watch his own sons play hockey. He missed weekends at home and never spent Christmas day with his family. Because he was absent for so long, a hockey player's kids often had the same one-dimensional relationship with their father that a fan had. When Casey Kelly was four, she looked out the window one day and saw her dad walking up the driveway with his suitcase. "Look Mommy," she said, "here comes Red Kelly."

It was hardest on the kids. All the wives said so. A hockey player's children enjoyed an elevated status among their peers, as if they lived with a movie star or the Wizard of Oz. "But we never knew if people liked us for us," said Jeri-Lyn Horton, "or because they wanted to meet Tim Horton."

Sometimes an injury came as a relief, if not to the player, then to his family. At last, he could spend some time at home, although he couldn't wrestle with the kids on the floor or go tobogganing in the park, not with his jaw wired shut or his arm in a cast. As time passed, though, the player and his wife would start to worry. "Players lived in constant fear of losing their jobs," said the writer Douglas Hunter. How would a wife feed her family if her husband couldn't work? What would happen to the kids if they had to move to another city in the middle of the school year?

"If you didn't come back from an injury," said Bob Baun, "some guy took your place and you'd wind up in the minors."

Betty Armstrong remembered when Larry Hillman had spent a week in the hospital and another two months recovering from surgery on his knee or his gall bladder or some other part of his body. He was twenty-four. Marjorie, his wife, was even younger. They'd moved that year to Toronto from Providence, Rhode Island, and rented a house in Etobicoke from a friend of Larry's brother, who played hockey for the Bisons in Buffalo. They didn't know a soul in the neighbourhood. Laurie, their daughter, was two years old. "I wondered all winter if Larry would still have a job when he recovered," Marjorie said.

When Hillman's injuries healed, he still had a job, but not with the Leafs. He and Marjorie gave their notice to the owner of their house, packed their furniture and dishes once again and moved to Rochester, where they rented another house that became their home for the next five years.

Players and their families learned to cope with trades, just as they learned to deal with injuries. What else could they do? "It's the kind of life he wants to lead," said Joan Ferguson. "Who am I to tell him not to?"

The owners and the managers had no sympathy for the players' families. Hockey was a business. If a player wanted to get paid for playing, he kept his mouth shut, and his family's mouths too. "You never argue with your meal cheque," said Punch Imlach.

Like families everywhere, some learned to adjust with grace and love, others fell apart. "What are the first two things to go on a hockey player?" asked Philadelphia Flyer Reggie Leach. "His legs and his wife." Pat Sawchuk threatened four times to leave her husband and would finally do it after he was sent to play in Los Angeles. The Cournoyers, the Pappins and the Keons would separate, as well. It could happen to anyone, of course. Dick Duff would never marry at all.

The couples who endured made amends, accommodated each other, learned how to cope and how to forgive. Some of them loved each other. "It's a way of life we're used to," said Andra Kelly. She and her husband, both accomplished skaters and light on their feet, took lessons in ballroom dancing. They learned the rhumba and the cha-cha and the Tennessee Waltz. Forty-five years later, long after Red had retired from the game, the Kellys were still dancing. Compared to a lot of players and their wives, the Kellys were the lucky ones.

While Terry Harper sat in the penalty box, the Leafs swarmed into the Canadiens' end. They came close to scoring when Frank Mahovlich took a pass from Jim Pappin and flipped the puck over Gump Worsley, only to hit the side of the net, six inches from the post. But when Harper's penalty ended, the Leafs hadn't scored, and now, more than five minutes had passed.

For only the second time in the period, the Canadiens had a full contingent of players on the ice. But neither team could make much headway. Fighting off Jean Beliveau in the corner beside the Leafs' net, Red Kelly fell forward onto the puck, and the referee blew his whistle.

For a second or two, Dave Balon loomed over the kneeling Kelly, jabbing him in the back with the butt end of his stick. But then, in front of six million television viewers, fifteen thousand fans and the referee, Balon thought better of his intentions to assault in public the former member of Parliament for York West, and he pushed himself away.

When the puck dropped from John Ashley's hand, Allan Stanley batted it toward the boards. It caromed off Tim Horton's skateblade toward the blue line, where Jacques Laperriere drew back his stick and fired a slapshot at the Leafs' goal.

Fans of the Canadiens joked that Laperriere's slapshot was so inaccurate, the only safe place to hide from it was in front of the net. This time, Laperriere's shot would have sailed about six feet wide of the Leafs' goal if Allan Stanley hadn't knocked it out of the air with his stick.

Snowshoes Stanley had studied every player in the NHL the way a botanist studies plants. He kept notes on each player's idiosyncrasies, including his own teammates'. "I ate, slept and played hockey," Stanley said, "twenty-four hours a day."

Not only could Stanley determine precisely the speed at which a player was skating toward him, he could also measure how fast a player skated away from him. So when he saw Red Kelly wheeling away from him and speeding past Laperriere toward the other end of the rink, with Ron Ellis just behind him, Stanley knew precisely how much force to use on the puck. His pass went fast enough that Kelly could skate after it at full speed, but not so fast that it would reach Terry Harper, the Canadiens defenceman, who was skating backwards about ten feet in front of Kelly.

Kelly caught up to the puck at the centre line. Now it was his turn to put his years of accumulated hockey wisdom to good use. In almost a hundred games against the Canadiens since Harper first joined the team, Kelly had watched the way the Canadiens defenceman played his position, and he knew Harper's characteristics in detail.

Asked to analyze this moment, forty years later, Kelly gave the same answer as he'd done in 1967: "The defenceman stayed between Ronnie and me. I had to shoot."

That was Kelly for you. Eighty years old, by hang, and still modest to a fault. As usual, Cornflakes Kelly left out most of the juicy details, in case someone might think he was bragging.

Kelly might have added, for example, that he'd played defence for twelve years before he became a full-time forward. In his first full year as a centre for the Leafs, he led the team with fifty assists and tied with Dave Keon, who was thirteen years younger, as the third-highest goal scorer on the team. Kelly and Frank Mahovlich set a Leafs record that year for combined goals and assists by two players. With "dazzling passes and astonishing rushes and fat rebounds," according to a local paper, Kelly helped the Big M score forty-eight goals, more than any other Leafs player had ever scored. Kelly would likely have been named for the thirteenth time to the all-star team if another player in tonight's game, Jean Beliveau, hadn't had an even better season. Kelly led the team in assists again in 1963 and, this year, at forty, he'd tied for second. "The hardest thing to learn," he said about playing forward, "was to take a pass from a defenceman in my own end and go out with it."

Thanks to Allan Stanley, he didn't have much trouble taking this one. Crossing the Canadiens' blue line, Kelly swerved toward the boards, then cut back toward the middle of the rink. As Kelly slowed down, Harper hesitated, thinking he might knock the puck off Kelly's stick. But when he reached out, Kelly tricked him and took a wrist shot. At the same time, Ellis sped past Harper.

"Worsley made the save," Kelly said, "but couldn't control the puck." That's the way Kelly had planned it. From Worsley's perspective, the puck came from behind Harper's leg, so high off the ice that he had to use his blocker to stop it. Unable to direct the puck away from Ellis, Worsley fell to his knees.

Kelly figured Worsley would do that, too. He'd seen him do it under similar conditions about three dozen times in the last ten years.

In front of fifteen thousand screaming fans, with Dave Balon whacking him repeatedly in the left arm with his stick, and with Worsley fluttering his arms, stacking his goalie pads and flapping his stick, Ellis felt the puck on his stick and prepared to shoot.

By now, Ellis had spent at least as much time on his hockey skills as a university student spends on his studies. He'd spent about an hour a day just practising his shot. "I shoot and shoot," he said, "aiming high and then low." Ten shots at each corner of the net, then ten more, over and over again, a thousand shots a week, until, by tonight, Ellis could put the puck exactly where he wanted it to go. And that's what he did. He shot the puck over Worsley and into the goal.

When the goal judge, Grant Eason, pressed the button and the red light flashed behind the goal, Ellis said, "Woo," swept to his left at full speed and skated toward centre.

It was, he said, "a highlight of my life."

...

The announcer's voice boomed from the Gardens public-address system, telling the world that the Leafs' first goal of the game had been "scored by number eight, Ellis, assist, number four, Kelly, and number twenty-six, Stanley. The time, six twenty-five."

Waiting on his wing for the face-off, John Ferguson took the announcer's words as a personal insult. He took pride, he said, in pushing hard under pressure. If any moment in his life demanded that he push hard under pressure, this one did. He hadn't come all this way to roll over and die when the Leafs scored a goal.

As the puck dropped from John Ashley's hand, the Canadiens centre, Ralph Backstrom, tried to bat it to Ferguson outside the face-off circle, but it dribbled between the feet of the Leafs centre, Pete Stemkowski. Both men strained to keep the other from touching it.

Bob Pulford took the puck across the blue line into the Canadiens' zone. From his backhand, his shot flew directly at Worsley's crotch. The goalie clapped his cumbersome gloves together as if he'd captured a fly with a pair of oven mitts. Ashley blew his whistle. Sixteen seconds had passed. Ferguson positioned himself once again for another face-off. Hopped up on anger and adrenaline, he could hardly keep his feet still.

Nothing in Ferguson's life had prepared him for a career in the NHL except his insatiable drive to win. He'd grown up in Vancouver, a city where more children had water wings than a pair of hockey skates. His father had come to Canada from Scotland, worked for a while as a shift worker in a meat-packing plant, and finally landed a job as a trainer at the Hastings Park racetrack. Ferguson had learned to read by perusing the green sheets, which gamblers studied for tips on horses before they placed a bet. Ferguson's mother made money doing piecework as a seamstress. Ferguson was nine when his father died. After that, his mom raised him on her own.

Losing his father made Ferguson vulnerable, frightened and angry. Other boys had fathers to support them. He didn't. He had to prove that it didn't matter, that he could do better than other boys who had fathers to help them. To do that, he had to beat them. He did it first by playing baseball and football. He also tried lacrosse and became one of the best players in Canada.

At the age of thirteen, Ferguson went with a friend to the Vancouver Forum, where he borrowed a pair of skates and skidded across the ice on his ankles, waving his arms like a windmill to keep his balance. Ferguson liked skating. Soon he landed a job as a sweeper at the rink and practised on skates that he lifted from the lost-and-found box. Eventually, he became a stick boy in the Western Hockey League for the Vancouver Canucks, whose equipment manager let him use the team's discarded skates. At nineteen, Ferguson was getting paid to play hockey with the Fort Wayne Komets.

A reporter once said that Ferguson skated like "a sackful of moose antlers." But what did he expect? Ferguson had won a job with the Montreal Canadiens only ten years after he'd worn a pair of skates for the first time, and despite his awkward style, he could skate as fast as half the players on the team. Besides, skating was just part of his job. Professionals, said Ferguson, didn't get paid just to play hockey. "We get paid to win." And no one wanted to win more than John Ferguson.

A fatherless, hook-nosed misfit with nothing to recommend him but his athletic ability, Ferguson had struggled without respite to earn himself a place on a professional hockey team, any team. More than anyone, he needed to feel that he belonged. The respect he earned from his teammates, his opponents and his fans could never compensate for the loss he'd suffered as a boy, so he kept pushing himself harder. To get to Montreal, he beat a path from Vancouver through Saskatoon and Cleveland, and he fought for every inch of his progress.

Ferguson had arrived in Montreal a few years earlier from Cleveland, where he'd lived with his wife near the south shore of Lake Erie in a one-bedroom apartment on Euclid Avenue. At the Cleveland Arena, a few blocks away, Ferguson played minor-league hockey for the Barons for three years, earning a salary of about $3,000 a year. In his spare time, he went to the horse races at Thistledown, a racetrack about ten miles out of the city. Ferguson had inherited his late father's passion for horses, and his job as a minor-league hockey player gave him the time, if not the money, to indulge it.

When Ferguson arrived in Montreal to join the Canadiens, he brought a suitcase containing one good shirt and a pair of pants. He didn't own a sports jacket, and he knew the other players on the Canadiens team only by reputation. Even after he passed the ordeal of training camp, his teammates didn't talk to him much, because many of them didn't speak English, and Ferguson spoke no French. At twenty-five, he occupied a no-man's land between the rest of the team's rookies, who were at least four years younger, and the team's three remaining veteran skaters, who were all over thirty, including Jean Beliveau, the player whom Ferguson had been hired to protect.

Before the first game of his first season with the Canadiens, in Boston against the Bruins, Ferguson sat by himself in the dressing room and hardly said a word to his teammates. Ferguson might have made the team, but he still didn't feel as if he'd earned his credentials as a Montreal Canadien.

Before the opening face-off, he skated onto the ice to take his first shift in the NHL, a stoop-shouldered, stumble-footed no-name, in front of fifteen thousand hostile fans. His two linemates, Jean Beliveau and Bernard Geoffrion, had played for the Canadiens for almost a decade and had won ten Stanley Cups between them. Beliveau had won an NHL scoring title. So had Geoffrion, known to his teammates as Boom, short for Boom Boom. Geoffrion had married the daughter of the late Howie Morenz, one of the first players to be inducted into the Hockey Hall of Fame, the first Montreal Canadien to have his number retired and the only Canadien at the time to have been honoured after his death with his body lying in state at centre ice in the Montreal Forum. The blood that flowed through the veins of Ferguson's two French-Canadian linemates was red, white and blue, the same colours as the French tricolour and the Montreal Canadiens logo. No one had ever heard of this maudit anglais named Ferguson or knew where he came from, but Ferguson intended to earn his place on this team just as he'd done on all the other teams he'd joined to get here.

As soon as the puck dropped, Ferguson dropped his gloves. Within twelve seconds, he'd engaged in a rip-roaring fight with a defenceman on the Bruins named Ted Green. Terrible Ted was two years younger than Ferguson and fifteen pounds heavier, and he looked at Ferguson as if he'd like to knock his head into the stands with his fist. In the two years he'd played in the NHL, Green had already broken five knuckles by punching opponents in the head and had spent about 240 minutes in the penalty box, the equivalent of almost four complete games, mostly for beating up other players, but also for harassing the Canadiens' best players, like Beliveau and Geoffrion. Ferguson and Green didn't grab each other's sweaters. They just squared off and dared each other to throw the first punch. Ferguson obliged and decked Green with a right cross. He also scored two goals in the game and recorded an assist. After that, his teammates called him Fergie.

Off the ice, while Beliveau smoked cigars and perused the novels of Victor Hugo, Ferguson was befriended by another veteran on the team, Jean-Guy Talbot, who'd played in tonight's game as a penalty killer for about five minutes. Talbot had played defence for the Canadiens for nine years by the time Ferguson showed up. He'd won five Stanley Cups and for a season or two had reluctantly fought with players on other teams to defend Jean Beliveau. When Ferguson arrived, Talbot was happy to give up fighting.

During that year, Talbot, who could speak English and French, tried to put Ferguson at ease and make him feel at home in the Canadiens organization. On road trips, Talbot roomed with the younger player. Every morning he did fifty push-ups on the floor beside the bed and talked to Ferguson in French. The brain was more receptive in the morning, he said. After practices, he invited Ferguson to join him and his teammates for lunch at Dunn's or Bens, a few blocks from the Forum. Like a surrogate father, he took Ferguson to Blue Bonnets, the local racetrack in Montreal. Talbot kept his own horse there, a gelding called Peter Gunn, named after a popular TV detective.

Thanks to Jean-Guy Talbot and some of his teammates, Ferguson settled down in Montreal. At home with his wife, Joan, in their duplex in Dollard-des-Ormeaux, he played with the kids, washed the floors, attended to Fluffy, the Pomeranian, and tried not to knock the Beswick china horses off their perch in the living room. Nancy Bower had known Fergie for years, ever since her husband, Johnny, had played in Vancouver for the Canucks when Fergie was the team's fifteen-year-old stickboy. "He was a real sweetie," she said of the NHL's toughest fighter.

Off the ice, Ferguson might have become more domesticated; on the ice, he hadn't changed a bit. Two years after Ferguson joined the Canadiens, a rookie named Danny Grant came to the team's training camp. As a junior, Grant had ripped through the Ontario Hockey Association like a fire through a dry forest. Convinced by his own newspaper clippings that he was the second coming of hockey's messiah, he upstaged guys who'd played for the Canadiens for years, as if he was trying not just to beat them but to humiliate them, as well. During a scrimmage, Grant made Jean-Guy Talbot look bad by stripping him of the puck and scoring a goal. Then he taunted Talbot afterwards. Ferguson had seen enough. Grant had violated the code that every Montreal player followed and that Ferguson himself enforced. Ferguson decided to teach him a lesson.

Later in the scrimmage, the puck slid into a corner of the rink, and Ferguson chased Grant to retrieve it. Grant got there first, but when he turned to look up the ice for an open man, Ferguson drove the shaft of his stick with two hands into his face, breaking his nose and leaving him unconscious on his back with his head in a pool of blood. Grant woke up with a concussion and stayed in the hospital for a week. To his credit, Grant fought his way back to the NHL with a vengeance and won the

Calder Trophy as the league's rookie of the year, but he did it not with the Montreal Canadiens but with an expansion team called the Minnesota North Stars.

"That's how hard it was to take a job away from somebody on the Montreal Canadiens," said Gilles Tremblay.

Ferguson skated now up and down the ice, but the puck didn't bounce his way. After almost a minute, Ralph Backstrom launched the puck high into the air from the Canadiens' zone toward the other end of the rink. As Backstrom looked up to follow the graceful arc of the puck, Pete Stemkowski drove his shoulder like a battering ram into Backstrom's upturned jaw. Backstrom's knees buckled, and he toppled to the ice. At the other end of the rink, the linesman blew his whistle to end the play.

John Ashley pointed at Stemkowski, called out his number, "Twelve, blue!" then headed toward the penalty box. Stemkowski, he said, had knocked Backstrom down with a cross-check.

Backstrom wobbled to his feet and made his way to the Canadiens' bench. Stemkowski skated without protest to the penalty box. John Ferguson watched him go. Ferguson hated to see his own teammate ambushed like that. He'd find a way to make Stemkowski pay for that dirty check.

In the Montreal goal, Gump Worsley spat into his goalie glove and slid his stick back and forth. Far down the ice, his teammates Beliveau, Duff, Cournoyer, Rousseau and J.C. Tremblay were attacking the Leafs' defences. Almost forty seconds had passed since Stemkowski had begun serving his penalty. That left another minute and twenty seconds for the five Canadiens on the ice to find a way to beat the four Leafs playing against them. Coach Toe Blake thought they could do it with speed. With the exception, perhaps, of J.C. Tremblay, all of the Canadiens players on the ice could skate faster than their opponents. Even Jean Beliveau, who was thirty-six, still maintained his speed by asking Yvan Cournoyer in practices to chase him up and down the rink. Then they would reverse roles, and Beliveau would chase Cournoyer, who was twelve years younger. He could never catch him, though. No one could catch Yvan Cournoyer.

All five practised their shooting, as well, until each of them could fire a puck so accurately, he could knock a match out of a man's mouth at twenty feet, ten times in a row. "In the NHL," said Beliveau, "you can't be close. You've got to be dead on."

Fast and accurate as they were, these five Canadiens could also score goals. There wasn't much that a player could do to practise that. "Goal-scoring is a gift that cannot be taught," said the former Canadiens goalie Ken Dryden.

To keep the Canadiens from scoring, Punch Imlach selected Tim Horton, Allan Stanley, George Armstrong and Dave Keon. Between them, they had fifty-eight seasons of experience in the NHL. Keon, the youngest of the four, had made the leap to the NHL from junior hockey by practising his defensive skills. The Leafs defencemen often socialized separately from the other players on the team. They invited only one forward to join them: Davey Keon. "He's almost a defenceman anyway," said Tim Horton.

When play resumed, Rousseau fed a pass to Cournoyer, who hesitated and then sped past the two Leafs defencemen. Horton tried to block Rousseau with his hip, but his skates slid out from under him, and now he was on his hands and knees sliding backwards into the boards. Cournoyer cut behind Stanley toward the goal. But because of his hesitation, he had only a few inches to spare, instead of a few feet. Even so, Stanley realized that he couldn't catch Cournoyer if he tried skating after him. So he chose an alternative. With both feet planted on the face-off dot to the left of Sawchuk, Stanley launched himself after Cournoyer as if he was diving off the end of a dock. With his arms outstretched and his stick extended six feet in front of him, he flew through the air like Superman. The tip of his stick touched the puck just hard enough to knock it off Cournoyer's stick.

But now two of the four Leafs were lying on the ice.

Stanley landed with a thud and slid on his Maple Leaf crest toward the end boards. Dave Keon had to jump over his teammate's legs to chase Cournoyer into the corner, but he caught his right skateblade on Stanley's heel and fell face-first into the boards.

Now there were three Leafs lying on the ice.

With no one but Terry Sawchuk to stop them from scoring, Duff and Rousseau skated close enough to the goalie to see him blink through the eyeholes in his mask. Cournoyer slid the puck to Duff. Rousseau circled between Duff and Sawchuk, hoping to block the goalie's view. Duff fired a wrist shot at the four-inch space between Sawchuk and the goalpost. Sawchuk dropped to his knees. The puck hit his left pad. He tried to scoop the puck with his glove, but it spurted away from him, directly back to Duff.

Rousseau collided with George Armstrong, the last Leaf standing. But now Horton had regained his feet and rushed back to defend his goalie. Cournoyer skated toward Horton, hoping to give his teammate more time to shoot. Horton stood his ground. Cournoyer fell backwards as if he'd run into a steam engine. Duff shot again. It went past Cournoyer, through Horton's legs, past Stanley, who'd also scrambled to his feet, and then past Sawchuk. Duff raised his stick to celebrate a goal, but the puck hit the post. Armstrong captured it and fired it down the ice.

With six minutes and thirty-seven seconds left in the period, Henri Richard accelerated from his own end of the rink toward centre. Instead of turning to skate ahead of Richard, Allan Stanley stayed at the Canadiens' blue line and tried to check him. Stanley was ten years older, twenty pounds heavier and seven inches taller. Before Richard had played a single period in the NHL, Stanley had completed more than three hundred games in the league. Now Richard cut past him like a Ferarri swerving past a lamppost, slid the puck to his left, to Dave Balon, crossed the centre line and cut back to his right to take the return pass. But Stanley caught up to him, reached out with his stick and hooked Richard under the shoulder. John Ashley raised his arm to signal a penalty.

Over the next minute, the Canadiens swarmed into the Leafs' end of the rink. They came close to scoring when Yvan Cournoyer skated alone with the puck thirty feet in front of Terry Sawchuk. Cournoyer not only skated like the wind, he'd also practised switching the position of his hands on his stick so that he could shoot from either the right side or the left. He became so adept at this manoeuvre that, during a playoff game, he swept down at full speed from the right side on a goalie named Cesare Maniago, switched hands and scored a goal. But this time, he misplayed the puck when Tim Horton hurled himself across the ice in front of him. On the next attack, Beliveau crossed the Leafs' blue line and slid a pass on his backhand to Ferguson. With Ron Ellis draped over his back, Ferguson chipped the puck off the ice so that it would catch the inside of the post. Sawchuk blocked the puck with his pad, placed his catching glove on top of it, and the referee blew his whistle.

With thirty-nine seconds left in the penalty to Stanley, Ron Ellis passed to Brian Conacher, but the puck crossed two lines. If Conacher touched it, he would be offside. Conacher caught up to the puck near the Canadiens' goal line. Instead of touching it, he just straddled it, keeping the puck between his feet. More time passed. J.C. Tremblay bumped into him, but because Conacher hadn't touched the puck, Tremblay couldn't hit him harder without getting a penalty. The puck remained between Conacher's skates. Bobby Rousseau skated up to Conacher. Rousseau had taken four shots at the Leafs' goal and missed each time. Now he saw this big English doofus insulting the Montreal Canadiens with a juvenile manoeuvre. Rousseau jammed his stick between Conacher's skates. He missed the puck but yanked Conacher's feet from under him. Conacher fell down. J.C. Tremblay touched the puck. The referee blew his whistle, pointed at Rousseau and ordered him to the penalty box. With his impetuous gesture, Rousseau had terminated the Canadiens power play prematurely. Judging by his posture and the grim expression on his face, Rousseau knew exactly what he'd done.

For almost two minutes, five Leafs skaters attacked four Canadiens, but they didn't get a single shot on Gump Worsley. The players were getting tired, and the ice was getting soft. The puck was visibly bouncing over chunks of slush, especially around the two goals. A player skating past his own goal with the puck had to bend forward to keep it cradled under his stickblade or else it would bounce away from him.

With one minute and two seconds left in the second period, Pappin and Pulford joined Stemkowski on the ice for the face-off.

As a teenaged junior with the Toronto Marlboros, Pappin had been a star. In his first year, he finished fourth on the team in scoring. In his second year, he finished first. "When you see a kid like that, you don't forget him," said Billy Reay, the former Leafs coach. "You just take his name and file it away somewhere."

The Toronto Maple Leafs under Punch Imlach seemed to have misfiled Pappin's name, even as he blossomed right before their eyes. Pappin bounced between the minors and the NHL, never knowing from one day to the next where he'd play tomorrow or what position. This year in Rochester, he'd played defence.

Pappin was devoted to the Maple Leafs. When Imlach kept sending him back to Rochester, as he'd done more than six times in the last four years, Pappin never had a bad word to say. "I'd sooner be farmed out in the Leaf organization than play elsewhere in the NHL," he said.

In Rochester, Pappin scored lots of goals, always ranking among the top three or four players. But until this year, he'd never scored more than twenty for the Leafs. After scoring twenty-one goals for the team this season, he'd accumulated another fourteen points in eleven games so far in the playoffs. But when this season ended, he had no confidence that Punch Imlach would keep him on the team. That didn't mean he wouldn't ask for a raise. He thought he deserved more money, even if Imlach didn't.

Although Imlach seemed not to know it, everyone else in the league regarded Pappin as a complete hockey player: As an individual, he might have been a surly dickhead, but as a hockey player, he backchecked with as much determination as he forechecked. He chased the puck into corners, where a defenceman who outweighed him by twenty pounds would invariably try to hammer him as hard as he could into the boards. He skated headlong into the area in front of the opposing team's net, knowing that an opponent would try to knock his head off when he looked down to receive a pass. He would stand in front of Tim Horton's hundred-mile-an-hour slapshot to tip the puck into the goal, then fight for the rebound if he didn't score. He was unselfish. Of the fifteen points he would accumulate in his twelve playoff games this year, eight of them would be assists. He might have made a dubious pal, but as a teammate, he was worth his weight in gold.

"If Pappin ever becomes available," said Billy Reay, "you grab him." And he did. Next season, Pappin would spend a few weeks in Rochester. Then the Leafs would trade him to Chicago, whose coach was Billy Reay.

Though none of them would ever admit that it mattered, some players in the NHL performed better when they felt appreciated by their team. Frank Mahovlich was one. Pappin was another.

In public, Pappin tried to disguise his sensitivity under a veneer of bluster and hard-edged callousness. "The only time I get discouraged is when I have to take a pay cut," he said.

Pappin felt pretty good tonight, though, despite the resentment and bitterness he'd begun to feel about the Leafs. Early this morning, before six, he'd driven to Woodbine Racetrack to work with a trainer named Jerry Meyer. This afternoon, Pappin's wife, Karen, had offered to fry up a slice of liver, but he'd said, no. He ate a hot dog instead.

When they'd first met in Sudbury, Karen had been a schoolteacher. Now they lived in Weston. Karen — at home with Merrill, the two-year-old, and Arne, who was born only a couple of months ago — was watching the game on TV. She knew that Pappin, like everyone else on the team, played best when his mind was free to think about hockey. Tonight, he was playing so well that the puck was bouncing his way, just as it always does when you don't have to think about what you're doing.

There wasn't much to think about anyway, with the final seconds of the period ticking away. Just don't make a mistake. Pappin took a pass from Pulford, then shoved the puck ahead to Stemkowski as they barrelled down the ice toward the Canadiens' blue line. When they crossed the line, Stemmer slipped the puck back to Pappin, then headed for the Canadiens' goal.

Laperriere chased Pappin into the corner to the right of Worsley and tried to make sure that Pappin didn't get a clear shot. It wasn't hard to do. Pappin was a right-handed shot. The only way he could get the puck past Laperriere was by taking a backhand, and that's what Pappin did. He lobbed the puck along the goal line, about three feet off the ice, toward the Canadiens' goal. He wasn't really aiming for the net. He was just trying to get the puck closer to Stemkowski, who was battling for position with Terry Harper.

Harper was facing Pappin. Stemkowski was behind him. When Pappin launched his diddly backhand, Stemkowski stepped forward, toward Gump Worsley. Worsley held himself firmly against the right post. Either Harper would block Pappin's shot or Worsley would. But when Stemkowski stepped forward, Harper spun to his left, away from Worsley, to avoid colliding with his goalie. The puck glanced off his leg and headed toward the far goalpost. Startled, Worsley twisted himself around and dived across the goal mouth to block the puck. But Pappin's shot was harder than Worsley thought. The puck glanced off the post and into the net, leaving Worsley sprawled on his stomach across his crease with his face buried in the damp leather of his catching glove.

Of the fourteen shots that the Canadiens had taken in the second period, Terry Sawchuk had stopped them all. The Leafs had taken sixteen shots on Gump Worsley. He'd stopped all but two.

The Canadiens were down by two goals. They had just twenty minutes left to even the score.

CHAPTER FIVE
Second Intermission

Well-heeled fans stood up from their seats behind the Canadiens' bench. The prime minister of the country was a few rows back, still sitting in his overcoat and hat, beside his wife. The premier of the province was nearby, smiling and laughing with Alan Eagleson. Compared to the grim intensity of the players filing past the Canadiens' assistant trainer, Eddy Palchak, their good humour seemed almost insulting.

Palchak made his way to the dressing room. In his pocket, he carried a miniature Stanley Cup attached to a sterling-silver keychain. The players on the team had pitched in to buy the trinket for him two years ago, after they'd won the real Cup against the Chicago Black Hawks. Palchak had just turned twenty-two that season. The players wanted to thank him for his hard work. They presented the keychain to him one morning at centre ice in the Forum, where they'd assembled in their uniforms for the team photo. When Jean Beliveau, the captain of the team, handed him the cup, the other players chanted, "Eddy, Eddy," and tapped their sticks on the ice.

On his Stanley Cup keychain he kept only one key. It opened the door to his bachelor apartment off De Maisonneuve, about a five-minute walk from the Forum. But he attached it to a bigger ring that held all the rest of his keys. He had keys to the first-aid room, the medicine chest, the skate-sharpening room, the equipment room, the trainers' room, the stick locker and the team's dressing room in the Forum. He had keys to about six different cubbyholes around the Forum where he stored bits and pieces of equipment and repair kits. He carried six different keys for all the trunks and stick racks that the team used to lug its equipment from one city to another. He had a key to a door that gave him access to the arena from De Maisonneuve so that he could let himself in when he had to work all night. When he walked through the empty corridors of the Montreal Forum, he sounded as if he had a tambourine in his pants. The keys had worn a hole through the pocket of his grey trousers. He usually repaired the hole himself, squinting through his glasses at the thick needle of the industrial sewing machine that the trainers used to repair the team's gloves, although sometimes he took the pants home to his mom. To make sure that the keys didn't drop right down his pantleg and onto the ground, Palchak fastened the big ring to one end of a cord. The other end of the cord was tied to a belt loop on his trousers, under his red Montreal Canadiens cardigan.

Palchak came from a family of hockey players. Cousins, brothers, uncles, nephews all played the game, including one named Mike Bossy, who would set records in the NHL and be inducted into the Hockey Hall of Fame. But Palchak still felt mildly surprised at the appearance of the players when they rested between periods. With their sunken eyes and hollow cheeks and their sweat-stained undershirts clinging to their chests, they looked as frail and skinny as a bunch of undernourished teenagers.

In the dressing room, Yvan Cournoyer sat in his bare feet with his skates on the floor between them. "Eddy," he said.

Palchak picked up Cournoyer's skates, one at a time, and ran his whetstone along each side of the blade to remove the burrs and notches inflicted on the metal by the game-worn ice. The sales rep from CCM had given the stone to Palchak one afternoon a few years ago, along with a couple of pairs of skates that the company had dispatched to the Forum for Jean Beliveau.

When Palchak first started working around the Montreal Forum, his mom worried that he might get into trouble. Some questionable characters loitered around hockey rinks, smoking cigarettes, scalping tickets, betting on games, chattering on the payphones that lined one wall of the lobby and delivering messages from their bosses, who placed wagers on games from strip bars and nightclubs. The timekeeper at the Forum had once been caught rigging the clock so that after a goal it would stop on an even number rather than an odd number. A gambler had paid him to do it to avoid making payouts on goals scored at odd-numbered times.

Like a gentleman's butler, Palchak had become the Canadiens' trusted retainer, competent, uncomplaining and discreet. Nothing that the players did could disconcert him. On weekday mornings before practice, Palchak had found players passed out dead drunk on the dressing-room floor and had cleaned up their vomit after they'd suited up and joined their teammates on the ice. At the instigation of mischievous teammates, he'd walked into hotel rooms to find women lying naked in the beds of players whose wives had kissed them goodbye before they'd boarded the train in Montreal, three hundred miles away. He'd been hit in the head by flying dinner rolls during team meals in hotel dining rooms, seen players knock down hotel-room doors and toss furniture from fourth-storey windows into hotel swimming pools. Hell, they'd thrown Eddy into a swimming pool, cardigan and all, and he'd never said a word. As much as the players relied on him to serve them, they trusted him never to talk out of school. For more than thirty years, turning down offers of money, fame and glory for the stories that he could tell, Palchak would keep their trust until he needed money. But by then, the secrets had lost their currency, and no one wanted them anymore. For all this, Palchak earned about $4,500 a year.

Every two weeks, Palchak walked upstairs in his soft-soled shoes to the manager's office in the Montreal Forum and fetched the players' paycheques. He also collected the players' mail in a sack from the team offices and left it for them on a table in the Canadiens' dressing room.

Jean Beliveau usually received more letters than anyone else on the team. But Dick Duff received a few hundred a month, as well. Many of them came from children, and the players answered every one of them.

In the days before an athlete's kindness had become a public-relations gesture, NHL players suffered children willingly and without much fanfare. Jean-Guy Talbot volunteered to dress up as Santa Claus for a couple of days a year at a local department store. Dick Duff found out that a dozen kids had to spend Christmas by themselves in a hospital and arranged to bring them all to a game on Christmas Eve, at his own expense. Henri Richard raised $120,000 one year from patrons of his tavern for an orphanage in Montreal's north end. Jean Beliveau played ball hockey on the street with kids in his neighbourhood and spent so much time trying to keep adolescents out of trouble that he'd once won a trophy from a fraternal organization called the Knights of Pythias.

Palchak honed Cournoyer's skateblade, hoping that it would help him in the third period. At the moment, nothing mattered more than the next period. Palchak hoped that the Canadiens would score two goals. He'd even bet on it, if he could. But he kept his hope to himself. He was superstitious enough to believe he'd jinx the team if he opened his mouth at the wrong time.

Even if they didn't gamble, hockey players paid attention to statistics and used them to calculate their chances of executing a play, scoring a goal, making the team, keeping their job, surviving for another season. When he'd first attended a Canadiens training camp, Henri Richard had calculated the odds and figured that he had a better chance of getting a job as a bricklayer. A couple of his brothers worked in construction and said there was always demand for a man who could build a wall. After Richard signed his first contract with Frank Selke, he'd worked for a year or two in the off-season as a sales rep for British Petroleum. Now Richard owned his own tavern, and he didn't have to work for anyone but himself. Things were going well enough that Richard had given his younger brother, Claude, a job as a waiter. Richard's reputation attracted customers to the tavern. So did the chance that he might talk to them.

It was Claude who had told Henri about Jean Drapeau's proclamation last week. Claude read the newspaper and paid attention to stuff like that. Drapeau, the mayor of Montreal, had stood up in front of a thousand dignitaries at the opening ceremony of Expo 67, with the Queen of England perched on the stage in her best wool suit. He'd puffed himself up in all his self-inflated grandeur and promised the audience that this year the Montreal Canadiens would win the Stanley Cup. Jean Beliveau had guaranteed it, he said. Only a politician would make a promise like that.

Since the end of April, more than a million people had visited Expo 67, on an island east of the city, and every one of them expected the Canadiens to return to Montreal tomorrow, win the seventh game of the series on Thursday and roll through the city a few days later with the Stanley Cup in the back seat of a Cadillac convertible.

Drapeau had even commissioned personalized trophies for the players, made by Bohemian glassmakers hand-picked by the Czechoslovakian minister of culture. The trophies had already arrived in Montreal and were sitting in padded boxes behind a locked door of the nearly completed Czech Pavilion. Two weeks from tonight, the mayor of Montreal and the lame-duck president of Czechoslovakia, Antonin Novotny, were scheduled to present the trophies to each of the Canadiens.

Players on the Canadiens usually spent the summer at home, working. When Henri Richard and Claude Provost formed a touring fastball squad to raise money playing charity games around the province, they couldn't fill all the positions, because most of their teammates had full-time jobs. But this year, most of the team intended to visit Expo. Jacques Laperriere had rented a cabin in the hills outside Montreal. Jean Beliveau intended to cross the bridge from his home in Longueuil whenever he could get a day off from his job with Molson. Rogie Vachon was twenty-two, unmarried and looking forward to summer nights of go-go dancing at the Youth

Pavilion. Dave Balon planned to stay in the city instead of taking the train back to Saskatchewan to spend the summer on the family wheat farm near Wakaw. Gilles Tremblay and Bobby Rousseau wanted to watch the Canadian Open at the municipal cow pasture that the mayor had tried to transform into a golf course. Tremblay's wife had just given birth to a daughter, though, so he wouldn't have as much time as his teammates to spend at Expo.

Richard's wife was pregnant again, as well. When they'd talked on the phone this morning, Lise said she'd had trouble sleeping last night. The baby hadn't kept her awake, though, as much as the thought of moving to another city. For wives who didn't speak the language, the prospect of moving to an English-speaking city filled them with dread. "We have always lived in the north end," Richard said in an interview, "and there is no reason at all to speak English there."

This summer, if one of the six new expansion teams in the NHL drafted their husbands, the French-speaking wives of the Montreal Canadiens didn't know what they'd do. Some of them thought they'd move home to Bagotville or Cap-de-la-Madeleine while their husbands spent the winter a thousand miles away in Minnesota or California. That's what their friends did, moved home when their husbands went off to work in the mines in British Columbia or the Yukon. But others thought they'd go with their husbands to Philadelphia or Oakland and live in linguistic purgatory for eight months. To prepare themselves for that possibility, some of them had enrolled in English courses.

Dick Duff knew how it felt to wake up as a member of a team in one city and go to bed that night as a member of another team in another city. He'd now played for three teams in the NHL: the Toronto Maple Leafs, the New York Rangers and the Montreal Canadiens. But his departure from Toronto hit him the hardest.

Duff played hockey with the elusive grace of a gust of wind. He was also one tough son of a bitch. Sure, he answered letters from children and blushed when he opened valentines from women he'd never met and felt sad when the Leafs sent him to New York. But he was also a tough son of a bitch. That's why his teammates loved him, and that's why he kept his sadness to himself.

The son of an underground gold miner who worked with Ralph Backstrom's dad for Teck-Hughes in Kirkland Lake, Duff had grown up with twelve brothers and sisters, including a few who'd become professional hockey players themselves, but Dickie was the best of them all. He'd made sure of it. Since he turned ten, he'd spent almost all his time playing hockey. When he wasn't playing the game, he was thinking about it. He thought about how he could manoeuvre the puck between his skates then kick it through a defenceman's legs and retrieve it when he darted past. He thought about shifting his head to fake a move to the left while swerving to his right at the same instant. He thought about the advice he'd received from a player named Ted Lindsay, another boy who'd grown up in Kirkland Lake and made it to the NHL. "Keep working," Lindsay said, "and don't take nothing from nobody."

When the school day ended, Duff went out on the ice and practised his moves until he perfected them. Then he'd work on them some more. The manners and conventions that he learned off the ice became irrelevant impediments when he started to skate. On the ice, winning mattered more than anything, and Duff would do anything to win.

There was no time for a conventional adolescence, Duff said later. "Growing-up time was somewhere else," he said. "The game didn't come without a price."

Duff learned early how to fight for what he wanted. He weighed about a hundred and fifty pounds, and he had to cut eight inches off the end of his stick before he could use it comfortably on the ice. But he backed down from no one. As one of the smallest players in the NHL, he didn't fight often, but when he did, he almost always chose the most fearsome opponent on the ice. Usually the guy outweighed Duff by twenty-five pounds, had knuckles the size of reef knots and spent far more time than Duff did in the penalty box. In his twelve seasons in the league so far,

Duff had fought Terrible Ted Green and Howie Young, whose nickname was Wild Thing. With the Toronto Maple Leafs, Duff had fought Reggie Fleming on two different occasions, and he'd fought him once again this year as a Canadien, after Fleming had taken on Duff's teammate Terry Harper. It didn't matter that Fleming averaged ten fights a year, spent seven times as many minutes as Duff did in the penalty box and had been described by the *New York Times* as one of the league's toughest players. Duff would do anything to help his team win a hockey game, and his teammates knew it.

"To play professional hockey," Duff said, "a guy has got to go out on the ice and pretend he's crazy." Some players didn't have to pretend very hard.

Duff was just as tough in practice as he was in a game. As a Maple Leaf, he tangled often with Bob Baun, the defenceman, who outweighed him by thirty pounds. As a Canadien, he went toe to toe with John Ferguson. And when the practice ended, the two players went out together for lunch.

Duff could also score goals. In his early days as a Maple Leaf, he'd scored more than twenty a season for three seasons in a row. He'd done it again last year with the Canadiens, when he was thirty. Duff was especially good at scoring goals when his team needed them most. In a year when he scored only once in every four games during the regular season, he improved his performance in the playoffs and scored a goal in every two.

Duff was sometimes compared to Dave Keon. Both players weighed about the same, and neither could change a lightbulb without standing on a stool. Duff grew up in Kirkland Lake. Keon grew up about fifty miles down the road, in Rouyn-Noranda. Both of them had travelled ten hours to Toronto at the age of fifteen and beaten sixty other boys for an available spot at St. Michael's College. Both players jumped as teenagers directly from junior hockey to the NHL. In their first seasons with the Leafs, Duff scored eighteen goals, Keon scored twenty. But the comparison ended with their temperament. In his first season in the NHL, Dave Keon received six minutes in penalties. Duff received seventy-four. "I didn't mind being mean," Duff said.

Duff was four years and thirty-two days older than Keon, and he'd played for the Leafs for five years when Keon joined the team in 1960. But within two years on the Leafs, Keon started to eclipse Duff as the most dazzling sprite in the NHL. He scored twenty-six goals in his second season in the league and finished twenty-four points ahead of Duff, although he also played thirteen more games because Duff had broken his ankle that year. At twenty-five, Duff looked as if he'd reached the end of the road as a Maple Leaf. And then the playoffs began. In twelve games against New York and Chicago, Keon recorded eight points, a respectable total for a twenty-one-year-old kid in his second year with the team. Duff recorded thirteen points, including the final goal against Chicago that won the Stanley Cup. He also received twenty minutes in penalties in the playoffs, more time than Keon received in eighteen years of NHL playoff games.

Duff's performance didn't persuade Punch Imlach to keep him on the team, though. After nine years with the team, he woke up one morning in 1964, turned on the radio and discovered from a news broadcast that the Leafs had traded him to New York. Duff was sharing an apartment in Weston with his brother, a mechanic, who'd already gone to work. So Duff left a note to tell his brother he wouldn't be home that night. He also suggested that his brother should find another roommate. Then he flew to New York and played the next night with the Rangers. In the years after that day, the Leafs and Dave Keon would win two more Stanley Cups. Duff would win four.

"Stay in motion," he'd said more than once when anyone asked for advice. "If you're always on the move, it's amazing how often you'll give yourself a second chance after a misplay. But it's mostly a state of mind."

Duff's state of mind on the ice brought him as close to Heaven as he could ever hope to get. Sometimes he wished that he could play hockey all day long. When Duff played hockey, his life became as pure as sunlight.

It had a purpose beyond hope or desire. When he played hockey, his life had no loose ends or ambiguities. It fit like a snug piece of a jigsaw puzzle within God's plan.

"The hard part," he said, "was the other twenty hours in a day." Off the ice, he couldn't stay in motion, and the second chances eluded him. After a few beers, his state of mind got the better of him. He felt bogged down, aimless, without purpose.

Duff had found it easier to fill his time in Toronto than in New York or Montreal. He'd been a star in Toronto since he'd played in high school with another of his brothers at St. Mike's. Later, in his first few years with the Maple Leafs, he'd lived as a tenant in a house in North Toronto. Pedestrians on Yonge Street said hello to him. When he took his loafers to get them repaired, the shoemaker did the work in return for Duff's autograph on a photo. Girls handed him their phone numbers on the back of chocolate-bar wrappers and empty gum packages. Sometimes he called them. Usually he didn't.

Players like Tim Horton and Tod Sloan had graduated from St. Mike's, too. They'd known about Duff since he'd come to the city from up north. He passed the time with his teammates, playing cribbage in the afternoons with Horton and Boomer Baun in a private room at George's Spaghetti House. In the off-season, he played tennis with George Armstrong. He was just as competitive in a tennis game as he was in hockey, and he could pester his opponents to distraction. Yapping one day after he'd skunked Horton in a crib game, he ended up dangling upside down from a second-storey window listening to the quarters falling like silver raindrops from his pockets to the sidewalk below, while Horton and Allan Stanley held him by the ankles. Even after his teammates on the Leafs settled down and got married, they still included Duff in their plans. When they had children, Duff volunteered to babysit. With the Hortons' kids, he'd played hide and seek in the living room of their home in Willowdale, stuffing himself behind the couch while they searched high and low for Uncle Duffy.

Things were different in Montreal. Duff was thirty-one years old now. He'd lived in Montreal for more than two years, but he didn't see much of the city. For the seven or eight months of the hockey season, he lived in a furnished apartment five storeys above the street. He didn't spend much time with his teammates, and they didn't know him very well.

The Canadiens were a close-knit team, especially on the road. On Sunday mornings, players would attend Mass together. In the evening, they'd go out for dinner. "I've often seen ten or twelve players, often the whole team, go out together as a group to eat," said Jean Beliveau, "or just sit around and hash over the game." Even after the season, players spent their vacations with each other. But Duff wasn't always among them. Some of his teammates didn't speak English very well, and Duff didn't speak French. Unlike Duff, most of his teammates were married, and they already had babysitters for the kids.

Duff had considered marriage. He'd met enough women during his career. He knew that a good hockey wife could make a big difference to a player's life. She protected her husband from harm and took umbrage when someone insulted him. When Toe Blake's wife, Betty, heard a hockey commentator joking on TV that the Canadiens might perform better without their coach, she refused to speak to the man for the rest of her life. But domestic bliss wasn't a priority for Dick Duff. Even the best marriage took more work than Duff wanted to give. And he didn't need a woman's help to protect himself. "I've got a life discipline that I'd have a hard time changing now," he said, if anyone asked.

That didn't stop others from trying to match him with eligible women. Couples felt mildly uncomfortable when single men joined their gatherings, so they sometimes invited a cousin to join them or a neighbour or a single woman from church. Duff appreciated their attention, but few of these women interested him. Trust was the problem — not of women, but of himself. Duff preferred the innocent company of children to a more complicated entanglement with an adult. More than anything, though, he preferred to play hockey. Hockey had given him everything in life that he could have asked for and more.

By the time a good hockey player like Duff was ten years old, school-teachers allowed him extra time to finish a test, knowing that he'd played hockey the night before, after most of his classmates had gone to bed. At fourteen, while his classmates earned money to buy a hockey stick by delivering newspapers or shovelling snow, hockey players like Duff competed against other teams from all over the district, some of whom were almost twenty years old. While their classmates repaired broken sticks with tape and nails rather than buy new ones, good players got all the sticks they wanted, free of charge, along with skates, pants, pads, sweaters and gloves. By sixteen, these players were getting as much as sixty dollars a week. Newspapers published their photographs. By twenty, they believed they deserved it all.

When he made it to the NHL, the most powerful people in the country deferred to a professional hockey player. He became almost untouchable. Police turned their backs on a hockey player's misbehaviour and offered to drive him home if they caught him behind the wheel after he'd spent a day in a bar. Once, when a pesky fan insulted Mike Walton once too often, Walton broke the guy's nose. The guy spent twenty-one days in the hospital recovering from his injuries, but criminal charges against Walton were dismissed. In Quebec City, Tim Horton was detained by police for heaving the Château Frontenac's garbage cans over the edge of a cliff into the St. Lawrence River. When a hotel pop machine took his money without delivering a Coke, Horton loaded the machine onto an elevator and sent it down to the lobby. It took four men to drag it away.

Horton was well past thirty, but his hijinks were treated as boyish pranks, hardly worthy of a reprimand. If he flashed past a police cruiser at more than a hundred miles an hour along the Queen Elizabeth Highway, the cops would recognize Horton's sports car and let him go.

Hockey players led privileged lives because their fans and the public wanted to believe that their heroes walked on water. "I don't see myself as special," insisted Yvan Cournoyer. But everyone else did. Sometimes it seemed as if the whole world conspired to relieve a player of his duties as a citizen.

Indulged, coddled, given special dispensation, some players would push the limits of their privilege until they crossed the inevitable line. A few would lapse into alcoholism and drug addiction. Some would risk their lives in cars and speedboats and come up short, their judgment impaired by a few beers. It would happen to Tim Horton, and it would happen to players who came after him such as Pelle Lindbergh, Bob Gassoff, Dmitri Tertyshny, Dan Snyder and Steve Chiasson, all of them good enough to play in the NHL, all of them dead before their time.

If a player's past caused a problem when he crossed the border into the United States, his team could contact a cabinet minister to obtain a passport for him. Judges allowed their courtrooms to be used by hockey players for practical jokes on their teammates. They dismissed charges against hockey players that would have earned any other man a term in jail. In Quebec, policemen offered to park Jean Beliveau's car.

Some players, like Jean Beliveau, remained humble and never took advantage of their status. "Instead of us being honoured," Beliveau said, "we athletes should thank God for being so kind to us."

Duff agreed with Beliveau. At St. Mike's, he had almost turned his back on a professional career in hockey to become a priest. Sometimes he still felt as if he'd answered a vocation in becoming a professional hockey player, and he felt privileged to play the game so well. In return, he made $10,000 a year — "for being a national hero," he said.

But at the same time as they idolized him, some people played tricks on a hockey player like Duff. They made him believe they enjoyed the honour of his company, when they really just wanted to sell him something. Duff tried to be on his guard. But in a cold city full of strangers, people seemed friendlier after a couple of beers, and after a couple of beers his guard would slip. After three or four, he and his drinking buddies would become best friends, and Duff would do anything to help them. By the time Duff retired, he'd squandered all his money.

Most players sensed the chasm that separated their private and public lives. In one moment, they revelled in the fans' adoration. In the next, they just wanted to escape from the demands imposed by their own notoriety. Haunted by the unexamined contradiction in their lives between fear and privilege, some players became belligerent after a few drinks.

Others just felt sad. Either way, it was almost impossible for a professional hockey player to talk about his feelings to people who didn't make a living from playing the game. With hard work and talent, he'd removed himself from the humdrum world of the common man. He was doing what thousands of men could only dream about. How could a professional hockey player admit that he felt as confused or sad, frightened or despondent, as any other man? Hockey accommodated sentiment, not emotion. Like Hallmark cards, NHL players celebrated milestones, anniversaries and reunions and lamented the passing of their predecessors by tapping their sticks on the ice in ceremonies before a game. But sentiment had the depth of a ten-cent mirror and demanded nothing from a player but his warm and fuzzy acknowledgement. Emotions were different. They were ambiguous, elusive, conflicted and unsettling. They distracted a player's attention. He could numb them with alcohol, but he couldn't escape from them.

Emotions exposed a player's vulnerability, and a man who made his living from his strength couldn't afford to reveal such weakness, so he kept the windows down and the blinds drawn. Most people wouldn't have understood a hockey player's emotions anyway. Most people had to pick up their own underwear, pay their own speeding tickets and put their childhood dreams aside. What did they know about the sadness of a professional hockey player?

It made Dick Duff sad to be traded from Toronto in mid-season. He wore a Leafs sweater on a Tuesday night, and the next night he pulled on the jersey of the Rangers in New York, five hundred miles away. He wasn't the only one. Ralph Backstrom would go home one afternoon after a practice at the Montreal Forum and tell his wife and their three kids, all under the age of ten, that he had three hours to get to the airport to catch a flight to Los Angeles, where a team called the Kings had acquired him. After waking up with his family that morning in Montreal, he'd go to bed alone that night in Los Angeles, and he'd stay there for the rest of the season.

"I went up to see the manager after practice," Backstrom said. "He said, 'You're going to LA. I've got [team owner] Jack Kent Cooke on the phone.' It was about noon. I talked to Mr. Cooke and I said, 'I'll be there tomorrow.' He said, 'You'll be here tonight. You've got a reservation on the 4 o'clock flight.'"

That was that. Hockey players might fight with each other, but no one argued with an owner. You just sucked it up and kept going.

Of all the Canadiens in the room tonight, Eddy Palchak could count on the fingers of one hand the ones who'd been here when he'd first started humping their laundry into the washing machine before school. Beliveau was one. Henri Richard was another. The rest of the players had disappeared from the team.

Rocket Richard had retired, but he still lived in Montreal, and he came to the Forum once in a while dressed in a shirt and tie, looking like a clerk in a liquor store. The Canadiens had given him a job as an ambassador for the team, whatever that meant. Most of the Rocket's teammates had retired, as well, or scattered to cities throughout the National Hockey League, discarded by the Canadiens like yesterday's newspaper.

The same thing would happen to half the players in the room tonight. Six new teams in the NHL would acquire players next month from the league's established teams. The Canadiens had protected Beliveau, Richard and eight other players. But Jim Roberts was up for grabs. So were Leon Rochefort and Dave Balon. Jean-Guy Talbot would go, too, after thirteen years with the Canadiens. In September, all of them could end up on the other side of the continent.

Of the twenty players who'd dressed for tonight's game, six would end their NHL careers with the Canadiens. The end would come first for Gilles Tremblay, two years from tonight, crippled before his thirtieth birthday by asthma that resulted from a flu shot. Tremblay already took as many as sixteen antibiotics a day to enable him to breathe properly.

"If you had Gordie Howe's elbow up your nose for ten years, you'd have asthma too," he said.

Jean Beliveau would retire next, after leading the team in scoring and completing seventy games in the regular season, the first time in fifteen years that an injury hadn't forced him to sit on the sidelines. John Ferguson would quit that year, as well, after five hundred games. In fifteen years of junior and professional hockey, Ferguson had never been traded. After Ferguson's arrival in Montreal in 1963, the Canadiens won Stanley Cups in four of the next six years. Possessing such a weapon, who would put it into the arsenal of a rival army? Ferguson finally quit because he felt distracted, he said, by the demands of the successful business that he'd built on his reputation as the Canadiens' tough guy. But he also worried that he might kill an opponent in a fight. "I was so mad," he said after a fight against a Chicago Black Hawk named Jerry Korab, "I would have killed him. Afterwards, I said to myself, 'Do I really need this? What kind of a guy am I for my kids, for my family?'"

Jacques Laperriere would go three years later, after playing with a broken bone in his foot, followed by a broken thumb, a torn knee ligament, an injured groin and a broken nose smashed into seven pieces by an opponent's stick — but hurt most of all by a coach who treated him like a stranger. Henri Richard would hang on as captain of the team until the mid-1970s, and when he relinquished his grip, Yvan Cournoyer would take over. After that, the only person left in the dressing room from tonight's game would be Eddy Palchak.

The other fourteen players here tonight would end up in St. Louis, Minneapolis, Philadelphia, Quebec City, even Toronto. Duff and Backstrom would both move to Los Angeles. So would Rogie Vachon. Only Palchak would stay in Montreal until he quit the game. Working non-stop for more than 250 consecutive days a year, sometimes twenty hours a day, he would outlast ten coaches, nine captains, thirty goalies and enough players to start another hockey league. Eddy Palchak would accumulate ten Stanley Cup rings, more than any player except Henri Richard, and survive on hot dogs, french fries and Pepsi Cola, seeing his girlfriend for an hour or two a week and sleeping when he could find the time.

At the end of it all, even Palchak would realize how much he'd sacrificed for a life with the Montreal Canadiens. At the age of sixty, he'd start auctioning his jackets, keychains and Stanley Cup rings on eBay to help make ends meet.

Players who retired from the teams in tonight's game would face a similar financial predicament. Like the common man they'd left behind as teenagers, they would have to work to make ends meet or scrape by on a pension that would hardly put food on the table. Players might have loved the game so much that they'd have played for nothing, but none of them wanted to retire that way.

Money was only part of the challenge that faced a retired hockey player. He also had to deal with the emotions that plagued him when he realized that, without hockey, his life had lost its meaning.

"You play hockey all winter from the time you're five years old," said Yvan Cournoyer. "You have the excitement, the camaraderie, the schedule to follow, and then, boom, it's over. And there's a very large hole in your life."

Players coming into the NHL after tonight's game would try to fill the hole with money. Mick Vukota, who tonight was a one-year-old baby in Saskatoon, stuffed into a bassinette near the TV while his parents watched the game, would grow up over the next twenty years to become a professional hockey player in the NHL. Vukota would appear in half as many games as Ralph Backstrom and one-third as many as Jean Beliveau. Over thirteen years, he would play only four full seasons in the NHL, about a quarter of the games that Beliveau, Backstrom and Duff would play. But when Vukota retired from hockey, at the age of thirty-four, he would have almost half a million dollars in the bank, and he would receive an annual pension of $129,000.

By comparison, Backstrom, Beliveau and Cournoyer, each of whom played more than one thousand games in the NHL and generated untold millions of dollars for his team's owners, received pensions of $1,000 a month. After contributing fifteen per cent of his income every year for twenty-six years to the players' pension fund, Gordie Howe, the game's most accomplished player before Wayne Gretzky, would receive less than $14,000 a year. While Rocket Richard's contemporary in baseball, Yogi Berra, retired after eighteen years with the New York Yankees on a pension of $165,000 a year, the Rocket received an annual pension of $7,200. Other players received even less because a crook named Alan Eagleson would systematically steal their money.

The referee and linesmen in tonight's game, along with the other NHL officials, were covered by the same pension plan as the players. They, too, would come up short when they tried to collect on their investment. Over nineteen years, a Hall of Fame linesman named George Hayes worked 1,704 games. When he died in 1987, his wife, a recreational coordinator in Ingersoll, Ontario, was offered monthly payments of $16.98 or a lump sum of $1,032.

Maybe Palchak's mother was right. A hockey rink was no place for a kid, especially if he didn't have a steady job like Eddy's.

Toe Blake's chest felt tight. The tightness had started more than seven months ago, before the Canadiens' first game of the season. The more games the team played, the tighter it felt. After the Leafs scored their first goal tonight, the pressure tightened like a hangman's noose around his torso.

The pain was nothing new for Toe Blake. He beat himself up with worrying, and he worried all the time. If the Canadiens lost, he worried that the team was sliding into a losing streak. If the team won three in a row, he worried that the streak would end. He worried more than ever in the playoffs, and he didn't stop until they ended. Then he worried about the next season.

"The game of hockey was his life," said Jean Beliveau.

Concerned that he might have suffered a heart attack, Blake had once consulted a doctor. The doctor found nothing physically wrong with him. "It must be mental," Blake said. After that, he didn't pay much attention to it.

Blake's life revolved around hockey and his family. In his lexicon, Blake's family extended beyond his wife and children to the Montreal Canadiens. He was a good husband and a good father. He took pride in his family's accomplishments, shared their anxieties, fretted about their problems and encouraged them when they faced difficult decisions. When they weren't playing hockey, his children wore Montreal Canadiens cardigans. Blake held his children to the same standards as his team.

"Toe liked a certain character," said Terry Harper. "He liked people who stood up and spoke for themselves and were honest."

By tonight, Blake and his wife, Betty, had raised three children of their own and a few dozen Montreal Canadiens. He'd guided the Canadiens through almost a thousand games over twelve seasons. For Toe Blake, every one of those games felt like an extended panic attack.

"He was like a father to me," said Yvan Cournoyer. "We were une grande famille."

When Cournoyer first joined the Canadiens, he was unmarried, twenty-one, well-paid and good-looking. With a contract in his pocket, he bought a sports car, rented an apartment and headed for the bright lights of the Montreal nightlife. Women called his number at all hours of the day or night and knocked on his door after home games in the Forum. Cournoyer also had a girlfriend, Ginette, whom he'd met as a junior in Lachine. Ginette was nineteen. Blake took Cournoyer aside that year and told him to move out of his apartment and live with his mother. "Think about getting married," Blake said.

There was nothing that Toe Blake wouldn't do for his family. At the end of one game in which the referee seemed biased against his team, Blake burst from the bench, skidded in his Oxfords across the ice and punched the ref in the cheek. When Henri Richard scored a goal that won the Stanley Cup by depositing the puck in the net as he slid on his stomach past the goalpost, Blake sent the entire team over the boards to celebrate. He figured the referee would have a harder time disallowing the goal if all fifteen thousand fans in the rink thought it counted, and he was right.

"This man loved to win, eh?" said Gump Worsley.

La rage de vaincre: the rage to win. It informed Blake as a father, a player and a coach. He cried when he watched his infant son, Bruce, take his first steps across the carpet in the living room of their house in Notre-Dame-de-Grâce. He cried again more than twenty years later, when the Montreal Canadiens won the 1960 Stanley Cup. By then, his team had won the Cup eight times. The next year, when the Canadiens lost in the playoffs, he burst into tears. But these tears expressed such rage that he rebuffed with a single glance a throng of experienced reporters from some of the biggest newspapers on the continent. Paid to ask sensitive questions at awkward moments, the reporters stormed into the Canadiens' dressing room, saw the fury in Blake's eyes and cowered in silence with their pens and pads in their hands. "I never saw anything like it," said Gilles Tremblay.

A well-known sports journalist in Quebec named Jacques Beauchamp had known Blake for more than twenty years. The first reporter to travel with the Canadiens, Beauchamp spent hours with Blake on road trips, playing cards and talking about hockey. In Montreal, Blake occasionally called on Beauchamp to practise with the Canadiens as the team's spare goalie.

But their friendship ended after a game when the Leafs beat the Canadiens by six goals to three. Red Kelly scored half the goals for the Leafs, including one on a penalty shot. Blake disputed the penalty, then disputed the goal. He continued to argue all night long with the referee, Eddie Powers. When the game ended, Blake was incensed. In the dressing room, he told a reporter that Eddie Powers had called the game "as if he'd bet on the Leafs."

When Powers read Blake's comment in the next day's paper, he sued everyone he could think of: the reporter, the reporter's boss, Toe Blake and the entire Montreal Canadiens organization. Powers would have sued the fans if he'd thought he could include them. It was more than a referee's job was worth to be suspected of betting on the outcome of a hockey game. It took two years of legal wrangling to settle the case, and in the end, Blake lost. The editor who allowed Blake's comment to appear in the newspaper was Blake's friend Jacques Beauchamp. Beauchamp worked in Montreal for another twenty years. The Canadiens created an award in his honour. But Toe Blake never spoke to him again.

Hard-nosed, demanding and tough, Blake expected no more from his family and friends than he demanded from himself. Most of the time, he got what he wanted.

"He had a way," said Gump Worsley, "like an earnestness, of making you feel that, since the idea of this game is to win, you've got to give it your best shot, every game."

There was no room in the family for anyone who fell short of Blake's standards. A defenceman named Doug Harvey joined the Canadiens during Blake's last year as a player for the team. A few years later, Blake became the team's coach. Under Blake's coaching, Doug Harvey won five of his seven Norris Trophies as the NHL's best defenceman and made the league's all-star team every year. But Harvey had a drinking problem, and he also joined some of his fellow players in organizing a union. No matter how hard Blake tried to influence his behaviour, Harvey wouldn't see things Blake's way. So Blake got rid of him. Harvey had played for the Canadiens for fourteen years and was still good enough to win another Norris Trophy the next year with the New York Rangers, but that didn't matter to Blake. The team came first.

Blake also unloaded Jacques Plante, an all-star goalie who'd spent ten years with the Canadiens, after Plante's stressful marriage began affecting his performance. By 1963, Plante had won six Vezina Trophies as the best goalie in the league, but Blake couldn't risk the security of his family on a distracted goalie, and he sent him to New York.

All his life, Blake had shouldered responsibilities without complaint. Growing up in Coniston, a few miles east of Sudbury, young Hector was out of bed before the sun rose over the slag heaps so he could hitch the horses at five a.m. to deliver milk each day before playing on the local hockey rink, heading off to school, coming home and playing hockey again. Money was tight in the Blake family, so Hector played goalie. Goalies didn't have to skate. He could play in his boots and save money on skates. His younger brother idolized him but couldn't pronounce his name properly. Instead of Hector, the kid called him Hec-Toe. By the time Blake started playing hockey for the Sudbury Cub Wolves, the team had given him a pair of skates, and everyone called him Toe.

As the Depression loomed, Blake's mom wanted her son to get a job in the mines rather than risk the uncertainties of a career in hockey. But Blake had other ideas. He also had talent, and he could score goals. With Blake on their side, the Cub Wolves won a Memorial Cup as the best junior team in Canada.

At twenty, Blake moved to Hamilton to play senior hockey for the Tigers. Not surprisingly, the team made it to the Allan Cup finals as one of the two best senior teams in the country. Blake played so well that the Montreal Maroons invited him to their training camp in Grimsby. A local girl named Betty Walters noticed Blake, as well, and invited him to meet her parents. When Blake boarded the train to Montreal to join the Maroons in 1934, Betty went with him. That was a good year for Toe Blake. He and Betty got married, and the Maroons won the Stanley Cup.

The Maroons traded Blake to the Canadiens, but nothing really changed for him except the colour of his sweater. The Maroons and the Canadiens were both owned by the Canadian Arena Company, and both teams played in the Montreal Forum, the company's rink. Betty watched Toe play hockey there for the next twelve years, although for most of her husband's career as a player, the Forum was no place for a lady. A chain-link fence separated the clamouring rabble in the six thousand cheap seats from the better-dressed, better-fed and better-behaved fans down below. Fans in the high-priced seats had access to washrooms and snack bars. The clamouring rabble behind them brought their own refreshments, tossed their empty bottles at the chain-link fence and looked for a dark corner under the stands if they needed relief. The fence protected the mucky-mucks from the hoi polloi, but it couldn't hide the stench of piss and cigarette smoke. Betty spent a lot of time in the corridor under the stands.

On the ice, Betty's husband won the Hart Trophy as the most valuable player in the NHL and the Lady Byng Trophy for combining talent with fair play. He also became the captain of the Montreal Canadiens. For four of those years, he played with Maurice Richard and Elmer Lach. Between them, Toe Blake or one of his linemates led the NHL each year in goals, assists and total points. They set a league record for the most points ever scored by a line, captured more than one-third of the available all-star spots and helped their team win two Stanley Cups. On both occasions, Toe Blake scored the winning goal. Both times, Betty cried for joy, and so did her husband.

Conn Smythe offered six players to the Canadiens in return for Blake. The Canadiens turned him down. No team gave away a player who loved to win as much as Toe Blake. "He couldn't stand to lose," said Gilles Tremblay.

Blake would have played forever for the Canadiens, but when he was thirty-five, he broke his ankle so badly that he couldn't skate fast enough to keep up with his linemates. The Canadiens replaced him as the team's captain with a goalie named Bill Durnan. By then, Blake had opened a tavern on St. Catherine Street, not far from the Forum, and Frank Selke had taken over as the team's manager.

Selke had won two Stanley Cups with the Toronto Maple Leafs during the Second World War, while the team's owner, Conn Smythe, was overseas leading a troop of Canadian athletes into battle. When Smythe returned, he took back his position as the Maple Leafs' boss and demanded that Selke salute him. Selke had a better idea. Having put together a good team in Toronto, he moved east to Montreal and built an even better one. In the process, he turned the Montreal Canadiens and their home arena into the pride of the city, although it didn't happen overnight.

"When I walked into the Montreal Forum in 1946," Selke said, "the place was filthy, and the smell of urine was enough to knock you over."

With the help of private detectives, Selke discovered that thousands of fans snuck every night past the turnstiles. Believing that everyone should pay to watch the Canadiens in action, Selke secured the entrances and made sure that every fan arrived at his seat with a ticket. Then, for the first time since the Depression, he raised the price of a ticket. It now cost more than fifty cents to watch the Canadiens play. When the owners had enough money to refurbish the Forum and install washrooms and snack bars where they belonged, Selke removed the chain-link fence. Now all the fans were part of the Canadiens' family, and they behaved accordingly.

Running the team for eighteen years, Selke transformed the Forum from a run-down dump, where drunks stumbled through the corridors with their pants undone, into a shrine, where the wives of lawyers and bankers in suits arrived from Westmount in limousines to show off their jewels and fur coats and worship les glorieux. Selke also built the Canadiens into one of the most successful franchises in sport. And when he had any time to himself, he raised chickens in his backyard in Côtes-des-Neiges, in pens made of wire mesh and sawed-off hockey sticks. Thanks to Selke, said John Ferguson, "The Montreal Canadiens had class."

Knowing that the future of the Montreal Canadiens depended on access to skilled young players, Selke purchased a network of amateur teams throughout Canada and hired a haberdasher's son with a passion for hockey named Sam Pollock to oversee the farm system. Pollock operated for several years as Selke's right-hand man. Like everyone involved with the Canadiens, he based every decision on its contribution to the team's success. Pollock also coached the pride and joy of the amateur ranks, the Montreal Junior Canadiens. When his players graduated from his junior team, Pollock didn't let them wander far from the nest. "He said he didn't want his kids going to the American League," said Gilles Tremblay.

In the American Hockey League, Pollock said, "there were a lot of old pros, drinking and all that." To protect his brood from developing bad habits, he persuaded the NHL to organize an entire new league, the Eastern Professional Hockey League, so he could keep an eye on them. Among others, Gilles Tremblay, Jim Roberts, Jacques Laperriere, Claude Larose and Ralph Backstrom all played in the EPHL for Hull-Ottawa before they joined the Canadiens in Montreal. Like Toe Blake, Pollock regarded the Montreal Canadiens as his family.

Selke made room in the Montreal family for Toe Blake, as well. When Blake recovered from his broken ankle, Selke sent him to Houston to coach one of Selke's minor-league teams, the Huskies. Under Blake, the team won the United States Hockey League championship.

The following year, the Canadiens sent Blake to Buffalo, where he became a playing coach for the Bisons in the AHL. At thirty-six, he was the oldest player on the team, but he thought he could still skate as well as anyone. While Betty took the kids to the Buffalo zoo, Blake limped around the ice on his gimpy leg, but after scoring only one goal in eighteen games, he stopped playing.

If playing frustrated him, coaching drove him crazy, especially in the AHL, where there really were a lot of old pros, as Sam Pollock said — "drinking and all that." The team's manager, a former Boston Bruin named Art Chapman, didn't share Blake's dedication to his players or his passion for winning, and he didn't particularly like sharing the Buffalo limelight with a former whiz-bang from the Montreal Canadiens who'd played with Rocket Richard, won three Stanley Cups and accomplished ten times as much in the NHL as Chapman ever did. But Chapman was the manager, Blake was the coach, and Chapman intended to stay in Buffalo. Either you do things my way, said Chapman, or you'll never work in this town again. The Blakes packed their bags and headed back to Montreal and the Toe Blake Tavern.

The owners of the Canadiens were furious. No one walked out on the Montreal Canadiens, not even Toe Blake. From a rising star in the pantheon of Canadiens' coaches, Blake became just another fan who ran a business and occasionally came to the Forum to watch a hockey game. When he did, he had to buy his own ticket, just like everybody else. Once again, Blake's rage de vaincre had got him into trouble.

One man's misery is another man's opportunity. In Valleyfield, a mill town on an island in the St. Lawrence, halfway between Cornwall and Montreal, a team called the Braves had struggled for four years in the Quebec Senior Hockey League, finishing out of the playoffs three times.

The owner of the local hockey rink was a former Montreal Canadien named Battleship Leduc. He'd won two Stanley Cups in his NHL career, and he recognized a winner when he saw one. When the Canadiens banished Toe Blake, Leduc invited him up the river for a chat.

Everyone in Valleyfield spoke French, which was fine with Toe, who'd learned to speak French from his mother and English from his father and now spoke both languages with equal fluency. Blake wasn't so happy about the downward trajectory of his career, though, from coaching a team of professionals, one rung below the NHL, to coaching a collection of amateurs who'd tumbled off the hockey ladder into oblivion.

In his first year in Valleyfield, Blake played and coached the team to the six-team quarter-finals, not especially impressive in a league of seven teams. The next year, though, the Braves finished in first place, nine points ahead of the Quebec Aces. The Aces' captain, Jean Beliveau, and manager, Punch Imlach, both figured their team would beat the Braves in the playoffs. But when the two teams met in the final series, Blake's team outscored the Aces. Over nine games, the Braves lost four but won five. The Braves went on that year to win the Alexander Cup as the best team from five major hockey leagues in Canada.

Blake's accomplishment didn't particularly impress the Montreal Canadiens. They didn't invite him to games or put his name back on the list of candidates for coaching jobs. When he walked down St. Catherine to the Forum to watch the Canadiens play, he still had to jostle in the queue with the rest of the fans until he reached the box office wicket and bought a ticket.

On the night when the city erupted in rioting after the NHL suspended

Rocket Richard, Blake ran to his tavern to protect his investment. When the rioting ended, the Toe Blake Tavern remained intact. Even in their outrage, the rioting hockey fans knew enough to keep their hands off the property of a former Canadiens star. Some people said the riot might never have happened at all if the Canadiens had been playing under a different coach than Dick Irvin. Irvin was an English-speaking native of Hamilton, Ontario, who did little to discourage violence even among his own players. Some people said he'd goaded Richard into the frenzy that led to the Rocket's suspension. When the story reached Richard, he didn't disagree, so the Montreal Canadiens started looking for a new coach.

Frank Selke considered several candidates to replace him: a former Maple Leaf named Joe Primeau, a former Canadien named Billy Reay, a minor-league player named Roger Leger. Selke's assistant, Ken Reardon, suggested Toe Blake, but Selke just shrugged. Then Rocket Richard appeared on a television show and suggested Blake, as well. With Montreal still picking up the pieces after the riot, Selke could hardly ignore the Rocket.

In 1955, whether Selke agreed or not, the team announced Toe Blake's appointment as coach of the Montreal Canadiens. Blake had been gone from the team for seven years. He'd spent his last few years coaching a team that no one had heard of in a place where no one ever went. But his teammates remembered Blake. "We love that old man," said Blake's former linemate Maurice Richard.

At forty-three, Blake rejoined the Canadiens as coach at the same time as the Rocket's younger brother, Henri, joined the team as a centre. For the next five years, Toe Blake, the two Richards and the rest of the Canadiens won the Stanley Cup every year. Without Blake, Rocket Richard probably would have quit the game. But under Blake's influence, the Rocket spent less time in the penalty box and scored more goals than he had as a rookie.

Like a good father, Blake not only had a calming influence on Rocket Richard, he also appreciated the qualities that distinguished one player from another. When Jean Beliveau became discouraged after he lost the knack for scoring goals, Blake told him just to take shots at the net until one of them went in. "Sure enough," Beliveau said, "a couple went in, and I did all right."

When Gump Worsley started to allow some easy goals, Blake took him into his office, closed the door and said, "You're not goin' so good. You're goin' down too much and when you go down, you're not gettin' up quick enough. Is there anything on your mind? Things okay at home?"

Worsley appreciated Blake's concern, especially after he'd played in New York for ten years under a coach who ridiculed him to the press for drinking too much beer. "I figured, now here's a guy concerned about me," Worsley said. "I dunno how he handled the others, but that's how he handled me."

When the Canadiens were in a slump, Blake walked across the dressing room one night and told Ralph Backstrom, number 6 on the team, that a painter had removed the numbers from the front of the Blakes' house. When the mailman stopped delivering mail, Blake said, he told the painter to put the numbers back. The painter told Blake that he could find all the numbers except the 6. "That's funny," Blake said, "we've got a 6 on our club, and I haven't been able to find him for the last two months, either." Everybody laughed at the joke. The players relaxed. Backstrom played better that night, and the Canadiens won the game.

Blake understood the pressures of playing for the best team in the best league in the world, and he tried never to criticize a player in public. Earlier in this series, a reporter asked Blake about the errors of the team's rookie goalie, Rogatien Vachon, who'd allowed a goal on a harmless shot from Marcel Pronovost. "Leave him alone," Blake said. "He's just a kid."

Blake nurtured Yvan Cournoyer to perfect his defensive play, inspired Bobby Rousseau to pass the puck more often than he shot, extended Dave Balon's career by moving him to left wing and put to rest the troubled thoughts of Gump Worsley. And at the end of each season, he invited everyone to his bar for a party. "I will never get a chance to play for a better coach than Toe Blake," said Bobby Rousseau.

With the third period about to begin, Blake stood now in the centre of the dressing room. "All I want you to do," he said, "is win the period." Not the game. Not the series. Just the period.

CHAPTER SIX
Third Period

The Leafs started the period as if they intended to stop the Canadiens in their tracks. Pappin, Stemkowski and Pulford faced off against Backstrom, Ferguson and Larose, just as they'd done to begin the first two periods of the game. Stemkowski lost the face-off but bulled his way past Backstrom, took two steps and knocked Terry Harper to the ice as soon as Harper touched the puck.

Larose carried the puck down the boards and into the Leafs' end. Marcel Pronovost swept the puck off his stick and into the corner. Pulford, who had raced back to his end of the ice, held the puck against the boards with his skates until the referee blew his whistle.

About a month after tonight's game, Bob Pulford planned to put his professional life on the line. On a Tuesday morning in June, he would say goodbye to his wife, Ros, and leave his house west of the city. While a taxi idled in the driveway, Pulford would check the rose bushes in the garden, which he'd nurtured like a doting parent for about ten years. Then he'd join his friend Alan Eagleson in the cab, and they'd drive a few miles to the airport in Malton.

Pulford and Eagleson had scheduled a meeting in Montreal with Clarence Campbell, the president of the National Hockey League, and the NHL team owners. Eagleson and Pulford intended to inform the owners that the players in the NHL had finally organized themselves into a union. Over the previous season, almost every player in the league had signed a pledge card and paid $150 in annual dues. From now on, the NHL Players' Association would administer their benefits, represent them in collective bargaining discussions with owners and managers and stand behind them when disputes arose.

Bob Pulford had just turned thirty-one. One of the few NHL players who'd graduated from university, Pulford had convictions that ran as deep as his athletic talent and his desire to win. In particular, he believed in supporting his teammates against unscrupulous owners and managers who capitalized on a player's naivety and inexperience to enrich themselves. Through Pulford, other players on the Maple Leafs and in the league had met Eagleson and been persuaded over the previous year to risk their jobs by recruiting their teammates into the NHLPA. Given his hard work, systematic personality and academic qualifications, the players figured Pulford would make a good president of their association.

Alan Eagleson was lean and wiry, wore horn-rimmed glasses and could light up a room with his big-jawed boisterous wit. The Eagle was not a particularly gifted athlete, but that didn't matter. He was smart, tough and ambitious and as competitive as any player in football, lacrosse or hockey. Like Pulford, he didn't back down from a fight. A foil for Pulford's self-contained reserve, Eagleson could blather on for hours with great gusto, about nothing in particular. It was no wonder that he'd become a lawyer and a politician. At thirty-four, he'd already run for a seat in Canada's Parliament and lost, then run for the provincial legislature and won. He also knew his way around a balance sheet, and he'd convinced Pulford and several of his friends that he could not only help them invest their money more wisely, but get them more money to invest, as well, by acting as their agent in contract negotiations. He'd done it for Bobby Orr, he said, and he could sure as hell do it for them, too. Mike Walton, Pulford's roommate on the road, would soon put his trust in Eagleson. So would Ron Ellis and several other Maple Leafs. On the recommendation of players like Pulford and Bobby Orr, Eagleson gained access to the closed world of professional hockey. Doing much more than negotiating contracts, he provided some of his clients with a surrogate father. He held power of attorney over their finances, advised them on business deals, attended their weddings and doled out a weekly allowance so that they wouldn't blow their paycheques like kids in a candy store. Above all else, Eagleson had a gift for inspiring trust. You stick to hockey, he told the players, I'll take care of the rest.

The players liked the way Eagleson stood up for them. He worked for the players, not the league, and they figured he'd stick to his guns on their behalf. He had nothing to gain, it seemed, by betraying them to the league's owners. He was fully on their side.

Eagleson took full advantage of the players' trust. They'd invited him into their world. He was one of them. The players asked Eagleson to become the NHLPA's executive director, and when he accepted the job, they felt relieved. Never in a million years would they have suspected him of collaborating with the owners, selling the players short and ripping them off.

In Montreal, Pulford and Eagleson would head directly downtown to the league's offices, on the sixth floor of the Sun Life Building on Dorchester Square. The imposing granite tower had once been the largest in the British Empire, and it represented everything that Eagleson wanted from life: money, prestige, power and class. The building stood now in the shadows of Place Ville Marie. Designed by I.M. Pei, the forty-seven-storey monstrosity made Eagleson feel insignificant. He preferred his buildings lower to the ground, with more classical lines. Just walking through the heavy brass doors into the marble foyer of the Sun Life Building, he felt important. The Eagle liked to feel important.

When Pulford and Eagleson announced to the owners that they represented the NHLPA, some of the owners would be furious. Others refused to believe that their players would betray them. Sam Pollock, the paternalistic manager of the Montreal Canadiens, always said that no one on his team would have supported a union. Why should they? He treated his players like his own sons. Pollock would be surprised and disappointed to discover that all but four players on the Canadiens had supported the NHLPA, and even the four hold-outs would sign within another three months. The drive to sign up the Canadiens players had been led by Bobby Rousseau and J.C. Tremblay. Pollock had known both players since they were teenagers. To acquire Rousseau for the Canadiens, Pollock had persuaded his bosses to buy an entire junior-hockey team. Tremblay's team in Hull had won a Memorial Cup under Pollock's management. In return for his care and concern, Pollock expected nothing but his players' loyalty and best efforts. Now they'd repaid him by organizing a union.

As Pulford would remind himself, this was no time for sentiment. NHL players wanted more than a pat on the back for a job well done from an employer who could bury them for years in the minor leagues at the drop of a hat. Their own fathers had joined unions as miners, sawmill workers and railway employees to get a better deal. Hockey players deserved a better deal, too. Rocket Richard's superlative skills had enabled his team's owners to generate a million dollars a year in profit, while Richard wondered from one game to the next if he'd still have a job and what he would do when his days in the NHL came to an end. "I've thought about nothing but money all my life," he said.

Compared to an NHL owner's income, Jim Pappin's $14,500 salary, Rocket Richard's $25,000 or Jean Beliveau's $30,000 were drops in the financial bucket. Hell, the entire payroll for the Montreal Canadiens amounted to less than $400,000. Just to get into the league next season, the owners of the six new expansion teams had paid the NHL $2 million apiece. The U.S. television network, CBS, had signed a three-year deal with the NHL for $3.6 million. Teams made another million apiece from ticket sales, and they made even more from soft drinks, popcorn, souvenirs, parking and lucky-number programs. Sam Pollock could argue till he was blue in the face that he treated his players the way a father treats his sons. But most players already had a dad. Now they wanted a bigger allowance, and they had Alan Eagleson to help them get it. "How does that song by the Contours go?" Eagleson had said, as he and Pully arrived for the meeting at the Sun Life Building. "'First I look at the purse.'"

But there was much more than money behind the formation of the NHL Players' Association. Players already made enough money to live comfortably, as long as they had NHL jobs. But none of them knew how long his job would last or what he would do when it ended. Even if a team no longer wanted him, a player's contract prevented him from selling his services elsewhere. Either a player performed for the team that owned his contract or he didn't perform at all.

With a union, all that would change. Rather than suffer the abuse or neglect of a team that didn't want him, as Frank Mahovlich had done for nine years under Punch Imlach, players would have a choice. They wouldn't obtain complete freedom over their working lives. Eagleson didn't ask the owners to go that far. But they could at least express their opinions and exercise choices, especially after the World Hockey Association began competing with the NHL.

At the heart of the players' concerns, however, lay the money, and after tonight's game, they started to get what they deserved. Within five years of tonight's game, players could afford to spend most of their time with bank presidents, entrepreneurs and rock stars instead of the labouring stiffs who'd once helped pay their wages. Hockey players became full-fledged celebrities, and their union collaborated with their employers to milk their adoring fans for all they could get. Under the direction of Eagleson, the NHL Players' Association would sell rights to its logo to a skate company, a food company and a toothpaste company. It entered the hockey school business through Sportsways Inc. in Detroit and Leisuresport Promotions in Toronto, and it began a relationship with a chain of Ontario milk stores.

By 1973, the NHLPA had become so successful at marketing its image that NHL team owners offered, unsuccessfully, to buy it for $1 million. By the time of the players' first strike, in 1992, the hockey cards that school kids once threw against a wall during recess generated $16 million in royalties for the NHLPA and the league. Players might have owed their fortunes in part to the same solidarity movement as the men and women who delivered their mail and manufactured their BMWs, but few players spent much time hobnobbing with their union brethren, unless they'd been paid by a memorabilia dealer to sign autographs at twenty-five bucks a shot.

Like the players it represented, the NHLPA had little in common with more conventional labour unions, and Bob Pulford was an ideal player to head the association. In his opinions about labour-management relations, Pulford spoke not with the voice of a wage-earning labourer but with the voice of the manager that he eventually became. When a baseball player named Curt Flood argued in a $1-million lawsuit that a clause in players' contracts violated U.S. anti-trust legislation, Pulford disagreed with him. NHL contracts contained a similar clause, called a reserve clause. The reserve clause bound a player for life to a single employer within his chosen profession and enabled a team to retain control of a player even after his contract expired. Pulford, who'd become the property of the Toronto Maple Leafs at fourteen, regarded the reserve clause as part of professional hockey. "If a man isn't willing to accept that," he said, "maybe he shouldn't be in the game."

The Liberal federal government, led by Lester Pearson, played into the owners' hands. Sitting with his wife among the fans tonight, Pearson had castigated corporations for collusion, union-busting and price-fixing, and his government had started to revise the nation's competition law, ostensibly to defend the marketplace against corporate greed. But Pearson was also a hockey fan, a former player and coach. In this capacity, he turned a blind eye to the dubious labour tactics practised by the NHL's owners.

When Pearson returned to Ottawa after tonight's game, two members of Parliament would ask his minister of justice, Pierre Trudeau, in the House of Commons why the government continually ignored the NHL's abuse of its players. Contracted for life to self-serving owners and their managerial henchmen, the MPs said, players worked under conditions comparable to indentured servants. Professional hockey players, said Reid Scott, a Toronto lawyer and member of the socialist-influenced New Democratic Party, work "under archaic and serfdom-like rules to be traded like cattle, regardless of their views."

Even if his opinions corresponded more to a manager's than a player's, Pulford still paid a price for his union activities. When Punch Imlach heard about Pulford's role in forming the NHLPA, he stripped him of his status as assistant captain of the team and removed the A from his jersey. That was more than a token gesture. Toronto had always held the captain and his assistants in high regard, and the appointment was an honour extended only to the most worthy individuals. "Losing the A might have been the worst thing that happened to me as a hockey player in Toronto," Pulford said.

Blinded by his paranoia, Imlach failed to recognize a kindred spirit in Pulford. As managers, the two men had a lot in common. Within five years, Pulford would resign his position with the players' union and turn his attention to ascending hockey's corporate ladder. He turned down an offer to join the PR and sales department of a food and beverage conglomerate in Toronto, instead becoming head coach and then manager of the Chicago Black Hawks, answering to the team's owner, "Dollar Bill" Wirtz, known only partly in jest for evaluating players by their price per pound.

Former teammates from the Leafs would contact him occasionally, hoping to land a job or at least a tryout with the team. But a manager's duties didn't include hoisting the baggage of old friendships, and Pulford didn't return their calls. Eventually he became a senior executive with the company that owned the Black Hawks. Long after Curt Flood's argument was vindicated and baseball players gained some control over their professional destinies, a reserve clause would remain in every contract that Pulford's and every other NHL team negotiated with a player and his agent.

More effectively than the players' union, the World Hockey Association challenged the NHL's reserve clause in court. After the rival league succeeded with its challenge, a player could join the WHA without fearing repercussions from the NHL. Yet the clause, in a modified form, remained in NHL contracts for another three decades. In 2004, when players insisted on further modifications, the league's owners locked them out of the league's arenas. So intractable did both sides become during the dispute that, for the first time in the history of professional sports in North America, a major league shut down for an entire season. And for the first time since 1919, when a flu epidemic led to the cancellation of the NHL finals, no team won the Stanley Cup.

On this night in 1967, though, Bob Pulford had never dreamed of player's salaries rising into the millions, the league generating revenues of US$2.5 billion a year or NHL goalies receiving offers of US$30 million a year to wear graphics on their jerseys representing hamburger restaurants, sports shoes, luxury cars, cellular phones and beer. Nor did he anticipate that the NHL would follow the money, moving its head office from the Sun Life Building in Canada, the birthplace of the league, to the forty-seventh floor of an office building in Manhattan, or that the position of president, currently occupied by a compliant former NHL referee named Clarence Campbell, would be assumed in the twenty-first century — along with the title of "commissioner" and a paycheque of more than US$8 million — by a U.S. lawyer named Gary Bettman, who'd never watched a hockey game until he got the job.

If Pulford wouldn't feel shocked by these developments, he would certainly feel shocked by the corruption of his bosom buddy Alan Eagleson. After twenty-five years as executive director of the NHLPA, the Eagle would be arrested, charged and convicted in two countries for stealing hundreds of thousands of dollars from the NHL players who had trusted him. For larding his own coffers with money from their pension fund, Eagleson would serve time in jail, although many players felt that he got off lightly, especially after they realized that their pension cheques amounted to half as much as they would have received if an honest man had administered their savings. The Law Society of Upper Canada would disbar Eagleson. He would be relieved of his Order of Canada, removed from the Hockey Hall of Fame, kicked out of Canada's Sports Hall of Fame and vilified by millions of hockey fans in Canada and the United States for betraying their heroes.

In private, Pulford might have condemned the behaviour of the man. But while hundreds of former NHL players castigated Eagleson in public, Pulford remained steadfast in his friendship. "For his entire life Bob has worshipped God and Eagleson," said former Maple Leaf Billy Harris. "I'm not quite sure in what order."

Though his judgment might seem questionable, his loyalty to his friend remained unimpeachable. When almost 1,400 former and current players sued the NHL over the way the league and Eagleson had manipulated and neglected their pensions, Pulford tended to his rose bushes and refused to participate. "The players owe Alan Eagleson a big thank you," he said. "We would never have got off the ground without him."

Without Pulford's help, the players still won their suit. Pulford himself received $11,044.09 as his share of the settlement. He took the money.

Ralph Backstrom won the face-off and slid the puck back to Claude Larose. But before Larose could control the puck, George Armstrong attacked him like a sprinter off the blocks. The puck slid toward the Canadiens' end of the rink, and Frank Mahovlich chased it.

As quickly as Mahovlich attacked, his teammates skated the other way, after the Canadiens retrieved the puck, to defend their goal. Keon knocked the puck off Backstrom's stick. Mahovlich slid it back to Allan

Stanley. Stanley banked the puck off the boards. Keon chased it, but he put himself offside.

Another whistle, another face-off, another interruption of the Canadiens' momentum.

"Gotta have it," Dick Duff shouted from the Canadiens' bench.

Duff had played in the NHL for eleven years and had started listening on the radio to NHL broadcasts before he could walk. He knew the six teams in the league as well as he knew his own brothers, and he'd memorized every nuance of every player as if he'd absorbed the information through the pores of his skin. Next season, when the league expanded, Duff would play against twice as many players and twice as many teams as he'd done this year. He'd play in cities that he'd never visited in his life, against players he'd never met. None of them could have landed a job this year in the NHL, but next year, NHL teams would beg them to play. Expansion sapped the blood from hockey, said the writer Trent Frayne in 1974, "spreading the talent thin." The quality of the game suffered. The value of the Stanley Cup was diminished. Average attendance fell by almost twenty-five per cent, and it would take the NHL more than twenty years to lure back the absent fans.

After tonight, a player might apply as much skill and perseverance as ever to win the Cup, but along the way he'd compete against opponents who ranged in talent from Bobby Orr to a no-name player from a minor-league team in Amarillo, who'd spent more time in a Texas penalty box than he'd spent in the NHL. If Duff wanted to win a Stanley Cup that still meant as much as it did when he listened on the radio to his first NHL broadcast as a boy in Kirkland Lake, this was his last chance to do it.

Until tonight, teams in the NHL met fourteen times in a season. "We played back-to-back games, home-and-home. Saturday and Sunday," said Henri Richard. During each of those fourteen games, players tried as hard as they could to beat their opponents in any way possible. They pushed, shoved, held, hooked, raced, out-skated, out-muscled, taunted, punched, grappled, slammed and swore at each other, and then did it all over again in the next game. "If you had a grudge against somebody, you knew the next night you were after the guy," said Richard. "The fans knew it too."

Players would detect patterns in their opponents' tactics and come up with new patterns of their own to beat them. They'd remember the way an opponent turned when he received a pass, then figure out how to stop him. They knew to the split second how long an opponent would take to skate from one blue line to the next, then time their own movements to get there first. "We played against everyone so often, we felt as though we were living with them," said Allan Stanley.

But next year, the NHL would add more than a hundred new players. Many of them had never participated in an NHL game, and their teams would play against each other less frequently. Veterans would no longer be able to predict the moves of all their opponents. They'd be lucky if they'd ever seen them before. "I was temporarily lost," Stanley said when the league expanded. "I'd look up and see a stranger and say to myself, 'Who the heck is this guy?'"

Former antagonists in the NHL were accustomed to becoming teammates, playing under coaches and managers whom they'd once tried to beat to a pulp. In the early 1960s, the New York Rangers hired Doug Harvey to coach the team, on the tacit recommendation of the team's assistant captain, Red Sullivan. As a Montreal Canadien, Harvey had once speared Sullivan so badly that he ruptured his spleen. Sullivan nearly died in surgery and was given the last rites by a priest. Would Sullivan mind playing under a man who'd almost killed him, the Rangers' owner asked. "You want to get in the playoffs?" said Sullivan. "Then get him."

After expansion, however, the whole world of professional hockey seemed to lose its bearings. Rivalries between teams and between players became less intense. "You play a team only four or five times a season," said Terry Harper, "you forget the trouble you had with someone and cool down before you see him again."

After tonight, even John Ferguson would start talking to his opponents, greeting former teammates as they warmed up at the other end of the ice.

"Hey, Bosey," he'd shout at Dave Balon, after Balon moved next year to Minnesota.

"Hey, Ralphie," he'd holler at Ralph Backstrom, who would be traded to Los Angeles.

"Hey, Jimmy," he'd shout at Jim Roberts in St. Louis.

His own teammates would razz him for violating his self-imposed sanction against fraternizing with the enemy. "But I played with these guys," Ferguson would argue. "What else can I do?"

Terry Harper, who'd fought a pitched battle one night in the Maple Leaf Gardens penalty box with Bob Pulford, would fly to Los Angeles in a few years to ask Pulford for a job. Pulford had become coach by then of the Kings. He carried no grudges and knew from personal experience what Harper could do. The Kings not only hired Harper, they paid him $125,000 a season. Later, Harper would sue the Kings for trading him to Detroit.

The careers of most players in the game tonight had already lasted longer than average. Only one player in five lasts ten years in the NHL. That adds up to 1,100 games at the most, assuming he's never been sick, injured or demoted to the boonies by a coach like Punch Imlach. Of the forty players in tonight's game, though, ten Maple Leafs and nine Canadiens would end up having played more than a thousand games each. Tim Horton would outlast them all, playing in 1,446 regular season games, and he would have completed more if he hadn't died in a car accident after a game against the Leafs.

Of those nineteen players, though, only four would remain with the same team throughout their NHL career. The rest would move from one city to another as often as an itinerant shoe salesman. Of course, a salesman could quit and take a job with a competitor. NHL players didn't have that choice. But at least the money improved, especially after the World Hockey Association began competing with the NHL for players.

With dozens of teams requiring hundreds of hockey players, a skilled veteran of the NHL could command a higher salary than he'd ever earned in his life. After his first year in the NHL, Ralph Backstrom had won the Calder Trophy as the league's rookie of the year, helped the Montreal Canadiens win the Stanley Cup and made $8,000 playing on the team's third line. Six years from tonight, at an age when many players had retired, Backstrom would hold his nose, sign a five-year contract with the Chicago Cougars and jump to the WHA. In his first year in that league, Backstrom would make $150,000, and he would receive another $100,000 just for putting his signature on the page. "I never dreamed that I'd sign a contract with a salary like this," he said.

Backstrom left the NHL with regret, but he and his wife had two sons and a daughter at the time, all under the age of twelve, "and my family's security comes first," he said.

For every team in the WHA or the NHL, two other teams emerged in minor-league cities throughout the United States. After tonight, players who could hang on long enough would find themselves on a gravy train that took them to strange towns to play hockey before stands crammed with befuddled fans who knew little about the game and wondered half the time what the players were doing. Third-string Canadian players who'd never stepped across the U.S. border in their lives found themselves playing in places like Greenville, South Carolina; Shreveport, Louisiana; and Austin, Texas, for teams with names like the Ice Bats, the Grrrowl and the Jackalopes. In Georgia, a team in Macon was called the Whoopee. On their jerseys, the players wore a logo representing a fig leaf. In El Paso, fans celebrated a goal by tossing tortillas onto the ice.

In the years after tonight's game, hockey would become so popular in Texas that the state would boast more professional franchises than all of Canada. Under the influence of a winning NHL team, the metropolis around Dallas-Fort Worth would nurture the creation of 40 high-school hockey teams and 350 youth and adult recreational leagues.

The officials, too, entered a new era, especially after the formation of a players' union and the WHA. Brent Casselman, one of the linesmen in tonight's game, became a referee in the new league. After earning about $9,000 a year as an NHL linesman, he made $50,000 a year in his new job. After three years, though, Casselman quit and went to work in Hamilton as a car salesman. "I promised my wife I'd quit after our daughter was born," he said.

For the players, joining an expansion team was like attending a high-school reunion. Dick Duff would play again with Bob Pulford and Eddie Shack for the first time in seven years, under the coaching of Larry Regan, a teammate twelve years earlier, when Duff had led the Leafs in scoring. In Buffalo, Duff would play again for Punch Imlach while living with a Sabres' rookie named Rick Martin in Mrs. Higgins's boarding house in Fort Erie. Larry Hillman would be his teammate. So would Eddie Shack, Jean-Guy Talbot and Reggie Fleming, the brawler whom Duff had challenged to one of his few fights in the NHL.

All this lay in the future, though. At the moment, Dick Duff and his teammates had no thought for anything but winning tonight's game.

"Gotta have it," Duff said again.

Since the opening face-off, Toe Blake had stuck to his game plan. But now they'd squandered three minutes and eighteen seconds, more than fifteen per cent of the third period, taking only two shots at Terry Sawchuk and making mistakes that would have embarrassed a peewee.

Blake dug deeper into his bag of tricks. He sent Dick Duff, Bobby Rousseau and Jim Roberts onto the ice.

Dick Duff had spent all but five minutes of the game on the bench. Roberts had played only when the Canadiens had a penalty. As for Rousseau, he'd spent two periods at right wing, on a regular shift with Jean Beliveau and Gilles Tremblay. But he'd begun to make mistakes, he'd allowed his temper to get the better of him, he'd cost his team a penalty and he hadn't appeared yet in this period. Now he was on the ice, not at right wing but at centre.

Dave Balon watched Toe Blake's manoeuvres from his spot on the bench. Balon had proven himself in the NHL. But under Blake, he never knew from one game to the next whether or not he'd play. Sometimes he'd spend the whole game on the bench. Sometimes he wouldn't even dress for the game. "I lost the two best years of my life in Montreal," Balon said.

Next season, a team called the Minnesota North Stars would have first choice of players, and the Stars would choose Dave Balon ahead of all the others, and he would live up to their estimation of his talent. At one point in the 1967–68 season, he would rank as the leading two-way player in the league, with a plus/minus average of plus forty-eight. In other words, with Balon on the ice, he and his teammates scored forty-eight more goals against other teams than they allowed other teams to score against them. "If you live by statistics," said Stan Fischler in the *Sporting News*, "Balon is the best all-round player in the NHL."

In Minnesota, as a member of the North Stars, Balon not only played in every game, he was also one of the four top players on his team. But Balon would remember his year in Minnesota for a much different reason. One morning in Oakland, California, he woke up in his hotel room before a game against the Seals. The temperature outside was in the low eighties. Palm trees grew around the swimming pool.

The game that night would attract about three thousand fans to an arena that held more than fifteen thousand. Few of them had ever seen a hockey game, and none of them knew Dave Balon or what he'd accomplished. In his hotel room, none of that mattered much to Balon. He had already played more than three hundred games in the NHL. He'd won two Stanley Cups with the Canadiens. After his year with Minnesota, he would be traded to the Rangers in New York, where he'd score thirty-six goals in one season and thirty-three the next. With teammates like Rod Gilbert and Walt Tkaczuk, Balon would lead the team in goals.

This morning, in this tropical paradise in Oakland, Balon's roommate was Bill Masterton. Masterton was the same age as Balon, almost to the day, and had grown up in Winnipeg, almost as far west as Balon's hometown of Wakaw, Saskatchewan. But while Balon was scuttling through the minor professional leagues, Masterton had played hockey at the University of Denver, then moved for a year to Hull to play with Terry Harper on a Canadiens farm team. Masterton had played for a season in Cleveland, as well, finishing second in scoring, ahead of John Ferguson and Jim Roberts, and for another two years in St. Paul, in the U.S. Hockey League, where he'd finished first in scoring with a team called the Steers. When the NHL expanded, the Minnesota North Stars gave Masterton his first chance to play in the big league, and unlike his roommate, he had absolutely no complaints. He was thrilled to be here. If Balon groaned about the years that he'd wasted in Montreal, Masterton just smiled and felt lucky.

Balon and Masterton were not only friends and roommates, they also played together on the same line. After their team played to a five-five tie that night against the Seals in Oakland, they travelled back to Minneapolis, where the same two teams met again a week later. Four minutes into the game, Balon skated down the ice with Masterton and saw his friend trying to manoeuvre between two Oakland defencemen. He saw the defencemen knock Masterton down, and he watched Masterton fall backwards near the front of the Oakland net. Above the noise of the crowd, he heard Masterton's head strike the ice with a sound like a watermelon landing on a sidewalk. Balon skated over to see if Masterton was all right. Blood ran from his friend's mouth and ears, and his eyes were closed. The referee and a couple of players were signalling to the bench for a doctor. After they carried Masterton away on a stretcher, the game continued and ended in another tie.

Two nights later, Balon and the North Stars travelled to Los Angeles. Balon stayed alone in his hotel room. Masterton had suffered a brain hemorrhage and was still in the hospital. While the North Stars and Kings played that night, Masterton died. He was the only NHL player ever to die from injuries suffered in a game.

When John Ashley dropped the puck, Horton slapped it across the Canadiens' blue line. Worsley tossed the puck behind the net. Ted Harris circled the goal, saw Dick Duff to his left, accelerating up the ice through the face-off circle, and angled a pass to him. Duff took three strides and was out of his end. Heading straight toward his old pal Tim Horton, he brought his feet squarely under his shoulders so that he could shift to his left or his right without hesitation.

Horton positioned himself to meet his friend, spreading his arms and hovering like a human fishing net in front of a salmon. Every player in the NHL knew about Tim Horton. He was six years older than Duff, with three years' more experience in the NHL. "Nobody coming down his side wants anything to do with him," said a former NHL coach named Keith Allen, who also played against Horton in the American Hockey League. "I don't blame them for passing the puck to a teammate when they get up to the Leaf blueline."

But with Ellis covering Rousseau, Duff couldn't pass the puck. And if Duff moved to his left, toward the boards, Horton could follow. If Duff moved to his right toward the middle of the rink, Horton could go that way, too. Either way, Horton had enough mobility and enough strength to block Duff's progress. He also outweighed Duff by twenty pounds and could lift a small pony with one arm. Still, he'd seen Duff slip like a shadow through the clutches of other defencemen. He waited for his buddy to make the first move.

Duff dropped his head and shoulders to the right, as if he might plunge into the middle of the rink. "Eight times out of ten," said Beliveau, "Duff will go outside. But he'll come to the middle just often enough to worry the defenceman, because he can't be sure which way he'll move."

Horton twitched as imperceptibly as a rose petal under a raindrop. But the movement gave Duff the opening he needed. He went the other way. Horton reached out with his stick and his arms, but Duff had flown past, and Horton hugged a column of air.

Duff was within ten feet of the end boards when Allan Stanley tried to ward him into the corner. He'd skated so far into the Leafs' end of the rink that he had to turn at a right angle to cross in front of the net. He still couldn't pass the puck because his linemates were covered. To block his path to the goal, Stanley just had to keep his body parallel to the goal line. He had Duff contained. Duff started to glide into the corner, and Snowshoes turned his feet to follow him. Suddenly, Duff cut to his right, pulled the puck to his backhand and headed past Stanley to the front of the net. Stanley had only one hope of stopping Duff. He stuck out his left leg and tripped him. Duff flew into the air. Both his skates were off the ice and both his hands were on his stick. John Ashley raised his arm to call a penalty. Terry Sawchuk crouched down, expecting Duff just to shovel the puck along the ice before he landed. Still in the air, Duff nudged the puck. Sawchuk leaned away from the post to cut off the angle. Then, in the time it took for his body to hit the ice, Duff flipped the puck into the air between the goalpost and Sawchuk's pads. By the time Duff landed on his chest, the puck was in the net.

"Toe Blake made two mistakes," Brian Conacher said later. The first was waiting till this game to use Gump Worsley in goal. The second? "He didn't use Dick Duff more regularly."

Dick Duff was earning more than $500 an hour tonight, but within five years, he would earn more than five times as much. Playing in two competing leagues, hundreds of players who'd never dreamed of a career in professional hockey would earn far more than Dick Duff made tonight for playing the game with a fraction of the talent.

A players' union helped. But the fundamental catalyst for their financial bonanza was the World Hockey Association. Started by two sports nuts from California, the WHA competed with the NHL between 1972 and 1979 for players, fans, advertisers and television revenues. Between them, the two leagues initially operated twenty-eight teams, and each team needed at least twenty players.

"The World Hockey Association is the best thing that ever happened," said Ralph Backstrom, who would spend four years in the league. "It opened a lot of doors for a lot of hockey people." And one of those doors led to the vault.

Competition shocked the NHL's owners, but it worked wonders for the players. Teams in the WHA drafted anyone with a pulse and a pair of skates, and sometimes even the skates were optional. In 1972, the Calgary Broncos drafted the premier of the Soviet Union, Alexei Kosygin, mistakenly assuming he was a Russian left-winger. WHA teams recruited teenagers as young as fourteen and offered million-dollar signing bonuses to the best prospects. The Houston Aeros offered $200,000 to Henri Richard, even though he'd said many times that he'd never play professional hockey for anyone but the Montreal Canadiens.

Richard stayed in Montreal, but many other players took the bait. From the teams in tonight's game, the WHA would snare Ralph Backstrom, J.C. Tremblay, Dave Keon, Frank Mahovlich, Larry Hillman, Bob Baun, Mike Walton and Al Smith, the goalie who sat tonight in the Maple Leafs' dressing room, watching the game on TV. By 1979, when the WHA folded and the NHL incorporated four of its franchises, players in the upstart league included Bobby Hull, Gordie Howe, Mark Messier and Wayne Gretzky. Over five years, the WHA lured more than seventy players from the NHL. All of them would openly admit that they played in the new league for the money. And who could blame them? Frank Mahovlich used to make $18,000 a year and take the subway to his games in Toronto. When he moved to Birmingham, Alabama, he drove to his team's WHA games in a Jaguar V-12 and earned $235,000 a year, more money than he'd made in his life.

Operating in a "never-never land atmosphere," according to the *Montreal Gazette*, teams in both leagues offered more than money to attract players. A WHA team in Ottawa offered Dave Keon $1 million over five years and an endorsement arrangement with Monroe Games, a U.S. toy and novelty manufacturer, owned by the team's financial backer. Goalie Bernie Parent was offered $750,000 for five years, along with a houseboat and a car. Wayne Connelly received $300,000 from the Minnesota Fighting Saints and his own show on a local TV station.

NHL owners — who'd treated their players like serfs, with the Canadian government's tacit approval — now had to scramble to keep their organizations intact or else watch their former indentured servants walk out the door with the silverware. An expansion team called the New York Islanders lost seven of its twenty draft choices to the WHA. The no-names who remained on the team couldn't win more than one game in four.

Knowing that fans wouldn't cheer for long for a losing team, NHL owners doubled or tripled the salaries of their minor-league players to prevent the same calamity occurring in their rinks. Then they sued the WHA for weakening the stranglehold they'd applied for thirty years to their players' lives. In return, the WHA slapped the NHL with a $50-million antitrust lawsuit, showing more initiative than even the prime minister of Canada.

When players continued to jump to the rival league, NHL owners raised their salaries even further. After one year of competition with the WHA, the average NHL salary rose by thirty-five per cent, according to Alan Eagleson, who knew the value of every dollar he ever stole. The league would spend forty-five per cent of its total revenues on player salaries, up from about twenty-five per cent the year before. Before tonight's game, players could convincingly say that they played the game for other reasons besides money, since they made so little of it. In the decades after tonight, no one would believe that they played for any other reason than money, whether they did or not.

The richer the players became, the less they paid attention to the men who ran their teams. By the 1980s, players like Guy Lafleur of the Montreal Canadiens took more advice from their financial advisors than their coach. Sometimes they refused to play at all without their advisors' approval. Lafleur once refused to start a game until he'd stepped out of his dressing room in his undershirt to confer with his agent, his lawyer and the team's general manager. "Only then did he play," said Ken Dryden.

The money might have made the players happy, but all the money in the world could do nothing for the quality of the game. "A bunch of wimps who couldn't check their grandmothers," said Don Cherry about the WHA. They couldn't "shoot a puck through a pane of glass." In the NHL, players were still good enough to check their grandmothers, but they might have had trouble with their sisters.

Even the broadcaster Foster Hewitt soured on the sport. After tonight's game, Hewitt would turn sixty-five and retire from broadcasting. He owned two radio stations, had been appointed a director of several mining companies and was a major shareholder of the Vancouver Canucks of the Western Hockey League. But he seldom attended an NHL game, perhaps because the league had turned down his team's application for a franchise. Hockey had become an absurd copy, he said, of the sport he'd once loved.

King Clancy, the Leafs' assistant general manager, noticed the change, as well. "The game's just not the same," Clancy said. "We don't have a soul who'll walk out there tonight when the whistle blows and hammer somebody into the seats. They're all thinkin' about their money, I guess."

Not only had Clancy played against Conacher's father, he'd also played with Ace Bailey, whose career had ended in 1933, when Eddie Shore knocked him out with a cross-check from behind and almost killed him. Two months later, they shook hands in front of a raging crowd of partisan fans at Maple Leaf Gardens. "All part of the game," Bailey said.

For better or worse, players like Shore and Bailey made a clear distinction between their behaviour on the ice and off. But by 2004, the distinction had disappeared into a swamp of money. When Todd Bertuzzi inflicted an injury on Steve Moore similar to Bailey's, the outcome was much different. Unlike Shore and Bailey, Moore and Bertuzzi didn't shake hands at centre ice before a benefit game to raise money for Moore's welfare, nor did Moore need anyone's charity to cover his expenses. Instead, the two players continued their dispute in court, where Moore, along with his parents, filed lawsuits against Bertuzzi for $19.5 million. Bertuzzi pleaded guilty in a Vancouver courtroom to a charge of assault causing bodily harm. He received a conditional discharge and one year's probation.

"Hockey used to be business ten years ago," said John Ashley, the referee. "It was a lot of fun, too. Now it's big business. But the fun has gone."

At centre ice, Ashley dropped the puck between the sticks of Ralph Backstrom and Pete Stemkowski, then pushed himself away. Stemkowski batted the puck and chased it. With the Leafs leading by one goal, his two linemates shadowed their two opponents to deny them an opportunity to score the tying goal.

Stemkowski was twenty-three. The Leafs team program called him "a swinging young newcomer." In the twelve games of this year's playoffs, Stemkowski had averaged a point a game. In his career as an NHL player, he would score about two hundred goals of his own, but he'd record almost twice as many points by helping other players score. After tonight's game, Imlach would promise to keep Stemmer on a line with Jim Pappin, his road-trip roommate, and Bob Pulford — "the kind of playoff line that a good hockey team needs," Imlach said.

"Stemmer belongs to the old school," Imlach would say. "He hits you with everything he's got. He booms in there full-tilt. He gets the puck. He creates scoring opportunities."

But Imlach wasn't really praising Stemkowski. He was promoting Stemkowski like a used car, making a public sales pitch to raise his selling price to another team. After five months of the season next year, with thirteen games remaining in the schedule, the Leafs would send Stemkowski packing to Detroit. Stemkowski would hear of the trade not from his coach or manager but from his friend and roommate, Jim Pappin. Thirteen games later, the Leafs would trade Pappin, as well.

At the moment, Pappin and Stemkowski were waiting for a pass from Larry Hillman. But instead of passing, Hillman decided to ice the puck and stop the play.

For some players on the team tonight, getting traded from the Leafs was the best thing that ever happened in their hockey careers. Pete Stemkowski would finish the season in 1974 with more assists than all but fifteen players in the NHL and with more points than all but two other players on his team. But by then, he was playing for the New York Rangers, and the two other players were Brad Park and Rod Gilbert.

This season in Toronto, Frank Mahovlich scored about one goal in every four games. In the fall, the Leafs would send him to Detroit, where he would score more than once in every two games. In his first full season with the Red Wings, Mahovlich scored forty-nine goals, a total surpassed at the time by only three other players in the history of the NHL.

Jim Pappin was almost thirty years old and had come close to quitting the game. He would never play a thousand NHL games because he'd spent so much of his early career in Rochester. But by the time he retired, Pappin would rank among the top one hundred goal scorers in the history of the league. Unfortunately for the Leafs, Pappin would score most of his goals while playing for the Black Hawks in Chicago, where the Leafs sent him in 1968. Six other players on the Leafs tonight would rank within the NHL's top one hundred goal scorers, but all of them would play at least 250 more games in the league than Pappin.

"Just getting out of Toronto made a world of difference," said the defenceman Bob Baun, who'd spent the entire game tonight sitting on the bench.

It wasn't always easy for players to leave a team that had occupied their dreams as teenagers, commanded their obedience as adults and, with their help, won the Stanley Cup. Allan Stanley never completely lost his allegiance to the Leafs, even after the team traded him to Philadelphia in 1968. When the Flyers played at Maple Leaf Gardens against the Leafs, Stanley would sometimes skate to the wrong bench. At the end of a period, he'd follow his former teammates down the corridor toward the Maple Leafs' dressing room. "I constantly had the urge to skate with the blue-sweatered team," he said. "It was amazing how many things I did wrong."

Stanley's partner, Tim Horton, would be one of the last to leave the team. Horton would walk into the arena in Oakland, California, one afternoon in 1970, before a game against an expansion team called the Seals, and discover that the Leafs, his team of twenty-one years, had traded him to the New York Rangers. His new team expected him to play the next day.

Rather than going to New York, Horton could have quit hockey altogether. He'd paid for his house. The donut business that he'd started with a partner was doing well. But most of his teammates tonight would not have the same luxury of choice. Few of them could make as much elsewhere as they did playing hockey, and none of them would receive a pension that would support him and his family, even if they spent twenty years in the NHL — not after Alan Eagleson had plundered their pension fund to keep himself and his wife in fur coats and Cadillacs. Even Gordie Howe continued playing into his fifties, not for love but for money.

The night of the trade, Horton packed his skates, elbow pads and sticks with the straight blades whittled down like daggers and flew back across the continent to New York. After about an hour of sleep, he appeared the next night with the Rangers against the Detroit Red Wings. Three former Maple Leafs playing that night with the Red Wings sent their greetings to him through the team's trainer, Lefty Wilson. Horton was forty years old. Without Horton, the average age of defencemen on the Leafs was twenty-three, and the oldest, Pat Quinn, was twenty-seven. None of them had ever appeared in a Stanley Cup final game.

For George Armstrong, who remained with the Leafs, the writing was on the wall. "Sometimes you get to thinking that some things are immune to big business," he said.

By the time the Leafs traded Horton, Armstrong had played for the Leafs for twenty years, twelve of them as captain, and he'd played even longer with Horton. They'd played together as teenagers in Copper Cliff, the company town outside of Sudbury. "When you go back that far," Armstrong said, "you get to know each other's habits. Instinctive things." Without Horton on the team, Armstrong lost his enthusiasm for the game. At the end of the season, fifteen games after Horton left the team, Armstrong retired. "Those instincts aren't any use any more," he said.

By the early 1970s, only Dave Keon and Ron Ellis remained from the players in tonight's game, and the spirit that moved them tonight had all but disappeared. Ballard even removed the inspirational slogan from the team's dressing room. "Defeat does not rest lightly on their shoulders," it said. Perhaps he no longer understood the meaning of the words.

Under Ballard, the Leafs no longer played for the fans. They played for the fans' money. For Ballard — sentenced to three years in prison for fraud and three years for theft, running a team that included only two players from tonight's game, that would finish out of the playoffs three times in six years and that would not come close to winning another Stanley Cup for more than fifty years — defeat rolled off the shoulders as easily as a bowling ball, as long as it made a profit on the way down.

"There used to be a time when the Montreal Canadiens and the Toronto Maple Leafs were on the same path of success, tradition and class," a fan named Tom Cormier wrote to Ballard, "but you were the fork in the road."

Pete Stemkowski tried to pass the puck after the face-off in the Leafs' end, but John Ferguson smothered him and forced him to his knees, and the puck dribbled away. Ralph Backstrom swept past, took the puck and skated with it to the other side of the rink, pursued by Jim Pappin and Bob Pulford.

Unable to cut past them, Backstrom bounced a backhand shot off the foot of Pappin, who retrieved the puck and shot it down the ice.

From the Canadiens' blue line, J.C. Tremblay relayed the puck back to Ferguson, who fired it into the corner to the left of Sawchuk. Larry Hillman passed it to Stemkowski, who skated with Jim Pappin across the Canadiens' blue line, cut across the ice and fired a backhand shot that missed the net and hit the glass behind the goal. When Pappin tried to pass the puck back to Larry Hillman at the blue line, Backstrom intercepted the pass. Ferguson ran into him, dislodging the puck. Pappin tried to shove the puck past Gump Worsley, chased it when Worsley slapped it away, then passed it from the corner toward Bob Pulford in front of the net. Backstrom intercepted this pass, as well, and nudged the puck ahead to Ferguson, who carried it across the centre line and fired it back into the Leafs' end of the rink.

The Canadiens took two shots in the next ten seconds. Terry Sawchuk stopped one, a low wrist shot by J.C. Tremblay from ten feet away. The other one, a slapshot from the blue line by Jacques Laperriere, sailed over the net.

The Leafs cleared the puck down the ice, then headed for the bench. By the time Jacques Laperriere circled the Canadiens' goal and skated with the puck back up the ice, a wave of fresh players had jumped onto the ice from the Canadiens' bench, as well. Laperriere passed the puck up the boards to Henri Richard. Frank Mahovlich took it away from him. Laperriere took it back, skated across the centre line and passed it to his right, to Leon Rochefort. But Rochefort had stepped across the blue line ahead of the puck. As he drew back his stick to shoot, linesman Brent Casselman blew his whistle.

The Leafs had successfully defended their one-goal lead for another two minutes. But the Canadiens had spent twice as much time buzzing around the Leafs' end of the rink as the Leafs had spent in the Canadiens' end. Thanks to a pass from behind the net by John Ferguson, J.C. Tremblay had skated within ten feet of the Leafs' goal and taken a shot. Tremblay would have scored if Terry Sawchuk hadn't blocked the puck by extending the rectangle of leather-bound plastic on his hand as if he was swatting a fly with a restaurant menu. The Canadiens hadn't scored. But they needed only a single misplayed shot, an ill-timed deflection or a misjudged bounce to tie the game. As Rochefort, Richard and Balon jumped over the boards, the Canadiens still had twelve minutes and forty seconds to score the tying goal.

Most hockey fans would have noticed if Henri Richard hadn't appeared again next season with the Montreal Canadiens. They would have noticed if anyone else had worn Richard's number 16 on his jersey.

Unlike Henri, who'd worn the same number since he'd started playing for the Canadiens, his brother Maurice initially wore the number 15. But when his wife gave birth to a nine-pound baby daughter, one of his teammates suggested that he change his number to 9, on the assumption that it might bring him luck. For about twenty years after that, the outstanding player on most teams in the NHL, including Gordie Howe, Andy Bathgate, Bobby Hull and Johnny Bucyk, wore the number 9.

When Henri Richard retired, the number 16 would retire with him. The Canadiens would hang it on a banner from the rafters of the Montreal Forum, along with the numbers of Jean Beliveau, Howie Morenz and Maurice Richard. Like them, Henri Richard would also be admitted to the Hall of Fame. If the fans hadn't seen the familiar number 16 on his jersey next fall, they'd have wondered where Henri Richard had gone.

The number on a player's jersey had more than sentimental value. For many players, it was a brand. John Ferguson wore the number 22 throughout his career with the Canadiens and later named his stable of standardbred horses Double Two. Yvan Cournoyer inherited the number 12 from Dickie Moore, his predecessor on the Canadiens, and opened a chain of hamburger restaurants called Burger 12. Later he ran a bar called Brasserie 12. The number appeared on placemats, menus and outdoor signs. Cournoyer even obtained from the phone company the number 637-1212. "The number's part of who I am," he said.

But when the next season began, in the fall after tonight's game, few people noticed the absence from the team of the number 20. And even though Dave Balon had worn that number when he'd assisted on Richard's overtime goal that won a Stanley Cup for the Canadiens, hardly anyone missed him or wondered where he'd gone. After a year or two, few people remembered that he'd even worn the number.

Sometimes Dave Balon wondered what a guy had to do to get a fair shake in the NHL. No matter where he played, he scored goals, assisted on other players' goals and prevented his opponents from scoring goals against his team. Once in a while, if he had to, he even beat up his opponents. When Balon had played in New York, his coach told him to cover guys like Gordie Howe and Bobby Hull, and he'd still finished among the top ten players on the team. In Montreal, he finished third in goal-scoring one year and sixth another, ahead of better-known teammates like Henri Richard, Ralph Backstrom and Boom Boom Geoffrion. For all his efforts, the Canadiens demoted Balon for a month to a minor-league team in Houston. What more could he do? he wondered.

Coaches recognized Balon's talent. Other players did too. But teams never seemed to build their future around his presence. Instead, they used him as trade bait. Teams always seemed glad to get him. But they never seemed glad to keep him.

Since his first game in the NHL, Balon had taken whatever number the team trainer gave him at the beginning of the season. He'd played his first NHL game in New York, when he was twenty-one. Back then, he wore number 11. He was thirty years old when the North Stars traded him back to the Rangers, after the season when Bill Masterton died. This time, he wore the number 17.

The NHL's Hall of Fame has admitted more players from the Montreal Canadiens than any other team but the Maple Leafs, but no one who wore the number 20 is among them. Only two players had worn it for longer than a season before Balon came along. One of them, Paul Meger, had also grown up in Saskatchewan, in Watrous, and he, too, had helped the Canadiens win a Stanley Cup. But then he'd cracked open his skull and lacerated his brain on the skate blade of a Boston Bruin named Leo Labine, and he had to quit playing altogether, even though he was only twenty-five. After Balon, no one on the Montreal Canadiens wore the number 20 again, for more than a few games, until Pete Mahovlich joined the team.

With the Rangers again, Balon joined Phil Goyette, the human currency for whom the Rangers had sold Balon to Montreal in the first place. Goyette had also worn the number 20 for the Canadiens, for seven years, and he kept wearing the number in New York. A few players became identified with their numbers even after one team traded them to another. Boom Boom Geoffrion wore the number 5 when he moved to New York from Montreal. Wayne Gretzky would wear the number 99 after the Edmonton Oilers sent him to Los Angeles. Frank Mahovlich continued to wear the number 27 when he played in Montreal.

Even if Balon wanted to keep the number 20, he hadn't distinguished himself enough to merit such a privilege, and he didn't have enough money to buy Goyette a yacht in return for the number, the way a player might do twenty years later. Balon didn't mind. If Goyette wanted the number 20, he could have it. Balon just wanted to keep playing hockey in the NHL.

On the ice, Balon figured he might finally get a fair shake in New York. His coach, Emile Francis, said he had great faith in Balon. Francis came from Saskatchewan, too. Balon lived up to his coach's expectations. He scored thirty-three goals in his second season with the Rangers and recorded thirty-seven assists. He finished among the top ten players in the NHL and third on the team in total points, ahead of his teammate Rod Gilbert. Balon also received a hundred minutes in penalties that year. He was a good, tough, productive hockey player, just as he'd always been.

Balon and his wife were happy in New York. A couple of other guys from Saskatchewan had joined the Rangers, and they'd brought their wives with them, too. The Balons, the Kurtenbachs and the Neilsons spent a lot of time at one another's houses on Long Island, playing cards at the kitchen table, laughing about the watery American beer they had to drink, smoking a few cigarettes, passing the time together the way people did at home in Wakaw, Cudworth or Big River. Unable to have children themselves, the Balons adopted a boy and a girl. After practices and games, Balon visited Rangers fans in local hospitals. He stood for hours signing autographs and giving away his sticks to kids who clamoured outside the door of Madison Square Garden and the Rangers' practice rink on Long Island. One day he gave a stick to a kid whose father controlled a Mafia-run union on Fulton Street in Manhattan. To thank Balon, the kid's father diverted a truckload of fish to the Balons' front door. "I was giving fresh fish to everyone on the street," said Balon's wife, Gwen.

The next season, Balon repaid his coach's faith in him again by scoring thirty-six goals. He didn't get so many assists, but he still finished fourth on the team in scoring, and he had the best plus-minus record in the NHL that year, ahead of Bobby Orr. In a vote by New York fans, Balon was named the most popular Ranger and won a trophy. Tim Horton was now playing for the Rangers. Pete Stemkowski had joined the team, as well. Stemkowski's pal, Terry Sawchuk, didn't play that year, though. Sawchuk had died before the season started, after injuring himself in a tussle with a teammate with whom he shared a house on Long Island.

The end didn't come so suddenly for Balon. When he returned for his fourth season with the Rangers, he felt weaker, less coordinated. He tried as hard as ever, and he kept on playing. But his body stopped accepting signals from his brain. Move left and pass, his brain would say, but his body would just stand there. "One minute I'd be solid as a rock," he said, "and then my legs would go numb."

Balon thought he might have a virus. He complained to the New York trainers and asked them for help. The men who rubbed ice cubes and horse liniment on torn muscles and used adhesive tape to stabilize a player's broken ankle didn't know what Balon was talking about. "I get the puck on my stick, and I can't control it," he said after missing goals, bobbling passes, losing the puck to the opposing team. Yeah, right, said the trainers. Tell us another one. "They just laughed at me," Balon said.

Balon might have finished fourth on the team the previous year, but that was yesterday's news, and the three players who'd finished ahead of him, Vic Hadfield, Jean Ratelle and Rod Gilbert, had continued to excel this season. All three would finish among the top ten scorers in the NHL. Hadfield would score fifty goals. They'd already left Balon in their dust. The Rangers would go all the way that year to the Stanley Cup finals. But Balon didn't go with them. The trainers had mentioned Balon's complaints to Emile Francis, the coach. Francis figured he'd unload Balon to another team while he still had some value as a player. After sixteen games, the Rangers sent Balon with two other players to a new NHL expansion team in Vancouver called the Canucks. In return, the Rangers received two younger players, a defenceman named Gary Doak, who helped the Rangers get to the Stanley Cup finals, and a forward named Jim Wiste, who would never play again in an NHL game.

Balon took the trade in his stride. He had two great kids and a wife who adored him. Despite the ups and downs, he'd played almost seven hundred games in the NHL, enough to collect a pension. Back in Saskatchewan, he and Gwen had invested in a house in Prince Albert. They also owned a cabin in a national park nearby. When he retired he'd still have half a lifetime ahead of him.

In Vancouver, Balon's symptoms continued. The puck would arrive on Balon's stick, but when he tried to shoot, his arms and hands would go on strike. He'd skate into the corner to wrestle with a defenceman for the puck, and then his legs would give out and he'd fall down. Fans accused Balon of apathetic play. They didn't think he was trying hard enough. Some of his teammates thought the same thing, and Balon, well-versed in the ethics of hard-working prairie farmers, didn't try to change their minds by drawing attention to his complaints. He just kept trying. He didn't want pity. He wanted to play hockey. Despite his faulty wiring, he still managed to score nineteen goals, which at least placed him ahead of the other two players the Rangers had traded with him to Vancouver.

The last year of his NHL career Balon spent on the bench. He scored two goals. He received twenty-two minutes in penalties because NHL teams had begun to rely by then on muscle rather than skill to overpower their opponents, and Balon had to defend himself. "But my coordination was gone," he said. "A four-year-old could knock me over."

Once in a while, his coach in Vancouver, a former player named Vic Stasiuk, sent Balon over the boards to see if, by some miracle, he might have regained his finesse. But he never did, and the fans booed when he stumbled around the ice, so Stasiuk benched him again, and the team's management wrote him off as another bad debt. Balon was making about $25,000, and the team's manager, Bud Poile, resented every dollar that found its way into Balon's pocket. "When they think you're finished," Balon said, "you're just another slab of meat."

After Vancouver, Balon tried again, this time for a minor pro team called the Dusters, in Binghamton, New York. The team dropped him after seven games. Thinking he could still give it one more shot, he contacted the coach of the Quebec Nordiques, a team in the World Hockey Association: former Canadien Jacques Plante, who had been traded to New York along with Phil Goyette in the trade that brought Balon to Montreal. Plante remembered Balon, of course. Come to Quebec, he said, and give it a shot. This time, Balon lasted nine games. Then he quit for good. At thirty-eight, he was finished.

With his wife, Gwen, their daughter, Jodi, and their son, Jeff, Balon moved back to Saskatchewan. For a couple of years, he coached a junior team called the Humboldt Broncos. He didn't skate much, at first because he didn't have to, and then because he couldn't. His arms and legs behaved like unruly kids when the teacher leaves the classroom. Finally, he went to Saskatoon to consult a doctor and discovered that he had multiple sclerosis.

Now Balon began to worry about his future. For $175,000, a local man sold Balon a gas bar and laundromat, knowing that Balon had MS and that the job required fourteen-hour days, most of them spent on his feet. "I couldn't do it," Balon said. He had to sell the business for $80,000 less than he paid. Balon still wondered when he'd get another break.

Finally, on a lake north of Prince Albert, Balon bought the *Neo-watin*, a forty-passenger stern-wheeled paddleboat. As Captain Dave, he could sit down in his peaked cap while he guided boatloads of sightseers up and down Lake Waskesiu. The passengers loved it, and so did he. "It's beautiful up there," Balon said.

Even as he drove the boat, his body continued to rebel against his brain. Balon used a cane at first, then two canes, and then a walker. He drove a Lincoln equipped with a hydraulic lift. One day, as he climbed into the front seat, he fell down and couldn't get up again. At the age of fifty-four, Balon could not stand up for longer than two minutes. "I'm ashamed of the way I am now," he said.

After playing more than eight hundred games in the NHL and contributing regularly to his pension plan, Balon received $500 a month. Former players tried to help their disabled teammate. Alumni from the Montreal Canadiens bought a customized van for Bosey that could accommodate his wheelchair. Former players from the Vancouver Canucks paid for some renovations to the family home.

Balon struggled on through his sixties, supported by his wife and daughter. When the disease left him paralyzed and attacked his voice box, his family moved him into a private room in a full-care nursing home where he could receive more attention than they could give him. Even as his body quit, his mind continued to function. In his room one day, his daughter asked a visiting reporter from a Canadian newspaper to encourage fans to write to her dad. "Tell them just send money," Balon growled.

In the nursing home, on the outskirts of Prince Albert, Balon lived for three years, watching TV with geriatric Alzheimer's patients and wondering once in a while what he'd done to deserve this bullshit. In the spring of 2007, at the age of sixty-eight, he died.

He and Gwen had been married by then for forty-seven years, and she couldn't remember a single day when she didn't feel lucky to be married to Dave Balon.

"He was kind, a lot of fun and just funny," said his daughter, Jodi. "He was just humble to the core... You'd never have thought he was an NHL player."

Five feet outside the Leafs' blue line, the puck fell from the hand of linesman Matt Pavelich toward the red dot on the ice. Before it landed, Henri Richard tapped it past Dave Keon toward the corner of the rink and skated after it. Tim Horton intercepted the puck and skated down the right wing toward the Canadiens' end of the rink. Richard blocked his progress, so Horton crossed the centre line and flipped the puck into the zone.

A moment later, Richard blocked another Leafs pass at centre, darted across the ice and sped toward the Leafs' blue line. Dave Balon skated with him to his left. Allan Stanley stepped forward to block Richard's progress. Richard moved the puck to his left, then passed from his backhand into the middle of the rink to Leon Rochefort. But Rochefort had paused at the blue line to avoid putting himself offside, and Richard's pass landed on the stick of Frank Mahovlich. When Mahovlich's slapshot missed the net, the Canadiens relayed the puck up the ice again to Richard.

Horton and Stanley faced Richard at the blue line. George Armstrong had skated back to catch him, as well. Richard darted toward the three Leafs players like a marlin into a net. When Richard reached the blue line, Stanley stepped out to close the net and knocked the puck off Richard's stick. Balon caught up to the puck, but Richard had crossed the blue line ahead of him, putting himself offside. Pavelich blew his whistle to stop the play.

Richard, Balon and Rochefort skated toward the bench. Of the three players, only Richard would appear again next year with the Montreal Canadiens.

...

Twelve players would stick with the Montreal Canadiens after tonight's Stanley Cup game. All twelve had practised, played, travelled, roomed, eaten, drunk and gone to church together. They'd visited each other in the hospital and invited each other's families to dinner. In the dressing room after practice, they'd asked each other for advice, not just about hockey but also about money, marriage, jobs, cars, vacation plans, insurance and their children's ambitions and run-ins with the law. That's how each of them had learned to become a Montreal Canadien.

The younger players who joined the team paid attention to the older guys. Yvan Cournoyer, now finishing his third full season, would play in the 1970s with a new player from Thurso, Quebec, named Guy Lafleur, who still wore white socks with his black pants and needed some help adjusting to the life of a Canadien in Montreal. Jacques Laperriere, a veteran of ten years, would set an example for Serge Savard. Rogie Vachon, the back-up goalie, would share a bench in the dressing room with Ken Dryden. Just by their presence on the team, the experienced players inspired a new teammate to live up to their accomplishments. In this way, the Montreal Canadiens remained winners.

As the older players in tonight's game retired or moved on, the newcomers would win the Stanley Cup another six times in the 1970s. Between 1975 and 1979, they'd win it four times in a row. The Canadiens in the 1970s became the first team in the NHL ever to win more than five hundred games in a decade. For every ten games they played, they won seven. It felt good to play for the Montreal Canadiens.

Sooner or later, though, even the Montreal Canadiens had to capitulate to the forces that swept over the NHL. And the most powerful force of all was greed. With more than 240 players in the league after tonight and another 200 in a rival league, all moving from one year to the next between two dozen cities throughout the continent, hockey players made money by the bucketful, even as they became as anonymous as the metal men on a table hockey game. Even the best ones couldn't put down roots in a town without wondering if a gust of big money would blow them somewhere else. "It's the money that counts now," said Henri Richard, as his own career came to an end in 1975.

The breeze would blow gently through the Canadiens' dressing room next year, when Toe Blake retired after thirteen seasons as their coach. Under Blake and his predecessor, Dick Irvin, the team had finished in first place fourteen times and won the Stanley Cup eleven times. Together, the two men had coached the team for twenty-eight consecutive years. In the NHL today, most coaches remain with the same team for about three.

Many of the players who left Montreal ended up in either Minneapolis or St. Louis. Jean-Guy Talbot spent time in both cities. So many former Canadiens played for St. Louis or Minnesota that a game between the two teams resembled a reunion. With their poise and attitude toward winning, the former Canadiens stood out among their new teammates. Three of them became captains of their teams.

In Montreal, the Canadiens replaced Blake with a twenty-eight-year-old former scout named Claude Ruel. Ruel had played in the minor leagues with some of the players on the team and coached a few others on the Junior Canadiens. But he hadn't distinguished himself as a player or a coach. He didn't have the same credentials as Toe Blake. He hadn't earned the respect of his players, and he didn't seem to respect them. In private, he seemed unpredictable, and he disparaged his players in public.

Under Ruel, the Canadiens seemed to lose their spirit. The tapestry of allegiance, respect and loyalty that held the Canadiens together began to unravel. Ralph Backstrom almost retired at thirty-three after Ruel told him before a game that a rookie who was ten years younger would take his place at centre. Jean Beliveau, the team's captain, talked Backstrom out of quitting.

Ruel antagonized Dick Duff before the Canadiens traded him to Los Angeles and argued with Gump Worsley until the team sent the goalie to Minnesota. Even Beliveau wasn't beyond the criticism of Ruel, who benched him for the third period of a playoff game in which he'd already scored four goals, after Beliveau argued with him.

Jacques Laperriere cracked next. Already anxious about Ruel's intense criticism of his play, Laperriere protested a penalty during a close game in Boston. After arguing with the referee, Laperriere cross-checked him into the boards, then shoved a linesman out of the way, as well. For his uncharacteristic gesture, Laperriere received two misconduct penalties, a three-game suspension and a seventy-five-dollar fine.

John Ferguson became disillusioned after he was hit in the face by a slapshot. He suffered a detached retina and a crushed occipital bone beneath his right eye. It took two operations to repair the bone with a plastic implant, and Ferguson spent six days over Christmas in Montreal's General Hospital "in excruciating pain," he said. "During that time," he said, "not one member of the Canadiens' ownership or management or coaching staff came to visit me or even sent flowers or a card. Only one of them even phoned — Toe Blake. Once.

"I felt betrayed," said Ferguson. He, too, decided to retire.

By then, Ferguson's clothing and textile business had become successful enough that he could afford to leave the game. His business had also started to distract him. Instead of winding himself up before a game like a propeller on a rubber band, he had to interrupt his preparations to deal with complaints about late deliveries of men's pyjama bottoms or the woof and weft of his company's worsted wool trousers. "It was mental anguish," he said, "to put on my uniform and concentrate one hundred per cent on hockey."

When Ferguson quit in the spring of 1970, the Canadiens lured him back with a salary of $35,000. If the team reached the finals, he'd receive $8,000 more, and another $7,000 if they won the Stanley Cup. The next season, the Canadiens won the Cup, and Ferguson earned $50,000, plus another $60,000 in deferred salary. "But really," he said, "I'm playing for the love of the game."

Perhaps he was. Less than a year later, he sold his business to the Macdonald Tobacco Company but remained on the payroll as head of public relations. He also helped design men's shirts, stewardesses' uniforms and the blazers and pants worn by Team Canada in the 1972 Summit Series against Russia.

The spirit was draining from the team. From a close-knit family of like-minded champions, the Canadiens were degenerating into a gaggle of resentful complainers, and a Montreal columnist named John Robertson castigated the Canadiens' management for allowing it to happen. "I don't know of any professional sports organization which is despised as unanimously by its former players as the Montreal Canadiens are," he said. The team had earned its reputation for winning Stanley Cups, he said, but now the men who ran the Canadiens organization had become as ruthless and venal as any other flesh peddlers in professional sport. "These people exude all the warmth and sentiment of a cobra's kiss," he said. "Management has rewritten the club credo: With grasping hands we pass the buck."

Punch Imlach sent Red Kelly, Ron Ellis and Brian Conacher onto the ice. They'd played for most of the game against Richard, Balon and Rochefort, but those three Canadiens had just left the ice. In their place, Toe Blake sent Jean Beliveau over the boards to play centre between Yvan Cournoyer and Gilles Tremblay, two of the fastest skaters on the team.

It didn't matter how fast you could skate if you didn't have the puck, and for the next minute, neither team controlled it for more than a few seconds. Beliveau won the face-off against Kelly, drew the puck back to J.C. Tremblay, then followed it into the Leafs' end after Tremblay slid it into the corner. Then Ellis grabbed the puck and skated the other way and took a shot that went past the Canadiens' goal and slid around the boards back to the Canadiens' blue line. J.C. Tremblay took the puck over the centre line, then lobbed another corkscrew shot toward Terry Sawchuk, the fifth time in the game that he'd tried to trick the goalie with a high, floating blooper. This one didn't reach its target, though, because Larry Hillman batted it out of the air with his stick. John Ashley blew his whistle to stop the play because Hillman had touched the puck with his stick above his shoulders.

Facing off against Kelly again, Beliveau let the puck slide between his legs to J.C. Tremblay. Tremblay tried another corkscrew. This one reached Sawchuk, who fell to one knee and steered the puck toward the corner, keeping as much of his body as possible between the puck and the net. Hillman shot the puck out of the Leafs' end. Harris blocked it. He passed it to J.C. Tremblay, who relayed it behind him, as if he had eyes in the back of his head, to Beliveau. The pass seemed to catch everyone by surprise except Beliveau. The two Leafs defencemen hadn't skated yet from their own end. Now they reversed their direction, but they couldn't back up much farther without skating into the goal crease. Beliveau fired a slapshot from the top of the face-off circle. Knowing that he might deflect the puck past his own goalie if he tried to block the shot, Hillman moved his leg out of the path of the puck, giving Sawchuk a clear view. Sawchuk raised his blocker and nonchalantly steered the puck into the corner. When Ellis caught up to it, he iced the puck.

The Leafs had allowed the Canadiens to take two shots on their goal. Without much difficulty, Sawchuk had stopped one hard shot from Beliveau and one blooper from J.C. Tremblay. Just a period ago, the Leafs had scored a goal on a harmless pass from the corner of the rink. If they could do it, so could the Canadiens. Any shot on goal was better than none.

"I miss the old days," Tim Horton said in 1973, "when a rookie came into the league and kept his mouth shut for the first two or three seasons because he knew his place."

Take Ronnie Ellis, for example. Ellis had joined the Leafs three years ago as a teenager, and he hadn't said boo from October to March. If some joker like Horton or Eddie Shack told him to ask the trainer for a left-handed jockstrap, a can of steam or a pair of reversible socks, he did it, and he smiled when he got the joke. Most of the time, the older players didn't talk to him at all, so Ellis just paid attention, the way he usually did. Some of his teammates were old enough to have played with his dad before Ronnie had learned to tie his own shoelaces, and he thought he could learn something from them. He watched how they put on their equipment, how they secured their shin pads with tape, how they filed and sanded their sticks, how they left their equipment after a practice for the trainers. He watched how they hung their towel on a hook outside the showers, how they wore a sport coat over their shirt and tie, how they walked through the dressing-room door into the real world.

"Hockey is a world of its own," Ellis said, and for most of his life, he'd felt more comfortable in that world than he did in the real one outside the door. He might have been a kid, but he'd adopted the same values as the older players on the team. Work hard, do what you're told, keep your mouth shut. In return, the team looked out for him, just as a father looks out for a son. The team made decisions for him, told him what to do, when to do it and how. The team even told its players how to think. When the team thought they needed focus and motivation, Punch Imlach gave each player a copy of *The Power of Positive Thinking*. When the team thought they needed spiritual guidance, the trainer, Bob Haggert, placed a personalized Bible bound in blue leather in front of each of their stalls during practice. All a player had to do was play hockey.

"I was dedicated to making myself part of a team," said Ellis, "and to making that team part of a proud Maple Leaf tradition." Ellis's dedication impressed everyone, and his obedience impressed Punch Imlach. He did what Imlach ordered, and he didn't talk back. "I was very introspective," he said.

Because of his slight resemblance to a well-known Canadian boxer, some of Ellis's teammates called him Chuvalo. The boxer, a heavyweight named George Chuvalo, fought ninety-three times, never quit and was never knocked out. Ellis fought on the ice about as often as Chuvalo stepped into a boxing ring with skates on his feet, but he was just as intense and just as stubborn in his determination to win.

Already, Ellis ranked consistently among the team's top goal scorers. That made him a target for stiff checks and harassment from other teams, but Ellis never retaliated and seldom took a penalty. This year, he'd spent only four minutes in the penalty box at Maple Leaf Gardens, hardly enough time to talk to the Leafs' penalty timekeeper, Ace Bailey. An old guy in a blue suit with a stopwatch, Bailey kept track of the time that a player served for breaking a rule on the ice. The job allowed him to study the team, as he'd done when he played for the Leafs himself. Ron Ellis played the game the same way Bailey had, even tying with Frank Mahovlich for the lead in scoring on the team in his rookie year.

When Bailey suffered his career-ending head injury, long before Ellis was born, the Leafs retired Bailey's number, 6. The Leafs didn't retire many numbers. They'd done it only twice, once for Bailey, because he'd almost died in his hospital bed, and once for Bill Barilko's number 5, because Barilko scored the Cup-winning goal in April of 1951, a few months before his disappearance in a plane crash.

Before Ellis began his fifth season with the team, Bailey asked the Leafs to bring his number 6 out of retirement. Bailey had worn the number in the first game ever played by the Leafs. Now he asked Ellis to wear it. That's when Ellis became an integral part of the proud Maple Leafs tradition. That's also when Ellis finally talked to Ace Bailey.

For Ron Ellis, the Leafs tradition mattered as much as the routines that he observed to prepare for a game: the steak and eggs he ate at one o'clock, the nap he took between two and four-thirty, the route he followed on the drive downtown to Maple Leaf Gardens. Ellis changed his routine only if he thought it might improve his performance. And he never tinkered with tradition. "We all tried to do that on the Leafs," he said.

The bequeathing of numbers was an honourable tradition — for the players, at least. George Armstrong, the team's captain, had inherited his number from a previous Leafs captain, Syl Apps. When Apps broke his leg in a game and couldn't finish the season, he offered to repay half his salary to the Leafs' owner, Conn Smythe. Horton, Pulford, Mahovlich: they were all part of the same tradition. They had their foibles, but they were decent men. Ellis felt proud to be among them.

Things changed after tonight, and not necessarily for the better. After tonight, confronted by the solidarity of the players' association, owners and managers would no longer pretend to act in their players' best interests. NHL teams would abandon their farm system, no longer posing as surrogate parents for kids who might someday make it to the big league. Without the paternal guidance of their teams, players hired agents to represent them, and when they did, they discovered how much money they'd lost to the owners who'd supposedly had their best interest at heart. Frank Mahovlich once invited an agent to accompany him in contract negotiations with Punch Imlach. The agent was his father, Pete, who placed a shopping bag on Imlach's desk and demanded that Imlach fill it with cash. Imlach had laughed at him. But NHL managers weren't laughing now, and neither were the players.

Knowing Ellis would need an agent, the Leafs' trainer, Bob Haggert, introduced him to Alan Eagleson, who was already representing other players on the team, like Mike Walton. He did a good job, too, much better than Ellis could ever have done on his own.

As the NHL changed, so did the Maple Leafs, in all sorts of ways. One by one, Ellis's teammates either retired or joined other teams. Bob Haggert packed away his towels and his liniment for good and set up his own marketing agency for NHL players who wanted to capitalize on their reputations. The players who took the place of Ellis's teammates came and went like commuters on a bus, and the owners seemed determined to sell the wheels if they could make a buck. Instead of aspiring to win another Stanley Cup, the Maple Leafs aspired to make more money. Ellis became disillusioned. He performed on the ice better than ever, but his personal accomplishments paled as the proud Leafs tradition fell apart. "I refuse to play hockey just for the money," he said in 1976.

After tonight, against teams that hardly belonged in the NHL, the Leafs never progressed beyond the quarter-finals. They missed the playoffs three times in six years. When George Armstrong retired, in 1971, he left Ellis behind as the only player on the Maple Leafs who'd earned the number on his jersey by living up to the team's tradition. Meanwhile, the owners pilfered the treasury. They used the money to line their own pockets, wine and dine cheap floozies and impress their pals from private school. One of the owners went to jail, and when he got out, he fired Ace Bailey.

Ellis felt more disillusioned than his teammates because he believed in the proud tradition of the team, and the owner, Harold Ballard, had coached his father and had become a family friend. How could a man like Ballard behave with such compelling bravado while plundering a Canadian institution like the Toronto Maple Leafs?

Carrying the Leafs tradition on his back, Ellis scored more goals than ever and consistently ranked among the top scorers on the team. But the harder he worked, the worse the team performed. By 1974, he had spent more uninterrupted seasons on the team than any other Leaf except Dave Keon. The two players had become the team's grizzled veterans. Keon was thirty-four, Ellis was twenty-nine. Both decided that year to quit the Leafs.

Anxious and introspective at the best of times, Ellis began to regard himself as a failure. He stood second on the team in scoring that year, but the Leafs finished the season in thirteenth place out of eighteen teams in the league. To Ellis, the performance of the team mattered more than his own accomplishments. After practice, he sometimes sat behind the wheel of his car for an hour or more, unable to turn the key in the ignition and get going. No matter how hard he tried, he couldn't resurrect the team's high standards, and he couldn't meet the expectations of the fans, his father or himself. The disappointment was killing him. Earlier that year, in a game against St. Louis, a player named Floyd Thomson, who once won the Central Hockey League's Iron Man Award, punched Ellis in the mouth so hard that his incisor punctured his lip. In better times, Ellis would have skated away. But this time, Ellis retaliated. He punched Thomson back. It was the first time in eleven years as a Maple Leaf that Ellis had thrown a punch. The fans went wild, but Ellis felt nothing but anxiety and remorse. The fans had no idea what was happening to him, and neither did he.

Ellis continued to perform on the ice, but spiritually he was in the slump of his life. He could have changed his routines, sanded, filed and whittled his sticks into toothpicks, driven to the rink backwards and eaten donuts for his pre-game meal like Bobby Rousseau did. Anything for an edge. But nothing would work. "You can break out of a slump with two or three goals one night," he said. "It's not like that in life."

When he left the team that season, he said he wanted to spend more time with his five-year-old daughter, Kitty, and his infant son, R.J. In fact, he was falling to pieces. "I was close to a breakdown," he said later.

He tried other jobs. He sold insurance, but selling insurance didn't get him out of bed in the morning. Most of his clients wanted to talk about the Maple Leafs, and the paycheque at the end of the month amounted to less than the lunch money that he'd received from the team on a road trip. Ellis was listless. For most of his life, he'd succeeded by skating as fast as he could up and down a hockey rink and shooting a puck into a net. He'd refined those skills until he could apply them as well as almost anyone in the world, but now they didn't mean much anymore. He might have felt more secure if he'd pursued an education beyond high school. But Punch Imlach had talked him out of doing that.

Without the conventions of hockey to impose order, his life lost its meaning. With no routine of any consequence, Ellis teetered every day over chasms of indecision. He worried about the discrepancies between what he did and how he felt. With no one to keep him on track, Ellis called Mel Stevens, the man who'd donated the blue leather-bound Bibles to the Leafs. Then he drove to the Teen Ranch, the Christian camp that Stevens operated in Caledon, about twenty minutes from Ellis's house. Over a few days, Ellis attended a retreat there for Christian athletes like Paul Henderson, a former Leaf, and Zenon Andrusyshyn, a place kicker for the Toronto Argonauts. "They had peace and contentment," Ellis said, "something I didn't have."

The presumptuous megalomania that informs the belief that we represent God's will on earth didn't bother Ellis. He just wanted to restore the order that had escaped from his life.

After selling insurance, Ellis took a job with a property developer managing Carrying Place Golf & Country Club, near Kettleby. But he was still only thirty-one years old, and, like many players, he'd had second thoughts about retiring. When the Leafs invited him to return to the team, he jumped at the chance. This time, the money helped a lot. With Eagleson negotiating his contract and the NHL Players' Association officially certified as a union, Ellis landed a four-year deal worth $450,000, along with a $100,000 interest-free loan. By 1979, he was the only player on the team after Dave Keon to have scored more than three hundred goals. And with Keon playing in the WHA, Ellis was the only player on the Leafs who'd ever won a Stanley Cup. "We'll retire him when he's about fifty," said the team's owner, Harold Ballard. As usual, Ballard's words weren't worth the air that blew them out of his mouth.

In Ellis's last season, which began in 1980, the Leafs used thirty-seven players, some for only one or two games. More than half of them were ten years younger than Ellis, and few of them had played more than a season or two in the NHL. The Leafs' dressing room resembled a nursery school, and the team's management expected Ellis to keep the kids from drinking the glue and chasing the girls through the corridors. Ellis started feeling the pressure again, and his performance suffered. Halfway through the season, Punch Imlach told him to sit in the press box and watch his team play.

One Saturday night in January 1981, Ellis heard that he would play again in a game against the Canadiens. He was excited as he drove to Maple Leaf Gardens, but when he arrived to dress for the game, as he'd done more than a thousand times before, he found no equipment and no sweater hanging up in his stall. His nameplate had been removed, and his sticks had been packed away. When he asked Punch Imlach for an explanation, Imlach said Ellis was no longer wanted on the team. The

Leafs would either buy out Ellis's contract, at a discount, or send him eight hundred miles away to Moncton, New Brunswick, to play in the American Hockey League. The choice was up to him. Ellis went home and called Alan Eagleson.

At the time, Ellis was among the three leading scorers in Leafs history, with Dave Keon and Darryl Sittler. In his first twelve years, he'd averaged twenty-five goals and fifty points a year. He'd scored twenty goals or more in more consecutive seasons than any other Leafs player. But all that was in the past. When a reporter asked why Ellis wasn't playing, Harold Ballard said, "We're not getting what we want out of him anymore."

The news of Ellis's abrupt termination filled two pages of the sports section in the *Toronto Star*. It included a prepared statement by Punch Imlach. "Ron Ellis has had a long and distinguished career," Imlach wrote, "and he's made an outstanding contribution to the Toronto Maple Leafs."

A reporter named Frank Orr said Imlach sounded like "the chairman of the board of some gigantic corporation who is recruited to present the gold watch to a retiring janitor whom the chairman wouldn't know if he found the man in his cornflakes." Twenty-two years after Imlach had persuaded Randy Ellis to send his teenaged boy to Toronto, nineteen years after Imlach had dissuaded the boy from attending university, fourteen years after he'd scored the first goal in the final game of the Leafs' last Stanley Cup victory, Ron Ellis realized once and for all that his relationship with Punch Imlach and the Toronto Maple Leafs was nothing personal. Ellis had just discovered, as Ken Dryden once wrote, that "what you have done before counts only until you can't do it again."

That January, Ellis walked out of the Gardens for the last time. He carried a gym bag and a new CCM hockey stick, with his trenchcoat slung over his shoulder and a cheque in his pocket for $100,000. He was "a little disturbed," he said, "with the way it had to end for me." He didn't understand the timing, he said, or the reasons behind it. For the rest of the season, the Leafs replaced Ellis on right wing with a player named Rocky Saganiuk, who wore number 7. Ellis deserved a far more heartfelt send-off, and he knew it. But when he signed the papers that terminated his career, he didn't complain. He just added a note in the margin to Punch Imlach. "Punch," he said, "I started my career with you, and I'm pleased that I finished with you."

It would take several years, several jobs, a stint as a teacher at a Christian school, another few years running a sporting goods store, a season coaching his son's junior-hockey team, and a desperate battle with depression before Ellis would finally come to terms with his life. He got no help from the Leafs.

For the second time in the period, Toe Blake sent Duff, Rousseau and Roberts onto the ice together. About four minutes ago, they'd caught the Leafs off-guard and scored a goal. Maybe they'd do it again.

Duff stood on the edge of the circle, behind the right shoulder of Rousseau, the Canadiens centre. If Rousseau won the face-off and drew the puck back to him, Duff would have a fraction of a second to score. Dick Duff had scored more than a few goals with just a split second of opportunity.

To gain that split second for his teammate, Jim Roberts would have to prevent Jim Pappin from springing forward to check Duff. Roberts didn't score many goals. His job was to get in the way of his opponents. He did that as well as Duff scored goals, but he did it more often, and he inspired his teammates with his spirit.

As a teenager, Roberts had played in Peterborough for two years under a coach named Scotty Bowman. In one of those years, the team won the Memorial Cup as the best junior team in the country. When he turned professional, Roberts spent three years playing for a Canadiens farm team in the Eastern Professional Hockey League. Scotty Bowman became his coach in that league, as well. In two of those years, his teams won the league championship. The year Roberts turned twenty-four, he played with four different professional hockey teams, in Omaha, Cleveland,

Quebec City and Montreal. In Omaha, he scored eighteen goals, more than he'd scored in any of his previous seasons with nine teams in four different leagues, and more than he would ever score in fourteen seasons in the NHL. His coach in Omaha was Scotty Bowman.

In his first full season in the NHL, Roberts won a Stanley Cup. He won another Cup the next year. After tonight, the Canadiens would send Roberts to the St. Louis Blues, the first expansion team to reach the Stanley Cup finals. In the four years that Roberts played for that team, they did it three times. His coach in St. Louis was Scotty Bowman.

From St. Louis, Bowman moved to Montreal to become the coach of the Canadiens. A few weeks after he arrived, he arranged to bring Roberts back to Montreal, too. Roberts spent five more seasons there, and the Canadiens won three more Stanley Cups. For Roberts, being in the right place at the right time had a lot to do with playing under Scotty Bowman.

John Ashley dropped the puck, and the face-off went like clockwork. Roberts stood his ground in front of Pappin, Rousseau drew the puck backwards, directly onto Duff's stick. Without hesitating, Duff snapped a quick shot toward the goal. But the puck hit Allan Stanley, who batted it ahead to Bob Pulford.

Pulford took a long-shot from centre. Terry Harper blocked it with his shin pad and deflected it back to Rousseau. Rousseau reached the Leafs' blue line and flipped a pass to Duff. Duff sped toward the goal and drew his stick back to fire a shot, but Tim Horton hurled himself head-first into the line of fire. To avoid knocking the teeth out of the mouth of his old friend, Duff had to shoot the puck wide of his intended target. Roberts and Stanley chased it into the corner, and Roberts reached it first. Without looking, he slapped it behind him into the centre of the rink. His linemates, Rousseau and Duff, had already skated past the goal. Seeing three Canadiens trapped deep in the Leafs' end, Jim Pappin skated as hard as he could toward the Canadiens' blue line. Tim Horton captured the puck and timed his pass to elude the long tentacles of Jacques Laperriere so it reached Pappin's stick as he crossed the line. When he saw Harper edging toward him, he shot the puck. It sailed past Gump Worsley and into the corner of the rink.

The puck reached Duff at centre, who tipped it farther ahead to Jim Roberts. Horton and Stanley scrambled to stop the two Canadiens. Seeing the defencemen's distress, a more shifty forward than Roberts might have deked his way around Stanley or dropped a pass back to Duff. But goal-scoring wasn't one of Roberts's strong points. Stanley took one look at Roberts and knew exactly what Roberts intended to do. Instead of shifting his weight, Roberts skated right toward Stanley. As Roberts prepared to shoot, Stanley stuck out his stick and nudged the puck. Roberts lost his balance, toppled forward and slid on his chest along the ice. The puck bounced into the corner. Duff chased it, but Stanley got there first and held it against the boards until the referee blew his whistle.

With this weird Montreal line threatening again to score a goal and tie the game, Punch Imlach sent three forwards onto the ice who seemed better matched to the three Canadiens. In fact, all three of the Leafs' forward lines in the game tonight had outscored Duff, Rousseau and Roberts in the regular season. Only one Leafs line, Kelly, Ellis and Conacher, had scored fewer points in the playoffs. Perhaps such numbers didn't matter. But then again, perhaps they did. Toe Blake thought so. A few minutes ago, he'd sent Duff, Rousseau and Roberts onto the ice to face that line. They'd scored the Canadiens' only goal. Anything for an edge.

The two teams played for another fifty-one seconds without getting a shot on goal. Allan Stanley blocked two shots, one by J.C. Tremblay, the other by Ted Harris.

One of the two union organizers on the Canadiens, Tremblay would leave the team in a few years to join the Nordiques, based in Quebec City, in the rival WHA. The Nordiques paid Tremblay $140,000 a season, more than twice as much as the Canadiens had offered to keep him. No one could blame him for taking the money. He was thirty-two years old, with two young daughters and little chance of making that much money after his hockey-playing days ended. "I'm interested in my security and my family," he said.

Tremblay earned his pay. He led the WHA in assists, made the league's all-star team four times and was named the league's top defenceman twice. In his fifth season with the Nordiques, his team won the league championship.

Despite that accomplishment, Tremblay hadn't felt well during the season. A week after the final game, with his health deteriorating rapidly, he entered Quebec City's Enfant-Jésus hospital, where doctors removed his right kidney. The Nordiques expected Tremblay's performance to suffer and reduced his salary by more than $40,000. The cut in pay offended Tremblay, but he played for two more seasons. Then he moved with his wife and two daughters, Myriam and Suzanne, to Switzerland to play a final year in Geneva. When he stopped playing, he became a European scout for his old team, the Montreal Canadiens. He was still working for the Canadiens when he developed cancer in his remaining kidney. He returned to Canada for treatment and died in Montreal General Hospital, at the age of fifty-five.

Tremblay now slid the puck past Bob Pulford onto Ferguson's stick. Ferguson bulldozed his way into the Leafs' end but ran into Allan Stanley. Pappin banked a backhand pass toward Stemkowski, who was dashing on a diagonal across the blue line, but Larose lifted his stick and took the puck the other way, toward the corner. Pappin tried to stop him, but his stick slid up Larose's arm and struck Larose in the face. John Ashley blew his whistle, pointed at Pappin and skated to the penalty box to report a slashing penalty.

Pappin looked straight ahead as he skated toward the penalty box, but as he passed the referee, he muttered, "Pretty fuckin' lousy call, John." Ashley ignored him.

...

From time to time, an ambitious gambler tried to fix a hockey game the way Arnold Rothstein had fixed the 1919 World Series. A gambler once phoned Terry Sawchuk on a Saturday afternoon and told him that if he didn't allow the other team to win that night he'd be killed. The ploy didn't work. Sawchuk got so angry that he played that night without allowing a goal. "He was really peeved off," said his wife, Pat. For a couple of weeks, he worried about the gambler's threat. Then he forgot all about it.

Even without a fix, the odds were stacked in the Leafs' favour at the moment. A local sports reporter named Henry Roxborough had calculated that the team that scored the first goal in an NHL game had seven chances in ten of winning. When a team scored the first two goals, according to Roxborough, the odds in its favour increased to nine in ten. Roxborough found that the Leafs had led their opponents at the end of the second period in 158 games. Of all those games, the Leafs had not lost one.

Big Jean Beliveau, le Gros Bill, orchestrated the Canadiens power play at centre while Yvan Cournoyer, skating for only the second time in more than thirty minutes, shook his sluggish muscles at right wing, and Dick Duff hovered like a sniper on the left. J.C. Tremblay and Bobby Rousseau perched on the blue line, ready to swoop toward the Leafs' goal when their chance came. Their presence on the blue line was symbolic. It had little to do with defending their goal and everything to do with scoring a goal for the Canadiens. Rousseau had led the Canadiens in scoring this year. Tremblay had scored more goals in this season alone than his team's three other defencemen had scored in three years.

For twenty seconds the Canadiens kept the puck in the Leafs' end of the rink. But the four Leafs on the ice had prepared themselves for the onslaught. As soon as Beliveau slid the puck back to J.C. Tremblay, Dave Keon darted from the face-off circle toward the blue line. So did George Armstrong.

They allowed Tremblay less than a second to control the puck and fire it toward the net. When he did, Keon and Armstrong turned, and each of them covered one of the Canadiens' forwards while their two teammates on defence, Marcel Pronovost and Larry Hillman, protected their goalie like two bodyguards, making sure neither Beliveau nor the puck came anywhere near Terry Sawchuk. If necessary, they would hurl themselves in front of a shot, taking a bullet for the man who'd kept them in the lead in this game for two and a half periods. When the puck bounced toward the corner, Pronovost chased it and tried to shoot it down the ice. Bobby Rousseau and Yvan Cournoyer pestered him from both sides. Pronovost lost control of the puck. It dribbled back to Tremblay at the blue line.

Tremblay fired the puck into the corner. It skidded behind the Leafs' goal. Pronovost tried to control it with his skates. Beliveau nudged him from one side. Cournoyer used his stick from the other side to pry him away from the puck. Beliveau took the puck. But Cournoyer caught his stick between Pronovost's skate and the boards and tore the blade from the shaft. Without a stick, Cournoyer couldn't score a goal and posed no threat to the Leafs. They ignored him and turned their full attention to Beliveau. They went after him like a pack of wolves. Larry Hillman pushed him one way. Marcel Pronovost pushed him the other way. Dave Keon swept past, blocking Beliveau's escape route. Beliveau fought back. With a forearm to the chest, he knocked Larry Hillman backwards onto the seat of his pants. He shoved Pronovost away with his other arm. He turned and kicked, stumbled, regained his balance, saw that he was outnumbered and that Cournoyer had no stick. Finally he leaned against Pronovost and held the puck against the boards with his feet until John Ashley blew his whistle.

Larry Hillman said he spent more time on the ice during these playoffs than any other player on his team. "I had more than half an hour of ice time per game," he said. "I killed over half an hour of penalties, and [Marcel Pronovost and I] never had one goal scored against us."

Considering that he hadn't played a full season with the team in seven years, Hillman's playoff performance should have earned him a little security, some acclaim and perhaps a little money, too. But Hillman played for the Toronto Maple Leafs, and the Leafs under Punch Imlach rewarded exceptional performance with an insult and a ticket to the minor leagues. Like Jim Pappin, who'd outscored all his teammates this year, Hillman found himself in the season after tonight's game not playing in the NHL in Toronto but dodging raindrops under the leaky roof of the War Memorial arena in Rochester.

In twelve years as a professional, Hillman might have lived and played hockey in more cities than all his teammates combined, but he was only thirty years old, and he would hang on long enough after tonight to reap the rewards that came from the expansion of the NHL, the founding of the WHA and the organization of a players' union. He just wouldn't do it in one place, even when he stopped playing and began coaching.

In the ten years after tonight's game, Hillman would play for professional hockey teams in nine cities. He would dress for a single playoff game with the Montreal Canadiens and win his sixth Stanley Cup. As a coach, he would win a WHA league championship with the Jets in Winnipeg, then lose his job when the Jets hired a new manager, John Ferguson, who was playing tonight against Hillman for the Canadiens.

Hillman wasn't the only player who would try coaching after he gave up playing. By choice or necessity, more than half the players in the game tonight would eventually occupy the coach's spot behind the bench of a hockey team. On the Leafs, Red Kelly, Bob Pulford, Johnny Bower, Bob Baun, Pete Stemkowski, Marcel Pronovost, George Armstrong, Ron Ellis and Brian Conacher would all try their hands at coaching. So would Larry Jeffrey, once his gimpy knees got better. On the Canadiens, Jimmy Roberts, Dick Duff, John Ferguson, Jacques Laperriere, Ted Harris, Ralph Backstrom, Claude Larose, Jean-Guy Talbot, Terry Harper, Dave Balon and Gump Worsley would become coaches. As Punch Imlach might have predicted, though, only a few of them did the job well enough to become established in the job. The best coaches unite their players by giving them a collective focus that binds them together as a team. Imlach did it by giving the Maple Leafs a collective focus for their anger. The Leafs players may not have had much in common, but all of them shared the binding conviction that Punch Imlach was a prick.

As coaches themselves, few players in tonight's game could duplicate the conditions that prevailed under Imlach's tyranny, nor did they want to. Brian Conacher drifted into a coaching job in the WHA, with a farm team of the Toronto Toros called the Mohawk Valley Comets. "I was coach, general manager, Zamboni driver, program salesman, you name it," he said. "My biggest score was renting our bus to the outfit making [the movie] *Slap Shot*, for $6,000. But it cost me $3,000 to repair the luggage door after that scene where the guy took an axe to the vehicle."

George Armstrong coached the Toronto Marlboros to the Memorial Cup on two occasions in three years and was named coach of the year by the Ontario Hockey Association in his first year. "We won games as much for him as for ourselves," said one of his players, Mark Howe. But Armstrong took no credit for his team's performance. "Players make a coach," he said. "Coaches don't make players."

Armstrong's biggest challenge as a coach, he said, was telling a teenager that he probably wouldn't make it to the NHL. "How do I tell him he just hasn't got it and will never become a good hockey player?" he said. "I find these things tough."

As coaches, none of the players tonight would surpass the record of the two men who'd led them to this game. Toe Blake coached the Canadiens to eight Stanley Cups. Punch Imlach coached the Leafs to four. Imlach helped crush the spirit of at least three of his players in the game tonight and neglected others who proved their talent only after they moved to other teams to play under other coaches. Yet he also remains the only coach of the Toronto Maple Leafs ever to win 365 games. The Leafs had now won three Stanley Cups under Imlach and were eight minutes away from winning a fourth. After tonight, he would never come close to winning another one.

As for Larry Hillman, his peripatetic life would come to a sudden halt when he became paralyzed with Guillain-Barré syndrome. At forty-seven, he couldn't walk, brush his teeth or tie his shoes. He received blood transfusions and several weeks of therapy. Eventually he recovered, despite occasional tingling in his hands and feet, to operate a hunting and fishing camp on the Englehart River, near Charlton, Ontario, not far from Jacques Laperriere's summer home on Lake Timiskaming.

With thirty seconds left in the penalty, the Canadiens continued to pepper shots at the Leafs' goal, but always from a distance. With three Canadiens and two Maple Leafs clustering around the net, a shot from the blue line hardly stood a chance of reaching its destination.

When Sawchuk stopped a shot from centre and left the puck behind the goal, Conacher jammed the puck against the boards with his foot to stop play.

Toe Blake reassembled the line that had started each of the first two periods: Ralph Backstrom, John Ferguson and Claude Larose. He sent Jacques Laperriere back onto the ice to replace Bobby Rousseau on the blue line, but rather than replacing J.C. Tremblay with Lappy's usual partner, Terry Harper, he left Tremblay out there and told him to move to the right point from the left.

Toe Blake had first started pacing behind his players on the bench eleven years ago. As coach of the Montreal Canadiens, he'd walked more than half a mile a game. The Canadiens had played 944 games under Blake, and he hadn't missed the opening face-off of a single one. He'd been thrown out of a few, but despite the tension, stress and chest pains that came with the job, Blake's health had never let him down, and neither had his shoes. He'd worn out three pairs. Tonight, he had another six minutes and thirty-seven seconds left in the game to pace up and down as he tried to find a way to penetrate the Leafs' defences.

Next year, Blake would retire after winning his eleventh Stanley Cup — three as a player and eight a coach. But Canadiens coaches would carry on his attendance record, not missing a game for another quarter-century. In 1993, Jacques Demers would catch the flu and miss two games, the first time in fifty-three years that poor health would keep a Canadiens coach away from his perch behind the players' bench. Tonight, Demers was twenty-two years old and driving a truck for Coca Cola.

That didn't mean that coaching in the NHL was good for a man's health. The job could turn his hair grey, set his heart beating like a tom-tom and make his nerves quiver like guitar strings. But if a coach's life was stressful, it also lasted a long time. The average Canadian man in the 1960s lived for sixty-seven years. All the coaches in the NHL this season would live longer. A few of them would last well into their eighties.

By then, there would be four times as many teams in the league, playing in cities such as Raleigh, Anaheim and Columbus, where Toe Blake had never been in his life, and four times as many jobs for the players. By the turn of the twenty-first century, NHL players would come from more than a dozen different countries, and they would make about twenty times more money than the players in tonight's game. A few of them would make $3 million a year. That amount would have covered the salaries tonight of all the players on both teams, along with their coaches, trainers and medical staff, plus the referee and linesmen. To an observer of a game, all of the $3-million-a year players would look almost identical, because the NHL would eventually require the players to cover their heads with a helmet. Even the referees would have to wear one — and there would be seventy-six refs.

All this would happen in the future, without Toe Blake. Soon, Blake wouldn't recognize anyone in an NHL game. The game itself would baffle him, and not just because it had changed. Blake would be afflicted with

Alzheimer's. For the last ten years of his life, he wouldn't recognize his own wife.

To kill the last twenty-three seconds of the penalty, Punch Imlach sent George Armstrong back onto the ice with Bob Pulford and put Hillman and Pronovost on defence. Once again, the four Leafs players prevented the Canadiens from mounting a sustained attack.

The harder the Canadiens attacked, the more risks they took. With all three Montreal forwards stranded deep in the Leafs' end, Jim Pappin took the puck down the ice, fooled Jacques Laperriere and swerved into the middle of the rink. Pappin's backhand shot bounced directly in front of Gump Worsley and slid toward the corner.

Gilles Tremblay streaked up the ice with the puck, but Richard and Rochefort were exhausted and couldn't keep up with him. Tremblay took a tricky backhand shot from the face-off circle that went over Sawchuk's shoulder. Then he caught up to the puck, spun around and took another backhand. Marcel Pronovost blocked it and fell backwards with the puck smothered in the folds of his jersey.

For the next minute, the Leafs players calmly shot the puck out of their end and across the centre line, forcing the Canadiens each time to regroup and attack again. By the time they did, all five Leafs players stood between the Canadiens and Terry Sawchuk in the goal.

At one point, Brian Conacher dragged the puck along the boards with his feet. As J.C. Tremblay and Yvan Cournoyer pestered him like excited puppies, Conacher kept the puck at his feet for seven seconds. Seven seconds amounted now to about four per cent of all the seconds left in the period, and here were the Canadiens, losing by a single goal, standing in their own end of the rink while their opponent kicked the puck around with his skateblades. Conacher and his linemates, Ron Ellis and Red Kelly, scrambled to their bench, then the Leafs iced the puck and stopped the play.

...

Red Kelly had just turned twenty when he crossed the U.S. border at Windsor to join the Detroit Red Wings and play his first game in the NHL. That season, he wore the number 20. In his second year, he became a full-time defenceman. His team's manager told him to replace the two-digit number with a single-digit number, 4. He told Kelly that NHL defencemen traditionally wore low numbers. He also said the single cloth numeral would weigh less on Kelly's wool jersey, especially when it got wet. Kelly wore the number for the next twelve years.

When Kelly joined the Maple Leafs and moved with his family to Toronto, his wife, Andra, asked the team to give her husband the same number, 4. "I was tickled pink," said Kelly after he saw the jersey hanging above his spot in the dressing room. Now he'd worn the number for nineteen seasons.

The number 4 had brought good luck to Kelly. His teams had made the playoffs eighteen times. He'd won seven Stanley Cups. And now, as he watched his teammate Davey Keon jump onto the ice, he was within three minutes of winning his eighth. Kelly wouldn't let himself think about that possibility, though, not if it might jinx his team's chances.

When this game ended, Kelly intended to hang up his skates for good. The contract that he'd negotiated this season with the Leafs said he could quit playing after tonight's game and start coaching in the NHL next season, and that's what he planned to do. The owner of an expansion team called the Los Angeles Kings had offered Kelly the job as the team's first coach. Before his fortieth birthday in July, Kelly and his family would pack up and move to California.

Of course, a contract didn't mean much unless both parties kept their word. Kelly would certainly keep his, by golly, but the Leafs were another story. "I knew there were plenty of problems," he said. But Kelly hadn't expected this one. "A doublecross," he called it.

The Leafs owned Kelly's contract, whether he played or not. No other team in the NHL could hire him — as a player, a coach or a Zamboni driver — unless the Leafs gave their permission. When the time came to honour his team's commitment, Punch Imlach decided that an expansion team should compensate the Leafs for Kelly's potential services as a player. Kelly had already stated publicly that he'd decided never to play again. Now he sent a registered letter to the Leafs confirming his decision. No one bothered to reply. Kelly had already arranged to move his family to Los Angeles. He'd found a place to live and enrolled the kids in school. But thanks to the Leafs, he wasn't sure anymore that he could work in Los Angeles once he got there. Kelly began to worry. "This is awful," he said. The Leafs, he said, were preventing him from working. "I go right to the prime minister about this," he said.

Eventually, Imlach and the Leafs got their way. In return for letting Kelly go to Los Angeles, the Kings gave the Leafs a player named Ken Block. It wasn't a particularly good deal. Kelly had played more than 1,400 games in the NHL. Block would play a total of one.

Given the inauspicious start to his coaching career, Kelly arrived in California with some foreboding. So did Terry Sawchuk. Expansion teams were allowed to hire any player in the league whose team didn't protect him. As of tonight, Sawchuk had won the Vezina Trophy as the best goaltender in the NHL four times. He held more records, had won more games and recorded more shutouts than any other goaltender in the NHL. A few days after tonight, the Leafs would announce that they were protecting one goalie, as the NHL allowed, but it wasn't Sawchuk.

Like every other player in the league, Sawchuk didn't appreciate his value in dollars. The Leafs did, of course, but they didn't tell him. As of tonight, Sawchuk earned $18,000 a year. Rookies who'd never played in the NHL were signing contracts for $25,000. "We couldn't believe it," said Johnny Wilson, a member of the Kings' coaching staff. In Los Angeles, the Kings said they'd pay Sawchuk $40,000 a year. When he heard the news, Sawchuk started to cry. "I've never seen that much money in my life," he said.

For the previous ten years, in a stormy marriage, Sawchuk had used his income to support six children, a wife, a girlfriend and himself. Now he couldn't thank the Kings enough. To celebrate, he took Wilson to a nearby Legion for a beer. "Terry could always find a Legion," Wilson said.

In Los Angeles, however, Sawchuk's life didn't go so smoothly. His wife had given birth in July to their seventh child, and he'd left them behind when he moved west. In Toronto, he'd had an affair with a woman who'd also become pregnant. In Los Angeles, he found a bag of marijuana on the front lawn of his rented house. He didn't know what it was and, when he found out, he refused to try it. "He probably sold it," said the team's announcer, Jiggs McDonald. Sawchuk preferred to drink, and he did a lot of that in Los Angeles.

On the ice, Sawchuk wore the same tattered shoulder pads and battered belly pad as he'd worn for eighteen years, but now he was thirty-eight, and the game had changed. Before the season was three months old, he suffered a series of injuries. In the thirty-six games that he did play, he allowed more than three goals a game, his worst record in years. The Kings still finished second in their division, much higher than anyone had expected, including the Kings themselves. In the playoffs, Sawchuk didn't improve. He allowed almost four goals a game over five games. In one of them, against Minnesota, he became the first goalie to give up a goal on a penalty shot in an NHL playoff game.

Red Kelly felt disappointed in his goalie, and he didn't feel much better about the city. With their home arena still unfinished, Kelly's team practised and played for the first five months of the season in a temporary facility in Long Beach. It sometimes took him almost an hour to get there on the freeway. With only one other NHL team within a thousand miles, the team's travel schedule was gruelling. "I used to be away so much," Kelly said, "I began to forget what home looked like."

The Kellys lived in a house in West Hollywood, near Benedict Canyon, where the smog sometimes became unbearable. "Hang," said Kelly, "they tell you that the view on a clear day is fantastic. They don't tell you when you can expect that clear day."

In the months after their arrival in California, two earthquakes shook the foundations of their house. The next big one, according to an astrologer named Jeane Dixon, would knock the entire state of California into the

Pacific Ocean. For the Kellys, who believed that the number on a player's jersey might influence the outcome of a hockey game, Dixon's prediction was unnerving. His wife, Andra, hated the place.

The Kellys had more immediate concerns. They'd hardly lived in LA for more than a year when the daughter of a neighbour was killed in a mudslide. A few months later, the followers of Charles Manson descended on a house in Benedict Canyon, about a mile away from the Kellys, and used knives and machetes to slaughter five people, including the actress Sharon Tate. By the time Kelly's contract was up, he and his family were more than ready to leave Los Angeles. "Even our dog was happy to get out," Kelly said.

From LA, Kelly moved to Pittsburgh to coach a team called the Penguins. But the unsettling occurrences continued. In the year before Kelly arrived, the Penguins had finished second and won the first round of the playoffs. That pleased the owners, who'd earned their fortunes from Heinz ketchup, Mellon banking and high-stakes gambling on thoroughbred horses. The more playoff games the team played, the more money the team made. Despite their success, though, the Penguins attracted fewer than seven thousand fans a game to an arena that accommodated more than twelve thousand. When the team's owners stopped paying their bills, the NHL took over the operation. Now they hoped that Kelly could work the same magic in Pittsburgh as he'd done in Los Angeles.

Kelly arrived in Pittsburgh expecting to build the team around a rising star named Michel Briere. But that summer, Briere went home to northern Quebec and drove his car off the road near Malartic, about fifty miles east of Rouyn-Noranda, and never regained consciousness. Without Briere, the team finished out of the playoffs. Shortly after the season ended, Briere died in a hospital in Montreal. He was twenty-one. As coach of the team, Kelly attended Briere's funeral.

The Penguins rallied in Kelly's second year, making the playoffs again, then relapsed in his third year. But if the Penguins didn't win games, they could at least attract fans, especially after Kelly hired his former teammate

from the Leafs, Eddie Shack. With Shackie on the team, attendance rose
by more than fifteen per cent. More than eleven thousand fans a game
flocked to the Igloo, the Penguins arena, to watch his slam-bang antics.
They also came to see Andy Brown, the last NHL goalie to play without
a facemask, in case he stopped a puck with his teeth. But neither Brown
nor the Penguins' three other goalies stopped many shots, with their
faces or any other parts of their bodies. Kelly had never felt so frustrated
in his life. In a game with the Maple Leafs, a referee named Bruce Hood
called a penalty that allowed the Leafs to beat the Penguins. That pushed
Kelly over the edge. "What the hell kind of an official is he?" Kelly said.
It was the first time in recorded history that Kelly had sworn out loud.

At the end of the season, the Penguins fired Kelly but agreed to pay
him $50,000 a year, under the terms of his contract, for the next three
years. He and Andra moved with the kids to a thirty-six-acre tobacco
farm near his childhood home in Simcoe, north of Lake Erie, and wondered
what they'd do next. They didn't wait long. When Kelly answered the
phone one morning, he heard the voice of Harold Ballard, the Leafs'
owner.

Ballard's partner, Stafford Smythe, had died of a bleeding ulcer, under
a cloud of suspicion and innuendo for his involvement in defrauding the
company's shareholders, and had been buried in Muskoka under a head-
stone that said he'd been "persecuted to death by his enemies." Ballard
had borrowed $7.5 million from the TD Bank to buy Smythe's shares in
the Leafs organization. Then, as the sole controlling shareholder, Ballard
started to reconfigure the Leafs in his own image. The image resembled
a dollar sign. He unloaded players who earned more than he wanted to
pay them. He reduced the width of seats so that the Gardens could accommodate a few thousand more skinny fans. He fired Tommy Smythe,
Stafford's son, as boss of the Toronto Marlboros and dumped the kid's
personal belongings onto the sidewalk in front of the Gardens. He sent
an employee to Etobicoke to repossess the company car from Stafford
Smythe's widow. Ballard even superimposed a photo of his own son Bill

over the face of his former partner John Bassett on a Leafs' calendar. By the time he died in 1990, Ballard might have ruined the Leafs, but he got what he wanted. His estate was worth an estimated $50 million.

When he made his phone call to Kelly, Ballard was confined in a minimum-security penitentiary called Millhaven Institution, serving a sentence for fraud, theft and tax evasion after pilfering the Gardens till. Since he couldn't travel to Simcoe, Ballard suggested that Kelly drive to Kingston to see him.

Marcel Pronovost, Kelly's teammate tonight, also aspired to become the coach of the Maple Leafs. Pronovost had begun coaching in Tulsa, Oklahoma. By coincidence, one of his nine brothers, Jean Pronovost, had just begun his NHL career with Kelly's team in Pittsburgh and now ranked second on the team in scoring. In Tulsa, Marcel, who was fifteen years older, won an award as coach of the year. Thinking that Harold Ballard might hire him to coach the Leafs some day, Marcel spent two more years preparing himself with the Leafs' affiliate in the Central Hockey League. But when the moment came to hire a new coach for the Leafs, Ballard said that he thought Pronovost was happy coaching in the minor leagues and that he couldn't afford to pay him anyway, and hired Kelly instead. Pronovost reluctantly took a job in the WHA, coaching the Cougars in Chicago.

Kelly was back where he'd left off in 1967, working for Harold Ballard with the Maple Leafs in Toronto. Kelly and Ballard negotiated a contract that paid Kelly $45,000 a year for four years. "Four has always been kind of lucky for me," he said.

By 1974, the only players from tonight's game who remained with the team were Dave Keon and Ron Ellis, and both of them would leave the team within two years of Kelly's arrival under a cloud of confusion, ill-will and regret. Continuing the Leafs' convention of abusing players in public, Ballard began criticizing Keon, who had become the team's captain.

Ballard probably felt more irritated by Keon's salary. By then, the Leafs were paying Keon $135,000 a year. But Ballard had just served a prison sentence for lying, cheating and stealing more money than he was paying Keon. So he attacked Keon's character instead. He said Keon was a failure as a captain, and he took him to task for antagonizing reporters who pestered players in search of a good story. "Keon was one of the first Leaf stars to be bad-mouthed in public by the owner," said the reporter Frank Orr, "a happening that has been repeated with nauseating regularity ever since."

Even as they lugged the managerial albatross of Harold Ballard around the ice, the Leafs under Kelly still made the playoffs for two consecutive years, and in the first of those years, Keon had a lot to do with the team's performance. Over fifteen years, Keon had led the team in total points three times and ranked among the top two or three players on the team in every year but one, his first in the league. Keon was the first player in the history of the Maple Leafs to score more than three hundred goals, and he'd scored more goals, more short-handed goals and more game-winning goals than any other player on the team, ever. He would remain the team's only player to win the Lady Byng Trophy for combining excellence with fair play, until a Russian named Alex Mogilny won it almost thirty years later. And he would remain the second-highest goal scorer on the Leafs, behind Darryl Sittler, for more than thirty years, until Mats Sundin surpassed his record in 2006.

None of this impressed Harold Ballard. He just wanted to save a few bucks. When Keon's $135,000 contract came up for renewal, Ballard refused to negotiate another one with his team's captain, and then he refused to let Keon play for another NHL team.

By the time Mats Sundin surpassed Keon's goal-scoring record, Harold Ballard was dead, and the Leafs were hardly breathing. Keon's son, Dave Jr., had become an employee of the NHL, and Mats Sundin was making $6.5 million a season, almost fifty times as much as Ballard had saved by alienating one of the best players in the history of the team.

By 2003, Keon had owned a Tim Hortons donut franchise, sold real estate in Florida for Realty World and coached a kids' hockey team in

Fort Lauderdale to the state championship. But he'd turned his back completely on the organization that he'd joined as a kid from Rouyn-Noranda. "I didn't leave the Toronto Maple Leafs," he said. "They didn't want me anymore."

Even as Ballard decimated his roster, Kelly continued to coach the Leafs for another two years. In both years, the team reached the second round of the playoffs, and in both years, the Leafs met the Philadelphia Flyers. Depending on the inclinations of the observer, the Flyers had become the scourge or the salvation of the NHL. Led by a coach named Fred Shero, and with the NHL's tacit approval, the Flyers won hockey games through violence and intimidation as much as skill. The players themselves admitted that their approach to the game resembled gang warfare. A magazine called *Sport* described NHL hockey as "the next best thing to a mass murder."

If the Flyers hadn't won hockey games, they might have changed their ways. But with violence and intimidation, Philadelphia became the first expansion team to win a Stanley Cup, so the other teams in the league changed their ways instead. Soon, every team employed a phalanx of players with necks the size of tree stumps and a predilection for running head-first into walls. And when Shero hired an assistant to help him coach the Flyers, every team in the league hired an assistant coach, as well. If Shero had coached his team to the Cup while wearing a kilt, every other coach in the league would suddenly have become a Scot.

By the time Keon left the team, the Leafs, too, had adopted the Flyers' intimidating tactics. Led by a player named Tiger Williams, the Leafs spent almost twice as much time in the penalty box as they'd done this season, and Williams accounted for a quarter of the penalties. But they still fell far short of the Flyers in their capacity for bullying, so Kelly resorted to a more exotic tactic. Kelly's two sons had taken a trip to Egypt and had impressed their dad with their tales of the power of the pyramids. If it worked for King Tut, Kelly figured, a pyramid might work for Tiger Williams, Pat Boutette and the rest of the Maple Leafs. He hung a pyramid from the ceiling of the Leafs' dressing room and placed a few more pyramids on the Leafs' bench for good measure. With his stick empowered by an Egyptian burial monument, the Leafs' captain, Darryl Sittler, skated onto the ice one night in April and scored five goals against the team's nemesis, the Philadelphia Flyers. In the playoffs, still soaking up the power of the pyramid, the Leafs pushed the Flyers to a seventh game before finally losing the series. No one could say exactly how the pyramid influenced the Leafs' performance, but what the hey, as Kelly would say, it couldn't have hurt.

When it came to influencing the behaviour of his players, pyramids certainly worked better than Kelly's more conventional coaching tactics. Coming from the old school of hockey, Kelly assumed that the coach of a hockey team deserved the respect of his players simply because of the authority inherent in his job. In Kelly's assessment of the game, a coach talked, and the players listened. But times had changed, and Kelly's players didn't share his views. When they grumbled about a lack of communication, unexplained benchings and dull practices, Kelly couldn't understand why they expected anything different. Kelly himself had never needed much coaching. If he needed to hone his skills, he practised until he noticed an improvement. If he needed motivation, he found it within himself.

Kelly tried to appeal to his players' pride and was surprised when his appeals didn't work. "They're pro athletes," he said, "and they should be proud of what they're doing." True to his Roman Catholic roots, he approached coaching with religious fervour. "I like to have faith and trust in my players," he said, "and I like them to have faith and trust in me."

But nothing seemed to work: not faith, not trust, not even pyramids. Still, Kelly didn't give up. He had more tricks in his bag. Before a game against New York, he carried a whip into the dressing room and joked that he'd flail the first player who made a mistake. When hecklers in St. Louis began getting under the skin of his players, he gave each of them a set of earmuffs.

He recorded games and the performance of individual players with a video camera, a practice that the Leafs had begun under Conn Smythe in the 1940s with film cameras. Unlike Smythe, Kelly didn't use the technology to gain an advantage over players in contract negotiations but to help them improve their game. "Videotape can fill the role of an assistant coach," said Kelly.

When these tactics didn't work, Kelly relented and hired his own assistant coach, Johnny Bower, his former teammate, to help the Leafs' goalies. He also pulled out the last gimmick in his repertoire. In his final season as the Leafs' coach, Kelly installed a generator in the dressing room to fill the air with negative ions. In theory, negative ions relieve the symptoms of seasonal affective disorder and improve a person's disposition. Maybe they'd help the Leafs win hockey games, too.

By the time Kelly emptied his bag of coaching tricks, the man who'd once aspired to his job, Marcel Pronovost, had fallen on hard times. Pronovost spent one losing season with the Cougars in the WHA. When he lost that job, he spent two years looking for another one. He also started drinking heavily. "I gave the game everything I had," he said. But after almost thirty years in the game, it seemed, hockey no longer wanted anything from Pronovost. "I became an alcoholic."

Around the same time as Kelly was festooning the Leafs' dressing room with pyramids, Pronovost pulled himself together long enough to become coach of a city-owned junior team in Hull, Quebec, called the Festivals. He lasted about a month until the Quebec Major Junior Hockey League suspended him for refusing to obey a referee's order to leave a game.

When his former coach Punch Imlach became general manager of the Buffalo Sabres, he asked Pronovost to coach the team. Pronovost didn't want to leave Hull. The city had given him another chance, and he'd given his word to stay with the junior team. Finally, the Festivals' president threatened to punch Pronovost in the nose if he didn't take the NHL job. So Pronovost relented and moved to Buffalo. "This is my thirty-fourth training camp [in forty-eight years]," he said. "And I get just as worked up now as I did when I was a junior."

Under Pronovost, the Sabres bulldozed their way into the second round of the playoffs. But Imlach hadn't changed since his days with the Maple Leafs. As he did with the Leafs, he antagonized the Sabres players by belittling them in public, aggravating their differences and undermining their confidence. The game and the players had changed, however, and they no longer took Imlach's abuse without comment. After twenty-four games of the next season, the Sabres released Imlach, and Pronovost went with him. Meeting their obligations under his contract, the Sabres continued to pay Pronovost, even after he returned to his previous job in Hull.

"The Sabres are a class organization," Pronovost said, "and I'm proud to have been a part of it." The owners of the Sabres, Seymour and Northrup Knox, took their role seriously in maintaining the integrity of their city. Unlike Harold Ballard, they treated their team, its players and their fans with respect. A few other owners did the same. In St. Louis, the Salomons, owners of the St. Louis Blues, rewarded their players one year for reaching the Stanley Cup finals with a two-week paid vacation in Florida with their wives and children.

Although Pronovost had lost another NHL job, the league chose that year to induct him into the Hockey Hall of Fame. At forty-eight, Pronovost invited his parents, his wife and his children along with five brothers and two sisters to attend the ceremonies.

"We slept two or three to a bed," he told the *Hockey News* before his induction. "The younger ones dressed in hand-me-downs from the older ones. We made do. We had happiness. Life has been wonderful to me."

After two more uneventful years in junior, Pronovost was hired by his former teammate in Detroit, Ted Lindsay, as an assistant with the Red Wings. Pronovost had started his professional career in Detroit at seventeen and had stayed there for more than fifteen years. This time, he lasted two. Fired by the Red Wings, he crossed the Detroit River to Windsor to coach another junior team, the Spitfires. Once again, Pronovost's temper cost him his job, after a referee tossed him out of a game and he refused to go. This time, he didn't get another chance. The league suspended him for ten games, and his team fired him. "It feels like they took all my toys away," he said.

In his mid-fifties, Pronovost still had something to offer to the game that he'd played all his life. The owner of the Red Wings gave him yet another break, hiring him as assistant coach of a team of fifteen-year-olds called the Detroit Little Caesars. After that, Pronovost drifted into scouting, ending up with the New Jersey Devils. Pronovost had won the Stanley Cup for the first time when he was nineteen years old. When the Devils won it in 2003, they included Pronovost's name on the Cup. By then, he was seventy-two. Pronovost had spent all but two years of his adult life involved in hockey.

As for Kelly, he ran out of options in his fourth year as coach of the Leafs, despite his application of faith, trust, whips, pyramids, negative ions and the number four. He gave up coaching in the NHL and made his last appearance behind a bench full of hockey players two years later, when he agreed to coach his son's midget team in the west end of Toronto.

Apart from his own family, Kelly's most loyal supporter was Marcel Pronovost. "Red Kelly is the greatest man I've ever met," said Pronovost. "He's the most honest, most dedicated and possibly the most intelligent."

When John Ashley dropped the puck, five players converged on it and started pushing and shoving in a scrum until the puck popped loose. Bobby Rousseau chased it, but Tim Horton pushed him aside and bulled his way up the ice. When Horton lost the puck, Jacques Laperriere took it and fed a pass to his right into the middle of the rink. Jim Roberts had replaced Laperriere's partner, Terry Harper, and he wasn't used to receiving one of Lappy's passes. The puck slid behind him. Roberts stuck out his stick to stop Bob Pulford. Pulford golfed the stick right out of Roberts's hands, then caught up to the puck and prepared to take a shot at the

Canadiens' goal. Without a stick, Roberts still managed to swing in front of Pulford and drag the player and the puck with him into the corner. When the puck became entangled in the skates of the players around him, John Ashley blew his whistle.

One minute and fifty-eight seconds remained in the period. Twenty-eight seconds had passed since the previous face-off, and the Canadiens had spent most of them in their own end of the rink. The fans in Maple Leaf Gardens could hardly contain themselves. Ashley stood with the puck in the face-off circle, thirty feet from Gump Worsley. Worsley couldn't leave the goal until his teammates carried the puck to the other end of the rink.

From high in the stands, someone threw an egg onto the ice. Two attendants in navy blue sweaters shuffled onto the ice. To calm the raving crowd, the arena staff turned on the sound system and played a recorded ditty called "Tijuana Taxi."

As the fans tapped their toes, Toe Blake called Worsley to the Canadiens' bench and replaced him on the ice with Henri Richard. The strategy of replacing a goalie with a forward had first been used by Art Ross in 1931, when he was coaching the Bruins in a game against the Canadiens in Boston. By 1967, teams pulled their goalie in the last minute more than sixty per cent of the time if they were losing by one or even two goals. With their goalie on the bench, the Canadiens had six players on the ice who could score goals, one more than the Leafs. An additional forward presumably gave the Canadiens an advantage, but how big was it?

A few years before tonight's game, Henry Roxborough, the Toronto reporter, had used a pad and pencil to examine the results of one hundred and seventy-five games. Roxborough found that teams had scored forty-eight goals within the last two minutes. Within the final sixty seconds, they'd scored twenty-nine goals. Those were pretty good odds for the Canadiens.

In a more precise analysis conducted more than forty years later, a Harvard researcher named Andrew Thomas used a computer to assess the results of NHL playoff games over a four-year period. He found that teams losing by one or two goals had pulled their goalies in sixty-four per cent of the games. "In 34% of those games," Thomas said, "a goal was scored with one net empty, and of those goals 30% were scored by the team that pulled their goaltender."

But with the Stanley Cup on the line, statistics had as much substance as the melting mush under the Maple Leafs' skates. Other big-brained statisticians had calculated that a team has about a six per cent chance of winning four games in a row after it loses the first three games in a seven-game series. Despite those odds, the Leafs had done it. Down three games to none in a series against Detroit, twenty-five years before tonight, the Leafs had won four in a row to claim the Stanley Cup. No other team in any North American major-league sports championship has ever done it.

In 1951, the Leafs had pulled their goalie in the last minute of the final game of a Stanley Cup series against Montreal. With thirty-two seconds left, Dave Keon's cousin, Tod Sloan, scored a goal to tie the game. The Leafs had already beaten the Canadiens three times in the series in overtime, and they did it for the fourth time when Bill Barilko scored the winning goal after less than three minutes. The Leafs won the Stanley Cup again. The Canadiens had lost four final games in overtime, the only time an NHL team has ever done that.

In other words, despite the statistical odds, the Canadiens could still tie the game.

Of the six Leafs on the ice at the moment, Allan Stanley, Terry Sawchuk and Red Kelly had played against Bill Barilko in the year when he'd scored his Cup-winning overtime goal. George Armstrong and Tim Horton had played a game or two with Barilko as teenagers before they joined the Leafs for good, four months after his Cup-winning goal. All of them had seen goals scored and games tied in the final fifty-five seconds.

...

With John Ashley watching closely to make sure the players lined up fairly, linesman Brent Casselman waited to drop the puck. To his right and left, Jean Beliveau and Allan Stanley waited to take the face-off.

Players on both teams fussed over their positions and conferred with each other like sorority sisters before a big dance. When Casselman finally dropped the puck, Stanley pulled it behind him and then slammed forward into Beliveau. "Face-off interference!" Beliveau hollered. "Face-off interference!" But the play continued.

By the boards, Red Kelly pounced on the puck and passed it to Pulford, who crossed the blue line and passed from his backhand just firmly enough for the puck to reach Armstrong's outstretched stick at centre ice.

With Ralph Backstrom one step away, Armstrong cradled the puck to make it sit on the ice, then fired a wrist shot at the empty goal. Jacques Laperriere, skating backwards, reached out, but the puck sailed past his stick into the empty Montreal goal. Leafs fans leapt out of their seats, tossed their hats into the air, spun empty popcorn boxes toward the rafters and hollered at the top of their lungs.

Later, when Armstrong's mother asked Pulford why he'd passed instead of shooting the puck, Pulford said he thought George was a pretty nice guy.

Forty-seven seconds left to play in this period, and the Leafs didn't want to play one second longer. They especially didn't want to play another game. If they did, they would have to play it on Thursday night in Montreal, and everyone on the team felt superstitious about trying to win in Montreal on a Thursday. Four of the Leafs' eleven playoff games this year had been played on Thursdays, and they had lost all four. So far, the Leafs had allowed thirty goals against in the playoffs; twenty-one of them had been scored on Thursdays. On Thursday, even the gods were Habs fans.

The next game would be the seventh and final game, and the Canadiens tended to win final playoff games at home. As of this year, the Canadiens had never lost a Stanley Cup final game in the Montreal Forum, and they wouldn't lose one for another twenty-two years after tonight. Forty-seven seconds amounted to 1.3 per cent of all the time available in a regulation hockey game. The Canadiens had to score two goals to tie the game. The chance of scoring two goals in such a short time was infinitesimal. But the Leafs would take no chances.

The Canadiens looked glum. Leafs fans in their jubilation had littered the ice with programs, coffee cups, paper airplanes and anything else they could find to throw into the air. It took ninety seconds to clear the debris. As the players waited, the Gardens announcer, Paul Morris, read the names over the public-address system of the Maple Leaf players who'd participated in scoring the team's third goal. "Toronto goal scored by number ten, Armstrong, assist, number twenty, Pulford, and number twenty-six, Stanley. The time nineteen-thirteen."

The Canadiens couldn't wait for the announcement to end. Each word poured over their heads like a bucket of slops. But Morris wasn't finished. "Official correction on the second Toronto goal," he thundered over the PA system. "Scored by number eighteen, Pappin, assist, number twelve, Stemkowski, and number twenty, Pulford."

Even after John Ashley dropped the puck at centre, Morris kept going, trying hard to keep moderate the gloating jubilation in his voice. "And official correction on the last Toronto goal, scored by number ten, Armstrong, assist, number twenty, Pulford, and number four, Kelly."

By the time Morris finished his oration, the teams had already started playing, and ten of the remaining forty-seven seconds had passed. As if he wanted to atone for his errors, Toe Blake sent Henri Richard, Yvan Cournoyer and Dick Duff onto the ice. The three Canadiens forwards buzzed around the ice like hostile hornets. Duff raked his stick across Pronovost's head as he sidestepped the Leafs defenceman and steamed over the blue line. Pronovost tried to retaliate but couldn't reach Duff with his stick. Hillman snared the puck behind the Leafs' goal and passed it up the boards to Bob Pulford. With nothing to lose, J.C. Tremblay skated deep into the Leafs' end to knock the puck away from Pulford, then swerved toward the front of the Leafs' goal, leaving only one defenceman, Jacques Laperriere, at the blue line. When the puck bounced free, Pulford and Armstrong sped away down the ice with only Laperriere between them and the Canadiens' goal. Gump Worsley sprawled to block Pulford's shot. The puck slid into the corner.

J.C. Tremblay tried one last time to move the puck up the ice, but his pass went beyond the reach of Henri Richard. The fans began counting. "Ten," they chanted. "Nine. Eight."

Pulford held the puck for a moment, then chucked it gently off the boards and watched it drift back into the Canadiens' end of the rink. By the time Richard flipped a half-baked pass to Duff, everyone in the rink knew that the game was over. The Toronto Maple Leafs had won the Stanley Cup.

CHAPTER SEVEN
Post-game Wrap-up

Terry Sawchuk feels as if he has spent the night under a sweaty elephant. Every bone in his body aches. His underwear is drenched. His back hurts, and he can't stand up straight. When he pulls off his jersey, he can feel the bruises on his arms and chest where the pucks stung like rubber bullets. Forty-one shots the Canadiens drilled at the Leafs' goal tonight, and Sawchuk stopped all but one.

He tosses his soggy jersey into the centre of the dressing room. An attendant picks it up as soon as it hits the floor. The Leafs never allow a player to take his jersey home at the end of a season unless he pays for it, even if he's helped the team win the Stanley Cup. Sawchuk takes a pack of cigarettes from the shelf above his cubicle. He sits down, lights a cigarette, slouches forward and rests his forearms on the tops of his goalie pads.

It feels good to win. The best feeling in the world. Nothing else comes close. What you do at other times seems pointless in comparison. Crossword puzzles. Beer. Women. Kids. Try as hard as you can, you'll never win a Stanley Cup for taking your son to the zoo. But the euphoria soon wears off, and then you have to do it all over again. Victory is addictive.

The door to the dressing room swings open. The hubbub in the corridor washes over the room, as if someone has turned up the volume on a radio.

Into the room march Sawchuk's teammates: Kelly he's known for seventeen years, and Pronovost, too; Keon, dour, self-contained and taciturn, even in victory; Mahovlich, like a big kid, happy despite himself to have won another Cup. Pappin walks in, followed by the Cup itself, perched on the left shoulder of George Armstrong. Army hoists the silver pillar onto the table in the centre of the room and starts to fill the bowl with champagne. Purchased by the governor general of Canada for fifty bucks from a silversmith in England, the Cup holds two gallons. Red Kelly once placed his infant son in the Cup without a diaper. Now he wouldn't drink from the thing if you paid him. As of tonight, the Leafs and the Canadiens together have won the Cup twenty-two times in fifty years, more often than the other four NHL teams combined.

A guy in a suit leads Armstrong away to the cubbyhole down the hall, where Ward Cornell and Frank Selke Jr. are interviewing players in front of a bank of lights and a TV camera.

Pete Stemkowski barges into the room, takes one look at Sawchuk, hollers, "Way to go, Ukie boy!" and pours a beer over his head. Sawchuk looks up, cupping his cigarette in his hand to keep it dry. Stemkowski hands the half-empty bottle to Sawchuk, then struts in his skates to the table. He puts his arms around the Cup and hugs it.

Sawchuk can't blame the kid for getting excited. This is Stemmer's first Stanley Cup. Stemkowski's brother, Ron, has moved to Alberta to sell cars, but he'll probably drive to Winnipeg to celebrate with Pete. Maybe they'll go hunting together.

Now the coach and the owners pile into the room along with the admen from MacLaren and the sponsors' reps from Esso, the executives in suits from Molson, an army of reporters and a cluster of photographers with cameras dangling from their necks. Stemmer and Horton grab Punch Imlach. They carry him into the showers and turn on the water. Clarence Campbell, the NHL president, stands inside the door, looking stern even when he smiles, as if he might hand out demerit points for bad behaviour. There's Conn Smythe, face like a lizard, heart like a skateblade, puffed up with pride that the team he started thirty years ago has just won another Stanley Cup. "The Smythe name is on the Stanley Cup eleven times," he says to a reporter. "Nobody else is gonna beat that, boy."

Lester Pearson, the prime minister of Canada, strolls from player to player like a general inspecting his troops. Alan Eagleson, the agent, is laughing and hugging Mike Walton. Stafford Smythe, keeping his distance from his father, is kibbitzing with Bob Pulford. Some of these guys can't stand the sight of each other, but here they are now, celebrating as if they all belong to the same big happy family. The spirit of victory is better than Christmas, and it ends just as quickly.

Sawchuk wishes the game would go on forever. It's the only time in his miserable life that he feels completely at peace. Twenty thousand people watching, and no place to hide. No ambiguity, no guilt, no shame, no haunting doubt, no crippling sadness, just win or lose, and you put everything you have into the effort: your head, your heart, your balls, your instincts, your memory. The game consumes everything. Sawchuk wants to hold the moment in his hand, pop it into his mouth, roll it around on his tongue like a marble. But the rock-hard certainty of victory dissolves like a pill, and once again his life becomes the same old doubt-laden crapshoot. You have no control. You make decisions even though you know one is no better than another and it doesn't really matter what you do. You do your best. Or sometimes, you don't. It's all the same, a monotonous shade of grey, like living in a cloud. One day, your older brother takes you under his wing, drives you to a rink to watch him play in goal for his hockey team. The next day, your brother dies, and instead of a brother, all you've got are his goalie pads. In the end, you die, too. All roads lead to the grave. Who really cares what you do on the way?

Sawchuk lumbers in his undershirt and his goalie pads across the room to stand in his skates beside Frank Selke Jr. and tell the world how it feels to win the Stanley Cup. "It's the greatest thrill of my life in hockey," he says. And even as the words tumble out of his mouth, he can feel the moment receding into the past like a distant light in a dark house seen from a passing train. No one will ever know how it really feels, not this guy with the microphone or that guy behind the camera, not the wives, the girlfriends, the kids, not his mom or his little brother. Even as the words tumble out of his mouth, no one will ever know how it feels to be Terry Sawchuk when the last game ends.

Sawchuk tells Selke about the gratitude he feels to the doctor who operated on his back, the people who helped him all winter and especially Punch Imlach. "And here I end up on a Stanley Cup team," he says. "I can't believe it."

And he really can't. It feels like a dream. But this guy with the microphone keeps waking him up, asking him to talk about the past. And now he wants to hear about the future. "What about next year?" Selke says. "I'll have to make that decision," Sawchuk says. "I'm not planning on retiring, and if I do, Mr. Imlach will be the first to know."

Sawchuk plods away and the interviews continue. Stemkowski wipes champagne from his eyes and says he hasn't felt so happy since he passed his economics exam three years ago. Keon, glum-faced, says he plans to play a little golf and work at the hockey school in July and August. Pulford cracks a bashful smile and says he's thrilled. Allan Stanley says winning the Cup is exciting "but it seems to be more satisfying than anything else." More than fifty years ago, Stanley's Uncle Barney won the Cup on a team with only ten men, who played fewer than twenty games a season, and the ages of the entire team didn't add up to the ages of Stanley and his four oldest teammates on the Leafs tonight. With an average age of thirty-one years and five months, the Leafs are the oldest collection of geezers ever to win the Cup. "I wasn't the slowest one on the ice," says Stanley. "I think maybe I'd like to play again next year."

Sawchuk, too, will decide to play again next year. How can he afford not to? He and his teammates have just earned themselves $3,000 apiece for winning the Cup, another $1,500 for winning the semi-finals and $750 for finishing third in the regular season. That money, along with his $18,500 salary, goes a long way to supporting his wife and six kids.

But not far enough, not with his wife and his girlfriend both expecting babies. When Sawchuk hears a few weeks later that the Leafs have let his contract go to a new team in Los Angeles, he will not be unhappy. Under the circumstances, maybe it's a good idea to get out of town. In a couple of months, Sawchuk will move to Los Angeles. When he gets there, he'll find $1,000, a gift from Punch Imlach, in a bank account opened in the name of his seventh child, Michael.

If he can hold on for a few more years, Sawchuk might even win another Cup and make even more money. Big money is just over the horizon, and Sawchuk can smell it. Six years from tonight, each member of the Cup-winning team will make more than Sawchuk earned this year for the entire season. But it won't happen, not for Terry Sawchuk. Within three years, his wife will divorce him. He'll live a thousand miles away from his children. His girlfriend will refuse to see him. He'll drink more than ever and gain twenty pounds. And in his final days in the league, he won't even have the unadulterated certainty of the game to relieve his misery. In his last year in the NHL, in New York, he'll sit at the end of the bench through more than sixty games and play in only eleven. Eleven hours of colour in a lifetime of black and white. At the end of the season, he'll get drunk in a bar one afternoon, go home and start bickering with a teammate in the backyard about cleaning the kitchen and paying the rent on the house they share in the suburbs. He'll take a wild swing at his roommate, stumble into the barbecue, fall on the guy's knee and damage his own gall bladder. A surgeon will operate but inadvertently nick Sawchuk's liver. Two more operations, a gallon of lost blood, and all the life will seep out of Terry Sawchuk forever. Twenty years as an NHL goalie, stopping hundred-mile-an-hour slapshots with his face, and he ends up dead on a spring day in May after a few beers and a tussle on the lawn with a pal in a Long Island backyard. His coach, Emile Francis, a Hall of Fame goalie who was the first to wear a catching glove attached to a protective cuff around his wrist, goes to the morgue to identify Sawchuk's body. He finds the two-hundred-pound corpse lying in a bag on the concrete floor with a tag around its neck. "There he is," says Francis, "the greatest goalie I ever seen."

The veteran hockey writers at tonight's game have chosen the three star players, a gimmick started to promote gasoline, but as meaningful now to the players as the gimmicks used to promote Christmas or Valentine's Day. They name Sawchuk as the first star. It's an honour, but it doesn't come with any money. A few weeks from tonight, the Leafs' board of directors will give Sawchuk the J.P. Bickell Memorial Award, named after the gold-mining magnate who backed Conn Smythe when he founded the team. The award distinguishes Sawchuk as the most valuable player on the team, but it doesn't come with any money, either. The Conn Smythe Trophy, given to the most valuable player in the playoffs this year, comes with $1,000 in cash and a $5,000 car, but Sawchuk doesn't win it. It goes instead to his teammate Dave Keon, even though many people think it should go to Jim Pappin for scoring the game-winning goal and leading the team in scoring throughout the playoffs. Pappin's mom thinks so, too.

That's all right. Sawchuk can at least drink for free tonight. A party at Pappin's house will rage till four a.m., when Pappin himself will drive home Tommy Nayler, the assistant trainer. Four hours later, Wednesday morning, the third day of May, Pappin will wake up to the sound of two workmen digging a hole in his backyard with a front-end loader to install a $3,200 swimming pool. Pappin's pal at the racetrack, Jimmy Black, promised to buy the pool for Pappin if the Leafs won the Cup. The odds against the Leafs were fifteen to one. But the Leafs did it, and Black made $30,000. The goal judge Eddie Mepham won his bet, as well, and made fifty cents from his wife, Myrt.

In a few months, some of the players in the room will return to the Leafs to begin another season. Others will disappear. One by one, all of them will drift away. "Players get older, players get traded, players go to expansion teams," said the trainer, Bob Haggert.

As of tonight, the Leafs have appeared in the Stanley Cup finals nineteen times in thirty-six years. They've finished out of the playoffs four times. After tonight, they won't reach a semi-final series for eleven years. Johnny Bower will take home a bottle of champagne that he intends to open when the Leafs win the Stanley Cup again. As of his eighty-ninth birthday, the bottle will remain unopened. "Some of the guys felt they'd won the last real Stanley Cup," Bower will say later.

After tonight, hundreds of players on dozens of NHL teams will disagree with him, including Wayne Gretzky, Guy Lafleur, Marian Hossa, Evgeni Malkin, Nicklas Lidstrom and Pavel Datsyuk. Some of them won't recognize the names of many players in the game tonight. But all of them will know how much it takes to compete for the Stanley Cup and how it feels to win it. If they look closely, they'll find Terry Sawchuk's name engraved on it, four times, and they'll know how much he paid for his four moments of unqualified joy.

Amidst the hullabaloo that follows the final whistle, Henri Richard has skated off the ice, walked down the corridor and shut himself inside the visitors' dressing room. Ten minutes have gone by, and he hasn't moved. His heart feels like lead in his chest. He can hear the buzzing of the fluorescent lights inside their metal cages on the ceiling. He feels as if someone has died. From the corridor the sound of shouting voices seeps into the room. No one in the room says a word. John Ferguson sits with his head between his hands. Bobby Rousseau is sobbing. No one has removed his jersey.

The assistant trainer, Eddie Palchak, places a cup of hot tea next to Gump Worsley. The goalie has said that cold drinks give him cramps. But Worsley doesn't even look at the cup, so Palchak takes it away again.

A year ago the Montreal Canadiens won the Stanley Cup as a team. Tonight, they've lost it as individuals, and each player blames himself for the catastrophe. Rousseau allowed his temper to get the better of his judgment, and his lapse in discipline cost the team a penalty. Ferguson's penalty at the end of the first period prevented the Canadiens from taking control of the second period and changed the momentum of the game. Yvan Cournoyer came within a fraction of an inch of scoring the tying goal, but his shot caromed off the goalpost. Dick Duff hit the post, as well. Such a shot might look like bad luck. They both know better.

In the second period, Gump Worsley allowed Ron Ellis to fire the puck over his shoulder and into the net. Jacques Laperriere allowed Jim Pappin to backhand the puck from the corner toward the Canadiens' goal, and Terry Harper allowed the puck to bounce off his leg and into the net. The Leafs have won the Stanley Cup, and each player on the Montreal Canadiens has, in his own way, allowed them to do it.

"Bad breaks are usually the result of some technical error," said Lloyd Percival in *The Hockey Handbook*. "If you hit the post, your accuracy is at fault. It does not mean that the gods of hockey have decided to turn sour on you."

Written sixteen years before tonight's game and based on four years of research, Percival's *Hockey Handbook* shows players how they can improve their skating, refine their passing and accelerate their shooting. It describes the way that a team can position itself to take better advantage of a power play and how it can defend itself when it receives a penalty. It prescribes a training regimen based on a Swedish program called Fartlek, which includes running on an outdoor track and hopping on one foot to improve a player's balance. It provides detailed recipes for a proper diet and encourages players to eat fruit and yoghurt before a game and save the steak for later, to replenish their protein reserves. NHL coaches have dismissed *The Hockey Handbook*, calling it impractical, fanciful and "the product of a three-year-old." But coaches in Europe and Russia have translated the three-hundred-page doorstopper into Czech and Russian and now apply every word of the book like holy scripture as they build their national teams.

After tonight, while the NHL remains hidebound, conservative and resistant to change, teams from Vladivostok to Stockholm will begin consistently to beat amateur teams from Canada and the United States. North Americans will scoff and say these garlic-chomping foreigners will meet their match if they ever compete against a team of NHL superstars. When the match-up occurs in 1972, the NHL superstars squeeze through to win the series. But twelve years after tonight's game, a team from the Soviet Union will skate circles around the NHL's best players. In three games in mid-season at Madison Square Garden, the Soviet team will prevent Guy Lafleur, Bobby Clarke, Mike Bossy, Darryl Sittler and their teammates from scoring a single goal in more than ninety minutes. Over the same ninety minutes, the Soviets will score nine times against the goalies Ken Dryden, Tony Esposito and Gerry Cheevers and defeat the NHL team thirteen goals to eight. For their success, Russian coaches will thank Lloyd Percival, a Canadian. "Your wonderful book introduced us to the mysteries of Canadian hockey," Anatoli Tarasov, coach of the Soviet national team for fourteen years, will say. "I have read it like a schoolboy."

Tonight, every player in the silent dressing room of the Montreal Canadiens comes from Canada. But in the years ahead, about one-third of Canadiens players will come from the Czech Republic, Sweden, Finland, Russia, Switzerland, Belarus, Denmark and the United States. Bigger, stronger, faster and more skilled in the basics of the game, they will feel no differently than the players in the dressing room tonight when they lose the Stanley Cup. They will feel as if the love of their life has deserted them.

Toe Blake sits alone on a table in the coach's room with his hat on his head and the door closed, staring at the floor, wishing he were dead. "Rough flight, eh, coach?" a reporter will say next year as Blake disembarks after a losing game on the road. "I wish the fuckin' thing had crashed," Blake will say, and he won't be joking.

Twenty-two years later, another Canadiens coach will feel exactly the same way after losing the Stanley Cup. "It really does hurt to lose," Pat Burns will say after sobbing by himself for fifteen minutes.

People criticize the Canadiens for being sore losers. After losing a game, they rant, rage, throw gloves, kick trashcans. Some of them cry. After losing the Stanley Cup, they lock themselves away. They shut out their wives and children, dwell on their mistakes and lament their missed opportunities.

But what do people expect? Owners pay their players to win, and fans pay to watch them do it. Nothing else matters to a player. If it does, he loses his job. If a man wants to make a living from the game, he puts his heart and soul and every ounce of his strength into winning. He doesn't have much left to spend on losing gracefully. Nor should he, not if he wants to keep his place on the team. In the last few years, the Montreal Canadiens have sold every ticket to every game that they've played at the Montreal Forum, not because they know how to accept defeat but because they don't. Bad losers sell tickets.

The Montreal Canadiens are such bad losers that they will accumulate enough Stanley Cup rings to fill a gumball machine. Yet no one in the room tonight can explain how they do it. Maybe their blood contains elevated levels of norepinephrine, but so does the blood of every other single-minded athlete who makes a living from hockey. Like Richard and Rousseau, some have brothers or fathers or uncles who've played for the Canadiens, but most don't. The culture of small-town Quebec might explain why Jean-Guy Talbot and Jacques Laperriere will win more than fifteen Cups between them. But what about Jim Roberts, who comes from Port Hope and will win five? Or Dave Balon and Terry Harper from Saskatchewan, Ted Harris from Manitoba or Ralph Backstrom and Dick Duff from Ontario? Hard work certainly helps, as Yvan Cournoyer knows from firing a five-pound puck at a brick wall for two hours a day during the summer. But lots of kids work just as hard, and they'll never win ten Stanley Cups the way he will. Maybe pushy parents explain it, but John Ferguson's dad died before Fergie learned to skate, and no one else pushed him to win five Stanley Cups. Terry Harper's mom worries about her son every time he steps onto the ice, and he'll win five Cups, as well. Jean Beliveau's dad wanted his son to get a steady job with the power company instead of hanging around with the rounders at the hockey rink, and Beliveau will win ten. Rosey Larose and J.C. Tremblay, five Cups apiece. Gilles Tremblay, three. Even Leon Rochefort will win two. And when those players leave the team, others will take their place and keep on winning. After Henri Richard retires, the team will make the playoffs every year for another twenty years and win six more Stanley Cups. Players come and players go, but the victories continue and the mystique endures. How do you explain it?

The players themselves can't explain it. They talk about how much they love the game. They talk about a winning spirit and their allegiance to the Canadiens family and blah blah blah. They talk about continuity and smart managers who make shrewd trades and pick excellent players. But other teams in the NHL don't hire stupid managers, at least not deliberately. And players in Detroit or New York love the game just as much as players in Montreal. All of them derive an identity from their team, but none of them will win the Stanley Cup twenty-three times in seventy-five years the way the Montreal Canadiens will do. There's something more.

"When my professors start talking about what makes a successful business, I often find myself thinking about the Canadiens," said Bobby Smith, who won a Stanley Cup with the team in 1986 before going to business school. "A first-rate business will build up a kind of folklore around itself — Rolls-Royce, Coca-Cola, whatever — and the Canadiens have done that brilliantly."

Nor has it happened by accident. It has happened by design.

Much of that design has come from the Molson family, founders of the oldest brewing company and the second-oldest corporation in Canada after the Hudson's Bay Company. The Molsons have owned a share of the Canadiens for more than eighty years. When the family bought the team outright, the Canadiens had already won two Stanley Cups in a row. All the family had to do was stand back and let the Canadiens win three more. As other teams have learned, however, that's not easy for a meddlesome owner with a big ego. According to a former Canadiens president, David Molson, "Our policy places considerable importance on the relationship between management and players." Or, in the words of Larry Hillman, who will play for the Canadiens himself after tonight, "It's all got to start at the top."

Hillman has played on defence tonight for Toronto, but when the league expands, he'll join the Canadiens and win a Stanley Cup in Montreal.

"The players know what to do to get the job done," Hillman said, "and they go out and do it. The managers and owners do, too. After all, if you've got harmony on your club you're a winner."

The fans certainly help. Fulfilling the dream of every marketing man in North America, fans of the Montreal Canadiens embrace the team with the fervour of religious zealots. To their favourite players, they send hand-crafted trophies, oil paintings, laboriously knitted Afghans and rugs in the team's colours, with the Canadiens crest in the centre. Schoolchildren send photographs of murals drawn in chalk on a blackboard with Jean Beliveau in the centre foreground. They send embroidery, wood inlay, metal work, portraits, photographs, sewing, knitting, slippers, baby blankets, etchings, sculptures in clay, papier mâché and metal, hand-worked books and albums. To Beliveau in particular, people write letters when they feel depressed and have no one else to turn to. They write to him when their businesses fail, when they separate from their husbands and wives, when they become sick, sad, lonely, confused and hopeless. "Not the usual run of tributes from fans," said the author Hugh Hood. "This is love." Beliveau answers each letter and feels privileged to do it.

Embracing such a personal relationship with the team, fans celebrate its victories and suffer its defeats. They trekked by the thousands to the airport, fifty miles at three in the morning, to greet the team's plane when the Canadiens arrived home from Chicago with the Cup. When the Canadiens miss the playoffs in 1970, the fans will become so persistent in accosting players on the street that players will stay indoors or leave town.

The news media succumb to the myth as well. "There is a mystic quality about the Canadiens in hockey as there is about the New York Yankees in baseball," said *Sports Illustrated*, "a quality rooted in talent, money, planning, good management, and good luck, but somehow sur-mounting them all."

By the end of the twentieth century, the Montreal Canadiens stop winning Stanley Cups, but their reputation as winners drives their value exponentially higher. Valued at more than $400 million, the team still looks the same in their red, white and blue uniforms, and they still play the same game. They play now in a new arena initially called the Molson Centre and later renamed the Bell Centre in return for an annual fee from the phone company of more than $1 million. The Montreal Forum, where the Canadiens played for more than seventy years, becomes a shopping mall and cinema complex. The Canadiens do a worthy job of herding the ghosts from the Forum into the nooks and crannies of the new facility. But something is missing. The mystique becomes a marketing tool to maintain the value of the franchise. Like a Rolls-Royce, a Coca-Cola or a bottle of Molson Canadian lager, the Montreal Canadiens become a commodity, and the players represent potential money-generating opportunities. Nurtured by agents, managers, personal trainers, fitness coaches, psychologists and dietitians, they have more skill than ever. They still love the game as much as any player tonight, but with an average salary of $1.8 million, none of them dares to say that he'd play the game for nothing. Beneath the helmets and the hype, they might even have the same unmistakable character as the silent players in the room tonight. But if they ever expose that character to their fans, most of them do it by email and Twitter. The name of the game in professional hockey has always been money, but now that name is written in capital letters.

"The 1950s idea in which *les canadiens* stood for the common destiny of the French-Canadian people," says writer Jean Harvey, "is now clearly defunct."

For tonight, at least, the Montreal Canadiens still amount to more than a line entry on a corporate balance sheet, and Toe Blake still regards the team as his family. Blake emerges from his cubbyhole. He walks over to the captain, Jean Beliveau, and shakes his hand. The others watch him make his way around the room, shaking the hand of each despondent player and thanking him for his contribution to the team. Then he goes to the door and opens it to let the reporters inside. Much as it hurts, Blake and the players will answer the reporters' questions and tell the world how it feels to lose the Stanley Cup.

"The toughest loss of my career," says Yvan Cournoyer, and he'll keep saying it even after he retires. "The toughest series I ever lost," says Blake, and for him, it will be the last series he ever loses. A year from now, the Canadiens will win the Stanley Cup for him one last time, and Blake will retire.

Henri Richard will play for the Canadiens for another eight years and run his tavern for another eighteen. In the 1980s, the Canadiens will hire him to make public appearances at Molson-sponsored car races, hockey banquets and golf tournaments, sometimes decked out in his Canadiens jersey, with his name and the number 16 on the back. As a symbol of the Canadiens' mystique, Richard's currency will remain strong. Forty years after tonight's game, the *Hockey News* will rank Henri Richard among the top thirty NHL players of all time.

After more than fifty years, the marriage of Henri and his wife, Lise, continues. They go to church every Sunday in the north end of Montreal, until the priest instructs the congregation one morning to shake hands with each other as a sign of their solidarity before Christ. Then people start bringing their children to church and competing for the premium seats in the pews so they can all shake hands with the man who has won eleven Stanley Cups with the Montreal Canadiens. Some will hold out their Bibles to get his autograph. Henri Richard will stop going to church. He'll say he has shaken enough hands in his life. He just wants people to leave him alone.

As an icon and ambassador for the team, Henri Richard represents the essence of the Montreal Canadiens. But as a father, he can't persuade his children to share his passion for the game. "One day I told my son Gilles to stop skating with his stick in the air," Richard says. "He told me it didn't matter. He didn't want to be a hockey player like me anyway. I never talked to him about the game again."

Waves of jubilant fans pour through the doors of Maple Leaf Gardens, swarm onto the sidewalks and across the wet pavement of Carlton Street, halting streetcars in their tracks. Streetcar drivers ring their bells, car drivers honk their horns, passengers wave and cheer through open windows.

Where Carlton crosses Church Street, fans fill the intersection, taking courage from the mob and the darkness to cross against red lights. They keep their enthusiasm in check and pass through the snarled traffic without incident. This is, after all, Toronto the Good, where stores remain closed on Sundays and a patron of a tavern can get arrested for standing up with a beer in his hand. But obedience doesn't temper their joy, and none of them will forget this night or the collective sense of triumph that spreads outward through the city from the yellow brick building where the Toronto Maple Leafs have just won the Stanley Cup.

But even as this moment becomes a milestone in the history of the team, the lustre of the yellow brick building has begun to fade. By the time the Maple Leafs abandon it, twenty-two years after tonight, Maple Leaf Gardens will have become a soot-stained monument to greed, negligence and corruption. Along the way, the team's performance will suffer, but the suffering will extend far beyond a group of hockey players and their fans. And as Larry Hillman said, it all starts at the top.

If the success of a theatrical performance depends on the audience's willful suspension of disbelief, the Leafs' owners will challenge their customers after tonight to shut down their critical faculties entirely. The owners will bicker, squabble and jockey for possession of the team while they squander talent, sell farm teams and squeeze new seats into small spaces. They will resist innovation, neglect tradition, turn their backs on veteran players and transform a storied franchise into a money-making symbol of futility. While their owners diminish the team's human values, the Leafs will remain financially the most valuable franchise in the National Hockey League. And even as it becomes abundantly clear that no other value matters to its owners, fans will remain loyal to the team. Forty years after tonight, one-quarter of all Canadians will say they cheer for the Toronto Maple Leafs. Few of them, though, will have enough money to attend a game.

Three men share ownership of the team tonight. Within four years, one of them will sell his shares to his partners for $6 million. The following year, Stafford Smythe will die. After postponing a game to commemorate his death, the team will play a regular-season game on a Monday night for the first time in its history. The sole surviving partner will buy Smythe's shares. Then the Leafs will belong lock, stock and Zamboni to Harold Ballard.

Whimsical, boisterous, self-indulgent, unpredictable, bloated and greedy, Ballard fits snugly into the pantheon of the NHL's more dubious owners. Before him come owners like Bill Dwyer, who shared an office in Manhattan with Dutch Schultz and Legs Diamond and went to jail for bootlegging; Tom Scallen, the initial owner of Vancouver's NHL franchise, convicted of fraud and theft; former NHL president Frank Calder, who tried to buy the Montreal Canadiens at the same time as he ran the league. Conflicts of interest abound in the closed shop of the NHL. Even one of its most illustrious builders, Lester Patrick, coached, managed, owned and played for the same team at the same time, hiring his players, negotiating their salaries and then firing them if he didn't like the way they performed.

After Ballard will come Boots Del Biaggio, sentenced to eight years in prison for defrauding lenders of US$110 million to pay for a stake in an NHL franchise in Nashville. Bruce McNall will drive the Los Angeles Kings into bankruptcy and receive a sentence of almost six years in prison for defrauding banks out of US$236 million. And while it isn't a crime to fleece investors, Wayne Huizenga will raise US$67.3 million from public shareholders by selling forty-nine per cent of an NHL team with a total estimated value of just US$45 million. Five years later, shareholders will remain underwater, receiving seventy-five per cent of their money back when a new owner buys the entire team for US$110 million.

By the time Alan Eagleson appeared in their midst, slick manoeuvring, questionable deals and conflicts of interest were no more unusual among NHL owners than hinges on a door. For years, Eagleson will play multiple roles as a players' agent, head of the players' association and organizer of international hockey tournaments that depend for their success on NHL owners. On behalf of 480 NHL players, he will haggle in the morning with owners over a collective bargaining agreement. After handshakes, backslaps and huzza-huzzas all round, he'll fly home in the afternoon on an owner's private jet, and by the time they land, he'll have negotiated a player's contract to the owner's satisfaction. In the evening, he'll urge owners and players in a conference call to work together in an international hockey tournament in which the players will represent their country for nothing and from which Eagleson will make a million dollars. "A joke," Harold Ballard will say about a collective bargaining agreement negotiated by Eagleson between the NHL and the NHLPA, "a joke" on all the players. And Ballard will laugh all the way to the bank.

As Dave Keon turns his back on the league and the team he has served for fifteen years, Ballard will defy the league, disrupt his team and neglect the fans while lining his own pockets. Fearing a loss of revenue, he'll contravene the NHL rule requiring him to stitch players' names on the backs of their jerseys. If a fan wants to identify a player, Ballard says, he can spend five bucks to buy a Maple Leafs program. Ballard will fire a coach before he can find a replacement, then offer to reinstate him if the coach agrees to appear behind the Leafs' bench on a Saturday night with a paper bag over his head. He'll fire the penalty timekeeper, a former player who has come close to death on the ice wearing a Maple Leafs uniform and who has reported for duty before every home game since then for almost forty years, and he will have neither the grace nor the courage to do it to the man's face, choosing instead to send him a typewritten letter. To make room in Maple Leaf Gardens for premium-priced executive boxes, Ballard will rip out the broadcast gondola, where Foster Hewitt has worked since the first game ever played in the building, and dump it into an incinerator instead of donating it to the Hockey Hall of Fame. And as he does all this, his team will collapse. Over a ten-year period under Ballard's ownership, the Leafs will lose more than half their games. In one of those years, they'll win fewer than one game in three. "Defeat does not rest lightly on their shoulders," says the motto in the Leafs' dressing room tonight. But as the weight of defeat grows heavier, Ballard will remove the words from the wall. In the meantime, he'll double the price of a ticket.

Giving less for more, Ballard sets a precedent that his successors will follow. Over the next forty years, the Leafs' owners will raise the price of a ticket more than twenty times. For people who choose to watch the Leafs in a bar or restaurant, the Leafs' owners will raise the cost of a commercial subscription to the team's cable channel to $1,500 a season from $2.50 a month. After forty years without a Stanley Cup, after decades of dismal performance and lacklustre play, after scandals, crimes and prolonged neglect, the Leafs' owners will charge fans more than any other team in the league to watch a game. Of the 122 teams in North America competing in the four major sports of baseball, basketball, football and hockey today, not one team charges its fans as much to attend a game as the Toronto Maple Leafs.

Playing at Maple Leaf Gardens "used to be like going to church," said Red Kelly. "But in later years you didn't get that sense of awe."

Despite the owners' neglect, the team colours will continue to stir the faith of Leafs fans with the same compelling intensity as the icons of a corrupt religion, and no one will believe in the team with more unadulterated passion than children. Almost by definition, professional sport appeals to the child in everyone, and children can overlook a dirty floor and a cramped seat if it allows them a glimpse of their heroes.

"I just wish all the players could understand how greatly they are idolized by the kids in this country," said Teedle Walker, the penalty-box attendant at Maple Leaf Gardens for twenty-five years. "The little tykes come down from the greys just to touch the bench where the players have sat or ask a question about their favourites. They even offer to pay for pucks and sticks and only want them because their heroes have used them. Sometimes I wish I had a bucketful of pucks so I could pass them out to every youngster who comes along."

Under Harold Ballard's ownership of the Toronto Maple Leafs, the man who controls the pucks will take Walker's advice to heart. From his office just inside the door to the Gardens, a pedophile named George Hannah will watch young boys congregate at the corner of Wood and Church Streets, where they can ambush an emerging player after practice for an autograph. Hannah has access to the team's used equipment and all the pucks he wants, and he knows how to use them to his advantage. One by one, he starts inviting boys into his office. He offers a boy a puck, a stick or a ticket to a game and watches the boy's eyes light up. And then he tells the boy what he wants in return.

Like rats sniffing cheese, Hannah's associates will scurry to the Gardens to work for Mr. Ballard. They'll get jobs as ushers, ticket-takers and part-time dogsbodies, and their jobs will give them access to a never-ending stream of unsuspecting kids who would give their left arm for a puck or a stick from a Toronto Maple Leaf. When the boys realize that these men want something more from their bodies than an arm, they pay the price and blame themselves. They go home with a souvenir and a secret, and they live for the rest of their lives with crippling guilt, shame, regret and anger. Some of them take more than forty years to speak openly about the assaults they've endured as teenagers. Some of them have the courage to confront the owners of the Maple Leafs with their allegations and to ask for some acknowledgement that they aren't entirely to blame for their sullied lives. Some never come forward at all. At least one of them kills himself. All of them agonize about revealing in public what they've done in private as kids to get a souvenir from the Toronto Maple Leafs. Eventually twenty-six of these grown-up boys come forward, alleging that they've been molested more than six hundred times. The team's owners offer them $60,000 apiece and tell them to stay quiet.

The owners can afford the payout. By 2007, according to the *Toronto Star*, Maple Leaf Sports and Entertainment generates profits of $83 million on revenue of $383 million. On every dollar it receives, the company makes a profit of twenty-two cents. By comparison, the Royal Bank of Canada, the country's largest bank, earns a profit of about thirteen cents on a dollar and receives nothing in return but criticism for its efforts. But then, no one goes to the bank to watch a teller score a goal on a slapshot.

With their team's heritage in shambles, the owners who succeed Ballard will devise a corporate marketing plan to regenerate the lost spirit of the Maple Leafs. As if they're selling laundry detergent or mass-produced beer, they will contrive a program of "mediated nostalgia" that will enrich the memories of Leafs fans with "a socially constructed discourse that conflates nationalism, recollections of a happier time, and the success of Canadian sporting teams."

After years of neglect, the Leafs' owners will also begin to recognize the value of the team's former players. Like bubblegum cards and autographs, George Armstrong, Marcel Pronovost, Johnny Bower and other players from tonight's game will become hot commodities on the memorabilia circuit. Even Dave Keon will reappear after refusing for decades to have anything to do with his former team. After decades of insult, the Leafs will begin to regain their capacity to accommodate a fan's dreams. Whether they feel manipulated or not, many fans who have put their faith in their team will feel vindicated.

Others don't care one way or the other. For them, a ticket to a Leafs game is just another way to entertain a client. Before one game, the owners will ask Leafs fans to demonstrate their solidarity and express their loyalty by wearing blue. But it won't work. "It was still a lot of investment bankers," a former Leafs executive will say, "coming to the game in suits."

By the time Allan Stanley closes the dressing-room door behind him tonight, the men in suits and the women in dresses have all gone home. Stanley and Pulford are always the last to shower and dress after a game. On some nights, Bob Haggert, the trainer, practically has to chase them out of the room. But not tonight. Tonight, there's a party at Pappin's house. There will be another one tomorrow at Stafford Smythe's and a parade on Friday that will shut down the city for half a day. Children will get the day off school. The 48th Highlanders will lead the parade. A flotilla of Buick convertibles from Addison Motors will cruise through twenty city blocks and end up at Nathan Phillips Square, in front of the new city hall.

Most of Toronto, it seems, will turn out for the parade, but some players won't bother attending. Bob Baun will go fishing with his three sons. Ron Ellis will go with his wife, Jan, to Parry Sound to help his parents open the family resort. "I left the Stanley Cup celebration to cut grass amongst the blackflies," he'll say.

By the day of the parade, Expo 67 will have drawn more than a million visitors to Montreal in a single week. Lester Pearson, who strolled earlier tonight through the Maple Leafs' dressing room, has opened the fair with a speech to seven thousand dignitaries, fifty-three heads of state and a thousand reporters, and the proceedings have been broadcast in colour via satellite to more than seven hundred million viewers. In the Czech Pavilion tonight sit two dozen glass sculptures, created especially for the Montreal Canadiens to commemorate their third consecutive Stanley Cup. But they will sit in their boxes, collecting dust, because the wrong team won the Cup. "We won the Cup," says Allan Stanley, "but we didn't even get an invitation to Expo."

Confident, self-assured, cocky, full of beans, Punch Imlach guides the family Lincoln Continental across the city to the west end of Toronto. Dodo Imlach, his wife, likes to spend time with her husband when he's in a good mood. At times like this, Punch reminds her of the young man with the big ideas who won her heart at the curling club almost thirty years ago.

Sure, he has his quirks. His superstitions get on her nerves. He won't touch a two-dollar bill, so he'll pay for a newspaper with a ten and ask the poor vendor for change. He can be a cheapskate. Just a few weeks ago, he got mad at her when she allowed some kids from the local high school to take his empty bottles from the garage so they could return them to the beer store. She has explained that the kids needed the money for a trip or a dance or cheerleaders' uniforms or something, but Punch says, "We're not made of money. We can't afford to give it away."

For as long as they've been married, Dodo has known that nothing in her husband's life comes before hockey. She doesn't mind. So far, hockey has provided them with a pretty good life.

Tonight, Punch has money in his pocket, and that always puts him in a generous mood. Not only have the Leafs won the Stanley Cup, but the Leafs' farm team in Rochester won their league championship last year for the second time in a row and made it to the finals this year, as well. Punch is a part-owner of the Americans. When they win their league championship again next year, Rochester players will receive commemorative rings, just like the Leafs, but set with glass chips instead of diamonds. The chips will eventually turn green.

Even on a happy occasion like tonight, though, Dodo has a bad feeling about the future. Just one look at those high-school kids who came to the door, and it isn't hard to see the way the world is going. It isn't Punch's way, that's for sure. Punch likes to give orders, and he likes hockey players who do as they're told. George Armstrong, Allan Stanley, Tim Horton, Bob Pulford, Red Kelly. He sent all five of them onto the ice tonight at the end of the game, just to show them how much he appreciated their efforts. At least, that's what he says now. But those guys will soon be gone and, apart from Ron Ellis, the younger players who replace them will seem to have puffed once too often from a pipe full of wacky tabacky.

So far, the NHL, like the army, has stood fast against the libertine currents of the sixties. But it's 1967, and the league can't hold out much longer. The players have organized a union, and soon the sixties will seep like a poison gas under the dressing-room door of every NHL team. Next season, players will wear longer hair and sideburns and dress like jugglers in a travelling circus, and no one will stop them, not even Punch. Instead of acquiescing to their coach's cockamamie strategies, they'll challenge him and demand answers. Dodo knows without a doubt that it will drive her husband nuts.

For a while, Punch will hold out and drive his players crazy first. For the first few months of the next season, he'll still have Frank Mahovlich to kick around. When the Leafs trade Mahovlich to Detroit, Punch will turn his attention to Mike Walton and drive him nuts, too.

Walton's getting married in a week or so, to a niece of Stafford Smythe's. They're on their way to Smythe's house now. But marriage to the owner's niece doesn't assure Walton of a place in Imlach's heart, and Walton knows it. "Yeah I'm married into the Smythe family," Walton says. "You know what that means? It means someday they'll give me a broom to push around Maple Leaf Gardens."

Like Mahovlich before him, Walton will become the leading scorer on the team. He'll begin to think that he has a lot to contribute to the Leafs. But even if it were true, Imlach can't tolerate such a self-centred attitude. To nip it in the bud, he'll take the necessary steps. He'll tell Walton to sit on the bench, and he'll find another player to take his place. As he did with Frank Mahovlich, he'll say it's for Walton's own good. "I've tried my damnedest to help the kid," Imlach will say, like a beleaguered father about his delinquent son.

Other teams will covet a player like Walton, who seems to score goals almost at will. "He might be a bit of a flake," says a rival coach in Philadelphia, "but he's a flake who can score goals. We got flakes on our club who can't score."

Ten years from tonight, Walton will score a goal in every four shots he takes, twenty-nine times in 115 shots. Against players like Guy Lafleur, Marcel Dionne and Steve Shutt, Walton will rank as the most accurate shooter in the NHL. But he won't do it in Toronto, because the Maple Leafs will practically kick him off the team. He'll do it in Vancouver, where he'll keep a shrunken skull in his stall and wear a gold pendant given to him for Christmas by Alan Eagleson. When his career in hockey ends, Walton will return to Toronto and become a real estate agent in the city's west end. His connections in hockey will serve him well. At the age of sixty-one, he'll sell a house belonging to Mats Sundin, the Leafs' captain at the time, for $6 million.

Tonight, Imlach takes much of the credit for winning the Stanley Cup. "I did it," he says as he drives up Royal York Road. "By Christ, I did it."

No matter how highly he regards himself tonight, Imlach won't do it again. Next year, with almost everyone back from tonight's team except Terry Sawchuk, the Leafs will play seventy-four games, a third of them against expansion teams staffed by cast-offs and no-names. Not only will the team lose the Stanley Cup, it won't even make the playoffs. Imlach will blame his players, but he will inflict his wrath even on the trainer, Bob Haggert. At the end of the season, he'll give a message to Tommy Nayler. "Tell Haggert he's fired," he'll say. Then he'll order the attendants in the corridor to bar Haggert from the dressing room. "I couldn't care less about being barred from the dressing room," says Haggert, who will soon start his successful agency to represent the NHL Players' Association in merchandising, public appearances and licensing. "What really disturbs me is that Imlach, the tough businessman, the tough coach, did not have the guts to tell me himself. He had to use a sixty-five-year-old man, Tommy Nayler, to inform me."

In the season after that, only seven players will remain from tonight's game. The Leafs will make the playoffs, but in the first round they'll lose four straight games to the Boston Bruins. In the first two, the Bruins will score seventeen times. The Leafs won't score a single goal. They'll lose the fourth game at Maple Leaf Gardens, by three goals to two. The writers Damien Cox and Gord Stellick have described what happens when the game ends. Stafford Smythe invites Imlach into a cubbyhole office outside the Leafs' dressing room. Standing face to face with Imlach, Smythe extends his hand. Imlach shakes it.

"Well, that's it," Smythe says.

"You're telling me I'm fired?" Imlach says.

"You're through," says Smythe. "I want to run the club now."

Afterwards, players like Johnny Bower and Tim Horton, who have won four Stanley Cups under Imlach, say they feel bad about the decision. Imlach's assistant, King Clancy, will say that he feels bad, too. Clancy is sixty-six years old. He has spent more than twenty years in Toronto, as a player and a coach, and he has stuck with Imlach from the day he arrived in the city. Friendly, open-minded, genuine and good-hearted, Clancy has filled in for Imlach when the coach got sick, phoned players when Imlach decided to send them to Rochester, attended to the chores that Imlach didn't want to do himself, and accompanied Imlach to dinner when the coach wanted someone to talk to. In sympathy, he says, he'll quit the Leafs, too. But like Bower and Horton, Clancy changes his mind.

He needs a job. Harold Ballard makes him a vice-president. Clancy never says an unkind word about Imlach, but the generosity of spirit is not reciprocated. At a league meeting a few weeks after Imlach loses his job, Clancy walks over to his friend to say hello. "Fuck you," Imlach says and turns his back on him.

After he leaves the Leafs, Imlach will make a quarter of a million dollars from the sale of his shares in a hockey team in Vancouver. But he still has something to prove. When the NHL expands again, he accepts a job as coach and general manager of the Buffalo Sabres. There, he hires Tim Horton and Larry Hillman to play defence. Apart from them, the average age of the leading players on the team is twenty-three. Imlach applies the same methods as he has used with cowed and grizzled forty-year-olds in Toronto, imposing sanctions against long hair, criticizing players in public and demanding blind obedience from his team. The team refuses to obey him. By the second year, the tension between the players and their coach has not only contributed to the team's lacklustre performance, it has also contributed to Imlach's first heart attack.

Although he accomplishes little of consequence, the Sabres will employ Imlach as general manager for eight years. When the owners fire him, Harold Ballard will come to the rescue and invite Imlach back to Toronto to take the helm of the disintegrating shipwreck that the Leafs have become under his guidance. Imlach resumes his customary approach to running a hockey team, ordering players to cut their hair and wear a tie and fining them for disobeying his orders. He takes other players to court, rails against their union and trades disobedient players out of spite rather than common sense.

The pressure becomes unbearable. Imlach suffers two more heart attacks and undergoes a quadruple bypass. He spends two months away from the team. On a November morning fourteen years after tonight, he drives his Lincoln Continental to Maple Leaf Gardens to go back to work. But when the big steel door opens at the back of the building on Wood Street, the attendant tells him he can't drive through. Harold Ballard has taken away Imlach's parking space and given it to a former goalie named

Gerry McNamara. McNamara, who played five games as a Leaf under Imlach more than twenty years earlier, has now taken Imlach's job as general manager.

Imlach parks his car in the lot across the street. He walks upstairs to his office in the Gardens and picks up the phone to call his wife on his private line, but the line has been disconnected. When he asks Harold Ballard for an explanation, Ballard gives Imlach a taste of his own medicine. "I've done this for your own good," Ballard says. "Well, call me when you need a manager," says Imlach.

One last time, Imlach will walk upstairs to the Gardens accounting office to collect payment for his outstanding expenses. Then he'll leave the Gardens, and this time he won't come back. This time, no one associated with the team will offer to quit in sympathy, and no one will call to offer him another job.

Every two weeks after that until his contract expires, Imlach's car will appear on Wood Street behind the Gardens and sit idling by the curb until an employee of the team comes outside with a cheque, which he'll hand to Imlach through the driver's window.

Imlach will suffer two more heart attacks, the first in a casino in Las Vegas, the second while watching football teams from Toronto and Edmonton compete for the Grey Cup on TV. The last one will kill him, at the age of sixty-nine.

Loyal to the bitter end, Johnny Bower and Allan Stanley will serve as pallbearers at Imlach's funeral and accompany the casket to Mount Pleasant Cemetery.

"Punch Imlach sometimes took some rather older hockey players, who others said were washed up, and made them into Stanley Cup champions," a provincial politician will say in tribute the next day in Ontario's Legislature.

"He put money in my pocket," says Bower. "I owe him a lot."

...

At the party at Smythe's house, Tim Horton asks Red Kelly if he'll change his mind about retiring. Sitting side by side in the Leafs' dressing room, Horton and Kelly have talked for the last three years about quitting the game. Each time Horton decides to do it, someone or something persuades him to change his mind. He loves his job, he loves the razzle-dazzle, he still feels strong on his skates, and he performs as well as ever. For six seasons in a row, four hundred and twenty games, Horton hasn't missed a single game. This year, he made the NHL all-star team for the fourth time. Next year, competing against twice as many players in an expanded league, he'll make it again, and the year after that, too, partnered with Bobby Orr, who was one year old when Horton played his first professional game. Horton's thirty-seven, but some days he feels like he's fifteen. On other days, he feels like he's a hundred, and that's the problem.

The money helps. There's no denying that. And it will get better over the next few years. But all good things come to an end, as Horton's mom would say. Or as Frank Mahovlich will say when his day comes, "Even Gene Autry has to climb off the horse sometime."

Through his milk-bottle spectacles, Horton peers at his teammates and their wives. Pete Stemkowski is singing along to the music. "What's it all about, Alfie?" Over there by the TV is Mahov, with Marie, talking to Brian Conacher and his fiancée, Susan Davis. There's George Armstrong, Army, the Chief, dressed in a turtleneck and slacks, puffing on his pipe and adjusting the glasses on his nose as he and Stanley talk about their plans for the summer. Stanley and his wife will go to Timmins. Army and Betty will go to Skead to visit his parents. Dressed in civvies, these guys look as unassuming as a couple of middle-aged inspectors for the gas company, until you look at their arms and legs. Big hands, big arms, big legs. Even their jaws look big. Horton himself can bench-press a Holstein cow. They make a living with their bodies, on skates. On skates, in a hockey uniform, they move with the power and menacing grace of a shark. In shoes, in Stafford Smythe's Humber Valley basement rec room, they stand awkwardly, as if they don't know what to do with all the strength in their limbs. "No one really wants to retire," says Horton.

Horton figures he can retire and still make a pretty good living from the donut business that he and a partner have started in Hamilton. They have about ten shops, and they're doing pretty well, but not well enough to pay him as much as he made this year as a hockey player. The business is doing even better when Horton decides in 1969 to quit the game for good. Mr. Ballard tries to talk him out of it. Horton has been one of the Leafs' most popular players, good for the box office. "If somebody said they'd double my salary I'd consider it," Horton says. So Ballard doubles his salary, to $85,000, and Horton changes his mind again. The money comes in handy when you own a growing business.

As a coach in Pittsburgh in 1971, Kelly will talk Horton into playing for another year. Horton is forty-one at the time, an age when some men think about buying a sit-down lawn mower. That season, in a game against Detroit, Horton will skate back to the bench and tell Kelly that he might have to sit out a shift. When the period ends, Kelly will look more closely at Horton in the dressing room and discover that his defenceman has played all period with a separated shoulder. Kelly will have to argue with Horton to keep him from going back onto the ice. Later in the season, Horton will break his ankle. Now he'll have no choice. He'll have to stop playing.

This time, Punch Imlach talks him out of it. Imlach is managing the Sabres in Buffalo, and he wants Horton on his team. He offers him a brand new Ford Pantera to join the Sabres and teach the kids on the team how to play defence.

A Pantera. If Horton has a weakness besides his bad eyes, it's a passion for fast cars. Made in Italy at the rate of three a day by a company called De Tomaso, the Pantera has been available in North America for only a year. Elvis Presley has one, although he'll fire a gun at it one day when it won't start. When it does start, a Pantera will go from zero to sixty in five-and-a-half seconds, as fast as a panther, which is what Pantera means in Italian. Low and sleek, it won't accommodate a driver over six feet tall. Fortunately, Horton's only five-ten. For most of the season, Horton can live at home and drive the car back and forth between Toronto and Buffalo, a straight shot down the four-lane Queen Elizabeth Highway. The commute takes only a couple of hours, a lot less if you drive the way Horton does, especially at night, when there's no traffic. A couple of times he'll make the trip in less than sixty minutes, going 110 miles per hour all the way.

Horton accepts Imlach's offer. Now he's forty-three, but he misses only one game in his first season. The only other player in the league who's older than Horton is Gump Worsley, and Worsley's not normal. He's a goalie.

As the Stanley Cup party rolls on, Stemmer starts singing along with another song, "Happy Together," by the Turtles. One of these days, even he'll have to retire. Everyone does, sooner or later. Horton's best friend, George Armstrong, will try four times.

With time on his hands, Army takes a bit part in a movie called *Face-Off*, but when he reads his steamy love scene to his wife, Betty confronts the director and tells him he can choose from three actresses to kiss her husband: "Our daughter, my mother or me."

Army goes back to hockey. "I was bored," he'll say. "I couldn't find anything to do to kill time."

Most players would agree. In retirement, they feel as lost as kids who run away from home. Most of them started playing the game when they were three or four or five years old, and they've never really had to grow up. They might have some money, but they'll have little education and even less incentive to join the rat race. Hockey has extended their childhood, and when it ends, they have to become adults overnight, when everyone else has had a fifteen-year head start. "It's hard to find your niche in life that can give you the same feelings you had as a player," said Ron Ellis.

By the time they start leaving the party tonight, a few of the players have hoovered enough beer to put a glow on their cheeks. Tim Horton wades through the crowd like a bespectacled bear in a forest and puts his arm around Stafford Smythe as if he's hugging a sapling.

Horton and Lori leave the party to drive home. Horton can drive tonight across the city to Willowdale, taking back streets, but he and Lori don't worry much about the law. If he gets pulled over on a night when the Toronto Maple Leafs have won the Stanley Cup, the cop will probably ask for Horton's autograph and give them an escort home. A lot of cops figure they play on the same extended team as the Leafs anyway, standing up for the forces of stability and order against an onslaught of long-haired anarchy. The brotherhood of warriors extends beyond hockey players to soldiers, cops, firemen, customs agents, game wardens and anyone else who wears a uniform, carries a weapon and risks his life in the course of doing his job.

Certainly Tim Horton feels like part of the brotherhood. His business partner is an ex-cop, and some of his closest friends are on the force. Of course, Horton is a friendly guy with everyone. "I never met anyone who didn't like Tim Horton," said the writer Scott Young.

But the application of a double standard to members of the brotherhood can have lethal results. Even players know it. "Quit letting people get away with things," Andrew Ference, an NHL defenceman, will say, forty years after tonight's game. But by then it will be far too late for Tim Horton and for at least a few other players whose identity as hockey players has distracted them from the consequences of their behaviour as men.

Seven years from tonight, Horton will crack his jaw in a practice with the Buffalo Sabres. He'll play despite the pain in a game against the Maple Leafs in Toronto. To do his job, he has to collide with other players about forty times in a period. Each time he does, he feels as if someone has shot him in the head.

For the third period, Horton sits on the bench, and his team loses the game. After the game, he takes a handful of pills to numb the pain and leaves in his Pantera for Buffalo. Along the way, he stops near Hamilton to visit his business partner. They now operate thirty-nine shops around the province. They have a few drinks, and Horton continues on his way. He passes St. Catharines, on the south shore of Lake Ontario, going more than 100 miles an hour. A provincial cop starts to chase him. Horton goes faster. Going 160 miles an hour, he loses control of his Pantera, drives into a guardrail, rolls end over end down the highway and dies.

After Horton's death, a fifteen-year-old girl will write a letter to the *Buffalo Evening News*. She will remember meeting Horton after a Sabres practice, just after the death of her own father. "We got to talking," she will write, "and I told him I didn't have no father, and he said, 'Just because someone's left the earth doesn't mean they're dead. You're only dead if you're forgotten and not loved. If you still have a place for that person in your heart, they're still with you and will never be dead. They've only taken a long trip.'

"I guess I've learned a lot from that," the girl will say. "But I never cried as hard as when I heard that Horton went on that trip."

Thirteen years after tonight's game, Gump Worsley will arrive in Toronto from Montreal with Doreen and the kids. They'll check into the Royal York Hotel. Worsley is fifty-one years old. He hasn't played in a professional hockey game in six years. He weighs even more now than he did then, but he worries a lot less.

A few weeks earlier, on another visit to Toronto, a reporter named Tim Moriarty gave Worsley the news that a selection committee had voted to induct him into the Hockey Hall of Fame. "I'd better call my wife," Worsley said.

Worsley seems remarkably calm when he hears the news, Moriarty says later. But when he goes to find a public phone, he walks into the women's washroom.

Now Worsley has come back to Toronto with his family for the induction ceremony. The New York Yankees have also come to town, for a baseball game against the Blue Jays. Worsley and his son Dean decide to visit Exhibition Stadium, where the Blue Jays play their games, and walk to the Hockey Hall of Fame nearby. On their way through the hotel lobby, Dean spots a player for the Yankees named Reggie Jackson. He walks over to the player and asks for his autograph. Jackson tells him to get lost.

Worsley shares his son's disappointment. "I hope the Blue Jays pitchers strike him out every time he's at bat," he says.

Worsley has spent $35 a ticket to the induction dinner so that his three sons can attend along with him and Doreen. At the table, he tells the story about the inconsiderate baseball player. "I always thought signing autographs was part of the job," he says. Most other hockey players agree. But then, hockey players aren't the same as other athletes.

By the time of Worsley's visit, the Hall of Fame has inducted 158 players, including eight from the final game of the Stanley Cup playoffs in 1967. Red Kelly was the first. Terry Sawchuk came next, then Jean Beliveau, George Armstrong, Johnny Bower, Tim Horton, Marcel Pronovost and Henri Richard. In a separate category, the Hall has also inducted Harold Ballard. The Hall applies an elastic definition to the good character of its members.

In return for the honour of membership in the Hall of Fame, players receive either a pair of cufflinks or a ring from the Board of Governors, but not both. If they want both trinkets, they have to pay $300. But money isn't really the point.

As in most other industries, the men who run professional hockey understand the importance of recognizing the high achievers in their midst. Membership in the Hall of Fame is one way to deliver this recognition. At first, the Hall existed only in the imaginations of the men who created it. But by the time Worsley gets the nod, the Hockey Hall of Fame operates as a non-profit corporation from its own building on the grounds of the Canadian National Exhibition. The Hall is also a museum, and fans of the game line up to buy tickets and get inside. Like the priesthood, hockey is a vocation. Some who are called rise from novitiate to bishop to monsignor. In the Hall of Fame, hockey players are canonized. When they give autographs, players who have been admitted to the Hall append the letters *HoF* to their signatures.

In the years after Worsley's induction, the Hall of Fame will give its blessing to more players from the final Stanley Cup playoff game of 1967. Frank Mahovlich and Allan Stanley will come next, inducted the same year as the referee, John Ashley. Yvan Cournoyer, Dave Keon, Jacques

Laperriere and Bob Pulford will all win spots in the Hall, as well. Altogether, ten Leafs from that night's game will enter the Hall of Fame, along with their coach, Punch Imlach. Five Canadiens, their coach, Toe Blake, and their manager, Sam Pollock, will be there, as well. A few years later, Dick Duff will join them.

Without a doubt, the Hall of Fame is another marketing ploy financed by corporate sponsors who see a money-making opportunity in associating their names with a sport that's loved by its aficionados. It's an industry boondoggle as well as a gesture of recognition, no different than a hall of fame for jewellers, mining engineers or grocery store operators. But while few children dream about selling a watch, they flock in the thousands to the Hockey Hall of Fame, and so do their parents, who were children themselves when they first played hockey and who feel like kids every time they watch a game.

Some of them will look with wonder at photographs and artifacts from players who never lost their love of the game, either. They'll stare at Terry Sawchuk's battered chest protector and wonder how a goalie could dare to stop a puck with such a flimsy shield. Some of them may even recognize the names of a few players from that 1967 final game.

As for Gump Worsley, until he dies at seventy-seven, he'll never turn away a kid who asks for his autograph. He'll take the kid's pad of paper, a crumpled paper napkin or a photograph that the kid has clipped from a magazine. He'll sign his name: Gump Worsley, HoF. And he'll say, "It's nice not to be forgotten."

Notes on Sources

More than thirty players participated in the final game of the Stanley Cup playoffs in 1967. Various trainers, timekeepers, goal judges, Zamboni drivers, owners, managers, physiotherapists, wives, children, mothers, fathers, teachers, reporters and announcers also played a role in their own ways.

I gathered most of the information in the book from written sources. I talked to a few players such as Red Kelly, Ron Ellis and Marcel Pronovost, and several times to the late Bob Haggert, the Leafs' trainer. But these interviews merely confirmed that I'd interpreted my information correctly.

I wondered if I should have pursued more interviews until the day when a friend kindly arranged to include me in a golf game with his son and Bob Baun, the former Leafs defenceman. While my friend and his son rode together in one golf cart, I rode with Baun and pestered him with questions between shots. I figured I'd never have this opportunity again, and Baun was a captive audience for my inquiries. I kept it up until the ninth hole, when he finally turned to me in exasperation and said, "Why don't you stop asking questions and just read my book?"

By the time I finished writing this book, I'd read Baun's and about sixty others. I'd read newspaper and magazine articles on every player in the game, provided by the staff of the Hockey Hall of Fame in Toronto. I'd hired two researchers, Jean-Patrice Martel in Montreal and Paul Patskou in Toronto. Both of them uncovered nuggets of information worth their weight in gold.

Since this book is a tapestry of details, different passages from the same page or paragraph may appear in several chapters. Some repetition of sources is inevitable, but I have used the full citation only for the first appearance of each, and shortened citations (author's name and short title only) thereafter.

Chapter One: Pre-game Warm-up

The first chapter describes the significant moments that have led to tonight's game, in the lives of the players, officials, owners, announcers, fans, and in the sport itself. At the same time, it shows how hockey developed from an amusing winter pastime, played by privileged amateurs before wealthy spectators in evening dress, into a strategic battle of wit, finesse and brutality, in which the unworldly sons of miners, farmers and lumberjacks risked serious injury for a chance to earn money and glory in the biggest cities on the continent.

Among the many sources of information in this chapter, the one that I relied on for much of the historical data is Dan Diamond, ed., *Total Hockey: The Official Encyclopedia of the National Hockey League*, 2nd ed. (Kingston, NY: Total Sports, 2000). Other sources, both entertaining and valuable, included: Zander Hollander, ed., *The Hockey News Hockey Almanac, 1999* (Toronto and Canton, MI: Visible Ink Press, 1998); Don Weekes and Kerry Banks, *The Best & Worst Of Hockey Firsts: The Unofficial Guide* (Vancouver: Greystone Books, 2003); Don Weekes, *The Big Book of Hockey Trivia* (Vancouver: Greystone Books, 2005); Michael McKinley's *Etched in Ice: A Tribute to Hockey's Defining Moments* (Vancouver: Greystone Books 1998); *Putting a Roof on Winter: Hockey's Rise from Sport to Spectacle* (Vancouver: Greystone Books, 2000); and *Hockey: A People's History* (Toronto: McClelland & Stewart, 2006), as well as Stephen Cole's *The Canadian Hockey Atlas* (Toronto: Doubleday Canada, 2006) and *The Last Hurrah: A Celebration of Hockey's Greatest Season '66-'67* (Toronto: Viking, 1995).

I not only relied on Michael Benedict and D'Arcy Jenish, eds., *Canada on Ice: 50 Years of Great Hockey* (Toronto: Viking, 1998), but read every word. This book contains some of the best articles about hockey ever written, by such accomplished writers as Trent Frayne, June Callwood, Scott Young, Peter Gzowski, Jack Batten, Roy MacGregor and Sidney Katz. They don't make 'em like that anymore.

For details about life with the Toronto Maple Leafs, I consulted several books, including: Kelly McParland, *The Lives of Conn Smythe: From the Battlefield to Maple Leaf Gardens; A Hockey Icon's Story* (Toronto: McClelland & Stewart, 2011); *George and Darril Fosty's Black Ice: The Lost History of the Colored Hockey League of the Maritimes, 1895-1925* (New York: Stryker-Indigo, 2004); Cecil Harris, *Breaking the Ice: The Black Experience in Professional Hockey* (Toronto: Insomniac Press, 2003); *Over the Boards: The Ron Ellis Story*, with Kevin Shea (Bolton, ON: Fenn, 2002); *The Glory Years: Memories of a Decade, 1955-1965* (Scarborough, ON: Prentice-Hall Canada, 1989) by Billy Harris, who played for the team over that period; Jack Batten, *The Leafs: An Anecdotal History of the Toronto Maple Leafs* (Toronto: Key Porter Books, 1994); *Hockey Is a Battle: Punch Imlach's Own Story*, with Scott Young (Toronto: Macmillan of Canada, 1969); *Heaven and Hell in the NHL: Punch Imlach's Own Story*, with Scott Young (Toronto: McClelland & Stewart, 1982); and Damien Cox and Gord Stellick, *'67: The Maple Leafs, Their*

Sensational Victory, and the End of an Empire (Toronto: J. Wiley & Sons Canada, 2004), which describes the malignancies that had begun to fester within the team even as the Leafs won their last Stanley Cup.

For details about Terry Sawchuk's triumphant and haunted life, I relied heavily on David Dupuis, *Sawchuk: The Troubles and Triumphs of the World's Greatest Goalie* (Toronto: Stoddart, 1998) and Kevin Allen and Bob Duff, *Without Fear: Hockey's 50 Greatest Goaltenders*, with special commentary by Johnny Bower (Chicago: Triumph Books, 2002). And for the suffering of Frank Mahovlich under the narrow-minded tyranny of Punch Imlach, I turned to Ted Mahovlich, *The Big M: The Frank Mahovlich Story* (Toronto: HarperCollins, 1999).

For Brian Conacher's observations, I relied on Brian Conacher, *So You Want to Be a Hockey Player!* (Richmond Hill, ON: Simon & Schuster, 1971; orig. publ. 1970 as *Hockey in Canada: The Way It Is!*).

For details of Tim Horton's life, Douglas Hunter, *Open Ice: The Tim Horton Story* (Toronto: Viking, 1994) is not only a valuable source of information, it's also a compelling story.

For background information about the Montreal Canadiens and their emergence as the most powerful professional hockey team in the world, I consulted Dick Irvin, *The Habs: An Oral History of the Montreal Canadiens, 1940-1980* (Toronto: McClelland & Stewart, 1991); D'Arcy Jenish, *The Montreal Canadiens: 100 Years of Glory* (Toronto: Doubleday Canada, 2008); Frank J. Selke, *Behind the Cheering*, with H. Gordon Green (Toronto: McClelland & Stewart, 1962); Andy O'Brien, *Les Canadiens: The Story of the Montreal Canadiens*, rev. ed. (Toronto: McGraw-Hill Ryerson, 1971; orig. publ. 1967 as *Fire-Wagon Hockey*); Ken Dryden, *The Game: A Thoughtful and Provocative Look at a Life in Hockey* (Toronto: Macmillan of Canada, 1983); *Jean Béliveau: My Life in Hockey*, with Chrys Goyens and Allan Turowetz (Vancouver: Greystone Books, 2005); and Chrys Goyens and Allan Turowetz, *Lions in Winter* (Scarborough, ON: Prentice Hall Canada, 1986).

For information and anecdotes about specific players, I referred to Lorne "Gump" Worsley, *They Call Me Gump*, with Tim Moriarty (New York: Dodd, Mead, 1975) and John Ferguson, *Thunder and Lightning*, with Stan and Shirley Fischler (Scarborough, ON: Prentice-Hall Canada, 1989).

A great number of quotations and valuable observations about life as a professional hockey player come from *Breakaway: Hockey and the Years Beyond*, by the talented Charles Wilkins (Toronto: McClelland & Stewart, 1995) and from James Duplacey and Charles Wilkins, *Forever Rivals: Montreal Canadiens — Toronto Maple Leafs*, ed. Dan Diamond (Toronto: Random House of Canada, 1996). Dick Irvin's *Behind the Bench: Coaches Talk About Life in the NHL* (Toronto: McClelland & Stewart, 1993) was also useful.

I read the late Trent Frayne's witty and entertaining book *The Mad Men of Hockey* (New York: Dodd, Mead, 1974) from cover to cover, then realized that I'd underlined almost every sentence and had to read it again to find the passages that I needed to include in my own book. Frayne remains one of Canada's best writers, and this book deserves to be reprinted.

For information on officials in the game, I consulted *Calling the Shots: Memoirs of an NHL Referee* (Toronto: Stoddart, 1988) and *The Good of the Game: Recapturing Hockey's Greatness* (Toronto: Stoddart, 1999), both by Bruce Hood (with Murray Townsend), as well as another book by Dick Irvin — *Tough Calls: NHL Referees and Linesmen Tell Their Story* (Toronto: McClelland & Stewart, 1997).

For the talent, accomplishments and treachery of Alan Eagleson and his betrayal of the men who trusted him, I turned to Russ Conway's *Game Misconduct: Alan Eagleson and the Corruption of Hockey* (Toronto: Macfarlane Walter & Ross, 1995); David Cruise and Alison Griffiths, *Net Worth: Exploding the Myth of Pro Hockey* (Toronto: Viking, 1991); and Bruce Dowbiggin, *The Defense Never Rests* (Toronto: HarperCollins, 1993).

For various details throughout the chapter about everything from the history of the Stanley Cup and the nature of competitive sport to the attitude of Conn Smythe toward the Vietnam War, I consulted: D'Arcy Jenish, *The Stanley Cup: A Hundred Years of Hockey at Its Best* (Toronto: McClelland & Stewart, 1992); *Dick Beddoes' Greatest Hockey Stories* (Toronto: Macmillan of Canada, 1990); David Remnick, *King of the World: Muhammad Ali and the Rise of an American Hero* (New York: Random House, 1999); Geoffrey Wheatcroft, *Le Tour: A History of the Tour de France* (London: Simon & Schuster, 2003); and David Whitson and Richard Gruneau, eds., *Artificial Ice: Hockey, Culture, and Commerce* (Peterborough, ON: Broadview Press, 2006).

In the Hockey Hall of Fame archives, to which I was allowed access by Ron Ellis and where I was assisted and treated with great sympathy by Miragh Bitove, Katherine Pearce and Craig Campbell, I sifted through a blizzard of clippings from newspapers, journals and hockey programs, including: *Hockey Pictorial*; Maple Leaf Gardens programs; Montreal Forum programs; Buffalo Sabres programs; *Toronto Star*; *Toronto Telegram*; *Liberty Magazine*; *Hockey News*; *Le Petit Journal*; *Le Nouvelliste*; *Sport*; *Canadian Magazine*; *Hockey World*; *Sports Illustrated*; *Weekend Magazine*; *Parlons Sports*; *Montreal Gazette*; *Toronto Sun*; *Detroit Times*; *Montreal Star*; *Globe and Mail*; and *Saturday Night*.

For tidbits and nuggets of information, I also consulted a vast number of websites. Some of these websites seem to come and go with the same regularity as professional hockey players. I've included only the ones that still exist as of 2014:

NHL.com, Hockey Hall of Fame (http://www.hhof.com/html/sitemap.shtml), Internet Hockey Database (http://www.hockeydb.com/), Society for International Hockey Research (http://www.sihrhockey.org), Montreal Canadiens (www.canadiens.com/eng/history) and the Toronto Maple Leafs (http://mapleleafs.nhl.com/)

Finally, when I started this book, a video of the entire game was available on the web. I also had a copy of the game recorded on DVD. By the time I finished the book, the video had been removed from the Internet, either by the NHL or by Molson, replaced by a 30-minute YouTube video of highlights from the entire playoffs (https://www.youtube.com/watch?v=gatNKICLmxM), complete with idiotic musical accompaniment that transforms the 1967 playoff games into quaint historical curiosities, the athletic equivalent of a Laurel and Hardy talkie. If you watch closely, though, the grace, skill and precision of the players shine through.

Chapter Two: First Period

The game begins. In describing the first period, the chapter draws attention to the skills of the players and the way in which they've acquired and refined those skills. It shows the challenges that a player faces in executing a play that looks, to a spectator, as if it requires no skill at all. Through meticulous analysis of the game and the personalities of the players, we appreciate the subtle differences in skill and the enormous advantage that an individual and his team may gain from the slightest mistake by an opponent. We also see that it takes more than skill in the 1960s to hold a job in the NHL.

In assembling portraits of the players, I consulted a wide variety of books and articles in newspapers and journals. I also incorporated comments made in interviews, in public appearances by some of the players — including a dinner at the Metro Toronto Convention Centre in March, 2007, at which several players from the Maple Leafs appeared — and in a conversation on CBC Radio on May 30, 2006, between Shelagh Rogers and Ted Nolan. In many cases, a single sentence or paragraph in this chapter may contain details from several different sources.

Books consulted in this chapter include Bruce Hood, *Calling the Shots*; Don Cherry, *Grapes: A Vintage View of Hockey*, with Stan Fischler (Scarborough, ON: Prentice-Hall Canada, 1982); Hugh Hood, *Strength Down the Centre: The Jean Beliveau Story* (Scarborough, ON: Prentice-Hall Canada, 1970); Billy Harris, *The Glory Years*; Stephen Cole, *The Canadian Hockey Atlas*; Zander Hollander, ed., *The Hockey News Hockey Almanac, 1999*; Lorne "Gump" Worsley, *They Call Me Gump*; Punch Imlach, *Hockey Is a Battle*; Charles Wilkins, *Breakaway*; and Trent Frayne, *The Mad Men of Hockey*.

For rare glimpses into the inner workings of the Leafs, I relied on Damien Cox and Gord Stellick's *'67: The Maple Leafs*.

For details about the career of Dave Balon, I consulted a number of articles in *Hockey World* and Joe O'Connor's sensitively written obituary of Balon that appeared in the *National Post* on May 30, 2007.

Details about the life of Henri Richard were accumulated from *Sports Illustrated*, *Sport*, *Hockey News* and the game program of the Detroit Red Wings.

As I did throughout the book, I relied on Ken Dryden's observations in *The Game* to confirm some of the details about the game and the way that players perceive it.

Material about players on the Canadiens came from sources examined through the tireless research of Jean-Patrice Martel, such as *Parlons Sport* and *Le Petit*

Journal, as well as English-language newspapers such as the *Toronto Star*, *Toronto Telegram*, *Globe and Mail* and *Toronto Sun* and magazines such as *Canadian Magazine* and the game programs of the Leafs and the Canadiens.

Other books consulted for details in this chapter include D'Arcy Jenish, *The Stanley Cup*; Don Weekes and Kerry Banks, *The Best & Worst of Hockey Firsts*; the invaluable *Canada on Ice*, edited by Benedict and Jenish; David Dupuis, *Sawchuk*; and Jack Batten, *The Leafs*.

Chapter Three: First Intermission
Behind the razzle dazzle and the excitement of the game, men in suits conduct the business of hockey with a relentless eye on profit. From the technology of ice-making to the play-by-play announcing of the game, all aspects of the game contribute to its profitability. Though the owners of the teams haven't fully grasped its potential, TV represents the pot of gold at the end of the hockey rainbow.

The men who run the game are greedy at best. Some are crooks. Most are bigots. Few of them have anything but their own interests at heart. Behind these men, the players, most of them hard-working, decent and slightly naïve young men, follow like lambs to the slaughter.

For details about ice-making and equipment, I consulted Jason Cohen, *Zamboni Rodeo: Chasing Hockey Dreams from Austin to Albuquerque* (Vancouver: Greystone Books, 2001); Eric Dregni, *Zamboni: The Coolest Machines on Ice* (St. Paul, MI: Voyageur Press, 2006); Billy Harris, *The Glory Years*; Damien Cox and Gord Stellick, *'67: The Maple Leafs*; and Benedict and Jenish, eds., *Canada on Ice*, as well as programs from Maple Leaf Gardens.

For observations about coaching the Maple Leafs, I relied on Douglas Hunter, *Open Ice*; Punch Imlach, *Heaven and Hell in the NHL*; Kelly McParland, *The Lives of Conn Smythe*; Hugh Hood, *Strength Down the Centre*; Benedict and Jenish, eds., *Canada on Ice*; Punch Imlach, *Hockey Is a Battle*; and interviews with the former New York Rangers captain Harry Howell and the late Bob Haggert, former trainer of the Toronto Maple Leafs. For the anecdote about Punch Imlach and his violin, I consulted the LA Memorial Sports Arena Official Programs from 1961.

For details about bigotry and racism in the NHL, I consulted Benedict and Jenish, eds., *Canada on Ice*; Michael McKinley, *Putting a Roof on Winter*; Whitson and Gruneau, eds., *Artificial Ice*; Hugh Hood, *Strength Down the Centre*; magazine articles in *Hockey Pictorial*, which confirmed the qualities that made George Armstrong such an exceptional man; *Canadian Magazine*, *Sporting News*, *Toronto Life*, *Toronto Star*, Maple Leaf Gardens programs and an article on ESPN's website (http://sports.espn.go.com/espn/blackhistory/news/story?id=1739870).

Other details in this chapter come from Brian Conacher, *So You Want to Be a Hockey Player!*, *Globe and Mail* and the *Simcoe Reformer*.

Finally, the observations about fighting in hockey and its impact on the game's popularity come from Ken Dryden, who says in *The Game* that "fighting degrades the sport." I agree.

Chapter Four: Second Period

As the game proceeds through the second period, the narrative addresses the job of the professional hockey player. From an early age, players spend most of their time and effort on obtaining a job in professional hockey. They calculate odds, analyze angles and apply their intelligence to playing their sport better than anyone else in the world. Against enormous odds, a player may keep his job, to the delight and entertainment of millions of fans. By the time their hockey careers end, they hope they can support themselves and their families on their wits and their reputation. Few of them have the education to pursue a career that will pay them as much as they've earned from hockey. None of them will receive again the adulation that the fans bestow on them tonight.

For comparisons between the relatively privileged lives of professional hockey players and the dangerous drudgery endured by their fathers, I incorporated material from John Vaillant, *The Golden Spruce: A True Story of Myth, Madness and Greed* (Toronto: A.A. Knopf Canada, 2005). On the job of the hockey player, books such as D'Arcy Jenish, *The Stanley Cup*; Billy Harris, *The Glory Years*; Douglas Hunter, *Open Ice*; Benedict and Jenish, eds., *Canada on Ice*; Hugh Hood, *Strength Down the Centre*; and Dick Irvin, *The Habs* were rich sources of information. I also incorporated details from *Parlons Sport, Toronto Sun, Toronto Star, Hockey News*, and Maple Leaf Gardens programs.

For details about Henri Richard, I relied on Michael McKinley, *Putting a Roof on Winter*; Dick Irvin, *The Habs*; Hugh Hood, *Strength Down the Centre*; and Andy O'Brien, *Les Canadiens*, as well as magazines such as *Sport* and *Canadian Magazine*.

The ordeal of negotiating a player's contract is described in several places including Billy Harris, *The Glory Years*; Damien Cox and Gord Stellick, *'67: The Maple Leafs*; Andy O'Brien, *Les Canadiens*; and *Le Petit Journal*.

Observations about the expectations placed on wives of NHL players come from Michael McKinley, *Putting a Roof on Winter*; David Dupuis, *Sawchuk*; Dick Irvin, *Behind the Bench*; Douglas Hunter, *Open Ice*; Trent Frayne, *The Mad Men of Hockey*; Punch Imlach, *Hockey Is a Battle*; Billy Harris, *The Glory Years*; Ken Dryden, *The Game*; Charles Wilkins, *Breakaway*; and Dan Diamond, ed., *Total Hockey*, as well as *Parlons Sport, Hockey News, Hockey World*, the *Canadian Parliamentary Review* 12, no. 3 (1989), Maple Leaf Gardens programs, *Weekend Magazine, Toronto Star, Globe and Mail* and a documentary film called *A Perfect Husband: The Life and Times of Tim Horton* (CBC: Danile Gelfant, Director, Lynn

Booth and Laurie Long of Make Believe Media), quoted in the *Toronto Star*, February 13, 2001.

Details about the first goal of the game, scored by Ron Ellis, appear in his *Over the Boards*; Stephen Cole, *The Canadian Hockey Atlas*; *Toronto Star*, *Parlons Sport*, Maple Leaf Gardens programs, *Hockey Pictorial* and an interview with Red Kelly.

For descriptions of John Ferguson's life and character, I consulted Charles Wilkins, *Breakaway*; John Ferguson, *Thunder and Lightning*; and Dick Irvin, *The Habs*, as well as *La Revue Sportive du Forum Sports Magazine*, 1959-1960; *Weekend Magazine*, *Toronto Sun*, *Hockey World*, *Parlons Sport* and *Canadian Magazine*.

The superlative skills of Jean Beliveau and the gift of goal-scoring are described in Hugh Hood, *Strength Down the Centre*; Ken Dryden, *The Game*; Frank Selke, *Behind the Cheering*; Stephen Cole, *The Last Hurrah*; and *Sport*, *Sports Illustrated*, *Star Weekly* and *Hockey World*.

Chapter Five: Second Intermission
The fifth chapter describes the role of the Montreal Canadiens in the culture of French-speaking Quebec. It illuminates the peculiarities that distinguish NHL hockey players in that province from their English-speaking counterparts beyond the province. It emphasizes the importance of hockey not just to the players and their families but to the fabric of French Canada, as well.

Details about the lives of individual players on the Canadiens, such as Henri Richard, Jean Beliveau and Dave Balon, and the team's assistant trainer, Eddie Palchak, come from Ken Dryden's *The Game*; Hugh Hood, *Strength Down the Centre*; and Andy O'Brien's *Les Canadiens*.

Sport, *Hockey World*, *Le Petit Journal*, *Parlons Sport*, *Le Nouvelliste*, *Toronto Star* and habbits.ca, a website devoted to the Canadiens (see: http://habbits.ca/news/?id=4ecc44007f75d), contain further details about the players as well as preparations made in Montreal for the Canadiens' anticipated playoff victory.

Details about the life and character of Dick Duff come from Douglas Hunter, *Open Ice*; Billy Harris, *The Glory Years*; *Toronto Sun* and Maple Leaf Gardens programs.

I found details about Toe Blake and his relationships with his family and his players in Dick Irvin, *Behind the Bench*; Hugh Hood, *Strength Down the Centre*; Andy O'Brien, *Les Canadiens*; Stephen Cole, *The Last Hurrah*; Dick Irvin, *The Habs*; Charles Wilkins, *Breakaway*; Trent Frayne, *The Mad Men of Hockey*; Frank J. Selke, *Behind the Cheering*; Michael McKinley, *Putting a Roof on Winter*; and Stephen Cole, *The Canadian Hockey Atlas*.

Further details appear in the *Toronto Telegram*, *Hamilton Spectator*, *Montreal Gazette*, *Globe and Mail*, *Toronto Sun*, *Toronto Star*, *Le Petit Journal*, *Le Nouvelliste*, *Parlons Sport*, *Canadian Magazine*, *Sport* and Montreal Forum programs.

Chaper Six: Third Period

This chapter looks toward the future of professional hockey after this night's game. It describes the changes that will occur within the next few years in professional hockey and the impact of these changes on conservative men who have resisted change throughout their lives. In particular, the chapter shows in some detail the characteristics that distinguish the men in the game tonight and that qualify them as leaders not only in their sport but occasionally in the much broader context of their lives, as well. The chapter also illuminates the venality of some of the owners involved in professional hockey and emphasizes graphically why the players need to organize themselves to win a fair deal. By the end of the chapter, the outcome of tonight's game seems anticlimactic, since the lives of the players and, in some ways, the sport of professional hockey, will soon change dramatically and forever.

Details about the roles of Bob Pulford and Alan Eagleson in the formation of the NHL Players' Association come from Ken Dryden, *The Game*; Billy Harris, *The Glory Years*; and Damien Cox and Gord Stellick, *'67: The Maple Leafs*, as well as the *Globe and Mail*, *Toronto Telegram* and *Weekend Magazine*.

The impact on players of the NHL's expansion and of the formation of the World Hockey Association is described in Trent Frayne, *The Mad Men of Hockey*; Dan Diamond, ed., *Total Hockey*; Jason Cohen, *Zamboni Rodeo*; Douglas Hunter, *Open Ice*; Benedict and Jenish, eds., *Canada on Ice*; Ken Dryden, *The Game*; Don Cherry, *Grapes*; and *Toronto Star, Washington Post, Globe and Mail, Toronto Telegram, Hamilton Spectator, Toronto Sun, Sports Illustrated, Sporting News* and Montreal Forum and Maple Leaf Gardens programs.

The average length of an NHL player's career is based on calculations at Quantum Hockey.com (http://www.quanthockey.com/Distributions/CareerLengthGP.php).

The fate of Maple Leafs players such as Frank Mahovlich, Tim Horton, Pete Stemkowski and Mike Walton after they moved to other teams is described in Douglas Hunter, *Open Ice: The Tim Horton Story* and in *Sports Illustrated, Hockey World, Toronto Sunday Sun, Toronto Telegram*, and Maple Leaf Gardens programs.

The challenges faced by Dave Balon are described in the *Vancouver Province, Globe and Mail, Prince Albert Daily Herald* and *National Post*.

Observations about individual players and the Montreal Canadiens after 1967 appear in *Canadian Magazine, Montreal Star* and *Globe and Mail*, and in Hugh Hood, *Strength Down the Centre*; Dick Irvin, *The Habs*; and Charles Wilkins, *Breakaway*.

Harold Ballard's shameful and abusive treatment of Ron Ellis is described in *Over the Boards: The Ron Ellis Story*; Damien Cox and Gord Stellick, *'67: The Maple Leafs*; and *Globe and Mail, Toronto Star*, Maple Leaf Gardens programs and an interview with Ron Ellis.

The attitude of team managers and owners toward their players is discussed in Ken Dryden, *The Game*; Damien Cox and Gord Stellick, *'67: The Maple Leafs*; David Dupuis, *Sawchuk*; Douglas Hunter, *Open Ice*; Ted Mahovlich, *The Big M:*

The Frank Mahovlich Story; Toronto Star, Toronto Sun and Maple Leaf Gardens programs.

Details of Larry Hillman's post-NHL life are included in his Hockey Hall of Fame Veteran Player Nomination Form in the Hockey Hall of Fame archives in Toronto.

Descriptions of Terry Sawchuk's life in Los Angeles are based on passages from David Dupuis, *Sawchuk*.

The experience in Los Angeles of Red Kelly and his family, including their apprehensions about the Manson murders in a nearby neighbourhood, is described in *Toronto Star, Globe and Mail, Toronto Telegram* and Maple Leaf Gardens programs.

The deterioration of the Maple Leafs' organization under Harold Ballard is described in all its dubious splendor in Benedict and Jenish, eds., *Canada on Ice*; Damien Cox and Gord Stellick, *'67: The Maple Leafs*; and *Toronto Telegram, Globe and Mail, Toronto Star, Sport, Hockey News, St. Catharines Standard, Welland Tribune* and Maple Leaf Gardens programs.

The original inscription on Stafford Smythe's gravestone was:

> *He was dearly loved by his wife, children, and many friends, he was persecuted to death by his enemies. Now he sleeps peacefully in the quiet north country that loved him for the person he was.* (http://www.cottageblog.ca/2008/11/28 conn-stafford-smythe-rip-in-beautiful-muskoka/)

It was written after Smythe's death in 1971 by his son, Tom, but was later removed by one of his daughters, without consultation with the rest of the family.

Chapter Seven: Post-game Wrap-up

A brief postscript brings the game of hockey and the players in the story into the present. It shows how the game has maintained and extended its appeal to a global audience despite the innumerable changes that have occurred. And it distinguishes the hard-nosed tactics of the sport and the business from the spark of inspiration that still illuminates the dreams of future players and even their most jaded fans.

Details about the aftermath of the 1967 playoffs appear in Ted Mahovlich, *The Big M: The Frank Mahovlich Story*; D'Arcy Jenish, *The Stanley Cup*; Damien Cox and Gord Stellick, *'67: The Maple Leafs*; David Dupuis, *Sawchuk*; Don Weekes and Kerry Banks, *The Best & Worst of Hockey Firsts*; Stephen Cole, *The Last Hurrah*; Charles Wilkins, *Breakaway*; and televised post-game interviews conducted with Conn Smythe, Terry Sawchuk and Bob Pulford, as well as the author's interviews with the late Bob Haggert.

Details about the rise of the Soviet Union as a hockey power and the contributions of Lloyd Percival to the science of hockey come from Lloyd Percival, *The Hockey Handbook* (Toronto: Copp Clark, 1951).

Observations about coaches, players and their adjustment to life after hockey come from Dick Irvin, *Behind the Bench*, and Charlie Wilkins, *Breakaway*.

The lasting heritage of the Montreal Canadiens is discussed in D'Arcy Jenish, *The Montreal Canadiens*; Andy O'Brien, *Les Canadiens*; Hugh Hood, *Strength Down the Centre*; Ken Dryden, *The Game*; Dick Irvin, *The Habs*; Whitson and Gruneau, eds., *Artificial Ice: Hockey, Culture and Commerce*; and *Sports Illustrated*, *Hockey News* and *Canadian Magazine*.

The continuing dismal saga of the Maple Leafs and the greed of its owners are discussed in Whitson and Gruneau, eds., *Artificial Ice*; Ron Ellis, *Over the Boards*; Billy Harris, *The Glory Years*; Maple Leaf Gardens programs, and an interview with Al Stuart, co-owner of the Pilot Tavern in Toronto and disgruntled corporate subscriber to Leaf TV.

The festering culture of pedophilia at Maple Leaf Gardens nurtured by management indifference and negligence is described in Damien Cox and Gord Stellick, *'67: The Maple Leafs*; Whitson and Gruneau, eds., *Artificial Ice*; Ron Ellis, *Over the Boards*; and *Toronto Star*.

Punch Imlach's ignominious retreat from the Maple Leafs spotlight is described in Damien Cox and Gord Stellick, *'67: The Maple Leafs*; Punch Imlach, *Hockey is a Battle*; Billy Harris, *The Glory Years*; and Stephen Cole, *The Last Hurrah*, as well as *Toronto Telegram*, *Hamilton Spectator*, *Globe and Mail* and Michael Breaugh's Member's statement in the Ontario Legislature, December 2, 1987: http://www.ontla.on.ca/web/house-proceedings/house_detail.do?locale=fr&Parl=34&Date=1987-12-02#P45_10347.

The implication of fame and the idolization of NHL players in the premature death of Tim Horton are discussed in Punch Imlach, *Heaven and Hell in the NHL*, and *Toronto Star*, *Toronto Sun*, *Globe and Mail* and a CBC interview with Andrew Ferrence on *The Current*, July 27, 2007.

Gump Worsley's reaction to his induction into the Hockey Hall of Fame and his encounter with Reggie Jackson are described in the *Toronto Star*, September 9, 1980, the *Toronto Sun*, June 15, 1980 and, in yet another superb article by the late Trent Frayne, in the *Toronto Sun*, September 9, 1980.

Index